JOHN WILKINSON first became acquainted with Jerusalem in 1961, when he went there as tutor of St. George's College.

Since then he has spent eleven years there, and is now Director of the British School of Archaeology in Jerusalem.

Among his writings on the Holy Land are *Jerusalem Pilgrims Before the Crusades,* in which he has translated the pilgrim texts from the centuries following Egeria, and *Jerusalem as Jesus Knew It.*

He is an Anglican priest and a canon of St. George's Cathedral.

EGERIA'S TRAVELS TO THE HOLY LAND

First published in 1971
by S.P.C.K.
London

Revised edition 1981
published by
Ariel Publishing House, P.O.Box 3328, Jerusalem
together with

Aris & Phillips, Warminster, England

ISBN   0 85668 169 5

Printed in Israel

EGERIA'S TRAVELS

TO THE HOLY LAND

Newly translated
with supporting documents
and notes
by

JOHN WILKINSON

Revised edition

Ariel Publishing House, Jerusalem

Aris & Phillips, Warminster, England

1981

FOR ALIX

CONTENTS

ILLUSTRATIONS

ix

ABBREVIATIONS

A.S.O.R.	*Annual of the American Schools of Oriental Research*, New Haven, 1920, etc.
A.B.	*Analecta Bollandiana*, Brussels 1882, etc.
A.L.	*Armenian Lectionary*, see pp. 253–77.
A.S.	*Anatolian Studies*, London 1951, etc.
Ball	J. Ball, *Egypt in the Classical Geographers*, Cairo 1942.
BASOR	*Bulletin of the American Schools of Oriental Research*, Baltimore, Md 1919, etc.
Bastiaensen, *Obs.*	A. A. R. Bastiaensen, *Observations sur le vocabulaire liturgique dans l'itinéraire d'Egérie*, Nijmegen-Utrecht 1962.
B.H.G.	*Bibliotheca Hagiographica Graeca*, Brussels 1909.
Bord	Bordeaux Pilgrim (see pp. 153–63).
C.S.E.L.	*Corpus Scriptorum Ecclesiasticorum Latinorum*, Vienna 1866, etc.
C.C.S.L.	*Corpus Christianorum, Series Latina*, Turnhout, 1953, etc.
CL	A. Baumstark, *Comparative Liturgy* (revised by B. Botte; E.T. F. L. Cross), London 1958.
C.S.C.O.	*Corpus Scriptorum Christianorum Orientalium*, Paris 1903, etc.
C.S.H.B.	*Corpus Scriptorum Historiae Byzantinae*, Bonn 1828–78.
DACL	F. Cabrol, H. Leclercq, H. I. Marrou, *Dictionnaire d'archéologie chrétienne et de liturgie*, Paris 1907, etc.
Egeria (E in additional note E)	*Egeria's Travels*.
EH (or HE)	*Ecclesiastical History*.
G.C.S.	*Griechischen Christlichen Schriftsteller der ersten drei Jahrhunderte*, Berlin-Leipzig 1897, etc.
Gingras	*Egeria, Diary of a Pilgrimage*, translated and annotated by George E. Gingras (=*Ancient Christian Writers* No 38, ed. J. Quasten, W. J. Burghardt, and T. C. Lawler), New York 1970.
Hennecke	E. Hennecke, *New Testament Apocrypha*, 2 vols, E.T. ed. R. McL. Wilson, London 1963, 1965.

xi

HG	Herzfeld and Guyer.
Hg	J. Jeremias, *Heiligengräber in Jesu Umwelt*, Göttingen 1958.
IJ	H. Michelant and G. Raynard, *Itinéraires à Jerusalem et Descriptions de la Terre Sainte*, Osnabrück 1966.
IRO	B. de Khitrova, *Itinéraires Russes en Orient*, Osnabrück 1966.
* J.E.H.	*Journal of Ecclesiastical History*, London 1950, etc.
J.P.O.S.	*Journal of the Palestine Oriental Society*, Jerusalem 1920, etc.
Kopp	C. Kopp, *The Holy Places of the Gospels* (E.T. R. Walls), London 1963.
LA	*Liber Annuus Studii Biblici Franciscani*, Jerusalem 1951, etc.
MF	M. L. McClure and C. L. Feltoe, *The Pilgrimage of Etheria*, London 1919.
MM	M. Avi-Yonah, *The Madaba Mosaic Map*, Jerusalem 1954
MUJ	*Melanges de l'Université St Joseph*, Beirut, 1906, etc.
On	E. Klostermann, ed., *Eusebius, Das Onomastikon der biblischen Ortsnamen*, Hildesheim 1966.
Pétré	H. Pétré, ed., *Ethérie, Journal de Voyage* (Sources Chrétiennes 21), Paris 1948.
PD	Peter the Deacon, *Book on the Holy Places*, (see pp. 179–210).
P.E.F.Q.S.	*Palestine Exploration Fund Quarterly Statement*, London 1868, etc.
PG	J. P. Migne, ed., *Patrologiae cursus completus, series Graeca*, Paris 1857, etc.
PL	J. P. Migne, ed., *Patrologiae cursus completus, series Latina*, Paris 1844, etc.
PM	J. E. Dean, *Epiphanius' Treatise on Weights and Measures, the Syriac Version*, Chicago Ill. 1935.
R.B.	*Revue Biblique*, Paris 1892, etc.
Renoux, *Codex*	A. Renoux, *Le Codex Arménien Jérusalem 121, Introduction aux origines de la liturgie hiérosolymitaine* (= F. Graffin, *Patrologia Orientalis*, 35, fasc. 1, No. 163), Turnhout 1969.

Renoux, *La Prière*	A. Renoux, "Liturgie de Jérusalem et Lectionnaires Arméniens. Vigiles, et Année Liturgique" in Cassien and B. Botte, *La Prière des Heures*, Paris 1963.
RSR	*Recherches de Science Religieuse*, Paris 1910, etc.
Segal	J. B. Segal, *Edessa " The Blessed City"*, Oxford 1970.
Telfer, *Cyril*	W. Telfer, ed., *Cyril of Jerusalem and Nemesius of Emesa* (Library of Christian Classics 4), London 1955.
VA	H. Vincent and F. M. Abel, *Jérusalem, Recherches de topographie, d'archéologie, et d'histoire*, Paris 1912–26.
VC	*Vigiliae Christianae*, Amsterdam 1947, etc.
Vermeer, *Obs.*	G. F. M. Vermeer, *Observations sur le vocabulaire du Pélerinage chez Egérie et chez Antonin de Plaisance*, Nijmegen-Utrecht 1965.
Zerfass	R. Zerfass, *Die Schriftlesung im Kathedraloffizium Jerusalems*, Münster Westfalen 1969.

ACKNOWLEDGEMENTS

The writing of this book has been a great pleasure to the author, and there is much gratitude to be expressed: first to the Society for Promoting Christian Knowledge, who suggested that I should begin, and have encouraged and helped me throughout its production, and then to the Trustees of the Gerald Averay Wainwright Near Eastern Archaeological Fund and of the Leverhulme Research Awards, through whose liberality I was able to journey to most but not all of the places Egeria mentions. For allowing me the time to visit them I am indebted to the United Society for the Propagation of the Gospel.

I am most grateful to the many scholars and others who have helped me either by answering the questions I have been sending them, or in other ways; especially to Dom A. Renoux, o.s.b. of En Calcat, the Reverend J. D. Crichton, and Fathers Pierre Benoit, Charles Coüasnon, and Roland de Vaux, o.p., of the École Biblique Française, Jerusalem; also to Mehmet Bey Belen, Dr I. E. S. Edwards, Canon E. Every, Dr G. H. Forsyth, Dr W. H. C. Frend, the Reverend F. Green, Dr Labib Habachi, Farid Bey Hamevioğlu, Mr R. W. Hamilton, the Reverend C. J. A. Hickling, Dr R. C. D. Jasper, Professor J. Jeremias, Dr N. Nováková, Mlle H. Pétré, Mrs E. Riefstahl, Dr S. Sauneron, Professor J. B. Segal, and Mr A. F. Shore.

I am specially grateful to Miss Ann Batten for her help with the indexes, and to Mr William Ball for contributing so much of his own knowledge and skill to the drawing of the maps, plans, and illustrations. For all her help my wife deserves more thanks than I can here express.

PREFACE TO THE SECOND EDITION

In the ten years which have gone by since the present translation was made
I have become more familiar with the writings of pilgrims who came to
visit Jerusalem in the centuries up to the arrival of the First Crusade. As
I read them I saw that I had made a number of mistakes in this book,
which I am now very glad to be able to correct. I am therefore most
grateful to Messrs Aris and Phillips for asking me to prepare this edition,
and for publishing the work on the later pilgrims under the title *Jerusalem
Pilgrims Before the Crusades.*

I am also grateful to Aris and Phillips for their determination to pro-
duce this book as economically as possible, since I hope that it will thus
find its way into the hands of students. Savings have been achieved by
grouping the new material together on pp. 298 − 333 and at the end
of the Notes. Where the reader needs to consult these pages we have
placed an asterisk in the margin.

I am most grateful for the useful criticisms which have been made by
reviewers and correspondents, and hope that where I have felt competent
to follow them I have made the appropriate alterations. In preparing
this edition I am particularly grateful to Dr. Robin Cormack, Father Joseph
Crehan, S.J., the Revd. Dr. Ronald H. Miller, and Professor Irfan Shahid.
Once more I am happy to express my thanks to Father Pierre Benoit, O.P.

London, 1981   JOHN WILKINSON

Introduction

The Author

Egeria's *Travels* was lost for seven hundred years. And when, in the late nineteenth century, a manuscript copy was found in Italy, it proved to be only the middle of the book. No doubt the name of the pilgrim and some clue about her date would have appeared either at the beginning or the end, but, since both are missing, we are left to rely on our own ingenuity. Plenty of guesses have been made, but at present it seems most likely that the pilgrim was called Egeria[1] and that she visited the East between A.D. 381 and 384.[2]

The bishop who met Egeria at Edessa was impressed by the fact that she had come "right from the other end of the earth"[3] and she herself compares the colour of the Red Sea with that of the "Ocean".[4] It is therefore safe to assume that her home country, and that of the beloved sisters for whom she wrote, was on some Atlantic coast. She may have been a Gaul from Aquitaine, or a Spaniard from Galicia. But equally she may have come from some other western province of the Roman empire, and even the most minute studies of the language she uses have failed to provide further pointers to the place of her origin.

There are teasing gaps in our knowledge about Egeria. But what we have of her text—possibly about a third—is enough to give a vivid idea of her personality and enthusiasms. She is an eager tourist with plenty of time at her disposal and, as she herself says, of unbounded curiosity. So it goes without saying that her book is full of enthusiastic comments on views (vast), buildings (famous), mountains (steep), and plains (fertile). But this traveller is decidedly Christian, and the things which interest her most are those which have to do with her understanding of the faith. Apart from her overriding eagerness to record the special characteristics of the East, its paragon monks, its holy places, and its model liturgy, she is on the look-out for every detail which will help her and her sisters to keep abreast of modern developments. So she is delighted when the Bishop of Edessa gives her a

[1] See Note A, pp. 235–6 below. [2] See Note B, pp. 237–9 below.
[3] 19.5. [4] See PD, Y10.

manuscript of the *Letter of Abgar*, since she rightly suspects that it is different from the text they have at home.[1] And she picks up all the details she can which will enable her sisters to picture what they read in the Bible: thus you cannot see the summit of Sinai till you are well up it, and this must surely have been intended by God.[2] This is a "marvel" which makes a considerable impression on her, but on the whole she speaks of "miracles" in a way which is little more than matter-of-fact. The sycamore at Rameses "does good" to those who pluck its shoots,[3] but Egeria is just as interested in the fact that it is very ancient. Nor is she credulous. She treats her guides with unvarying courtesy, and never expresses doubts about what she is shown. But in writing down what she has seen she often qualifies the story she has been told: the sycamore is "said to have been" planted by the patriarchs.

Between Egeria and the modern Christian traveller there are two striking differences. The modern tourist comes to the East mainly to see buildings and places, but Egeria is equally interested in the local church. Indeed some of her most enthusiastic descriptions are those of monks, nuns, and bishops. Then again the modern traveller spends much time viewing non-Christian sights, and admiring a non-Christian civilization. But Egeria, as a Roman citizen within a Roman and still largely pagan world, displays an almost complete indifference to anything non-Christian. It is of course impossible to say with confidence what Egeria did *not* describe, since we now have only a fraction of what she wrote. But the part we have is enough to show that for her the non-Christians are usually important only when they affect the Church—like the people of Carrae who outnumber the Christians,[4] or the Isaurians who raid them.[5] The only surviving remark which treats pagans as having an interest of their own is that about the men who live in the desert of Paran,[6] a place where her guides probably had little else to describe.

Egeria has a keen eye for liturgical arrangements, especially for those she finds exceptional. But while she is full of admiration for the marathon course of services held in Jerusalem at the great

---

[1] 19.19.   [2] 2.7.   [3] 8.3, 4.
[4] 20.8.   [5] 23.4.   [6] 6.2.

festivals, she is also sensitive to the fatigue of those who attend them.

Energetic, observant, determined, appreciative, Egeria punctuates her narrative with acknowledgements of her gratitude both to the people who were her guides and her hosts, and also to God, who has allowed her, humble and unworthy as she is, to carry out her wonderful journey. "Journeys are not hard when they are the fulfilment of hopes",[1] and her hopes were amply fulfilled.

Despite her many excellent qualities Egeria gives no evidence that she had studied the Latin classics. Indeed the unusual Latin in which she writes has set many problems for scholars, and some (for example, the writer of the first translation into English) have dismissed it as so "slipshod and tedious" that it did not deserve to be put into good English.[2] But this judgement has not been unanimous; another critic finds in her language a "hieratic grandeur",[3] enhanced by her frequent repetitions.

The present translation has been made on the assumption that Egeria wrote much as she spoke. By classical standards her writing is deplorable, but so is conversation in any language if it is judged by criteria which are inappropriate. And, if Egeria intended to do no more than pass on to her sisters as accurately as possible what she had seen, we may forgive her haphazard syntax and also, it may be, begin to appreciate her rich vocabulary, and her eye for the pointed word and phrase.[4]

It would be a mistake to see in Egeria's style no more than conversation. Egeria was steeped, if not in the Latin classics, at least in those of the Church, and her language often echoes that of the Bible or of formal prayer. It is also larded, like that of most travel-books, with foreign expressions (all Greek) which she picked up.

Egeria's dependence on the Bible affects not only her style, but also much of the content of her work. When she quotes it, she uses titles for the books[5] which indicate that she knew it in one of

---

[1] 3.2.
[2] J. H. Bernard, *The Pilgrimage of St Silvia of Aquitania to the Holy Places* (Palestine Pilgrim's Text Society) (London 1891), p. 9.
[3] L. Spitzer, "The Epic Style of the Pilgrim Aetheria" in *Comparative Literature* I (1949), pp. 225ff.
[4] Of which Bastiaensen, *Obs.* and Vermeer, *Obs.* provide many examples.
[5] E.g. "Books of the Kingdoms" (4.2), and "Actions of the Apostles" (37.5).

the Old Latin versions translated from the Greek.[1] For the Old Testament this means that she was familiar with a text which had received a number of additions not found in the Hebrew. The Septuagint was completed in Alexandria by about 130 B.C., and sometimes provides contemporary Greek names for places: thus in the two versions of Genesis 46.29 we read:

IN THE HEBREW	IN THE SEPTUAGINT
And Joseph . . . went up to meet his father, to Goshen	And Joseph . . . went up to meet Israel his father, to Heroöpolis.

Egeria gives no sign that she used any other reference book apart from her Bible.[2] But she gives a useful clue to her method of writing when she tells how she met a presbyter at Sedima, and goes straight on to say, "Later on we became acquainted with a good many bishops who spoke highly of the way he lived."[3] In this case it is clear that she did not write her description of the presbyter till a good deal later, and we should probably assume that on her journeys she made notes as she went along, and wrote them up later. We know that some of her writing was done during her stay in Constantinople.[4]

Egeria's unassuming account of her travels and the services in Jerusalem would be less important if any similar accounts had survived. As it is, however, we must depend on her information alone for many questions of fourth-century topography and liturgical arrangements. We are fortunate that she was at such pains to be both communicative and accurate.

[1] This assumption is borne out by some of her spelling—e.g. "Quodollagomor" (14.3), and the form of her quotations—e.g. *Quid tu hic Helias* (4.2); see J. Ziegler, "Die *Peregrinatio Aetheriae* und die Heilige Schrift" in *Biblica* 12 (1931), pp. 162–98.

[2] J. Ziegler, in his article "Die *Peregrinatio Aetheriae* und das Onomastikon des Eusebius", in *Biblica* 12 (1931), pp. 70–84, argued that she used Eusebius' *Onomasticon*. But the disagreements in spelling and interpretation outweigh the resemblances he noticed; and the distances given in the parts of Peter the Deacon's work which come from Egeria almost always disagree with Eusebius' measurements. The most striking agreement with Eusebius is at 12.8 in the words "Fogor, which was a city of the kingdom of Edom", which seem to derive from *On*, p. 301. But Egeria is here saying what the monks told her, and in any case Eusebius wrote the equivalent of *Fogo*, not *Fogor*: see p. 220 below.

[3] 14.2; cf. 17.3.

[4] 23.10.

The Text and its Context

DISCOVERY AND PUBLICATION

The one surviving manuscript of Egeria's *Travels* was copied out in the eleventh century, probably in the renowned monastery of Monte Cassino. It later passed into the hands of the Community of St Flora at Arezzo, perhaps in 1599, when Ambrose Rastrellini came from Monte Cassino to be Abbot at Arezzo, and at Arezzo it stayed, though in 1810 it became the property of a Lay Fraternity in the city. When it was taken into this library, it was bound up with a treatise, *On the Mysteries: with three Hymns*, by St Hilary.

The importance of the manuscript remained unrecognized till 1884, when it was discovered, fortunately by the great scholar J. F. Gamurrini, who immediately began to prepare it for publication. His first edition appeared in 1887, and the second, considerably corrected, followed in 1888. In the following year it had already been translated into Russian, and was first published with an English translation by J. H. Bernard in 1891.

Since then the *Travels* (under a variety of titles) has become widely known, and translations exist in most European languages. A new English translation by Mrs M. L. McClure was published by S.P.C.K. in 1919.

In its present state the manuscript consists of three quaternions (sections of eight folded leaves making sixteen pages). But the middle one has lost its outside leaves, and thus comprises only six leaves (or twelve pages). What remains of the text divides into two nearly equal sections, of which the first describes journeys beginning with an approach to Mount Sinai and ending at Constantinople, and the second the services of the Christian year in Jerusalem.

EARLY REFERENCES TO EGERIA

When Egeria finished writing her *Travels*, she doubtless sent or took the original manuscript back to her sisters in the West. It must have reached them towards the end of the fourth century.

8 INTRODUCTION

Near the end of the seventh a monk called Valerius wrote a letter
to his brethren at El Vierzo in north-western Spain. He described
a courageous pilgrim whom he called "the blessed nun Egeria".[1]
The letter is specially valuable since it speaks of several places
which must have been mentioned in the original manuscript, but
are missing from the copy we possess. The *Letter* is written in the
style of a sermon, and makes no attempt to quote verbatim what
Egeria herself may have said, so it does not enable us to reconstruct
her text. But it is at least a clue to her name, though unfortunately
not to the place where she lived.

A Glossary of the eighth or ninth century quotes from a passage
in the manuscript as we have it and ascribes it to "Egeria",[2] and
an anonymous and unnamed Madrid manuscript of the ninth
century quotes two passages we still have, a third which must
come from the missing leaf which occurred in *Travels*, chapter
16,[3] and a fourth which is hard to place.[4]

In 1137 Peter the Deacon, a monk of Monte Cassino and the
abbey's librarian, wrote a book on the holy places, in which he
made extensive quotations from the *Travels*. Some can be placed
beside passages from the manuscript of the *Travels*, and they show
how slightly he altered Egeria's style. But others correspond with
some of the places which are missing from our manuscript, but
are mentioned by Valerius. These provide not only a valuable
rendering of what Egeria said, but also a much better view of the
general pattern of her travels.[5]

No more such clues are given us after Peter's time. There are
some references to her name but no further information.[6]

[1] The name appears in various forms; see Note A, p. 235 below, and a translation of the *Letter*, pp. 174–8 below.
[2] The "Ansileubian" *Liber Glossarum*, either from Spain or France, ed. W. M.
Lindsay and J. F. Mountford, *Glossaria latina* (Paris 1926), vol. I, p. 110, n. 377.
[3] Bib. Nac. Tolet. 14.24; see Franceschini-Weber, p. 93. The two quotations are
also from *Travels*, ch. 16.
[4] See PD, Y15, n. 1.
[5] Annotated extracts from Peter the Deacon's work are given below, pp. 179–
210.
[6] See Note A, pp. 235–6 below.

TABLE OF DATES

9

The Orient in the Fourth Century

THE EMERGENCE OF THE "HOLY LAND"

After A.D. 325, and the Council of Nicaea, the Emperor Constantine embarked on a grand policy of church building in the eastern part of the empire. His friend and adviser, Eusebius, bishop of Caesarea, says that Palestine was specially chosen to benefit by this activity, "since it was from that source that the river of life flowed forth to mankind".[1] Eusebius describes what he did in significant terms: "He chose there three places, each distinguished by a sacred cave, and adorned them with rich buildings."

Fifteen years before the Council Jerusalem had seemed little different from any other Romanized city of the Empire. In the year 310 an official was interrogating a Christian about his place of residence, and, when he received the reply "Jerusalem", was none the wiser. He knew the city only under the name Aelia Capitolina,[2] which Hadrian had given it two centuries before. Some of the places connected with Christ's life and ministry were known in Christian tradition, and occasionally shown to visitors, but they remained inconspicuous.[3] It was not till Constantine put his plans into effect that Palestine began to attract foreign pilgrims in any numbers. Indeed, Egeria's is the first vivid account of pilgrimage which exists, and, though she saw several buildings which had been erected since the days of Constantine, the principal and most glorious churches were his.

Fourth-century authors naturally interpreted earlier travels as pilgrimages. Thus Eusebius speaks of a visitor called Alexander who came to Jerusalem before 213 "for the purpose of prayer and investigation of the [holy] places", phrases which are echoed in
* the vocabulary of Egeria herself.[4] But these earlier visits do not seem to have been pilgrimages in the sense which later became

---

[1] Eusebius, *de Laud. Const.* 9, PG 20.1369.
[2] Eusebius, *Martyrs of Palestine*, 11.10, PG 20.1504.
[3] E.g. Justin Martyr (c. 150) who describes the cave at Bethlehem in *Dial.* 70, 78, PG 6.640, 657–60.
[4] Eusebius, *EH* 6.11.2, PG 20.541, (Alexander later became Bishop of Jerusalem); cf. Jerome *Vir. Ill.* 62, PL 23.674, and Egeria 17.1, and 13.1.

EASTERN ROMAN PROVINCES IN THE FOURTH CENTURY

HONORIAS
Claudiopolis
Constantinopolis
EUROPA
Nicomedia
ARMENIA
MESOPOTAMIA
GALATIA
Ancyra
BITHYNIA
CAPPADOCIA
Nisibis
Caesarea
AVGVSTA
Edessa
OSRHOENE
Iconium
CILICIA
LYCAONIA
Tarsus
Hierapolis
EUPHRATENSIS
ISAURIA
Seleucia
Antioch
COELE SYRIA
EASTERN FRONTIER
PHOENICE
Damascus
Bostra
Caesarea
ARABIA
PALAESTINA
Aelia
Alexandria
Pelusium
Petra
AEGYPTUS
AUGUSTAMNICA
ARABIA
ARCADIA
Antinoe
THEBAIS

0   100   200   300 miles

* normal. Melito of Sardis, who came before 190, said in a letter[1]
that he went to the East and "came to the place where these
things [i.e. the events recorded in the Bible] were proclaimed and
done", but he says nothing of visiting any particular sites. And,
when the theologian Origen came in about 230 "ostensibly to see
the holy places"[2], we only have evidence that he saw Bethlehem
and the holy wells near Ascalon.[3]

If the flowering of the Roman province of Palestine into a place
of pilgrimage, the "Holy Land", is to be ascribed to a single
man, that man is certainly Eusebius, the church historian and
bishop of Caesarea. He first came in contact with the Emperor at the
Council of Nicaea, and the friendship which began there lasted the
rest of their lives. Constantine already had some picture of Palestine
in his mind, since he had travelled through it as a young soldier in
296. But in Eusebius he met a man whose enthusiasm for the
country knew no bounds: Jerome, who later translated many of
his works, lists among them four which were directly concerned
with Palestine: "After explaining the names of various nations
which were or are in any way used among the Hebrews, after
his *Topography of Judaea and the various Inheritances of the Tribes*,
and his concise *Description of Jerusalem and its Temple*, he at length
worked on this . . . biblical gazetteer known as the *Onomasticon*."[4]

Eusebius certainly seems to have imparted some of his enthusiasm to the Emperor: according to Eusebius' *Life of Constantine*
the Emperor said, as he received baptism on his death-bed, "I
had thought to do this in the waters of Jordan."[5] At least he spared
no effort to adorn the traditional holy places.

Constantine wished to make it clear to the East that he was
Emperor, and that he favoured Christianity, and one of the ways
in which he pursued this policy was by the time-honoured
practice of pulling down shrines built by previous rulers and
substituting buildings of his own. Splendid churches were built

---

[1] Preserved in Eusebius, *EH* 4.26.14, *PG* 20.396.
[2] Jerome, *Vir. Ill.* 54, *PL* 23.665.
* [3] Origen, *contra Celsum* 1.51, 4.44, *PG* 11.756, 1100.
[4] Jerome, *Liber locorum et nominum*, preface, for which see E. Klostermann,
Eusebius Werke III.1, *Das Onomastikon*, GCS (Leipzig 1904), p. 3. All references
to the *Onomasticon* are to this edition, which includes Jerome's version.
[5] Eusebius, *Vit. Const.* 4.62, *PG* 20.1216.

in all the provincial capitals, and still greater ones in Constantinople, the New Rome.[1] Eusebius describes eight of them, four
of which are in or near Jerusalem. And, although the Emperor
himself could not personally supervise the works at Jerusalem, he
sent not only experts, materials, and funds,[2] but also his mother
Helena. Her visit to dedicate the buildings at Bethlehem and on *
the Mount of Olives was never forgotten.[3]

Eusebius' descriptions are remarkable for the care with which
he deals with the demolitions and clearing of the sites.[4] This is an
illuminating trait, for it was not Constantine's policy simply to
build churches. Rather he intended by his resplendent churches
both to efface the memory of pagan worship and superstition, and
also to display himself, and the Christian faith, as victorious. This
policy is further illustrated by the dedications of his churches.
Eusebius reports that the vast and superb church at Nicomedia,
the capital of Bithynia, was erected as a memorial of his victory
over Licinius,[5] that the churches at Bethlehem and the Mount
of Olives were "to immortalize the memory of his mother,
Helena",[6] and that at Constantinople his own tomb was to be
placed among those of the apostles.[7] All these reasons are certainly
consistent with piety, but they are equally consistent with the
political aims of his building policy.[8]

FOURTH-CENTURY PILGRIMS

The first writer to record a pilgrimage to the holy places was an
anonymous traveller who came overland to Palestine from Bordeaux[9] in A.D. 333. He shows which places were being pointed
out when Christian pilgrimage was still in its infancy, and

---

[1] Ibid. 3.48,50,58, PG 20.1108, 1109, 1124–5.
[2] See Note D, pp. 242–52 below.   *
[3] Eusebius, Vit. Const. 3.42–7, PG 20.1101–8; see pp. 240–1 below.
[4] Cf. ibid. 3.26 (p. 164 below) for Jerusalem; ibid. 3.48, for Constantinople;
and EH 10.4.26f, PG 20.864–5 for Tyre.
[5] Eusebius, Vit. Const. 3.50.   [6] Ibid. 3.41.
[7] Ibid. 3.58, but cf. Philostorgius EH, fr. 2, PG 65.480–1 who says that the
tomb was next to the Church of the Apostles.
[8] On this policy see further M. H. Shepherd, "Liturgical Expressions of the
Constantinian Triumph" in Dumbarton Oaks Papers 21 (1967), pp. 59–78.
[9] The part of his work relating to the holy places is translated below, pp.
153–63.

(despite its laconic style) his account is of great interest. The next writer to speak about the holy places is St Cyril of Jerusalem, whose *Catechetical Lectures* were delivered in the church on Golgotha in about A.D. 348. In the year when Cyril became Bishop of Jerusalem, A.D. 351, St Basil of Caesarea came to visit Palestine,[1] and, like Egeria, went on to visit Alexandria and the rest of Egypt, Coele-Syria, and Mesopotamia. Basil hardly mentions the holy places. He states that the object of his journey was to visit the monks and ascetics, to stay with them, and to learn the secret of their holy lives.

Holy places and holy men gave the East a double attraction for the Western Christian, and most of the travellers described in the second half of the fourth century sought out both. They would see the holy places of Palestine with their great churches. They would see the *martyria*, which by then lay in profusion along routes which, less than a century before, had appeared simply pagan. But they would also be within reach of living heroes of their faith, whose discipline, holiness, and sufferings had rendered them famous throughout the Christian world. These too, at least as monks and confessors, were a relatively new phenomenon, since the great Egyptian pioneers of monasticism, Paul the first hermit (228–343) and his famous successors, Antony (251–356) and Pachomius (c. 275–c. 349), had still been alive, all three of them, only forty years before Egeria's journey; and persecutions were so recent that Egeria met two bishops who had been exiled under Valens (who died only five years before her journey) and thus merited the honourable title "confessor".

Egeria is a notable example of a traveller who came to see both holy places and saints; but there were many others like her, of whom the most famous are Melania the Elder and Rufinus who came in 373,[2] Jerome and Vincent in 385,[3] soon followed by the noble lady Paula and her daughter Eustochium,[4] and Poemenia, a member of the imperial family.[5]

---

[1] Amphilochius, *Vita S. Bas.* I, PG 29. CCC and Basil *Ep* 223.2, PG 32.824.
[2] Jerome, *Ep.* 4 ad Florentium, PL 22.336.
[3] Jerome, *adv. Lib. Rufin.* 3.22, PL 23.473.
[4] Jerome, *Ep.* 108, PL 22.878–906.
[5] See p. 51.

THE HOLY PLACES

One of the words most frequently used by Egeria is "holy"; she applies it impartially to mountains, buildings, and people, and among the holy men and women to saints of the Old as well as of the New Testament. Thus she sets off as enthusiastically to the tomb of Saint Job as she does to that of Saint Thomas, since she shared with most ordinary Christians of the fourth century the belief that the Old Testament no less than the New was concerned throughout with Jesus Christ. This belief had a profound effect on pilgrimage. Not only were most Jewish holy places likely to be considered sacred by Christians as well, but the land was used in a much fuller way than it is by today's Christian visitor, who is on the whole both less familiar and also less deeply involved with the Old Testament.

To one who shared Egeria's high regard for the Old Testament Palestine's interest was increased enormously. For where the New Testament mentions fewer than fifty place-names in this region, the Old Testament names roughly a thousand. Thus the places visited by Egeria comprise three main types: first, there are the caves, "houses", and other buildings connected with the saints of the Old Testament and some (far fewer in Egeria's time than later on) connected with people mentioned in the New Testament; secondly, there are the martyria, a word usually applied to the tombs of martyrs, biblical or more recent; among these it should be remembered that prophets were in Egeria's day generally understood to have been martyrs; and thirdly, the places of Christ's ministry, particularly those which had been adorned by Constantine.

Most Muslim villages in Palestine today contain the tomb of some local worthy or *weli*, often a character from the Bible, and the choice of possible places of pilgrimage is enormous. In practice the places visited today, as in Egeria's time, are usually selected because adequate roads lead to them. Roman roads provided a network which made it possible to travel widely, and the maps (see following pages) show that most of the places regularly visited by fourth-century pilgrims were on or very close

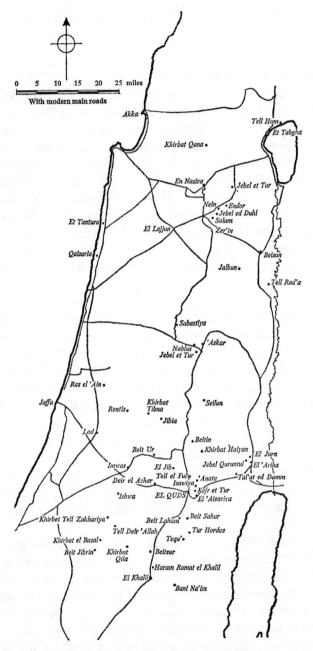

ARABIC NAMES OF FOURTH-CENTURY PLACES OF PILGRIMAGE

16

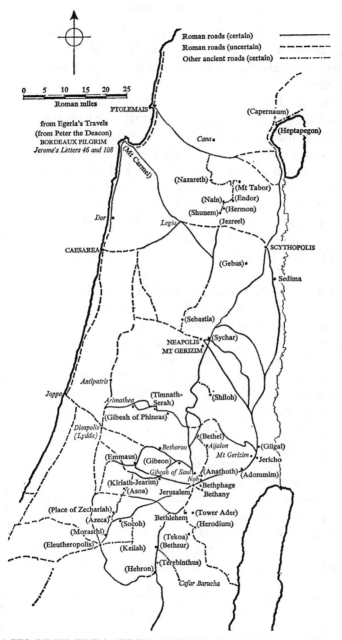

Roman roads (certain) ——————
Roman roads (uncertain) – – – – –
Other ancient roads (certain) —·—·—·—

0   5   10   15   20   25
Roman miles

*from Egeria's Travels
(from Peter the Deacon)*
BORDEAUX PILGRIM
Jerome's Letters 46 and 108

PTOLEMAIS

(Mt Carmel)

Cana

(Capernaum)

(Heptapegon)

(Nazareth)

(Mt Tabor)

(Nain)   (Endor)
(Shunem)   (Hermon)

Dor

Legio

(Jezreel)

CAESAREA

SCYTHOPOLIS

(Gebus)

Sedima

(Sebastia)

NEAPOLIS
MT GERIZIM

(Sychar)

Antipatris

(Timnath-
Serah)

Joppa

Arimathea

(Shiloh)

(Gibeah of Phineas)

*Diospolis
(Lydda)*

(Bethel)

(Emmaus)

Bethoron

Aijalon
Mt Gerizim

(Gilgal)

Jericho

(Gibeon)

Gibeah of Saul

(Kiriath-Jearim)

Nob

(Anathoth)

(Adommim)

(Asoa)

Jerusalem

Bethphage
Bethany

(Place of Zechariah)

(Tower Ader)

(Azeca)

(Socoh)

Bethlehem

(Herodium)

(Morasthi)

(Eleutheropolis)

(Keilah)

(Tekoa)
(Bethsur)

(Hebron)

(Terebinthus)

Cafar Barucha

PLACES OF PILGRIMAGE IN FOURTH-CENTURY PALESTINE

to a road. Egeria's own exceptions tend to prove the rule, since she describes in some detail the hardships of her expedition to Sinai, and makes special mention of leaving the road on the way to Nebo.[1]

The fact that so wide an assortment of places was visited in the fourth century by no means implies that they were then regarded as all of equal importance. Thus, when Jerome is describing the pilgrimage of Paula, he mentions Antipatris only to point out that it was named after Herod's father, and Eleutheropolis occurs in Peter the Deacon's book only as a place from which miles are measured. Even Egeria mentions a few places, such as forts, which were of topographical rather than devotional interest.

Nor can we take it that all the places shown to Egeria were what they were said to be. On the whole she was shown places which were hallowed by local tradition, but there were traditions of many different kinds. Thus the monks of Mount Sinai seem to have been the first to fix on Jebel Musa as the scene of the giving of the Law, and by the time Egeria came they had already built up a detailed topography of the mountain and its area. This strangely shaped rock, that ruin, this lonely bush, that spring were drawn into the service of their interpretation of the place where they spent their life. And a similar process could be traced in many other holy places, but not all. There were others where the building of tradition had already been done for the Christians by other users of the Bible, Samaritans or Jews. And there were yet other places, at times almost lost among the wealth of traditional interpretations, which were very likely to have been the same places of which the Bible speaks. This is clearly true of large or famous towns such as Memphis, Jericho, or Jerusalem, or of unmistakable geographical features such as the Sea of Galilee. But it is also true of some of the smaller spots. The pool of Siloam, the Pool of Bethesda, and the Jerusalem Temple enclosure were none

---

[1] If the places mentioned by Peter the Deacon are also taken into account, this general impression is not altered. There is no special road leading to Gebus, the village on Mount Gilboa (V.5), but it seems that the traveller saw it from a distance, rather than visiting it. Nor are there definite remains of the road to Tekoa (L.2). But these are the only two which are any distance from a good road.

of them in the same condition when Egeria saw them as when Christ had come to them. But they were undoubtedly authentic.

Egeria spent three full years in Jerusalem, and must have visited all the places on the normal pilgrim round. What we have in the manuscript is the last part of her journey, when she pays visits to such out-of-the-way places as Mount Nebo. Most of the more ordinary places are mentioned by Valerius and by Peter the Deacon, and to obtain a balanced view of Egeria's pilgrimages it is useful to begin by reading at least the extracts from Peter's work, even though they are less attractive than their lively original.

Apart from Jerusalem itself the normal fourth-century pilgrim visited holy places in four distinct areas. From north to south these are: first, those in Galilee, which was at that time still a strongly Jewish area; then, those near Neapolis, particularly the Tomb of Joseph and Jacob's Well; third, those near Jerusalem, particularly Bethlehem and Bethel; and fourth, those to the south, in and around Hebron and near Eleutheropolis.

Relations between Christians and Jews in Palestine were too competitive to guarantee an unbroken continuity in the devotional use of the Jewish holy places.[1] Even by Egeria's time not all the late Jewish traditions remained undisturbed. But seven hundred years later, after four centuries of Muslim rule, a far greater number of sites had been reinterpreted or forgotten. When Christians returned to the Holy Land as Crusaders, they created an entirely new tradition of topography in many parts of * Palestine.

THE MEANING OF PILGRIMAGE

The fourth century is a time of rapid development in the understanding of pilgrimage. The ideas begin to take shape with Eusebius, though he was not himself a pilgrim, but a native who had witnessed the triumphant finding and adorning of the holy places. To him they are holy first and foremost because they are visible witnesses to the truth of the biblical narrative.[2] The Pilgrim of Bordeaux may perhaps have seen them in this light, though his

[1] See Note K, pp. 296-7 below.
[2] Cf. *Vit. Const.* 3.28 (p. 165 below).

narrative is too condensed for us to be certain; but Cyril of Jerusalem constantly appeals to the holy places as confirmation of his baptismal lectures: "Should you be disposed to doubt it [the crucifixion], the very place which everyone can see proves you wrong, this blessed Golgotha . . . on which we are now assembled." "Deny not the crucified . . . Gethsemane bears him witness, where the betrayal took place".[1]

Even when he describes the discovery of the Lord's sepulchre, Eusebius says not a word about prayer. The revealing of the monument is wonderful, but rather as a support for faith than as a stimulant to devotion.[2] Cyril, it seems,[3] developed his belief about the holy places into an elaborate public liturgy, and the same formalized reaction is seen on its modest scale in the short offices experienced by Egeria on her private pilgrimages. The ejaculations of prayer which punctuate her narrative are not so much inspired by her emotional reaction to this or that holy place, as by God's goodness in permitting her to reach them.

A new warmth appears in Jerome's account of Paula. True there are occasions when her reactions are those of a polite pilgrim bearing with an embarrassingly learned guide: "She did not choose to go to Kiriath Sepher (the Village of Letters), for, despising the letter that kills, she had discovered the Spirit that gives life."[4] But Paula has her own emotions as well:

She prostrated herself before the Cross, and worshipped as though she could see the Lord hanging there. Entering the Sepulchre of the Resurrection, she kissed the Stone which the angel had removed from its mouth. And with faithful lips she touched the place where the Lord's body had lain as a thirsty man drinks welcome water. Jerusalem is witness to the tears she shed and to her moanings: the Lord is her witness, to whom she prayed.[5]

Pilgrimage became a practical possibility through the combina-

---

[1] *Cat.* 10.19, 13.38, *PG* 33.688,817.

[2] Compare the words of Melito of Sardis quoted above, p. 12, n. 1.

[3] There is no direct evidence that this liturgical development was due to Cyril, but it took place during his episcopate; see G. Dix, *The Shape of the Liturgy* (London 1945), pp. 349–50 and cf. pp. 54f below.

[4] Jerome, *Ep.* 108.11.

[5] Ibid. 108.9. For an interesting comment on later developments in the approach to pilgrimage see Vermeer, *Obs.*, pp. 58f, 67f, 79, 85f.

tion of Eusebius' learning and Constantine's bounty. But it was nowhere commanded to Christians in holy Scripture, and could not be taken to be a Christian obligation. A strong criticism of pilgrimage along these lines appeared in about 380 from the pen of St Gregory of Nyssa, who had been sent at public expense to Jerusalem to settle a quarrel among the clergy, and wrote a disgruntled letter[1] on his return home. Jerome is very likely to have read this letter, and it is tempting to think that two of his own letters are designed to refute Gregory's arguments. One of them was an invitation to pilgrimage written to the Roman lady Marcella,[2] and the other a reply to Paulinus of Nola who proposed to come and live in Jerusalem as a monk;[3] Jerome in fact dissuades him, but not for reasons which would hold against pilgrimage.

Jerome readily admits that pilgrimage is not an obligation: "Nothing is lacking to your faith, although you have not seen Jerusalem: and I am no better because I live where I do [in Bethlehem]." But this is no defence against Gregory's principal argument, which runs as follows:

If God's grace were more plentiful in the Jerusalem neighbourhood than elsewhere, then its inhabitants would not make sin so much the fashion. But as it is, there is no sort of filthy conduct they do not practise—cheating, adultery, theft, idolatry, poisoning, quarrelling and murder are commonplace. . . . Then what proof have you, in a place which allows things like that to go on, of the abundance of divine grace?

Speaking to Paulinus Jerome has to agree that Jerusalem displays the scenes of Christ's passion and resurrection "in a crowded city with the whole variety of people you normally find in such centres—prostitutes, actors, and clowns".[4] But Bethlehem was a different matter:

What we are saying does not deny that the kingdom of God is within us, nor that there are saintly men in other places. But we do say most

[1] Known as *On Pilgrimages*, PG 46.1009–16.
[2] *Ep* 46, written in 386, PL 22.483–92.
[3] *Ep*. 58, written in 395, PL 22.579–86. Note that Paulinus, like a number of the early monks, was a married man; for another example see Sulpicius Severus, *Dial*. 1.23, PL 20.198.
[4] *Ep* 58.4.

decidedly that the leading saints in the world are those who gather here. . . . They speak many different languages, yet have but one rule of life. . . . Most important of all Christian virtues, there is no arrogance, no conceit about religious discipline. The only competition we have is in humility.[1]

Gregory had asked what advantage there was for the man who has reached "those celebrated spots": "He cannot imagine that our Lord is today living there in his body, but has abandoned us foreigners; or that the Holy Spirit is plentifully present in Jerusalem, but unable to travel so far that he reaches us." Christ is not, of course, confined. Jerome does not "presume to restrict to a narrow strip of earth him whom the heaven cannot contain",[2] and asks a pertinent question:

If the tombs of servants and men[3] are glorious, why should we not consider glorious the tomb of the Lord and God? After all, everywhere in the world we venerate the tombs of the martyrs, and hold their holy ashes to our eyes or, if we may, kiss them—then how can anyone think we should neglect the tomb in which they placed the Lord![4]

Gregory's final complaint was that he had received no spiritual benefit from his visit: "We knew his incarnation by the Virgin before we saw Bethlehem, we believed in his resurrection from the dead before we saw his tomb." Yet for Jerome the Christian comes to Jerusalem as the Greek scholar to Athens.[5] He insists that "the places which witnessed the crucifixion and resurrection are of profit only to those who are bearing their own crosses, and are daily rising again with Christ, thus showing themselves worthy of so holy an abode".[6] Many who do not come to Jerusalem are saints. Yes. But if Marcella accepts the invitation to visit her friends in the Holy Land she will be able to say with them, "I have found him whom my soul desired."[7]

VISITING THE ASCETICS

St Antony had first established himself as a hermit in his ruined fort at Pispir in 285, only a century before Egeria's visit to the East. His determination pointed the way to new possibilities in an

[1] *Ep.* 46.10.   [2] *Ep.* 58.3.
[3] In the context he is referring to those of the Apostles Peter and Paul.
[4] *Ep.* 46.8.   [5] *Ep.* 46.9.   [6] *Ep.* 58.3.   [7] *Cant.* 3.4.

Empire long conscious of its decadence, and he had many follow-ers. By Egeria's time the hermits and monks of the East had long been famous. Their lives are known in considerable detail, since Palladius, their most famous historian, went on an extended visit to Egypt only two years after Egeria's visits, and ten years later he was followed by John Cassian, whose works were widely read in the West and had a great influence on monastic life there. But in 400 many of the Egyptian monks fled elsewhere. Egeria and the two historians were thus among the last to see Egyptian monasti-cism in its most flourishing state.

What drew so many visitors to see the monks and hermits? Cassian and Palladius were already monks before they made their visits, Egeria was a nun, and they no doubt wished to learn about the religious life from the acknowledged originators and experts. The same motive prompted visits by those who were intending to become monks, and attached themselves for a time to the men who would be best able to set an example. St Basil, for instance, visited the famous monks soon after 350, and twenty years later described his visit in these terms:

I read the Gospel, and I saw there that a great means of perfection was the selling of one's goods, the sharing of them with the poor, the giving up of all care for this life, and the refusal to allow the soul to be turned by any feeling of sympathy to the things of earth. I prayed that I might find some one of the brethren who had chosen this way of life, that with him I might cross life's deep and troubled strait. I found many in Alexandria, many in the rest of Egypt, and others in Palestine, Coele Syria, and Mesopotamia. I wondered at their continence in living and their endurance in toil; I was amazed at their persistence in prayer, and at their triumphs over sleep.[1]

The asceticism of the monks was a feature new to the Roman world, and to those who came to it from the easy-going atmos-phere of the great cities it was almost incredible. In the *Life of St Paul the First Hermit* which Jerome wrote when in 375 he was beginning his own ascetic apprenticeship in Syria, these words occur:

I call Jesus and his holy angels to witness that I have seen, and still see

[1] Basil, *Ep.* 223, *PG* 32.824.

among the monks of the tract of desert between Syria and the Saracens'
country, one who was shut up for thirty years and lived on barley
bread and muddy water, while . . . another kept himself alive on five
dried figs a day.[1]

Such feats of endurance certainly attracted would-be followers to
the cells of the great monks and hermits. But as their fame spread
they ran the risk of becoming a tourist attraction.

Visitors could be a problem. Cassian reports the shame of John,
an Egyptian abbot, at the anchorites who, "under pretence of
hospitality and welcoming guests have actually begun to keep a
blanket in their cells".[2] The New Testament itself enjoined the
virtue of hospitality,[3] and the clergy and monks of Egeria's
acquaintance clearly obeyed with generosity; but the monks had
deliberately retired from the world to seek solitude, and the
influx of visitors placed them in a dilemma. So St Hilarion,[4]
began his religious life by attaching himself to St Antony, but it
was not long before there were streams of visitors:

At last, unable any longer to endure the crowds of those who visited the
saint because they suffered from various illnesses or the attacks of
demons; and thinking it very strange that in the desert he should have
to endure the crowds of cities, he thought it better to begin as Antony
had begun. "Antony", he said, "is reaping the rewards of victory. He
is a veteran who has proved his bravery, but I have not even begun my
military service."[5]

For Antony solitude was less important than service to people in
need, but this was because he had already had years of solitude to
prepare him.

It went without saying that in distant places the monks should
provide necessary food for their visitors, and this too might have
caused difficulties. But by Egeria's time their normal practice was
to provide small tokens of hospitality rather than full provision.
Egeria calls these tokens "Blessings" (*eulogiae*), and they often

[1] *Life of Paul* 6, PL 23.21.
[2] Cassian, *Coll.* 19.6, PL 49.1136.
[3] See I Tim. 3.2; Titus 1.8; Rom. 12.13; I Pet. 4.9.
[4] Hilarion founded the first "Laura" in Palestine. Laura was the Palestinian
name (not, however, recorded by Egeria) for a community of individuals who
lived separately but under the direction of a single abbot.
[5] Jerome, *Life of Hilarion* 3, PL 23.30.

take the form of fruit. There is no indication that Egeria saw any connection between these "Blessings" and the celebration of the Eucharist.

Egeria treats the monks and ascetics with her accustomed straightforwardness and appreciation, and they respond with unvarying courtesy, spending a great deal of time and energy in talking to her and showing her the holy places. This cordial relationship probably reflects the relation between disciple and master, which is echoed (though in a different idiom) in Jerome's description of Paula's arrival at Alexandria:

There came to meet her the holy and reverend bishop and confessor Isidore, with innumerable crowds of monks. . . . Was there one whose cell she did not enter? Was there one at whose feet she did not prostrate herself? In each of these men she believed she was seeing Christ, and the gifts she offered them she rejoiced to have given to the Lord.[1]

Some of the visitors came in need, and others with the intention of learning about a life which they saw as their own vocation. But there were also those who came on a combined search for edification and pious entertainment. When Postumianus returned to Narbonne after three years in the East,[2] his friend Sulpicius Severus asked him how the faith of Christ was flourishing there, and "with what signs and miracles Christ is working in his servants". After some polite hesitation Postumianus proceeds to unfold amazing stories of monks whose exemplary obedience enabled them to go unharmed through fire, to tame wolves and lions, and to vanquish demons.

As the Emperor Julian had complained, some of the monks were no better than tramps.[3] Thus Pachomius introduced an important change when he supplemented Antony's system by his own. For whereas Antony's hermits had lived in groups in which each was independent of his neighbour, Pachomius established a system whereby the members of a group all acknowledged the authority of a single abbot. Antony's "monastic' 'and Pachomius'

---

[1] *Ep.* 108.14.
[2] He spent six months with Jerome in Bethlehem. His visit is recounted in Sulpicius Severus, *Dialogue* I, *PL* 20.183–202, written in 404, like Jerome's *Ep.* 108.
[3] Julian, *Orat.* 7 in *Works* (Teubner, Leipzig 1875), p. 290.

"coenobitic" system continued to exist side by side, and others were added, such as those based on the *Rules* of Saint Basil and John Cassian. The following passage from Cassian's *Conversations* describes the two Egyptian systems, and something of the confusion which existed in their terminology. Germanus interviews Abbot Piamun, a priest and leader of anchorites:

Germanus: Is there any difference between a "coenobium" and a "monastery", or do the two words mean the same?
Piamun: There are many people who make no distinction between them, and speak of monasteries as coenobia. But the difference is this: "monastery" means the dwelling, that is, simply the place where the monks live, while "coenobium" describes the character of life and its system. "Monastery" too may mean the dwelling of a single monk,[1] whereas "coenobium" can only mean the place where a number of men live together in a united community. The places where groups of Sarabaites[2] live are also called "monasteries".

Egeria thus visited men and women living under several distinct types of religious discipline. But, although she may well have written an extended description of their varying ways of life, any such description is certainly lacking from the manuscript we have, and it is impossible to make any clear distinctions between those who are there mentioned.[3]

---

[1] *Coll.* 18.9–10, *PL* 49.1110–11.
[2] For Sarabaites see below, p. 35.
[3] See further pp. 34–5 below, and D. Chitty. *The Desert a City* (Oxford 1966).

Egeria's Route

Egeria's text as we have it plunges straight into a description of her approach to Mount Sinai. But the journeys described in the text seem to have occupied only about four months, and she tells us that she was out in Jerusalem for "three full years".[1] A good deal of this time was no doubt spent in Jerusalem itself, where she was making notes on the liturgical improvements she discovered there; but we must visualize a good deal more travelling as well.[2]

Valerius' *Letter* and Peter the Deacon's *Holy Places* together provide an assortment of information which enables us to fill in a good deal of what is now missing from Egeria's own text. Unfortunately for our present purpose Peter the Deacon made Bede's book *On the Holy Places* the outline of his compilation, and we cannot therefore rely on him for the order in which Egeria made her visits. But we can often tell where she went.

It is thus possible to make a guess at her programme during the three years, though guesswork is the best we can do. Her travels seem to divide themselves into ten distinct sections:

1. EXPLORATION OF JERUSALEM AND THE AREA (A.D. 381)

Arriving from Constantinople in time for Easter,[3] Egeria visits the main holy places in the city of Jerusalem.[4] She goes on to explore other holy places which could be reached by short excursions from Jerusalem,[5] and makes the slightly longer excursion to those near Neapolis.[6]

2. VISIT TO ALEXANDRIA AND THE THEBAID (381–3)

She makes her first journey to Egypt, comprising a long tour of the monks and clergy in Nitria and the Thebaid, and returns through Goshen.[7]

3. VISIT TO GALILEE (383)

After visiting the neighbourhoods of Nazareth and Capernaum she goes down to Scythopolis, then west across the great plain to

---

[1] 17.1. [2] Her own text demands this; see 9.1,6.
[3] 17.1; 23.8. [4] See PD, E, I, L.I, N.I.
[5] See PD, L.2, P.2. [6] See PD, R.
[7] See 9.1,6; 7.1, and PD, Y1–3.

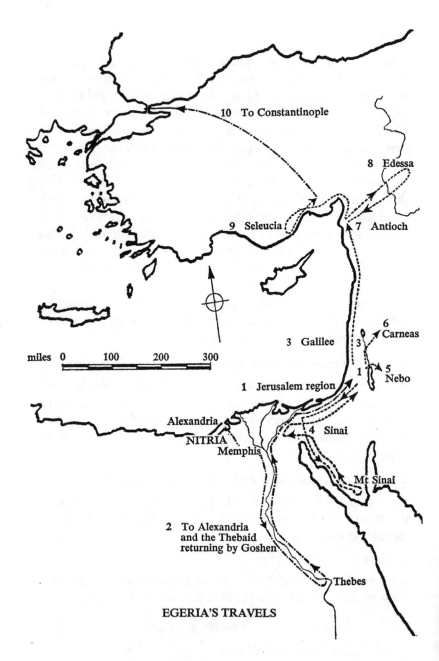

10 To Constantinople

8 Edessa

9 Seleucia   7 Antioch

6
Carneas

3 Galilee   3

1 Nebo
5

1 Jerusalem region

Alexandria
NITRIA
Memphis   4 Sinai

Mt Sinai

2 To Alexandria
and the Thebaid
returning by Goshen

Thebes

miles 0   100   200   300

EGERIA'S TRAVELS

Carmel, and back to Jerusalem by way of Sebastia. Here it seems that Peter the Deacon gives the place-names in the order of the itinerary.[1]

4. THE JOURNEY TO MOUNT SINAI (383–January 384)

At some stage before her journey to Sinai Egeria must have spent a long continuous period in Jerusalem, making notes on its liturgy.[2] Then, in late November, she sets off on her second visit to Egypt, going first to Mount Sinai.[3] On her return journey she makes a slight detour in order to pay a second visit to Goshen.[4]

5. THE EXCURSION TO MOUNT NEBO[5] (January or February 384)

6. THE JOURNEY TO CARNEAS[6] (February or March 384)

7. DEPARTURE FROM JERUSALEM FOR ANTIOCH (March 384)

It is likely that Egeria would have stayed in Jerusalem to take part in the celebration of Easter Day (24 March). If she had left on the following day, she could comfortably have reached Carrae by 23 April.[7] The first stage of her journey to Constantinople took her as far as Antioch.[8]

8. RETURN JOURNEY FROM ANTIOCH TO EDESSA (April 384)

Egeria's object in making this journey was to visit Edessa,[9] but she also found that there was much of interest to see in Carrae before she returned to Antioch.[10]

9. THE JOURNEY TO ST THECLA'S (May 384)

From Antioch Egeria covered more distance on her main route to Constantinople. But from Tarsus she made another return journey along the coast to Seleucia of Isauria to visit St Thecla's martyrium and her friend Marthana.[11]

---

[1] See PD, V2–7a; V7b–8 is an account of excursions to the south of Jerusalem.
[2] 24—49.   [3] PD, V9–Y17 and Egeria, 1.1—6.4.
[4] 7—9.   [5] 10—12.   [6] 13—16.
[7] See 20.5.   [8] 17.
[9] 17—19.   [10] 20—21.   [11] 22.1—23.6a.

10. THE ARRIVAL IN CONSTANTINOPLE (June or July 384)

As she writes to her sisters, Egeria is planning to make a further pilgrimage to St John's at Ephesus.[1]

[1] 23.6b–10.

Jerusalem—The Christian Community

The modern system of dioceses and parishes as areas of jurisdiction covering the whole map had begun to take shape in some parts of the Church in the time of Egeria. But she describes the older system; for, although church buildings had multiplied rapidly under the Christian emperors of the fourth century, there were still many towns and villages with no Christians, and the church communities still normally assembled in town centres, to worship with the bishop of the town.

The Jerusalem community, of which Egeria gives a detailed picture, was in several details unusual. Since it attracted pilgrims and residents from many parts of the world, it had its own special language-difficulties.[1] It also had an unusually large number of monks and nuns. But Egeria makes no comment which suggests any fundamental difference between the structure of the Church in Jerusalem and that of her own branch of the Church in the far West.

The bishop was essentially the leader of a community of Christians in a town or large village. As the father of the Christian family he sits in the chief seat at services,[2] and, when he has blessed the people, they come to him one by one to kiss his hand.[3] His ∗ attitude to the people is delightfully expressed in the words he addresses to them at a moment of special fatigue in the course of the ceremonies on Holy Thursday.[4] And he is their chief priest; as the High Priests of the Jewish Temple alone entered the Holy of ∗ Holies,[5] so he alone goes into the holy caves while the congregation remain outside.[6] He takes the principal part in the Eucharist,[7] and leads many of the prayers.[8] He is also the principal teacher of

[1] See 47.3–5.
[2] At Jerusalem his seat seems to have been portable; it was normally in the Anastasis, where it was used daily at Lucernare (24.4), but was placed elsewhere as necessary, in the Martyrium (45.2; 46.1) or near the Cross (37.1,5).
[3] The expression used is *ad manum accedunt*; see p. 83 below and, for example, 24.2.
[4] See 36.5.　　　　[5] See p. 165, n. 4 below.
[6] See 24.2,10; 25.3; 33.2; 47.1.　　　　　　　　　　　　　　　　∗
[7] See 29.3 "the bishop offers". Egeria usually says the equivalent of "they offer" or "we offer"; see, for example, 43.3 and 4.8.
[8] E.g. 24.2,3,6.

the community, though presbyters also teach; thus he reads some of the most important lessons,[1] gives the final sermon on Sundays,[2] and personally instructs those who are preparing for baptism.[3]

Egeria records the fact that a number of bishops had started their ministry as monks,[4] and one of the greatest compliments she pays bishops (and other clergy) is that they are "learned in the Scriptures".[5]

Presbyters occupy seats of honour round the bishop on any solemn occasion,[6] like the elders (*presbyteroi*) of Revelation 4.4. They take their part in preaching on Sundays, read lessons,[7] and lead prayers[8] and psalms.[9] The presbyters sit round the bishop, like his "councillors, the crown and senate of the church",[10] while he conducts the baptismal preparation,[11] and the initial registration of the candidates is also the task of a presbyter.

Presbyters were thus the bishop's lieutenants, and seen to be so as they sat round him. But the bishop might send them to act on his behalf as leaders of subsidiary communities, too remote to be able to come regularly to the services in the central church where he personally presided. Egeria mentions several such communities,[12] and it is interesting that, when she arrives among them, the presbyters show her round and explain the sights, as the bishops do in other places.[13] Presbyters who were put in charge of churches out of range of the episcopal centres presided at the Eucharist, but they do not seem to have given blessings, which were probably the bishop's prerogative.[14]

The deacons, like the presbyters, lead prayers[15] and psalms,[16] but Egeria does not mention an occasion on which they read lessons,

---

[1] E.g. 24.10; 33.2.   [2] See 25.1.   [3] 45—47.
[4] Bishops of Arabia 8.4, Batanis 19.1, Edessa 19.5, Carrae 20.2, Seleucia 23.1.
[5] See 9.2; 14.2; 20.9; cf. Eusebius *VC* 4.43.   [6] Cf. 43.5; 45.2.
[7] These seem to have been specially important lessons; see 29.5; 34; 43.3.
[8] E.g. 24.1   [9] E.g. 24.9.
[10] The description in *Const. Apost.* 2.28, PG 1.673.   [11] See 45.1,3.
[12] See, for example, 3.1; 4.8; 10.8; 14.1; and 25.12.
[13] See 12.3; 14.2.
[14] See 10.3 for a presbyter presiding at the Eucharist; and compare the blessings in 20.3; 21.1 (where a bishop leads prayer) with the same forms of prayer without blessings in 4.4; 10.7 (where a presbyter leads).
[15] E.g. 24.8,12.   [16] E.g. 24.9.

and they do not preach. When the bishop takes his seat, they remain standing round him like a bodyguard[1] (a function which on some occasions is more than a formality[2]). A deacon reads the names of individuals at the intercession at Lucernare (though the bishop reads them in the Morning Hymns[3]), and it falls to him to make announcements, as when he calls for the people to bow their heads for the bishop's blessing.[4] The deacon is "the ear, eye and mouth of the bishop, his angel and prophet, who ought to set him free from all unnecessary tasks".[5] Egeria shows that the recently introduced title of "archdeacon"[6] was applied to the leading deacon in Jerusalem, and that it was this deacon who gave out the special notices during the pre-Easter ceremonies.[7] It may well be that the archdeacon was elected by the other deacons.[8] She also uses the title "deaconess" for one of her friends who was in charge of some nuns, but what she says of her does not enable the reader to give any definite connotation to the title.[9]

The word "clergy" includes for Egeria both presbyters and deacons,[10] but it included other orders as well, since a *clericus* is on one occasion distinguished from presbyters and deacons.[11] The clergy carried out the daily exorcism of the baptismal candidates during Lent,[12] so we may assume that some belonged to the order of Exorcists, which had already been in existence in the West for a century.[13]

The congregation at ordinary services comprised three distinct groups of lay people: the monks (to be described later), the faithful,

---

[1] See 31.1. [2] See 37.2.
[3] 24.5; cf. 24.2. [4] 24.6.
[5] The words of *Const. Apost.* 11.28,44, PG 1.673,704.
[6] First found in a work of A.D. 367, Optatus, *de schism. Donat.*, 1.16, PL 11.916. Compare Gingras, p. 232, n. 344.
[7] See 29.3; 30.2; 35.1; 43.3.
[8] As described by Jerome, *Ep.* 146.1, PL, 22.1194.
[9] 23.3; *Didascalia Apostolorum* 16, ed. R. H. Connolly (Oxford 1929), pp. 146f, assigns to deaconesses the tasks of helping at the baptism of adult women and relieving the poor.
[10] See 44.3 and 24.1.
[11] 24.9, as in, for example, Augustine, *c. Emer.* 1, cited by Gingras, p. 219, n. 288.
[12] 46.1.
[13] Exorcists are first mentioned in a letter of Pope Cornelius (before A.D. 253), in Eusebius, *EH* 6.43.14, PG 20.624.

and those not yet baptized, who were known as catechumens. The bishop's blessings are given separately to the faithful and to the catechumens, and there is a marked distinction between them. For, although the catechumens are expected to be assiduous in attending the daily services and in fasting,[1] they are not permitted to be present at Baptism or the Eucharist, nor at the teaching by which candidates are prepared to receive them. Under such circumstances the use of the word "catechumen" is odd, since its literal meaning is "one who is being catechized"; but, when Egeria describes the beginning of the catechetical instruction, she uses a different word (*competentes*[2]) to describe those who are enrolled, and immediately they are baptized the candidates become *infantes*,[3] a word which means rather that they were newborn babes in Christ than that they were infants by age (indeed Egeria describes them as "men and women",[4] and the questions they are asked at their scrutinies are designed for young adults[5]). The word "catechumen" may well refer to people who have been accepted to serve for a probationary period,[6] and, if so, the scrutinies would refer to their conduct during this period, for which their godparents would be able to give evidence.[7]

The whole congregation of faithful and catechumens is described as "the people",[8] "the Christians",[9] or "the brothers and sisters";[10] but these descriptions seem to be given without reference to the monks.[11] When Egeria wishes to distinguish ordinary lay people from monks and nuns, she calls them "secular men and women".[12]

Monks and nuns were among the people whom Egeria came to visit in the East, and she describes many. The ones she specially admires are the great monks who (at least at Sinai and Mount

[1] 27.5. [2] Meaning "postulants" (45.2).
[3] See 38.1; 39.3, and p. 62 below.
[4] 46.1. [5] See 45.2–3.
[6] Like the three-year period mentioned in Hippolytus, *Ap. Trad.*, 17.1.
[7] See 45.4. Note that, though Egeria speaks of the catechumens being dismissed before the central act of the Eucharist (25.2 q.v.), she does not use the phrases "Mass of the Catechumens" and "Mass of the Faithful" which seem to have originated in the eleventh century.
[8] Usually *populus* as in 29.4, sometimes *plebs* as in 39.3.
[9] 43.8,9. [10] 47.4; and see Bastiaensen, *Obs.*, pp. 3–7.
[11] Cf. 40.1. [12] See 49.1.

Nebo) were called "ascetics",[1] normally living in remote places, but sometimes coming into the cities for great festivals.[2]

But, though Egeria uses several different words to describe people who have set themselves apart from the world by religious vows, her vocabulary is too confused to make it possible to distinguish technical terms. For this lack of precision she is hardly to be blamed, since different technical terms were used in Egypt from those of Syria and Palestine, and there were no doubt many local variations as well. Indeed Palladius himself in the *Lausiac History* uses "ascetic" and "monk" interchangeably.

It is noticeable that Egeria normally uses the word *monachi* (monks) to describe religious outside Jerusalem,[3] and *monazontes* for those who attend the services in the city, a word often used by Cyril[4] of the same group. But the words are not mutually exclusive,[5] and Egeria explains that *monazontes* meant monks and *parthenae* (= virgins) nuns according to the local usage of Jerusalem.

Another local word,[6] equally meaning "monks and nuns"[7] is "apotactites" (literally, "people set apart"), and there is no reason to suppose that these had a rule of life[8] distinct from that of the *monachi* or *monazontes*. Though the name was new to Egeria, it was one of the ordinary words for monks in Egypt. It is interesting that, whenever she uses "brother" to refer to monks, she explains what it means,[9] which suggests not so much that she found this usage novel but rather that "brother" was also one of the ordinary words for "baptized Christian".[10]

[1] 3.4; 10.9. [2] E.g. 20.5; cf. 49.1.
[3] E.g. 3.1; 49.1; cf. 29.4. See Bastiaensen, *Obs.*, p. 19.
[4] Cyril, *Cat.* 4.24; 12.33; 16.22, *PG* 33.485; 768; 949.
[5] In 25.12 they are used to describe the same group.
[6] 28.3. [7] Cf. 24.1 and 44.3.
[8] Thus they should not be identified with the Rebomoth of Jerome, *Ep.* 22.34, *PL* 23.1194, and to identify them with Sarabaites would be possible but meaningless; see Cassian, *Coll.* 18.5,7, *PL* 49.1094,1102.
[9] 10.3; 15.3; 16.2. [10] Cf. Bastiaensen, *Obs.*, p. 20.

The Jerusalem Buildings

Egeria came to a Jerusalem which had been transformed since the time of Christ. What she came to know was in its main features the city which was given a new shape and name by Hadrian in A.D. 135 after the demolitions following the Jewish rebellion under Bar Cochba. For a time Jews were completely excluded from the city, and it may be that at first Christians were also exiled.[1] But, whether they remained in the city or left it for a time, the headquarters of Christian life was in the part of the city which Egeria calls Sion, the south-western hill which looks down over the rest of Jerusalem. By her time the emphasis had changed, yet Sion retained an importance in the Jerusalem liturgy which cannot be explained only in terms of the biblical events which were believed to have taken place there.

Whatever may have been the form of the Christian centre on Sion before the fourth century, it was of little architectural significance compared with the site of the Jewish Temple. The vast Temple court, as extended and remade by Herod the Great still crowned the eastern hill of the city; but the Temple itself had been rendered unusable by Titus in A.D. 70, and Bar Cochba failed in his attempt to restore it in 132. Hadrian left the site in ruins, since he was determined that the destruction of the old Jerusalem should not be forgotten amidst the new glories of the paganized city renamed as Aelia Capitolina. One further attempt was made to restore the Temple, when in 362 the Emperor Julian, in reaction against the Christians, granted aid to the Jews to rebuild. But owing to an earthquake this undertaking also was abandoned.

Thus throughout the fourth century the Temple site remained in ruins. In 333 the Pilgrim of Bordeaux was shown a selection of minor sites there, but no building,[2] and in 348 Cyril of Jerusalem says it is in ruins.[3] To this site the Christian attitude was

---

[1] This need not necessarily have been so; see Telfer, *Cyril*, pp. 54–6.
[2] See 589–91, pp. 155–7 below.
[3] Cyril, *Cat.* 10.11; see also 15.15 which has a special interest because it was written before Julian's attempt, *PG* 33.676–7,889.

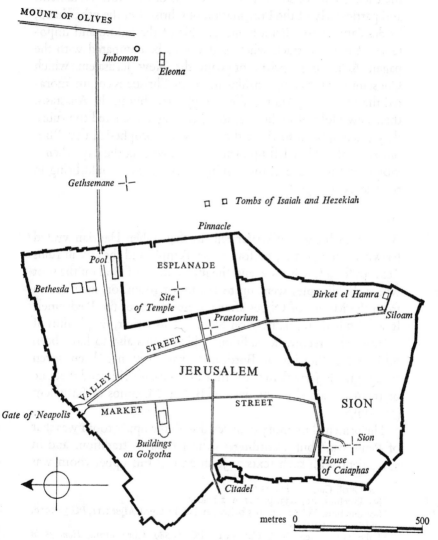

MOUNT OF OLIVES

Imbomon ○   ⊟
        Eleona

Gethsemane —|—

        ▢   ▢ *Tombs of Isaiah and Hezekiah*

Pinnacle

Pool ▯   ESPLANADE

Bethesda ▢ ▢   *Site*
       of Temple   *Birket el Hamra* ▯ ▯
                        Siloam

       Praetorium

STREET

VALLEY   JERUSALEM

              STREET   SION

Gate of Neapolis   MARKET

Buildings
on Golgotha   *Sion*

               House
               of Caiaphas

←⊕   *Citadel*

metres 0 ▬▬▬▬▬▬ 500

FOURTH-CENTURY JERUSALEM

ambiguous: on the one hand, the site was holy[1] since it had formed the background of so many of the events of the New Testament, and particularly of the Presentation of Christ. On the other hand, its desolation provided a living parable of the failure and impotence of the old Israel, whether it was to be compared with the pagan Aelia of Hadrian, or with the New Jerusalem which Constantine erected to outshine it.[2] Thus Christians commemorated the Presentation not in the Temple area, but in the Anastasis, their new Holy of Holies.[3] And when they considered the ruins, they often applied to them the text which prophesied that "not one stone should be left upon another", awaiting the day when it would be fulfilled, and the coming of Antichrist would bring in the end of the age.[4]

SION

A late fourth-century writer tells us that, when Hadrian visited Jerusalem in A.D. 130, he found the Temple and the city in ruins "except for a few houses, and the little church of God on the spot where the disciples went up to the upper room, on their return from the Mount of Olives after the Ascension of the Redeemer. It was built there, namely on Sion."[5] This writer, Epiphanius of Salamis, also records a tradition, which seems also to have been told to the Pilgrim of Bordeaux, that there had been seven synagogues in Jerusalem at the time of Hadrian's visit, and that one of them remained in the days of Bishop Maximos of Jerusalem (335–49).[6]

The principal memory connected with the upper room was that of Pentecost,[7] but according to the Jerusalem tradition, and in agreement with such texts as John 20.19,[8] this upper room was

---

1 See Cyril, *Cat.* 7.6, PG 33.612.
2 See Eusebius, *VC* 3.33, p. 167, n. 2 below.
3 See Eusebius, *VC* 3.28, p. 165 below, and cf. Ps-Cyril, *Myst* 1.11, PG 33.1076, and Jerome *Ep.* 46.5.
4 Luke 21.6–8; see Cyril, *Cat.* 15.15, PG 33.889, Chrysostom, *Hom 75 in Matt*, PG 58.686, and PD,E.
5 Epiphanius, *PM* 54c, Dean, p. 30 (PG 43.261); discussed by Kopp, pp. 323–34.
6 *PM* 54c; Bord 592, p. 158, n. 2 below. In A.D. 370 Optatus of Milevis reports that even this one remaining synagogue had disappeared (PL 11.994).
7 Egeria 43.3; cf. Cyril, *Cat.* 16.4., PG 33.924.
8 Egeria 39.5; 40.2.

also the place where, after the crucifixion, "the disciples were gathered together for fear of the Jews", and the risen Christ appeared to them. Egeria gives no hint of any connection between this upper room and the room of the Last Supper in her account of the Thursday before Easter, but it seems that the connection was made in Jerusalem in the fifth century,[1] and from then on became generally accepted.

Since Eusebius makes no mention of a church built on Sion by Constantine when describing the Emperor's works in 336, and no church was seen by the Pilgrim of Bordeaux, we must assume that the older church was renewed soon afterwards. At any rate Cyril speaks clearly of it in 348, calling it the "Upper Church", which may refer to its position in the highest part of the city area.[2] Thus the Sion mentioned by Egeria was a church built between 336 and 348, but of its plan and arrangements at this time nothing coherent is known.[3]

THE BUILDINGS ON GOLGOTHA

The Temple site is irrelevant to the Jerusalem liturgy which Egeria described, and we know little of Sion. But year by year we are learning more about the buildings on Golgotha, and the discoveries which have been made in the course of the current restoration have done much to assist our understanding of the services which took place there. The aim of the three communities who have agreed to restore the building has been to render it sound and serviceable, and to reveal it in the form of its twelfth-century rebuilding by the Franks. But in the pursuit of this aim the architects have undertaken new studies of the building, and made many new and valuable discoveries about its earlier forms. Much is now known about the western end of the site, and much

[1] See AL, No. 39, p. 267 below, and Hesychius (about 450) in PG 93.1480. Outside the Jerusalem context the connection was made already in about the time of Egeria in the Didascalia Addai, cited in VA, Jérusalem, p. 453.
[2] Cat. 16.4, PG 33.924.
[3] As B. Bagatti points out, "Ancora sulla data di Eteria", in Bibbia e Oriente 10 (1968), pp. 73–5, a seventh-century calendar attributes "the first building ✳ of Sion" to Bishop John II (397–417). But this in no way alters the fact that both Cyril and Egeria knew a church there. For its remains see VA, Jérusalem, pp. 421–40, and J. Pinkerfeld, "David's Tomb", Bulletin of Louis M. Rabinowitz Fund (3) (Jerusalem 1960), pp. 41–3 and pl. 9.

has long been known about the eastern entrance;[1] but no new discoveries have been made in a potentially important area between, and a good deal remains in the realm of conjecture.

The basilica is mentioned by the Bordeaux Pilgrim,[2] but the main early description is that given by Eusebius in his *Life of Constantine*, of which extracts are printed below (see pp. 164-71). Eusebius leaves a large number of questions unsolved, but he provides a clear guide to most of the main features of Constantine's work. The one major point on which more information would have been welcome is whether or not he yet knew of a church building round the "holy cave", believed to be the tomb of Christ. Most commentators believed that he had concentrated on the tomb with such enthusiasm that he forgot to speak of the building which enclosed it. But in 1952 Erik Wistrand challenged this view,[3] and in 1966 his suspicions were to a great extent confirmed by excavation.[4] It now seems probable that at the early stage when the buildings were begun, and probably still in 333, when they were visited by the Pilgrim of Bordeaux,[5] there was only one church on the site, the one which Egeria called the Martyrium.[6] Egeria certainly speaks of a second church building, which she called the Anastasis, which surrounded and enclosed the holy cave. But, since it is not expressly mentioned by Eusebius, the Bordeaux pilgrim, or Cyril of Jerusalem in his *Catechetical Lectures*, it was probably built at some stage between A.D. 348 and 381.[7]

---

[1] The great doors described by Egeria (43.7).
[2] 593-4, p. 158, notes 6-8 below.
[3] See p. 164, n. 2 below.
[4] See Eusebius, *VC*, p. 168, n. 1, and sections 33-4, p. 167 below. In order to diagnose the engineering and structural weaknesses of the building the architects had to make various soundings which had the additional value of revealing traces of the earlier buildings. It is much to be hoped that the evidence thus gained will soon be published. In the meantime the author is most grateful to those who have discussed the new evidence with him.
[5] See 594, p. 158, below.
[6] She explains the name in 30.1; cf. Eusebius, *VC* 3.28, p. 165, n. 4 below. Cyril, *Cat.* 14.6, PG 33.852, connects the name with the Greek version of Zeph. 3.8: "Therefore wait for me, saith the Lord, on the day of my resurrection (= *anastasis*) at the Martyrium"; see Telfer, *Cyril*, p. 43, who suggests that this may derive from the sermon which Cyril preached at the dedication of the buildings.
[7] See below, *Life of Constantine* 3.34 and notes, p. 167.

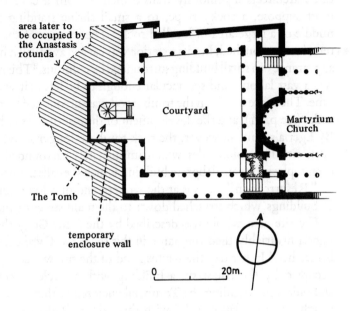

area later to
be occupied by
the Anastasis
rotunda

Courtyard

Martyrium
Church

The Tomb

temporary
enclosure wall

0   20m.

THE PRELIMINARY COURT ROUND THE CAVE
The shaded wall on the left is that of the later Anastasis
building which replaced the preliminary court.

As Eusebius describes it, the first event was the clearing of the
site, and the recovery of the rock tomb in which Christ had been
buried. This tomb was the main thing on the site, and Constantine's architects ingeniously transformed it from a cave in, one
must suppose, a rocky slope, to a small shrine standing in the
middle of a large area of levelled rock.[1] The interior of the tomb
* remained untouched, but its exterior was carved away till it had the
appearance of a small building surrounded by columns.[2] This in itself
was a vast labour, and spectacular enough to be left as it was for a
time. The space in which the tomb stood was surrounded by colonnades (see p. 41), and the development of the rest of the site began.
By Egeria's time, however, the rock tomb no longer stood in the
open air. The colonnades which immediately surrounded it had
been replaced by an elaborate building which she calls the Anastasis
or "Resurrection". It was at the western end of a long complex
of buildings which stretched down to the main street of the city.

The site as a whole was described by the name Golgotha, and
Egeria invariably used the name in this sense,[3] as Cyril often had
before her.[4] In her day the western end of the site was completely
occupied by the Anastasis, a building with a circle of columns
and pillars surrounding the Tomb, all enclosed within a wall very
roughly in the plan of a D, with three doors leading out into a
courtyard. The Tomb itself had a small porch on the east side,
and the porch was surrounded by a grill or screen between its
pillars. Hence Egeria speaks of people going "inside the screen"
when she means entering the Cave. In this porch there was
probably the stone believed to have sealed the mouth of the
tomb, and on which the angel sat on Easter morning.[5]

Leaving the Anastasis by the central door the visitor found
himself looking across a court to the apse end[6] of a large church,

---

[1] See VC 3.35, p. 168, n. 1 below.
[2] On its appearance see Note D, pp. 242–52 below.
[3] See, for example, 25.1.
[4] E.g. Cat. 1.1, PG 33.372. But 10.19, 13.4, PG 33.687, 776 may refer to the
outcrop of rock which Egeria indicates by her phrase "At the Cross"—see
24.7, etc.
[5] See Note D, p. 242, n. 1 below.
[6] Its position was disputed until the foundations were revealed in the current
restoration.

the Martyrium. On either side of the court were colonnades, and under those to the left (the north) a door led through into rooms which were used as living-quarters for the clergy. In the far south corner was the tall stump of rock which came to be called Golgotha, though Egeria called it "At the Cross". At one stage * she uses a phrase which might imply that there was a cross set up on this rock, but it is unfortunately impossible to be certain that this is her meaning.[1] The stump of rock was "rent",[2] but it is not possible in the present state of the evidence to be certain how it was incorporated into the general scheme of the buildings, and it is important to remember that Eusebius makes no mention of it.

Through an entry in the colonnade on the right and outside the main site were cisterns which probably had a paved court over them, and near by was the baptistery.[3]

The visitor crossed the columned court to the Cross, and passed through a door beside it into a chapel which Egeria calls "Behind the Cross". In this place the holy Wood of the Cross[4] was venerated on the Friday before Easter,[5] but it was often used at other times as well. Through another door the visitor went on and found himself inside a splendid church, the Martyrium. Immediately to the left was the apse,[6] which was surrounded by twelve pillars bearing silver bowls.[7] The altar stood in front of it, and eastwards of it stretched the nave with its resplendent coffered ceiling.

Passing on down the nave of the basilica the visitor came out of its central eastern door into a second court surrounded by colonnades, and in front of him were the three large doors which opened into the market. *

[1] In 37.1 she speaks of a cross, and then of a chair, then writes "which stands * now", leaving it uncertain whether what stands is the cross or the chair, and whether "now" means on this one day, or at this time, as contrasted with the days of Christ.
[2] Matt. 27.51; see Cyril, *Cat.* 13.39 and perhaps also 10.19, *PG* 33.820, 687.
[3] See Bord. 594, p. 158, notes 9–10 below.
[4] On the tradition of its discovery see Note C, pp. 240–1 below.
[5] Egeria 37.3: also *AL*, No. 68.
[6] Egeria 46.5.
[7] See Eusebius, *VC* 3.38, p. 170, notes 1–2 below, and *Breviarius* (*c.* A.D. 500?) 1, *C.C.S.L.* 175, p. 109.

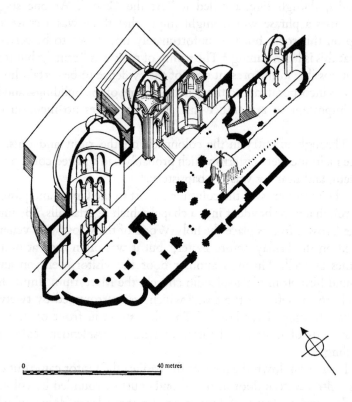

`0` _____ `40 metres`

THE PRESENT CHURCH OF THE HOLY SEPULCHRE
A Twelfth-century Building
incorporating the Anastasis building of the fourth century

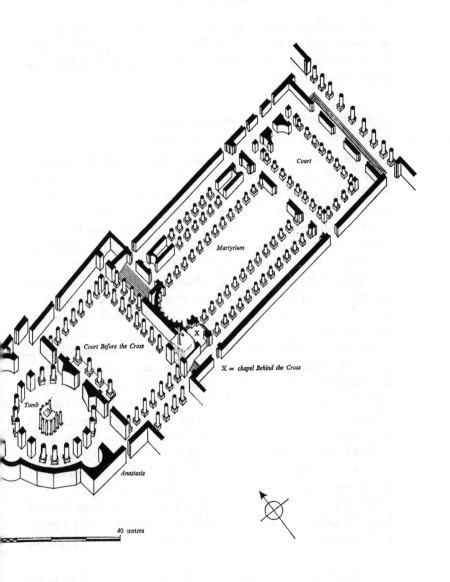

Court

Martyrium

X

Court Before the Cross

X = chapel Behind the Cross

Tomb

Anastasis

40 metres

NSTANTINE'S BUILDINGS ON GOLGOTHA IN THE TIME OF EGERIA

This was the church complex in which the normal daily services were held, and where the central mysteries of the Christian faith found their liturgical expression in the Great Week which culminated with Easter.

OTHER BUILDINGS IN THE REGION OF JERUSALEM, BETHLEHEM, AND THE MOUNT OF OLIVES

Eusebius praised Constantine for adorning not only the Anastasis Cave, but also two others: "the cave of God's first manifestation" in Bethlehem, and that "of his final taking-up on the mountain top" on the Mount of Olives. The buildings at these places are ascribed both to Constantine and also to the Empress Helena his mother, though Eusebius' vocabulary does not make it clear how far Helena's responsibilities extended, apart from the fact that she visited and "dedicated" them.[1] Though early writers[2] inform us of various details about these two churches, our knowledge of their form rests almost exclusively on the work of modern archaeologists.

Though the Bible does not indicate a cave as the birthplace of Christ, the earliest statements about the place agree that such it was. In about A.D. 150 this information is given in a widely read account of Christ's birth and childhood known as the *Protevangelium of James*,[3] and St Justin Martyr, writing at the same time, reports that Mary bore Christ in a cave "very close to the village of Bethlehem".[4] Origen, writing about a century later, says that he was shown the cave and the manger which were well known in the region of Bethlehem as the birthplace of Christ.[5]

The Cave of the Nativity had not apparently been isolated. Indeed, Jerome tells us that it had been overshadowed by a grove of Thammuz,[6] and in 348 Cyril says that "a few years ago the

---

[1] Eusebius, *VC* 9.41–2, *PG* 20.1369f; cf. *VC* 3.41, 43, *PG* 20.1101f; but see also Bord 598, p. 162, n. 2 below.
[2] Bord 595, p. 160, n. 1, and 598, p. 162, n. 2.
[3] See Hennecke I, p. 383.
[4] *Dial.* 78, *PG* 6.657f; see Kopp, pp. 8–9.
[5] Origen, *contra Celsum* 1.51, *PG* 11.756.
[6] *Ep.* 58 *ad Paulinum*, *PL* 22.581.

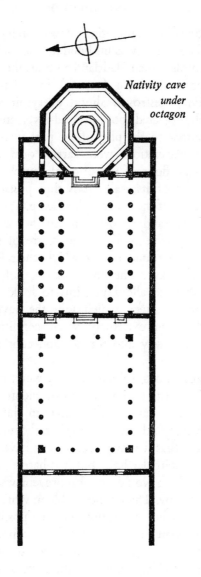

Nativity cave under octagon

0   10   20 metres

BETHLEHEM
Constantine's Church of the Nativity

47

place was woody ".[1] Constantine's new church no doubt abolished this grove as completely as his buildings on Golgotha supplanted the pagan temple which Hadrian had built there.

*   The Emperor Justinian (527–65) in enlarging the Church of the Nativity destroyed almost everything of Constantine's church which projected above ground-level, and apparently made radical alterations to the plan of the part surrounding the cave. But in 1934 excavations were carried out[2] which located not only the mosaic floor of the original church, but also many of the foundations of its walls. It is thus possible to speak with some confidence of the general plan (see p. 47), which comprised a court, a nave, and an octagon which was built round and above the holy cave itself. In the centre of the octagon floor steps led up to a round railing which encircled a large hole in the roof of the cave. The object of this hole can hardly have been other than to allow pilgrims to look down inside, and the fact that the steps which join the nave to the octagon were found in an extremely worn condition suggests that people went this way into the octagon constantly and in great numbers.

But the excavations, valuable as they were, were insufficient to supply any answer to two important problems. The first problem is that there must have been an altar in the church, but it is extremely hard to find any place for it in the suggested plan; it has been suggested that it may in some way have been arranged to stand above the circular hole, but it is hard to imagine any such arrangement which would not also prevent visitors seeing down into the cave below. The second problem, which would no doubt be resolved if further excavations became possible, is to discover how pilgrims went down into the cave to pray at the manger, and how the sacred ministers entered the cave for liturgical acts.[3] When the steps which connected the nave to the octagon were excavated, it was discovered that a stairway leading down into the cave had been cut into them; but these stairs have not been

---

[1] Cyril, *Cat.* 12.20, PG 33.752; cf. Ps. 132.6.
[2] See W. Harvey, *Structural Survey of the Church of the Nativity, Bethlehem* (London 1935), esp. pp. 17–22, 25–30.
[3] See, for example, *AL*, No. 1 and note.

dated, and can in any case hardly belong to the original arrangement of Constantine's church.[1]

The Eleona, Constantine's church on the Mount of Olives, is ✻ less hard to understand. In its original intention it commemorated two events which Eusebius describes in these words: "The feet of our Lord and Saviour . . . stood upon the Mount of Olives, by the cave which is shown there; from which, having first prayed and revealed the mysteries of the end of the world to his disciples on top of the mountain, he ascended into heaven".[2] The Bordeaux Pilgrim speaks of Christ's teaching at this place before his passion;[3] but it seems that Eusebius was referring to the preaching during the forty days after the passion and resurrection.[4] In fact the Bordeaux Pilgrim mentions a hillock near by, but he says that it is the place of the Transfiguration rather than of the Ascension, which may indicate that in 333 the Ascension itself was also commemorated in the cave in the church.

The cave was, as Fr Hugues Vincent discovered in his campaign ✻ of excavations,[5] enclosed under the sanctuary platform of the church (see p. 50), and it is through Vincent's work that we are able to visualize the church in its original condition. From the documents we learn little apart from the interesting fact that by Egeria's time it was the custom to bury bishops of Jerusalem at the Eleona or near by.[6]

The near-by Hillock (or "Imbomon"[7]) was used for services ✻ during the Great Week and at Pentecost, and, since Egeria tells us that the people "sat down" there,[8] sometimes for as long as two hours, it must have been in some way arranged for worship. Yet Egeria provides no evidence that it was a church. If she describes it

---

[1] On these two problems see Kopp, pp. 16–19 and R. W. Hamilton, *The Church of the Nativity, Bethlehem, A Guide* (Jerusalem 1947), pp. 13–14.

[2] Eusebius, *Dem. Evang.* 6.18, *PG* 22.457; cf. *VC* 3.43, *PG* 20.1101; also Cyril, *Cat.* 10.19, 13.38, *PG* 33.688, 817.

[3] Bord. 595 p. 160, n. 1 below; cf. Mark 13.

[4] See Acts 1.3.

[5] See VA, *Jérusalem*, pp. 337–60.

[6] Milik, *R.B.* 67 (1960), p. 555.

[7] Cf. *AL*, No. 40. "Imbomon" is probably derived from ἐν βουνῷ, meaning "On the Hillock".

[8] 31.1; see also 35.4.

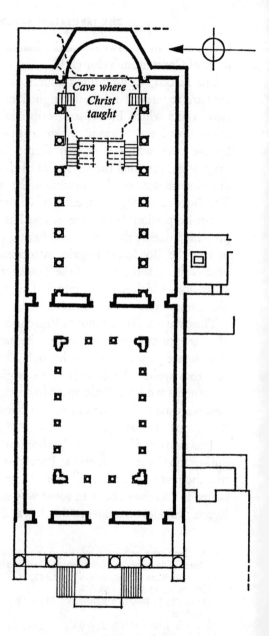

Cave where
Christ
taught

THE MOUNT OF OLIVES
CONSTANTINE'S CHURCH
ON ELEONA

0   10   20   metres

at all, it is simply as a "place",[1] and we can have little doubt that it lacked a church at her time. Three clues lead us to this conclusion: the first is that she never mentions the Imbomon among the major churches which were specially decorated at the great festivals; secondly, she never mentions it as a place where the Eucharist is celebrated; and thirdly, she clearly says that Ascension Day was celebrated not at the Imbomon, although it was "the place from which the Lord ascended into heaven",[2] but at Bethlehem.[3]

A church was in fact built at the Imbomon very soon after Egeria's visit, and Jerome mentions it in A.D. 392.[4] Later on it was known as "The Holy Ascension".[5] This church was built by Poemenia, a member of the imperial family who visited Jerusalem not long after Egeria,[6] and a small part of a fourth-century

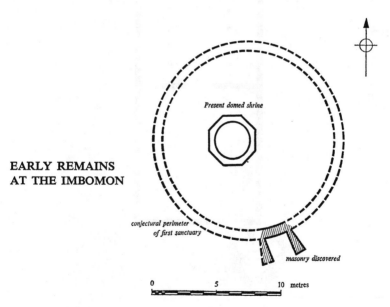

Present domed shrine

EARLY REMAINS
AT THE IMBOMON

conjectural perimeter
of first sanctuary

masonry discovered

0   5   10 metres

---

[1] 31.1, 35.4, 39.3, and 43.5 all contain the word "place", but there is little emphasis on the word.
[2] 31.1.   [3] See below, pp. 77–8.
[4] Jerome, *Com. in Zeph.* 1.15f.
[5] Cyril of Scythopolis, *Vita Sabae* (*BHG* 1608), and perhaps *AL*, No. 57.
[6] Mentioned by Palladius, *Hist Laus.* 35, and *Peter the Iberian*, ed. R. Raabe (Leipzig 1895), p. 35. See the important article by P. Devos, "La 'Servante de Dieu' Poemenia", *AB* 87 (1969), pp. 189–212.

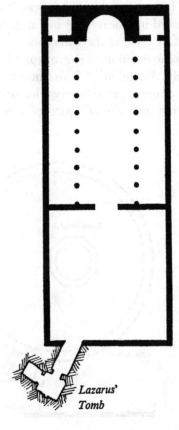

Lazarus'
Tomb

0   10   20   metres

THE FIRST CHURCH AT THE LAZARIUM

building on the "Hillock"—probably belonging to her church
—has been excavated.[1]   *

GETHSEMANE

Eusebius speaks of "a place on the Mount of Olives where once
Christ prayed, and where now the faithful are diligent in offering
prayer",[2] and the Pilgrim of Bordeaux speaks of a stone on the
east of the Valley of Jehoshaphat where Judas betrayed Christ.[3]
According to the Gospel account of Christ's agony these two
places ought to be a stone's throw apart from each other, but, *
since Egeria (36.2) seems to place them some distance apart, the
place of the prayer with its "graceful church" was probably some
way up the Mount of Olives,[4] and the place of the arrest near the
foot—perhaps at the present Church of All Nations, though there
was probably no church there till a little after Egeria's time.[5]

THE LAZARIUM

There seems to have been no church at Lazarus' Tomb in the
early fourth century, since Eusebius and the Pilgrim of Bordeaux
mention it only as his "vault" or "crypt".[6] But Jerome reports
that "the church now [that is, in about 390] built there shows the
place of his tomb",[7] and the celebrations there in the octaves of
great feasts[8] which were held during Egeria's visit show that in
her time this church was already built. In an exceptionally
complicated excavation Fr Sylvester Saller[9] discovered some of its
remains, which show clearly how the church and the tomb were
linked (see p. 52).

[1] See Milik, op. cit, p. 557 and V. Corbo, "Scavo archeologico a ridosso
della basilica dell'Ascensione" in *LA* 10 (1959–60), pp. 205–48.
[2] *On, Gethsemane.*
[3] Bord 594, p. 159, n. 3 below. Cyril also speaks of the place, but in vague
terms; see *Cat.* 10.19, 13.38, *PG* 33.688, 817.
[4] See Egeria 36.1. Milik, in *R.B.* 67 (1960), pp. 500–5, suggests that the place of
the prayer was at the site called *Dominus Flevit*, but his evidence is slight.   *
[5] Jerome, *On, Gethsemane* seems to be mentioning a different place from   *
Eusebius "at the foot of the Mount of Olives", and says that a church has
been built there. This may well be the predecessor of the present Church of
All Nations.
[6] Eusebius, *On, Bethania*; Bord 596, p. 160, n. 3 below.
[7] Jerome, *On, Bethania.*   [8] See 25.11; 39.1.
[9] See S. J. Saller, *Excavations at Bethany* (Jerusalem 1957).

The Jerusalem Liturgy

At the time of Egeria's visit the liturgy of the community in Jerusalem had begun to settle into a general pattern which is remarkably familiar to a modern reader. Some of its features she took for granted and did not bother to describe for her sisters,[1] but most of what she saw she recounts with an enthusiasm which shows that it was new to her. She particularly admired the careful way in which the psalms and lessons were chosen to fit the time and place at which they were used.[2] By a happy chance we have a manuscript which, though it represents a later period of development, nevertheless enables us to identify a great many more of the psalms and lessons than would have been possible from Egeria's text alone. This is an Armenian Lectionary of the fifth century which contains a wealth of details which often supplements what we know from the *Travels*, and sometimes shows in which direction the services developed after Egeria's time.[3]

The situation revealed by Egeria is not, even as she describes it, that of a liturgy in which all has been irrevocably decided. We see that there are certain services (for instance, the Sunday Eucharist) which are attended by all clergy and laity of the city, but there are others, such as the weekday dawn service, which are attended mainly by clergy and monks. There is also an informal night, or very early morning, service, which appears only to have been held because it was demanded by the monks. We are therefore witnessing a time when the relatively simple pattern of worship of the ordinary clergy and laity was being pressed to expand by the needs of the constantly growing number of monks and nuns who apparently used the same buildings for their daily worship.[4]

The recent developments which Egeria so admired in 383 were presumably due to the genius of none other than the Bishop of

---

[1] E.g. the Paschal vigil (38.2) and perhaps also the Sunday Eucharist (25.1).
[2] This admiration strongly suggests that at her home in the West the readings were only very seldom appropriate, as would be the case if the books of the Bible were read straight through in course.
[3] See Note E, pp. 253–77 below, for further details.
[4] See *CL*, p. 111, and cf. Egeria 24.1,8.

Jerusalem, the very Cyril who had preached the Catechetical Lectures as a priest in 348. And, since in those lectures he said nothing of any of the special observances which Egeria describes, he may have introduced them later, during the years of an episcopate frequently interrupted by exile.[1] The resulting services we shall now examine in three stages, looking first at such elements as psalms and lessons which formed the material for them, then at the different services, and finally at the distribution of the different services through the day, the week, and the year. We shall also seek to assess some of their ceremonial elements, and see something of their influence and subsequent development.

THE ELEMENTS OF THE SERVICES

PSALMS

When Egeria speaks of hymns, psalms, and antiphons, she seems to make no particular distinction between them.[2] Most were clearly from the Bible, psalms and perhaps also canticles, but it is also possible that metrical hymns such as "O gladsome light"[3] were in use, and perhaps other non-biblical texts as well.[4] The words of the psalm seem to have been sung by a soloist[5] who is answered at intervals by the congregation, who respond with one of the verses of the same psalm (which is used as an antiphon[6] or refrain). Other ways of singing were certainly used by monks at this time;[7] but Egeria gives no hint of them, and she is in any case describing congregational services, at which the lay people neither had their own books nor, presumably, knew the psalms by heart, as did some of the monks. Thus their way of singing psalms was probably the one which demanded least knowledge

---

[1] Cyril was bishop from c. 351 to 386. He was exiled three times, in 358-9, ✱ 360-2, and 367-78. See F. L. Cross, St Cyril of Jerusalem's Lectures on the Christian Sacraments (Texts for Students No. 51, London 1966), pp. xxvii-xxix.

[2] See, for example, 24.1,2.

[3] Apparently cited by St Basil, de Sancto Spiritu 73, PG 32.205; cf. Const. Apost. 7.48, PG 1.1057.

[4] See AL Lists A and B, p. 276 below.   [5] See 24.9.

[6] AL provides one exception where the antiphon is from a different psalm; see No. 39, 4th gobala.

[7] See especially Basil, Ep. 207 ad Cler. Neocaes., 3, PG 32.760-6, and Cassian, Inst. 2.11, PL 49.99-101.

of the text. The existence of the boys' choir in Jerusalem[1] enabled the service to contain at least some specially rehearsed singing which may have taken a more elaborate form.

The only psalms normally indicated in the Armenian Lectionary are those sung at the beginning of the Eucharist and the verse before the Gospel. But we know from other sources that a psalm in general use at the morning office was Psalm 63,[2] and that Psalm 141[3] was a regular constituent of the office held in the evening.[4]

PRAYERS

Between the psalms prayers were "interspersed"[5] and Egeria mentions many other occasions on which prayers were said; she expresses admiration for the way in which they were made to fit the theme of the occasions when they were being used, but, though we have this single clue about their content, we know nothing of their form.

These prayers were normally said by a presbyter or a deacon,[6] and sometimes by the bishop.[7] It seems to have been an accepted practice to attach a prayer to each psalm at this period,[8] and "psalter collects" are provided in some later rites.

Another type of prayer which was used in Jerusalem is what Egeria calls the "prayer and commemoration for all".[9] It was used by the bishop himself at the end of each hour service before the dismissal, and we learn that he mentioned the names of any he wished.[10] At the afternoon service called "Lucernare" this type of prayer took a more solemn form: the bishop takes his place outside the Cave of the Anastasis instead of staying inside it, as he does at the other services, a deacon makes the mention

[1] See 24.5.
[2] Other morning psalms mentioned in contemporary sources are 51, 67, 118, 148–50; see Zerfass, p. 12, n. 33.
[3] Others were 12, 113, 130; see Zerfass, p. 12, n. 34.
[4] See CL, pp. 112–13.
[5] See 24.9 and cf. 31.1; 32.1.
[6] Who sometimes attended particularly for this purpose; see 24.1; 44.3.
[7] See for example, 35.4.
[8] Cf. Cassian, Inst. 2.5,7,8,10, PL 49.84, etc.
[9] 24.9.
[10] There is no hint that he was reading from diptychs; see 24.2.

of the individual names, and he is answered by a boys' choir whose response, Egeria notes, is *Kyrie eleison*. This litany of intercession is brought to a close by the bishop's recitation of the "Prayer for All" which we may thus understand to be a "collect-prayer" in the sense that it "collects" the intercessions which have preceded it, even though it may not have been in a form which would be called a collect today. The response *Kyrie eleison* "or, as we say, 'Have mercy, Lord'" seems new to Egeria, or she would hardly have taken the trouble to translate it for her sisters. It does not seem to have been usual in the West till the sixth century,[1] though by Egeria's time it was probably in general use in the East,[2] having taken the place of the simple response *Amen*, inherited from Jewish sources. This use of *Amen* as a litany-response survives only, it seems, in the Nestorian Liturgy.[3]

DISMISSALS

All regular assemblies for prayer ended with an elaborate dismissal:[4] when the bishop had said the final Prayer for All, the deacon called on the catechumens to bow their heads,[5] and the bishop blessed them. He then said another prayer and blessed the faithful. Then he came forward and all "came to his hand", presumably to kiss it.

The Latin word for "dismissal" is *missa*,[6] but, though Egeria uses it in this sense, she is also able to use the word to refer to the whole service of which the dismissal is a part.[7] But, although Egeria often uses *missa* in the sense of "service", she is certainly not using it in the sense it was later to acquire of "Eucharist". One contemporary writer uses it in this more restricted and technical sense,[8] but such a usage does not become normal until the end of the fifth and the sixth centuries.[9]

[1] J. A. Jungmann, *The Early Liturgy* (London 1966), p. 294.
[2] See *Apost. Const.* 8.6,8, *PG* 1.1077, 1084.
[3] See *CL*, pp. 45–6, and F. E. Brightman, *Liturgies Eastern and Western* (Oxford 1896), pp. 263–6.
[4] See, for example, 24.2,6.
[5] The Roman Missal provides for Lent final prayers before the dismissal for which the introduction includes a similar invitation by the deacon.
[6] E.g. 24.2 end.   [7] E.g. 39.1.
[8] Ambrose, *Ep.* 20.4f, *PL* 16.995, written in 385.
[9] See C. Mohrmann, "Missa", *VC* 12 (1958), pp. 67–92.

On two occasions Egeria does in fact use *missa* (= "service") of
the Eucharist, but on the first occasion the identification of the
service as the Eucharist is unmistakably implied by the context
(25.10) and on the other she at once explains the word (27.8).

LESSONS AND PREACHING

One of the most unexpected features of the Jerusalem liturgy is
the absence of Scripture readings from the daily offices. Lessons
were for special occasions such as the celebrations of the Eucharist,
or other major services, and they were particularly used to mark
feast-days. Egeria remarks not on the fact that there are so many
services without readings, but rather on the appropriateness of the
lessons when they were read,[1] and this she does constantly. The
principles on which the lessons were chosen can to a great extent
be deduced from the old Armenian Lectionary,[2] which reflects
Jerusalem's liturgical life at a time not long after that of Egeria's
visit.

Among the readings the Gospel had pride of place. Thus at the
first service on Sundays the bishop himself read the Gospel
account of Christ's passion and resurrection,[3] and during Eastertide this Gospel was read every day.[4]

At the Sunday Eucharist (and at other synaxes[5]) the Old and
New Testament lessons and Gospel were followed by preaching,
"so that the people will constantly be learning about the Bible
and the love of God".[6] From the way Egeria speaks of the preaching, it seems that she was unused to such frequent sermons. Nor
was frequency the only unusual feature, for if there was any
preaching at all it lasted a long time. Any presbyters present were
allowed to preach, and, when they had finished, there was always
a final sermon from the bishop. Applause or groans from the
congregation marked their enthusiastic participation in what was
being read or preached.[7]

---

[1] See especially 47.5. The lessons were read from a *codex* or book (33.2).
[2] See pp. 253–77 below.   [3] See 24.10.   [4] 27.2.
[5] On the meaning of the word "synaxis" see p. 66 below.
[6] 25.1.
[7] As at the resurrection Gospel, 24.10 (cf. 34; 36.3; 37.7), or the catechetical
instructions, 46.4 and 47.2 (and Cyril, *Cat.* 14.1, PG 33.825).

Just as Egeria is impressed by the lessons chosen to mark special times and seasons, so she praises lessons read in particular places. Many of the feasts and fasts she describes were marked by "stational" services, in which the worshipping community went together to one of the holy places and read there the passage of Scripture which expressed its meaning. Such services have a clear parallel in the short acts of prayer used by Egeria when she made her own pilgrimages to holy places,[1] though these should not be conceived simply as private acts of devotion, since in the instances we have they were always conducted by local clergy.[2]

THE MYSTERIES

Egeria provides such full descriptions of the daily offices and the celebration of feast-days that it comes as a surprise to discover that nowhere in her book is there a systematic description of Baptism or the Eucharist. Since part of her manuscript is missing, it may possibly be that she had written such a description, but that it has been lost. But it is more likely that she was unwilling to commit to paper her knowledge of the Christian mysteries. When she speaks of the way in which this knowledge was imparted to the newly-baptized, she shows that this part of Christian teaching was strictly confined to baptized persons, and that the unbaptized were deliberately excluded.[3] Nevertheless, Egeria provides some valuable evidence for accessory features of both these sacraments, and we are fortunate that we have an almost (or even exactly) contemporary description of both in the *Mystagogical Lectures* ascribed to Cyril of Jerusalem.[4]

THE EUCHARIST

Our main evidence for the shape of the opening part of the Eucharist (the synaxis) in Jerusalem comes not from Egeria but from the Armenian Lectionary. There were five main elements:

[1] See, for example, 4.3 and 10.7.
[2] As at the approach to Sinai (1.2).
[3] See 47.2.
[4] The description of the Eucharist is partly reproduced below, pp. 172–3, and should be compared with that of the Syrian rite in *Const. Apost.* 8.12.6–39, *PG* 1.1076–1141.

1. A psalm with antiphon, which presumably formed the first
   element in the service, but not necessarily an introit.[1]
2. A lesson or lessons (from the Old or New Testaments).
3. A verse of a psalm sung as an Alleluia.
4. The Gospel.
5. The preaching.

The second part of the service, which Egeria calls the Offering
(*oblatio*), and the synaxis together made up the Sunday Eucharist.
But synaxes could take place separately, as they did on special
occasions during Lent,[2] and there were occasions on which the
Offering was offered twice without a repetition of the synaxis.[3]

After the Offering in the Martyrium on a Sunday there was a
"Thanksgiving" in the Anastasis.[4] It has been argued that this
was one of the instances of a second Offering without a repeated
synaxis,[5] but there is evidence of a thanksgiving for communion
in a nearly contemporary source, the *Apostolic Constitutions*,[6] and
Egeria neither uses the word "Thanksgiving" elsewhere to
describe the Eucharist, nor ever in her descriptions of this ceremony does she use a word which suggests that it was a eucharistic
offering.[7]

The fact that the Eucharist was on several occasions celebrated
twice in the same day[8] (and on Easter Day twice in the same
building[9]) does not in itself suggest that people received Holy
Communion at only one of the celebrations which they attended.
From the emphatic way in which Egeria speaks of receiving we
cannot avoid the impression that this was so,[10] but even though
she may be speaking of non-communicating attendance, her
language shows that she felt that all present were offering, and not

[1] The Eucharist was sometimes celebrated in the same church where another
   service had just taken place: e.g. 27.7; 29.3.
[2] See pp. 263–5 below, and Egeria 27.6.
[3] See *AL*, Nos. 39 and 44, and Egeria 35.2.
[4] 25, 2–3.
[5] Bastiaensen, *Obs.*, pp. 27 and 85–8.
[6] *Const. Apost.* 7.26 (*c.* A.D. 400), PG 1.1017.
[7] See 27.3; 30.3; 35.2; 41.
[8] On the Sunday when Egeria was on Mount Sinai (3.6; 4.2); on the Thursday
   before Easter (35.1,2); on Easter Day (38.2); and Pentecost (43.2,3).
[9] 39.2.
[10] See 3.6; 16.7; 23.6; 27.9; 35.2.

only the president: "We made the Offering there (4.3); "We could not make the Offering" (4.8).

Normally in Jerusalem the Eucharist was celebrated between dawn and 4 p.m. with exceptions on the Thursday before Easter[1] and at midnight on the vigils of Easter and Epiphany.[2] It is possible that on ordinary days of the year the celebration was not permitted after 4 p.m., since this is said to have been too late on the day when she came down from Sinai. But equally it is possible that on this occasion she was prevented by some quite different reason or perhaps a purely local rule.

BAPTISM

Egeria describes the preparations for baptism in some detail, and witnesses to a highly developed scheme of baptismal instruction.[3] Moreover, her account happens to be supplemented by the very catechetical lectures of the man she saw as bishop. Cyril of Jerusalem had first preached them as a presbyter nearly forty years before, but, since the text was apparently still being used in the following century, it may be assumed that, when Egeria heard him, she was listening to something very like the *Catechetical Lectures* as we now have them.[4]

Egeria's own description is so clear that little need be repeated here. She speaks of five stages:[5]

1. *Registration.* Those catechumens who wish to be baptized give in their names before Lent.[6]

2. *Examination and Enrolment.* On the first Monday in Lent those seeking baptism presented themselves individually with their godparents before the bishop and presbyters. They were then examined as to their character, and the godparents acted as their

---

[1] 35.2.
[2] 38.2, *AL*, No. 44 (and see Renoux, *La Prière*, pp. 181–7); 25.6, *AL*, No. 1.
[3] Chapters 45–7.
[4] Cyril's authorship of the last five (*Mystagogical*) *Lectures* has been disputed. See W. J. Swaans' article in *Le Muséon* 55 (1942), pp. 1–43; F. L. Cross, *St Cyril of Jerusalem*, pp. xxxiv–xxxix, and Telfer, *Cyril*, pp. 39–40.
[5] Comparison of Egeria's text with previous evidence is simplified by the use of E. C. Whitaker's, *Documents of the Baptismal Liturgy* (2nd edn, London 1970).
[6] 45.1.

witnesses; this examination was more than a formality, but
presumably applied only to the period during which those present-
ing themselves had been recognized as catechumens.[1] If the
catechumens satisfied their examiners, the bishop enrolled them,
and they became accepted candidates or what the Roman Church
called *electi*. Egeria does not use this word, but its synonym,
competentes, by which she seems to mean "those seeking ad-
mission". She also speaks of the godparents as "fathers" and
"mothers";[2] but it is clear both from the description of the
candidates as "men and women" and by the nature of the
questions asked them that they were not young children. The
name *infantes* is applied to them only when they first emerge
from the baptismal font and appear "now born unto Christ, who
hitherto were born unto this world", in the words of St Augustine.[3] Another word Egeria applies to them after their baptism is
"neophytes".[4]

3. *Exorcism and Catechesis.* Throughout the seven weeks of Lent
the candidates were exorcized daily by the clergy—perhaps by
persons specially ordained as exorcists.[5] They then received three
hours' instruction from the bishop; for the first five weeks this
consisted in the literal and spiritual exposition of the Scriptures,
and during the sixth and seventh week the bishop taught them
the Creed (also explained literally and then spiritually[6]), which
they repeated to him individually on the last day of their instruction, the Saturday before Palm Sunday. Any lay people who
wished could come and listen to the instructions together with
the candidates and their godparents; but catechumens were not
admitted.

This was a solid and valuable course of instruction. But, combined though it was with the exorcisms, it was not enough to

---

[1] See 45.2–4 and Whitaker's citations of Hippolytus xvii, p. 3 and xx, p. 4.
[2] 45.2.
[3] 38.1; Augustine, *Serm.* 228.1, *PL* 38.1101: "Those who just before were
called *competen es* are now called *infantes*—'*infantes*' because they are now
born unto Christ", etc.
[4] 47.2.
[5] 46.1; see also Telfer, *Cyril*, p. 33, and Jerome, *Ep.* 46.8.
[6] 46.3.

"cleanse" the candidates.[1] Only when they had been finally purified by the washing of baptism itself were the deeper mysteries revealed to them, which included the explanation of Baptism, the Holy Chrism,[2] and the Eucharist.

4. *The Baptism.* While the congregation (Egeria, it seems, included) kept the paschal vigil in the Martyrium, the candidates received baptism at a "font" which was elsewhere.[3] As soon as they received their white clothes, they were taken with the bishop to the Anastasis, where there was a psalm, and he said a prayer for them.[4] Then he took them to join the congregation of the faithful in the Martyrium,[5] with whom they received Holy Communion for the first time.

5. *Instruction in the Mysteries.* Throughout Easter Week after the   *
morning thanksgiving after the Eucharist the bishop stayed in the Anastasis with the neophytes or newly-baptized in order to instruct them in the meaning of the sacraments they had now received. Egeria's account suggests that these lectures took place   *
every day, but in fact only five *Mystagogical Lectures* remain to us from shortly before or after her time.[6]

THE STRUCTURE OF THE SERVICES

In studying the structure of the Jerusalem services two things should be borne in mind. First, these structures are those of a cathedral rite, designed to serve the needs of a full Christian community of bishop, presbyters, deacons, baptized persons, and

---

[1] See Cyril, *Procat.* 1.4; cf. *Myst.* 1.1 (Whitaker, op. cit., pp. 24, 27).   *
[2] This rite, the confirmation by chrismation, is not mentioned by Egeria. Perhaps she took it for granted as part of the baptism (cf. *Myst.* 3) but more probably she avoids describing it because it was one of the mysteries.
[3] This is the "bath" "behind" either the Anastasis or the cisterns beside it; see Bord 594.4, p. 158 below.
[4] 38.2.   [5] Cf. 15.5.
[6] A. Renoux, in "Les Catéchèses Mystagogiques dans l'organisation liturgique hiérosolymitaine du IVᵉ et du Vᵉ siècle", *Le Muséon* 78 (1965), pp. 355–9, suggests that mystagogical instruction was regarded as inseparable from the Anastasis. Thus when, by Egeria's time, some of the principal services of Easter Week had come to be held elsewhere (e.g. on Sion or the Eleona, 39.2) the lecture which should normally have followed them was omitted because of the inconvenience of returning to give it at the Anastasis. See also Egeria 47.1 and *AL*, No 52 and List D, p. 277 below.

catechumens. They are not therefore comparable with the structure of services designed for use in communities comprising only monks (who might all be laymen). Secondly, the forms now to be discussed are the simplest. Egeria shows that the basic forms were enriched in various ways on feast days, especially by the addition of short acts of prayer which might include a procession to a holy place, or the reading of a special Gospel, or both.[1]

Prayer in the Holy Places. Two types of prayer in holy places are mentioned: there is the short pilgrimage office which Egeria used privately on her visits to holy places, which seems to have been conducted either by clergy who had accompanied her on her journey or by local clergy or monks, and there are the stational services of the Jerusalem congregation held during processions.

Egeria's clearest description of the short act of prayer which was used on her private pilgrimages is in 10.7: It comprised:

> Prayer
> Appropriate lesson
> Appropriate psalm
> Prayer[2]

to this form there is added, when a bishop is present, a

> Blessing[3]

Although the congregation's stational services are not all described in identical terms, it appears that the normal form was:

> Prayer[4]
> Appropriate psalm
> Appropriate lesson[5]
> Prayer
> Blessing (the bishop is always present)[6]

---

[1] A valuable discussion of these additions will be found in Zerfass, pp. 20–37, and a comparison with contemporary and earlier witnesses on pp. 39–52.

[2] Only prayer and a lesson are mentioned in 4.8; 23.5, and a single prayer in 1.2.

[3] See 20.3; 21.1; and cf. 19.16.

[4] This was not invariable; but see 36.1,3, and 29.4; 36.4; 37.8; 40.3; and 43.8–9.

[5] All the stations mentioned have lessons from the Gospel narrative, and Gospels are provided in *AL*, No. 58 for the Pentecost stations which are described, but not all as having lessons, in Egeria 43.8.

[6] There were probably blessings at the stations described in 36.1,3,4.

Egeria's descriptions of these forms of prayer often seem imprecise, and it may be that, since they differ only in one respect, she was in fact describing only one type of stational prayer.

The First Service on Sundays. This appears to be a slightly elaborat- *
ed form of the structure of prayers in the holy places. It followed this pattern:[1]

In the Anastasis

> Three psalms with their prayers
> Commemoration of All
> (Incense is brought into the holy Cave)
> Resurrection Gospel

At the Cross

> One psalm with its prayer
> Blessing and dismissal

Here is a service which was celebrated on the day of the resurrection, and in the very place which was its testimony. Where the bishop reads the Gospel the angel once sat and announced the same news to the women. It is even possible that the incense (mentioned only in connection with this particular service) is used to recall the spices which they had come to bring.[2] But the dramatic quality of the first service on Sundays is not the only thing which sets it in a category of its own. It takes place at cockcrow, which is the end of the night, rather than at first light, the beginning of the day, and is thus like a short vigil,[3] and unlike the Morning Hymns, the cathedral office which began each weekday.[4] And for this service (though not for Morning Hymns) the bishop is present from the start.[5]

The Offices. Offices have an invariable structure, though clearly

---

[1] See 24.9–11; cf. Zerfass, pp. 15–19.   [2] Zerfass, p. 27.
[3] Egeria seems to be calling it a vigil in her description of Pentecost (43.1,9); but she also uses this word to describe the daily service (44.2, perhaps a monastic service).
[4] See Zerfass, pp. 26–8. It is uncertain whether there were Morning Hymns in Jerusalem on Sundays.
[5] 24.9; cf. 24.2.

Lucernare was the most solemn form, and was preceded by the lighting of lamps:[1]

> Psalms[2] with their prayers
> Prayer for All
> Dismissal

Vigils. Egeria describes vigils only in a summary fashion, and their varieties can be deduced only from the Armenian Lectionary.[3]

The Synaxis. This pattern of psalmody and lessons seems to be normal for solemn assemblies, whether or not it was leading up to the Offering.[4] Normally it is used in the full form:

> Psalm with antiphon
> Lesson(s) from the Old or New Testament
> Alleluia (which includes a verse from a psalm)
> Gospel

But there are instances of its use without a Gospel,[5] and during the Lenten week-days a psalm with antiphon took the place of the Alleluia.[6] Ordinarily when it was a self-contained rite this synaxis contained no preaching, but ended with a prayer and dismissal. But, if it was a eucharistic synaxis to be followed by the Offering, the sermons immediately followed it.[7]

TIMES AND SEASONS

THE DAY

The celebration of Sunday, as Egeria describes it, sets it apart from week-days in several ways, though we cannot be certain that her silences should always be strictly interpreted. We shall therefore

---

[1] 24.4–7.   [2] See above, p. 56, n. 3.
[3] See Note E, pp. 253–77 below, and Zerfass p. 35, n. 91.
[4] For instances without an Offering see, for example, 29.4 (*AL*, No. 33); 32.1; 33.2; 34 (where the pattern is followed in a rite which moves from the Martyrium to its conclusion in the Anastasis); and 37.5–7, the Three Hours' service on the Friday before Easter, which has the form of a succession of synaxes (see *AL*, No. 43) lacking the second psalm.
[5] See *AL*, Nos. 38 and 43.   [6] See, for example, *AL*, Nos. 18,35.
[7] As on Wednesday and Friday afternoons, even in Lent when the Offering was not in fact made, see 27.6.

begin by examining the services which were held on ordinary week-days. It is immediately clear from what Egeria tells us that the two main cathedral services were Morning and Evening Prayer or, as she named them, "Morning Hymns"[1] and Lucernare (the Service of the Lamps). Morning Hymns began at first light[2] and Lucernare at 4 p.m.,[3] and these services were attended not only by the bishop and his clergy, but also by any of the lay people and catechumens as wished to be present. The Jerusalem monks and nuns formed a regular part of the congregation.

Of these two services Lucernare was displaced only on rare occasions, and Morning Hymns only slightly more often, with exceptions in the case of the regular weekly vigil to be mentioned below. But the minor hour services at noon and 3 p.m. (and also in Lent at 9 a.m.), though they were normal, were apparently more easily displaced or omitted. Thus, on Wednesdays and Fridays there is never a service at 3 p.m., since a more important service takes its place.[4]

These cathedral day hours were usually held in the Anastasis, though Lucernare normally ended with a procession to the Cross.[5]

The observance of Sunday seems to have involved fewer but considerably longer services. At cock-crow the first service[6] took place in the Anastasis and its Cave; the Eucharist[7] lasted from full daylight till about eleven o'clock in the Martyrium, and was followed by a Thanksgiving in the Anastasis; and Lucernare with an extra procession added began at its usual time in the Anastasis.[8] *

But we cannot be sure whether this pattern did or did not include the recitation of the Morning Hymns, since Egeria, when she has described the first service, only tells us that from full daylight

---

[1] This name is also used by others, for example, Epiphanius, *Exp. Fid.* 23, *PG* 42.829.

[2] 24.2. *

[3] 24.4. When another service clashed with this time, Lucernare was usually postponed rather than omitted, as on the Monday in the Great Week, 32.2; cf. 34; 43.6.

[4] See 27.5.

[5] For some exceptions see, for example, 29.2 and 43.5. Also 32.2; 33.1; 34, where the presence of specially large congregations probably made it necessary to hold the service in the Martyrium rather than in the Anastasis.

[6] 24.8-11.   [7] 25.1-3.   [8] 25.4.

"they do what happens everywhere on a Sunday",[1] which may imply either the Eucharist on its own, or Morning Hymns followed by the Eucharist, depending on the pattern which she regarded as normal in her own country. Nor are we entirely clear whether or not there was a minor hour at 3 p.m. The manuscript as it stands says (apparently rather pointlessly) that there was such a service,[2] but most scholars prefer to believe that in this passage the word "not" has dropped out.

The contrast between a week-day and a Sunday will appear from the following timetable:

*

TIME	WEEK-DAY	SUNDAY
Cock-crow		First Service
First Light	Morning Hymns	—
Full Daylight	—	(Morning Hymns?)+ Eucharist
9 a.m.	Minor Office (only in Lent)	
11 a.m.		Thanksgiving
Noon	Minor Office	
3 p.m.	Minor Office	(Minor Office?)
4 p.m.	Lucernare	Lucernare with extra procession

Since, in comparison with Morning Hymns and Lucernare, the minor "hour" offices were fairly often replaced by other and longer observances, we might guess that they had been adopted as public services more recently, and were perhaps a monastic innovation. But the tradition of private prayer at these hours went back to remote antiquity, and Egeria gives no indication that she regarded the "hours" as specifically services for monks.

[1] 25.1; see Zerfass, p. 35, n. 91.
[2] At 27.3 Duchesne conjectured that the manuscript originally read *nona* (*non*) *fit* (cf. 25.4). 44.3 seems to refer to week-days.

Indeed she tells us that they were attended by the bishop and clergy, and some lay people.

The system described has many parallels in contemporary writings.[1] But, wherever these describe monastic services, they mention also services at night. Cassian describes as well an extra service after Morning Hymns, one of the main objects of which was to keep the monks from the temptations of returning to bed.[2] It seems that the Jerusalem monks did the same on Sundays,[3] accompanied by some of the laity. Egeria also tells us that the monks arrived for Morning Hymns early, even before the doors were opened, and spent some time singing psalms. At both these apparently monastic occasions members of the bishop's clergy are sent to say the prayers. The fact that they attend by rota[4] confirms the impression that these acts of devotion were not seen as part of the regular public round of prayer. Egeria explains the monks' early arrival in the mornings by saying that they were afraid that otherwise they might be late for the opening of the doors,[5] but it is more probable that they met to hold their equivalent of the night office.

THE WEEK

The climax of the Jewish week was the Sabbath, and the New Testament witnesses to the Pharisees' practice of fasting twice in the week.[6] The Christians seem to have taken it for granted that this rhythm must be preserved, even though they worked towards a new climax, the first rather than the seventh day of the week;[7] and deliberately altered the fasts from the Monday and Thursday observed by the Jews to Wednesday and Friday.[8] In the new

[1] 24.1–7. See Zerfass, pp. 39–55 and cf. *Const. Apost.* 8.35,37, *PG* 1.1137,1140; Basil, *Longer Rule* 37, *PG* 31.1009–16; Cassian, *Inst.* 3.3–4. On the history see especially E. C. Ratcliff, "The Choir Offices" in *Liturgy and Worship*, ed. W. K. Lowther Clarke (London 1954), pp. 257–61, and C. W. Dugmore, *The Influence of the Synagogue on the Divine Office* (London 1964), pp. 90–101.

[2] Cassian, *Inst.* 3.4, *PL* 49.127–8.

[3] 24.12.   [4] See 24.1; 44.2.

[5] 24.8.   [6] Luke 18.12.

[7] Egeria does not seem to have assimilated the idea that the first was also the "eighth" day, since in 24.8 she calls Sunday the "seventh" day.

[8] See Dugmore, op. cit., pp. 37–42, and J. A. Jungmann, *The Early Liturgy* (1966), pp. 19–24. Gingras, p.227, n. 327 shows that though the Wednesday

scheme the status of the Sabbath was doubtful. St Ignatius, for instance, had warned Christians not to keep the Sabbath, but to live in the spirit of the Lord's Day;[1] but apparent rejection of this kind did not prevail, and in the fourth century Saturdays were marked by some special observance in every known part of the Christian world.

Egeria thus describes a scheme which was in general use, even though the detailed observances she describes were not exactly those of Churches in other regions. In Jerusalem, for instance, it seems that there was a full celebration of the Eucharist on Wednesday and Friday afternoons.[2] Thus it would appear that the fasting on those days was understood as a eucharistic fast, and this is confirmed by the fact that in Eastertide, when fasting was suspended,[3] the Wednesday and Friday Eucharist was celebrated in the morning, and the necessary fasting was thus curtailed. Egeria tells us that Saturday was never a fasting day, even in Lent, with the one exception of Easter Even,[4] and that the Eucharist was celebrated on Saturday[5] mornings throughout the year.[6]

THE YEAR

Egeria's account of the Christian year in Jerusalem has a gap which deprives us of most of her description of Epiphany, and does not continue beyond the major feasts; but the Armenian Lectionary shows that few if any major feasts are missing. It is

---

and Friday fasting had been regarded by Tertullian (de Ieiunio 2, PL 2.965) in the second century as voluntary, authors of the fourth century treated it as an obligation (Epiphanius, Exp. Fid. 22, PG 42.825, and Const. Apost. 5.14).

[1] Ignatius, ad Magn. 9.1, cited by Dugmore, op. cit., p. 29. For the name "the Lord's Day" cf. Rev. 1.10.

[2] This seems to be the implication of 27.6. During Lent the synaxis alone was held without the Offering.   [3] 41.

[4] See 27.1; 44.1,2. This was a general practice. See Gingras, p. 226, n. 322, for other fourth-century references.

[5] Though modern names for week-days have been used in this translation, they, like their Roman counterparts, would have been abhorrent to Christians of Egeria's time because of their pagan implications: Saturday for instance is "Saturn's day". Apart from "the Lord's Day" Christians retained the Jewish nomenclature. So in Egeria's own text Monday is "the second weekday", Tuesday "the third", and so on, and Saturday is "the Sabbath". St Augustine, Enarr. in Ps. 18.3, PL 36.1192, shows that the avoidance of the pagan names was sometimes deliberate.

[6] 27.8.

probable that Egeria went on from her account of the Dedication octave to describe the martyrs' days which she mentions elsewhere in passing.[1]

The major feature of the year was the Easter cycle.[2] Eight weeks before Easter, according to Egeria,[3] all began their fasting, and the candidates for baptism started their daily instructions, which lasted until the Great Week preceding Easter Day. The observance of Eastertide lasted a further seven weeks, with a feast on the fortieth day,[4] and its conclusion in the feast of Pentecost, after which normal fasting was resumed on Wednesdays and Fridays. The two other great feasts described are Epiphany[5] (in part) and the Dedication, and a feast of the next rank is the fortieth day after the Epiphany, now known as the Presentation of Christ in the Temple.

Besides these feasts the Armenian Lectionary mentions a large number of saints' days which were celebrated with a Eucharist. The saints so commemorated are interestingly distributed in the light of the number of Old Testament sites venerated by Egeria: six refer to the Old Testament, twelve to the New, and eight to the time since the apostles. And, although the number of such days was certainly fewer in Egeria's time, they may well have been in roughly the same proportion.

Lent

At the time of Egeria's visit Lent lasted eight weeks,[6] a time when the clergy and lay people underwent an intensification of their regular round of worship, and the candidates for baptism received the immediate preparation for the night when they were to receive the sacraments of Baptism and Holy Communion.

---

[1] 27.5.

[2] *Dies paschales* (27.1) is her description for the whole cycle, including Lent, and presumably also the fifty days following.

[3] Her statement has been questioned; see Note F, pp. 278–80 below.

[4] See below, pp. 77–8.

[5] Celebrated as the Feast of the Nativity, as appears from the lessons appointed in *AL*, Nos. 1–2. December 25 seems also to have been celebrated as the Nativity at Antioch at this time; cf. John Chrysostom's sermon, *In diem natalem* 1, *PG* 49.351, delivered in 386, in which he says it was first celebrated there within the previous decade. The date in December is first appropriated to the Nativity by the Philocalian Calendar, referring to Rome in 336, but was long resisted in Jerusalem; cf. *AL*, No. 71.

[6] See Note F, pp. 278–80 below.

For those who were already members of the Church, as well as
for the candidates and catechumens, there was fasting on all days
except Saturdays and Sundays, as will be described below. But
there were also a number of extra services which were added to
the normal round. An extra office which resembled those normally held at noon and 3 p.m. was held at 9 a.m.[1] and on Friday
night Lucernare was the beginning of a vigil which lasted till the
celebration of the Saturday Eucharist before sunrise.[2] The
services which were held throughout the year on Wednesday and
Friday afternoons took place as usual, except that the synaxis was
not followed by the Offering.[3] Egeria's description suggests that
the amount of preaching was increased.

For the candidates, and for the bishop and clergy who mini-
stered to them, the first seven weeks of Lent brought considerable
exertion[4]. The instructions then ended, but this seems to have been
because the Great Week itself brought so many extra services
that further instruction was impossible.

The Lenten fast was kept not according to a general rule, but
according to the capacities of the individual.[5] Egeria reports that
it is known as "the Feast"[6] which sounds strange to modern ears,
but is an interesting reminder of the early Christians' ability to
combine penitence and joy, and may well be connected with the
idea that the Passover was a "feast of bitter herbs" (an idea
expounded by Origen[7]).

The regime described by Egeria is exceptionally austere, since
not only were oil and fruit given up, but even bread;[8] it may be
that she was describing the practice of the monks. She tells us that
some people kept the fast for a week, which meant that they ate
nothing between the dinner after their Sunday Communion and

---

[1] 27.4.   [2] See 27.9.

[3] 27.6; compare the 49th Canon of Laodicea (slightly earlier than Egeria);
"During Lent the Bread must not be offered except on the Sabbath and the
Lord's Day."

[4] See 46.   [5] See 28.

*   [6] *Heortai* (cultic plural for singular), like *ieiunia* 27.9, *octavae* 40.1, or *quadragesimae* 42.1).

[7] V. Peri, reviewing Bastiaensen, *Obs.*, in *Aevum* 37 (1963), p. 192, cites Origen,
Hom. in Hierem. 14.16 and *Const. Apost. 5.13* as parallels.

[8] 28.4; see R. Weber's note in *VC* 12 (1958), pp. 93–7. Cyril, *Cat.* 4.27, speaks
only of abstention from wine and flesh.

their breakfast on the following Saturday;[1] but, though she thinks highly of them, she emphasizes that no one was forced to undertake a fixed amount of fasting, and that the amount chosen was not made the subject of criticism.[2] Those who did not wish to keep a whole week might eat one meal (at midday on Thursday[3]), and there were also those who ate each evening.[4]

The Great Week

Lazarus Saturday and the Day of Palms. The distinctive ceremonies of the Great Week[5] began "six days before the Passover",[6] that is to say, on the Saturday before the Thursday on which the Last Supper was commemorated, which in the Armenian Lectionary is called "The Passover of the Old Law".[7] The Pasch, or Passover of the new law was Easter Day itself.

The observances began with a vigil from the Friday evening (i.e. the beginning of Saturday by the Jewish reckoning) till the Saturday morning which according to Egeria took place not, as in other weeks of Lent, at the Anastasis, but on Sion. At the Eucharist which formed its conclusion the archdeacon made the first of his announcements[8]—necessary throughout the Great Week—of the time and place where people were to assemble for the special service later in the day. He warned the people to be ready at the Lazarium at Bethany at one o'clock. They went there, and the bishop and the monks went with them. On the way they paused for a short station at the church where Mary, Lazarus' sister, met Christ,[9] and they then went on for an afternoon synaxis at the Lazarium itself, with the raising of Lazarus as its theme.[10]

---

[1] These were known as *hebdomadarii*, or "people who kept a week" (28.1–2). The word is a hybrid of Greek and Latin, which may be a sign that Egeria moved among the Latin-speaking community in Jerusalem (she mentions it in 47.4). Augustine, *Ep.* 36.12, *PL* 33.148, mentions a man who fasted throughout the whole forty days. For some further varieties of individual practice see Gingras, p. 230, n. 335.

[2] Cf. Rom. 14.5–6, and Jerome, *Ep.* 46.9.

[3] Presumably to avoid eating on Wednesday or Friday (28.3).

[4] The apotactites ate only once a day throughout the year.

[5] This name for the week preceding Easter was also used by John Chrysostom, for example *Hom. in Ps.* 145.2, §1, *PG* 55.519, and in *Const. Apost.* 5.15 (title), *PG* 1.880, and 833, *PG* 1.1133; see Bludau, pp. 119–21.

[6] John 12.1; cf. 29.5.   [7] See No. 38.

[8] 29.3; cf. 30.2; 35.1; (37.9); 43.3.

[9] This station is not mentioned in *AL*.   [10] 29.5; *AL*, No. 33.

On the next day (which Egeria describes simply as the opening of the Great Week, though in the Armenian Lectionary it is called the "Day of Palms") there were normal Sunday services in the morning, but in the afternoon they spent from one to five o'clock holding services at the Eleona and Imbomon, ending with the Gospel about the triumphal entry.[1] Then they went down the Mount of Olives carrying palms and escorted the bishop into the city until eventually they arrived at the Anastasis for Lucernare at a late hour.[2]

Monday, Tuesday, and Wednesday before Easter. On the first three week-days of the Great Week the services were as usual except that there was an additional synaxis in the Martyrium which began at three in the afternoon, and lasted for four hours. It was followed by Lucernare in the same building; then on the Monday there was a psalm and dismissal at the Anastasis,[3] and the same on Tuesday with the addition of a further evening service on the Eleona. This was a station to read Christ's apocalyptic teaching in the cave where it had traditionally been uttered on the eve of the passion.[4] On the Wednesday, after Lucernare and before the final dismissal, they went to the Anastasis, and a presbyter read from the Gospel about Judas' plot with the priests, and Jesus' anointing in the house of Simon the Leper.[5]

From Thursday to Saturday morning. On the Thursday morning there were the usual services till midday. Then at two o'clock began a continuous round of observances which, apart from one short break for the evening meal, lasted till dawn the next day.[6] The service at two o'clock was a synaxis on the theme of Judas' betrayal of Christ and subsequent death,[7] which seems to correspond to the afternoon synaxes on the previous three days; then the catechumens are dismissed, and the faithful remain for a synaxis on the theme of the Last Supper, followed by the Offering celebrated first in the Martyrium and then "Behind the Cross".[8]

---

[1] 31.1–2; cf. *AL*, No. 34.   [2] 31.4.
[3] 32.2; cf. *AL*, No. 35.   [4] 33.1–2; cf. *AL*, No. 36.
[5] 34; *AL*, No. 37.   [6] See 35.1–36.4 and cf. *AL*, Nos. 38–42.
[7] 35.1; *AL*, No. 38, supplies the lessons.
[8] 35.1–2; cf. *AL*, No. 39.

Since "Behind the Cross" appears to have been a small vestibule, the people probably remained in the Martyrium for both of the Offerings,[1] then going to the Anastasis for a service which was probably the Thanksgiving for Communion.[2] They went home to snatch an evening meal before going up the Mount of Olives for the night services.

From about seven to eleven o'clock they remained on the Eleona, holding Lucernare, and then singing psalms.[3] They read a second version of the teaching which Christ had given "in the cave",[4] and then went up to the Imbomon for a further office and a third version of the teaching which led on to a description of the arrest and trial.[5]

They then set off, according to Egeria, to the place of Christ's Agony,[6] where they held a short station service appropriate to the place; then, going down the mountain by torchlight to Geth- *semane, they made another station and read about the arrest.[7] The procession then went up on its final stage into the city to read at the courtyard Before the Cross the Gospel about Christ's trial by Pilate.[8] By this time it was morning, and the people were sent home for a short rest. The notice on this occasion was given out not, as in the ordinary way, by the archdeacon, but by the bishop himself.[9] At this point there were some courageous spirits who instead of going home to bed went to Sion to pray at the Column of the Flagellation.[10]

At seven o'clock the people were back again on Golgotha for the Veneration of the Cross, which went on Behind the Cross till

[1] Cf. 37.3. Note that there is no remark about the weather as in 37.4.
[2] Cf. 25.3.   [3] See *AL*, No. 39.
[4] 35.3; *AL*, No. 39. See Renoux, *La Prière*, pp. 187–91.
[5] 35.4; cf. *AL*, No. 40.
[6] 36.1; but *AL*, No. 40 says to the "Room of the Disciples" which may mean the same as "On Eleona". In any case the place seems to have been near the summit of the Mount of Olives, since the descent to Gethsemane is described after this station both in 36.2 and in *AL*, No. 40.
[7] 36.3; *AL*, No. 40. Note that *AL* gives a Gospel for both this and the last station which covers both the agony and the arrest.
[8] 36.4; *AL*, No. 42 gives a reading which describes also the trial before Caiaphas.
[9] 36.5.
[10] 37.1. This was perhaps for the same reason as the extra morning service for the monks on Sundays, see p. 69 above.

noon;[1] then they gathered in the courtyard Before the Cross for a three-hour office which resembled a series of synaxes on the theme of the passion.[2] This was followed by a synaxis of the normal form, except that the prophecies were read in the Martyrium, but the people moved across into the Anastasis to hear the Gospel which described Christ's burial in the new tomb, and to have the dismissal.[3] After such exertions it is not surprising that the vigil of Friday night was kept only by the young and vigorous, though even these formed a considerable crowd. Any people unable to keep vigil the whole night came and watched at the Anastasis as they could.[4] This vigil ended as usual at dawn, but on this one Saturday in the year there was no celebration of the Eucharist; the offices at nine o'clock and noon took place as on an ordinary week-day, and there were then no further services until the paschal vigil in the evening.

Easter Day. The paschal vigil opened with Lucernare in the Martyrium,[5] after which the people remained there for the office of the vigil.[6] In the meantime the candidates were baptized and brought in,[7] it would appear at about midnight, to take part in the Eucharist. The synaxis had the theme of the resurrection, and the Offering was made first in the Martyrium and then, after a reading of the resurrection Gospel, again in the Anastasis. The people then went home until the third celebration of the Eucharist at dawn.[8]

In the afternoon the bishop took the newly-baptized up the Mount of Olives for special offices at the Eleona and Imbomon, which were also attended by monks and anyone else who wished.[9] These offices took place each day in Easter week. Afterwards on Easter Day they returned to the Anastasis for Lucernare, and then
* held a final station in Sion, going home at about eight o'clock.[10]

---

*   [1] 36.5; *AL*, No. 43.   [2] 36.6–7; see *AL*, No. 43.
*   [3] 36.8; see *AL*, No. 43.   [4] 37.9; cf. *AL*, No. 44.
     [5] See *AL*, No. 44 for the form of the office.
     [6] The paschal vigil was a well-established institution, familiar not only to Egeria (see 38.1), but mentioned as long before as c. A.D. 225 in *Didascalia Apostolorum*, 5.20.9, ed. F. X. Funk (Paderborn 1905), vol. I, p. 296.
     [7] 38.1,2; *AL*, No. 44.   [8] See 39.2 and *AL*, No. 45.
     [9] 39.3; cf. *AL*, No. 45.   [10] 39.5; *AL*, No. 45.

Easter Week. On five of the eight days of Easter Week the daily Eucharist was celebrated in the buildings on Golgotha, but on Wednesday on the Eleona and on the Friday on Sion.[1] Morning Hymns and Lucernare took place as usual in the Anastasis, and every morning there were mystagogical lectures by the bishop to the newly-baptized which also took place in the Anastasis.[2] Each afternoon they continued to hold the offices at the Eleona and Imbomon before Lucernare, and on the Sunday after Easter the people once more ended the day with a station on Sion as they had done on Easter Day itself.[3]

From Easter to Pentecost. Eastertide was distinguished from the rest of the year chiefly by the absence of fasting, even for the monks.[4] This meant that the Wednesday and Friday Eucharists were celebrated in the morning, not the afternoon, and the previous eucharistic fast was thus reduced to a minimum. The office which had been held at 9 a.m. was discontinued at Easter, and not resumed till the following Lent.

The Fortieth Day after Easter. The Bible provided the date of Lazarus Saturday, "six days before the passover",[5] and the interval of fifty days between Easter and Pentecost.[6] And it was because the Bible demanded a week's festival at Passover that the Christians kept Easter as a feast of eight days' duration.[7] By the same token it was inevitable that a Feast of the Ascension came to be held forty days[8] after Easter.

To the modern reader it would seem equally inevitable that the feast should have been celebrated at the Imbomon, as indeed it seems to have been in the Armenian Lectionary,[9] since this was the site which had already been identified in tradition as that of Christ's ascension since the early fourth century.[10] But, although we can now be sure that the main eucharistic celebration must in $*$ Egeria's time have been elsewhere, since Poemenia had not yet

[1] 39.1; cf. *AL*, Nos. 46–52.
[2] 47.1; see *AL*, No. 52 and List D, p. 277 below: cf. also p. 63, n. 6.
[3] 40.2; *AL*, No. 52. [4] 41. [5] John 12.1.
[6] Lev. 23.16; Acts 2.1. [7] Exod. 12.15.
[8] See Acts 1.3. [9] No. 57.
[10] See *Vit. Const.* 3.41, *PG* 20.1101, and compare Egeria 31.1.

built her church at the Imbomon, we still have to explain Egeria's surprising information that the feast was kept in Bethlehem.

It is of course possible that in the year of which Egeria is speaking there was some feast of special importance to Bethlehem which coincided with and replaced the celebration of the Ascension, as has been argued by Dom E. Dekkers[1] and Père P. Devos,[2] and this line of argument would explain Egeria's remark that the preaching was "suited to the day and place".[3] It is also possible that, as Professor J. G. Davies has shown,[4] contemporary theology was so accustomed to considering together the mysteries of the incarnation and ascension that Bethlehem would have been a natural second choice after the Imbomon. We know too little to give a confident reason for the choice of Bethlehem. But it may be that this important feast[5] was held in Bethlehem simply because, without a special church, it could not be held in Jerusalem, and because the bishop desired to celebrate some feast other than Epiphany with the important religious community at the Bethlehem Church.

Pentecost. Pentecost, itself the feast of the coming of the Holy Spirit, was also the Fiftieth Day, the end of Eastertide.[6] It had no all-night vigil, but from dawn and the first Sunday service in the Anastasis[7] until midnight, when the people were finally dismissed, they were continuously occupied, except during a short break for lunch.

After an early (and brisk) celebration of the Eucharist in the

---

[1] E. Dekkers, "De datum der 'Peregrinatio Egeriae' en het feest van ons Heer Hemelvaart", in *Sacris Erudiri* 1 (1948), pp. 181–205.

[2] P. Devos, "Egérie à Bethléem: La 40ᵉ jour aprés Pâques à Jérusalem en 383", in *A.B.* 86 (1968), pp. 87–108. This article gives a useful summary of opinions previously put forward.

[3] 42.

[4] J. G. Davies, "The *Peregrinatio Egeriae* and the Ascension", in *VC* 8 (1954), pp. 93–101.

[5] Mentioned, for example, by Chrysostom, *Cur in Pentec* 5, *PG* 51. 105, and Augustine, *serm* 262.3, *PL* 38. 1208, and *AL*, No. 57. Note that F. C Conybeare inexplicably omitted the Feast of the Ascension (ibid., No. 57) from his translation of the Armenian Lectionary in *Rituale Armenorum* (Oxford 1905), which has added to the confusion of scholars who have discussed the problem raised by Egeria.

[6] It had no octave for Egeria, though one is given in *Const. Apost.* 5.20, *PG* 1.900–1.

[7] 43.1; cf. *AL*, No. 58.

Martyrium, which was over by 9 a.m., the people took the bishop to Sion for a second full celebration. In the afternoon a synaxis was held at the Imbomon[1] followed by Lucernare on the Eleona.[2] This in turn was followed by a procession which arrived at the Martyrium at about eight o'clock. An office was held there and at the Anastasis,[3] and last of all on Sion, from which the people left for home at midnight.

From the Monday after Pentecost Jerusalem reverted to its normal pattern of weekly worship, with Wednesdays and Fridays kept as fasting days.[4]

Dedication, Epiphany, and Presentation. Two feasts in the year were celebrated with a dignity comparable with that of Easter.[5] They were accorded an octave, the churches were specially decorated,[6] and crowds of monks came in to Jerusalem to join the community in their celebrations.[7]

Dedication or "Encaenia" was kept for eight days like Solomon's dedication of the Temple, to which Egeria refers.[8] Egeria tells us that on this occasion many bishops were present among the visitors, a tradition perhaps going back to the assembly of bishops organized by Constantine at the original dedication of the buildings on Golgotha.[9]

An additional reason for celebration in Egeria's time was the belief that on the very day of the dedication the holy cross had been found.[10] This belief became so firmly established that in the following century the cross was exposed for veneration on

[1] 43.5–6; cf. *AL*, No. 58.
[2] 43.6.
[3] See 43.7–8, and cf. *AL*, No. 58.
[4] 44.1. Gingras, p. 248, n. 448, shows evidence for a special fast after Pentecost in other parts of the world at the time of Egeria. But her description seems to imply no more than the resumption of the normal fasting which had been suspended during Eastertide.
[5] Cf. 25.6.
[6] 29.1; cf. 25.6–9; 49.3.
[7] 25.12; 49.1. No visitors are said to have come at Easter, no doubt because this was the climax of the local church year everywhere, and thus to be observed in every local congregation. But Egeria was there, and there may have been other pilgrims as well.
[8] 48.2; cf. 2 Chron. 7.8–9 and see 1 Kings 8.65–6.
[9] 49.2; cf. Eusebius, *VC* 4.43, *PG* 20.1193.
[10] See Note C, p. 240 below, on the Finding of the Cross.

the second day of this feast in the same way as on Good Friday.[1]

Epiphany, though Egeria's description of it is mainly missing, is provided in the Armenian Lectionary with lessons which are all concerned with the Nativity.[2] From the same source we learn that the proceedings at Bethlehem began in the afternoon with a synaxis "At the Shepherds",[3] and continued with a Gospel in the Cave of the Nativity,[4] and Lucernare in the Church, which formed the beginning of the vigil.[5] The vigil culminated, like that of Easter, with a midnight celebration of the Eucharist, and, when it was over, the bishop and the Jerusalem monks left for Jerusalem in order to celebrate the feast there. Egeria's description is resumed at the point of their arrival just before dawn,[6] and their station at the Anastasis. At this point the people went home for a short rest, but the monks remained to sing psalms in the Anastasis in the way they usually did on Sundays.[7] At eight o'clock the people assembled to celebrate the Eucharist in the Martyrium. The Festival of Epiphany continued for eight days with a daily Eucharist in the various holy places.[8]

The Presentation of Christ in the Temple, known to Egeria simply as the Fortieth Day after the Epiphany,[9] had its own

---

[1] The belief no doubt accounts for the connection between the Encaenia and the Feast of the Exaltation of the Cross. Baumstark (*CL*, p. 183) points out that the Encaenia was held on the date of the Roman feast of the dedication of the temple of Jupiter Capitolinus, and M. Black connects Encaenia with the Jewish *Hanukkah* in "The Festival of the Encaenia Ecclesiae in the Ancient Church with special reference to Palestine and Syria", in *J.E.H.* 5 (1954), pp. 78–86.

[2] See *AL*, Nos. 1–9. These were probably the same as those of Egeria's day, since the name of the feast seems to be connected with the first word of the Epistle—ἐπεφάνη (Titus 2.11). During the octave the lessons in *AL* are either connected with the places where they are read or with the Nativity. The visit of the Magi is one of the subjects of reading at the first Eucharist in Bethlehem, St Stephen's martyrdom at the Eucharist on the second day, and the Innocents on the third. On the eighth day there is a reading about the Circumcision (cf. Luke 2.21). It is interesting that there is no reading about the Lord's baptism.

[3] See *AL*, No. 1, and compare the afternoon synaxis on Lazarus Saturday (29.5).

[4] Cf. the readings in caves at the Eleona (33.2) and Anastasis (24.10).

[5] See *AL*, No. 1 and List A.   [6] 25.6.

[7] 25.7; cf. 24.12.

[8] See 25.11.

[9] 26; *AL*, No. 13. See Luke 2.22 and Lev. 12.2–4.

Eucharist with suitable readings at the synaxis, but she says that it was celebrated with the same solemnities as Easter.

Octaves in the Holy Places. During the Great Week there is seldom any difficulty in understanding why particular services are held in the places mentioned by Egeria. The services such as that at the Lazarium on Lazarus Saturday, or the Palm procession on the following day, not to mention all the special stations made between the Thursday afternoon and Easter morning, are purely and simply chosen to enable the people to follow out on the original sites the historical events which preceded Christ's passion and resurrection. Indeed this is the very feature of the Jerusalem liturgy of which Egeria seems most appreciative.

But this explanation in terms of sacred history applies hardly at all to the places chosen for the keeping of octaves. The Armenian Lectionary shows remarkable discrepancies between the places where the daily Eucharist is celebrated and the subject of the readings; it is true that the celebration at the Lazarium in the Epiphany octave[1] seems to be concerned exclusively with the raising of Lazarus and not at all with the Epiphany; but all the other readings for this week[2] are to do with the subject of the octave being celebrated rather than the place where the service takes place.[3] None of the readings for the octave of Easter has $*$ any specifically historical relation to the place where it is read; indeed two of the Gospels about the Burial are read in the Martyrium when they could presumably have been read equally well in the Anastasis.[4]

Since the available evidence thus provides nothing to connect the different places chosen for the celebration of octaves with the historical motive which clearly prompted the choice of the stational services of the Great Week, we have to seek another

[1] *AL*, No. 7; cf. 25.11.
[2] Except *AL*, No. 3, whose readings are concerned with the martyrdom of St Stephen as well as with the Epiphany; but this station did not exist in Egeria's day.
[3] Though note that the Anastasis may have been felt to represent the Temple, and thus to have been suitable for the Circumcision readings of *AL*, No. 9. But this could not apply to Egeria's description (25.11).
[4] See *AL*, Nos. 45–6.

explanation; and a clue may be forthcoming from Egeria when she remarks that during the Epiphany octave the bishop has to be in Jerusalem.[1] What brings him back from Bethlehem? Perhaps it is the need to lead the worship of the Jerusalem community in their principal church on the first days of the feast, and then to progress at least to some of the other important churches of the city to lead the celebrations there. Bethlehem was far enough away for the monks whose residence was there to continue the feast in their own church under the presidency of their own Bethlehem presbyters, but it seems that the great crowds whom Egeria saw at feasts in Jerusalem included not only the visitors who had travelled specially to join the Jerusalem community, but also the clergy, monks, and people who were near enough to the bishop's church to join him in normal celebrations of the Eucharist. The bishop moved from one church to another during the octave simply in order to celebrate the feast in as many of his churches, and with as many of his people, as possible. The tradition thus established seems, from the inconsistencies in the lists given by Egeria and the Armenian Lectionary,[2] to have had no deeper motive.

CEREMONIAL AND ORNAMENTS

As an intelligent Christian Egeria was delighted at the appropriateness of the psalms and Bible readings of the Jerusalem liturgy; but it was as a visitor from a distant province that she saw the splendour of the festal decorations of the churches. The characteristic ornaments were special hangings, "curtains and veils",[3] and there may also have been special clothing for the ministers, since we know that Constantine had presented Jerusalem with a gold vestment for the bishop to wear at the Baptism.[4] Nothing but the

---

[1] See 25.12.

[2] See *AL*, Nos. 2–9 and 25.11 for Epiphany; Nos. 45–52 and 39.2 for Easter; and compare Nos. 67–8 with 49.3 for Dedication.

[3] These may have hung between the pillars like those represented in the mosaic of Theodoric's palace in St Apollinare Nuovo, Ravenna. See M. Gough, *The Early Christians* (London 1961), pl. 74.

[4] See G. Dix, *The Shape of the Liturgy* (London 1945), pp. 398–9, and Theodoret *Eccl. Hist.* 2.23, PG 82.1066. If other vestments were used in Jerusalem, the city would have been ahead of the West in this matter, since Pope Celestine I (†432) still expressed his disapproval of their use.

best was used, whether it was candlesticks, books, lamps, or eucharistic vessels, and large numbers of extra lamps and candles were lighted as they still are today for great festivals in the churches Egeria describes.[1] The value of these possessions was considerable, and one of the accusations made by his enemies against Cyril was that he had sold some of them to provide for the poor. In effect they provided a reserve of wealth for hard times, even though they may have been given with other motives.[2]

Egeria is not particularly interested in the minutiae of ceremonial, but it is possible to glean some information from her casual descriptions. In at least some of the processions the bishop came last,[3] and at many services he sat in his chief seat, surrounded by presbyters who also sat, and deacons who stood. The people were also permitted to sit on some occasions.[4] On other occasions the bishop immediately on entering a holy place went straight into the sanctuary, that is, the holy cave.[5] When he read the Sunday resurrection Gospel, incense was first brought into the Anastasis cave,[6] at Lucernare the light was brought out of the cave itself,[7] and some special acts took place before the cave.[8]

In the dismissals the people were called to bow their heads before the bishop blessed them, and after the blessing they "came to his hand" individually, which probably means that they kissed it.[9] ∗

The ceremonial at the veneration of objects seems to have been elaborate: when the people venerate the cross, they bow over it,

---

[1] For Epiphany see 25.7,8, and for Sundays cf. 24.9. The innumerable lamps carried in the processions at night (15.5(?); 36.2; 43.7) were not so much festive as practical.

[2] See Telfer, *Cyril*, pp. 25–6. [3] See 25.2.

[4] See 31.1 and also 40.1; 25.1; 45.2; 43.5.

[5] E.g. the Anastasis (24.2,10), Eleona (33.2), and for Bethlehem see *AL*, No. 1 and Renoux, *La Prière*, pp. 186, 192–3.

[6] 24.10; cf. p. 65 above.

[7] 24.4. This act lies behind the present-day ceremony of the Holy Fire. See *CL*, pp. 146–8. See p. 88 below.

[8] 24.5, 34.

[9] 24.6, 24.2, etc. This hand-kissing is probably what is intended by the phrase ∗ "coming under the hand" of the bishop, used in the (Greek) Canons of Laodicea, Canon 19 (A.D. 363) to describe the blessing at the dismissal of catechumens and penitents. See Gingras, p. 217 n. 274. Kissing the hands of bishops and priests is still a common practice in Italy, in parts of eastern Europe and in the middle East.

first touch it with their forehead and their eyes, and then kiss it. When a similar action is taught to the newly-baptized in the context of receiving Holy Communion, it is explained as a "hallowing of the senses":

When thou hast hallowed thine eyes by the touch of the Holy Body, partake thereof... bending and saying in the way of worship and reverence, "Amen", be thou hallowed by partaking also of the Blood of Christ. And while the moisture is still upon thy lips, touching it with thine hands, hallow both thine eyes and brow and other senses.[1]

SUBSEQUENT MODIFICATIONS

* In A.D. 348, when Cyril of Jerusalem preached his *Catechetical Lectures* for the first time, he made no mention of the liturgical pattern described by Egeria. Indeed it can hardly have existed at that time, since it seems unlikely that there was a roofed building at the Anastasis, and this building was the most regularly used, winter and summer, by Egeria's time. It therefore seems reasonable to suppose that Cyril between roughly his thirtieth and his seventieth year was making constant liturgical experiments, and that the elaborate pattern recorded for us by Egeria was still being modified at the time of her visit, most often by additions, and the inclusion of new holy places. Certainly the resulting calendar, though vivid, was often overcrowded and impossibly demanding. On a day like Pentecost the people were expected to attend services almost continuously from dawn until midnight.

The Armenian Lectionary shows various ways in which this overcrowded programme was lightened. It is possible that Lent as a whole was reduced from eight to seven weeks, since no provision is made for a Wednesday and Friday synaxis in the seventh week.[2] But the reaction is most obvious in the Great Week itself. The afternoon service in the Eleona which is held before the Palm Sunday procession is shortened by two hours,[3] and the afternoon services of the Monday, Tuesday, and Wednes-

[1] Pseudo-Cyril, *Myst.* 5.21–2 (tr. Church), *PG* 33.1124–5, and cf. Egeria 37.3, and Jerome, *Ep.* 46.8, cited above p. 22.

[2] This week is particularly mentioned by Egeria (see 27.2), and *AL*, Nos. 20, 21, 23 may, as Baumstark suggests (*Oriens Christianus* I (1911), p. 68) have belonged originally to the extra week, perhaps the first.

[3] 31.1; cf. *AL*, No. 34.

day, as well as that of Lazarus Saturday, are all abbreviated,[1] thus allowing the people a longer rest between the morning and afternoon services. The eucharistic celebrations on the Thursday afternoon were moved to an earlier hour,[2] originally no doubt to save the people from hurrying over the meal which followed them.[3] But, though this may have been the original reason, the Armenian Lectionary strangely makes no provision for any meal, but sends them straight to Sion, and then on to the Lucernare which formed the opening of the night services.

Between the time of Egeria and that of the Armenian Lectionary several new churches had been built, and included in the liturgical programme. The Martyrium of St Stephen is visited during octaves,[4] and there was less time spent in Bible reading at the Imbomon on the night of Thursday in the Great Week, presumably to make time for the additional station at the Court of the High Priest and the Palace of the Judge,[5] which involved a considerable detour in comparison with the procession described by Egeria. On the Day of Pentecost a longer rest was allowed after lunch.[6]

Another modification, if the Armenian Lectionary is speaking in the same terminology as Egeria, is the removal of ceremonies which had been held in the cramped vestibule Behind the Cross to the more convenient court Before the Cross.[7] No readings are provided for vigils either on the night of the Friday in the Great Week[8] or before Lazarus Saturday;[9] but Egeria makes it clear that these were purely voluntary as far as the laity were concerned,[10] and it may well be that they were monastic occasions for which the cathedral clergy had no special arrangements to make.

---

[1] 29.3; 32—34; *AL*, Nos. 33, 35–7, where the two afternoon services may be combined into one.
[2] *AL*, No. 38.   [3] See 35.2.
[4] 25.10; 39.2 omit; see *AL*, Nos. 3, 47, and Renoux, *Codex*, p. 177.
[5] *AL*, No. 41. See Renoux, *Codex*, p. 143.
[6] *AL*, No. 58; cf. 43.3.
[7] The Veneration of the Cross (37.1–3; cf. *AL*, No. 43), and the afternoon Eucharist of Thursday (35.2; cf. *AL*, No. 39).
[8] 37.9; cf. *AL*, No. 44.
[9] 29.2; cf. *AL*, No. 33.   [10] 37.9.

INFLUENCE

The Jerusalem liturgy of Egeria's time merited careful description because it was so novel, a fact obscured for the modern reader because so much of what she describes has since become common usage. But she is the earliest witness to a type of liturgical procedure which spread from Jerusalem to affect almost all Christians in the world.[1]

St Leo speaks in a sermon of "the festivity of the Lord's passion, which does not allow us to be silent, so great is the exultation of spiritual joys".[2] We may compare Egeria's use, half a century earlier, of the word "Feast" (Heortae[3]) to describe Lent, or her equally unexpected use of the word "resurrection" to describe a Gospel which clearly included much of the passion.[4]

The very fact that such phrases come unexpectedly to modern ears, and that we believe we can make a separation between the joyful and the penitential aspects of our faith, is a sign of the extent of Jerusalem's (and presumably Cyril's) influence on the Christian world. As the heir of a Jerusalem glorified by its newly erected churches, he determined to work out a liturgy which would give expression to the Christian understanding of its setting. He alone of all bishops in the world could read of the events of the passion and resurrection in the very places mentioned in the Bible, and he made good use of his opportunity, as Egeria bears witness. She and thousands of other visitors were given the new experience of hearing lessons which were suitable both to the day and to the place, and many left Jerusalem with the resolve to attempt the same in their home church. In so doing they introduced an historical quality into the liturgy which had a widespread effect, not least in the West.

It is not to be supposed that Cyril's reforms were complete, nor that all the effects they had were deliberate. The resurrection-Gospel[5] in the Jerusalem manuscript of the Armenian Lectionary is in fact part of a scheme of continuous reading of the passion-

---

[1] As regards the offices this development can best be followed in Zerfass.

[2] Leo, *Serm.* lxii *de Pass. Dom.* 11.1, *PL* 54.349, cited by Baumstark (*CL*, p. 172 *q.v.*).

[3] 27.1.   [4] 24.10.

[5] Namely John 19.38—20.18. See *AL*, 44, and Renoux, *Codex*, pp. 158f.

narrative, and only in the Paris manuscript do we find it shortened to be fully appropriate to the "day and place" of Easter
morning in the Anastasis.[1] But the preference for a shorter and
less repetitive lectionary was widespread,[2] and the process initiated
by Cyril was soon becoming the norm.

It is always tempting to claim too great an influence for any
early source-document, and especially so when there is so strong
a combination of evidence as that provided by Egeria and the
Armenian Lectionary. But the influence of the Jerusalem liturgy
can be followed by means of many clues, provided by small
details which Egeria describes as belonging to Jerusalem: so some,
where the Jerusalem church had a station "At the Cross", had a
station at a magnificent cross set up for the purpose in their
church, or perhaps in the baptistery.[3] This is found after the
Mattins of certain great feasts in Milan, and after Lucernare in the
prescriptions of a tenth-century Greek lectionary now in Sinai.[4]
The Roman double celebration of the Eucharist on Christmas
Day has its origin in the two Epiphany celebrations at Bethlehem
and Jerusalem.[5] The lectionary too has left its mark, since some of
the lessons heard by Egeria continue in use in Eastern churches,
especially the Armenian.[6] And in Jerusalem itself the daily
ceremony of bringing the first lamp from the holy cave of the
Anastasis[7] is still performed once a year on Easter Eve. Cyril's
Great Week has left the clearest traces of all. Without the reforms
which he initiated there would be no Palm Sunday procession,[8]
nor Veneration of the Cross on Good Friday.[9] And even if in

[1] See Renoux, *Codex*, pp. 158–62, and note 10.
[2] See Renoux, *Codex*, pp. 52, 127f, 141f, and 153.
[3] See *CL*, p. 41.   [4] 24.7; see *CL*, pp. 40–2.
[5] 25.6–8; cf. *AL*, No. 1, and *CL*, pp. 156f. The *Benedictus* (25.6) serves as the
Gradual of the second Christmas Mass at Rome.
[6] Renoux, *Codex*, pp. 185ff, mentions four in the Georgian lectionaries, seven
in the Byzantine, and fifteen in the Armenian.
[7] 24.10; see *CL*, pp. 146–8.   [8] 31.2; see *CL*, pp. 148–50.
[9] See *CL*, pp. 142–3. The practice remained in the West, but was lost in the East
till revived at the Phanar in 1864. For other features of later liturgies which
owe their origin to Jerusalem see *CL*, pp. 150 (Presentation), 85 (Benedictus),
195 (Sexagesima), and 142 (Pentecost). Note that the Three Hours' Devotion
on Good Friday (which in *AL* seems to be a four-hour devotion) has no
continuous history. The present practice was introduced in Peru by Jesuits after
an earthquake in 1687.

Egeria's day there was no special Holy Fire ceremony at the Paschal vigil[1] in Jerusalem, it is from the Jerusalem custom that the Holy Fire developed, with its symbolism of turning darkness into resurrection light.[2]

---

[1] The usual Lucernare was held on that day, only in the Martyrium instead of the Anastasis, see *AL*, 44, and Renoux, *Codex*, pp. 84, 94.

[2] On the development of the ceremony see also Egeria's emphasis on the illumination produced at Lucernare (24.4–8), Renoux, *Codex*, p. 91, and Baumstark, *CL*, p. 148.

Egeria's Travels

The manuscript begins as Egeria is approaching Mount Sinai. For the places she had visited before see the extracts from Peter the Deacon, pp. 179–210 below.

The numbered notes at the foot of the page give biblical references or draw attention to points likely to help the reading. Other notes, which raise questions, indicated in the text by [n], are given on pp. 213–32 below and are referred to by the paragraph number in the text.

Egeria's Travels

1.1   ... biblical sites[1] were pointed out. In the meanwhile we were walking along between the mountains,[n] and came to a spot where they opened out to form an endless valley[n]—a huge plain, and very beautiful—across which we could see Sinai, the holy Mount of God. Next to the spot where the mountains open out is the place

2 of the "Graves of Craving".[2] [n] When we arrived there our guides, the holy men who were with us, said, "It is usual for the people who come here to say a prayer[n] when first they catch sight of the Mount of God", and we did as they suggested. The Mount of God is perhaps four miles[3] [n] away from where we were, right across the huge valley I have mentioned.

2.1   The valley lies under the flank of the Mount of God, and it really is huge. From looking at it we guessed—and they told us—that it was maybe sixteen miles long[n] and, they said, four miles wide,[n] and this valley we had to cross before we reached the   ✳

2 mountain. This is the huge flat valley in which the children of Israel were waiting[n] while holy Moses went up into the Mount of God and was there "forty days and forty nights".[4] It is the valley where the calf[5] was made, and the place is pointed out to this day, for a large stone stands there on the spot. Thus it was at the head of this very valley[n] that holy Moses pastured the cattle of his father-in-law and God spoke to him twice from the burning

3 bush.[6] From here we were looking at the Mount of God; our way first took us up it, since the best ascent is from the direction by which we were approaching, and then we would descend again to the head of the valley (where the Bush was), since that is the better way down.

So this was our plan. When we had seen everything we wanted and come down from the Mount of God, we would come to the place of the Bush. Then from there we would return through the middle of the valley now ahead of us and so return to the road

---

[1] For these sites see PD, Y16–17. Egeria returns this way, see 2.4.
[2] Kibroth-Hattaavah, where the Israelites were buried who had craved for the plenty of Egypt, Num. 11.34.
[3] A Roman mile is about ninety-five yards less than an English mile.
[4] Exod. 24.18.   [5] Exod. 32.   [6] Exod. 3.1.

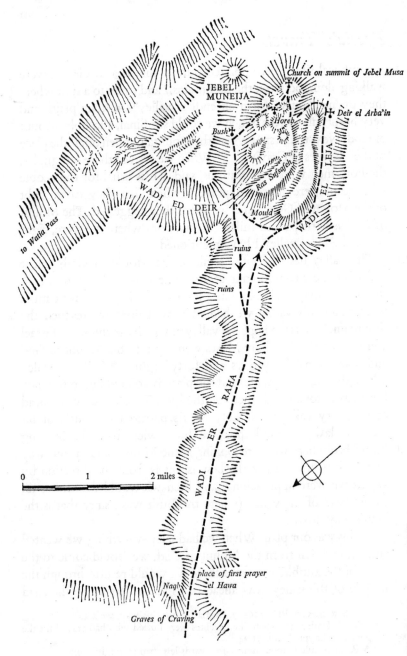

Church on summit of Jebel Musa

JEBEL
MUNEIJA

Deir el Arba'in

Bush

Horeb

WADI ED DEIR

Ras Sufsafeh

WADI EL LEJA

Mould

to Watia Pass

ruins

ruins

WADI ER RAHA

0   1   2 miles

place of first prayer

Nagb   el Hawa

Graves of Craving

THE APPROACH TO SINAI

with the men of God, who would show us each one of the places mentioned in the Bible. And that is what we did.

4   So, coming in from Paran,[n] we said the prayer. Then, going on, we made our way across the head of the valley and approached

5 the Mount of God. It looks like a single mountain[n] as you are going round it, but when you actually go into it there are really several peaks, all of them known as "the Mount of God", and the principal one, the summit on which the Bible tells us that "God's

6 glory came down",[1] is in the middle of them. I never thought I had seen mountains as high as those which stood around it, but the one in the middle where God's glory came down was the highest of all, so much so that, when we were on top, all the other peaks we had seen and thought so high looked like little hillocks far

7 below us. Another remarkable thing—it must have been planned by God—is that even though the central mountain, Sinai proper on which God's glory came down, is higher than all the others, you cannot see it[n] until you arrive at the very foot of it to begin your ascent. After you have seen everything and come down, it can be seen facing you,[n] but this cannot be done till you start your climb. I realized it was like this before we reached the Mount of God, since the brothers had already told me, and when we arrived there I saw very well what they meant.

.1   Late on Saturday, then, we arrived at the mountain and came to some cells.[n] The monks who lived in them received us most hospitably,[n] showing us every kindness. There is a church there with a presbyter;[n] that is where we spent the night, and, pretty early on Sunday, we set off with the presbyter and monks who lived there to climb each of the mountains.

They are hard to climb. You do not go round and round them, spiralling up gently, but straight at each one[n] as if you were going up a wall, and then straight down to the foot, till you reach the

2 foot of the central mountain, Sinai itself. Here then, impelled by Christ our God and assisted by the prayers of the holy men who accompanied us, we made the great effort of the climb. It was quite impossible to ride up, but though I had to go on foot I was

---

[1] Exod. 19.18,20.

not conscious of the effort—in fact I hardly noticed it because, by God's will, I was seeing my hopes coming true.

So at ten o'clock we arrived on the summit of Sinai, the Mount of God where the Law was given, and the place where God's
3 glory came down on the day when the mountain was smoking.[1] The church[n] which is now there is not impressive for its size (there is too
4 little room on the summit), but it has a grace all its own. And when with God's help we had climbed right to the top and reached the door of this church, there was the presbyter, the one who is appointed to the church, coming to meet us from his cell. He was a healthy old man, a monk from his boyhood and an "ascetic" as they call it here—in fact just the man for the place. Several other presbyters met us too, and all the monks who lived near the mountain, or at least all who were not prevented from coming by their age or their health.

5   All there is on the actual summit of the central mountain is the
6 church and the cave[n] of holy Moses.[2] No one lives there. So when the whole passage had been read to us from the Book of Moses (on the very spot!) we made the Offering[3][n] in the usual way and received Communion. As we were coming out of church the presbyters of the place gave us "blessings",[4][n] some fruits which grow on the mountain itself. For although Sinai, the holy Mount, is too stony even for bushes to grow on it, there is a little soil round the foot of the mountains, the central one and those around it, and in this the holy monks are always busy planting shrubs, and setting out orchards or vegetable-beds[n] round their cells.[n] It may look as if they gather fruit which is growing in the mountain soil, but in fact everything is the result of their own hard work.

7   We had received Communion and the holy men had given us the "blessings". Now we were outside the church door, and at once I asked them if they would point out to us all the different places. The holy men willingly agreed. They showed us the cave where holy Moses was when for the second time he went up into

---

[1] Exod. 19.18.   [2] Cf. Exod. 33.22.
[3] "The Offering" is Egeria's normal word for the second part of the Eucharist. No doubt the reading from the Book of Moses occurred in the first part.
[4] See pp. 24–5 above.

the Mount of God and a second time received the tables of stone[1] after breaking the first ones when the people sinned.[2] They showed us all the other places we wanted to see, and also the ones they 8 knew about themselves. I want you to be quite clear about these mountains, reverend ladies my sisters, which surrounded us as we stood beside the church looking down from the summit of the mountain in the middle. They had been almost too much for us to climb, and I really do not think I have ever seen any that were higher (apart from the central one which is higher still) even though they only looked like little hillocks to us as we stood on the central mountain. From there we were able to see Egypt and Palestine,[n] the Red Sea and the Parthenian Sea[3] (the part that takes you to Alexandria), as well as the vast lands of the Saracens[n]—all unbelievably far below us. All this was pointed out to us by the holy men.

4.1   We had been looking forward to all this so much that we had been eager to make the climb. Now that we had done all we wanted and climbed to the summit of the Mount of God, we began the descent. We passed on to another mountain next to it which 2 from the church there is called "On Horeb".[4] [n] This is the Horeb to which the holy Prophet Elijah fled from the presence of King Ahab, and it was there that God spoke to him with the words, "What doest thou here, Elijah?", as is written in the Books of the Kingdoms.[5] [n] The cave where Elijah hid can be seen there to this day in front of the church door, and we were shown the stone altar which holy Elijah set up for offering sacrifice to God. Thus 3 the holy men were kind enough to show us everything, and there too we made the Offering[n] and prayed very earnestly, and the passage was read from the Book of Kingdoms. Indeed, whenever we arrived, I always wanted the Bible passage to be read to us.   *
4   When we had made the Offering, we set off again, with the presbyters and monks pointing things out to us, to another place not far away. It is where Aaron[n] and the seventy elders stood[6]

[1] Exod. 34.   [2] Cf. Exod. 32.19.
[3] The "Sea of the Maiden", i.e. the eastern Mediterranean, also known as Mare Isiacum or "Sea of Isis".
[4] Compare the names Opu Melchisedech (15.5), and Ad Pastores (PD, L.1).
[5] I Kings 19.9.   [6] Exod. 24.9–14.

while holy Moses received from the Lord the Law for the children of Israel. There is no building there, but it is an enormous round rock with a flat place on top where the holy men are said to have stood, and a kind of altar in the middle made of stones. So there too we had a passage read from the Book of Moses and an
5　appropriate psalm,[n] and after a prayer we went on down. By then I suppose it must have been about two in the afternoon, and we still had three miles to go before emerging from the mountains which we entered on the previous evening. As I have already mentioned, we did not have to come out by the way we had gone in, because we had decided to visit all the holy places and cells in the mountains, and to come out at the head of the valley, of which I have spoken, below the Mount of God.

6　　　Our way out took us to the head of this valley because there the holy men had many cells, and there is also a church there at the
7　place of the Bush[n] (which is still alive and sprouting). It was about four o'clock by the time we had come right down the Mount and reached the Bush. This, as I have already said, is the Burning Bush out of which the Lord spoke to Moses, and it is at the head of the valley with the church and all the cells. The Bush itself is in front of the church in a very pretty garden which has plenty of ex-
8　cellent water.[n] Near by you are also shown the place where holy Moses was standing[n] when God said to him, "Undo the fastening of thy shoes", and so on.[1] Since it was already four in the afternoon by the time we got there, it was too late for us to be able to make the Offering, but we had a prayer in the church, and also in the garden by the Bush, and as usual the appropriate passage was read from the Book of Moses. Then, because it was late, we had our meal with the holy men in the garden near the Bush, and stayed there for the night. Next morning we were awake early, and the presbyters made the Offering there at our request.

5.1　　Our path lay through the middle of the valley which stretched out in front of us, the valley in which, as I have told you, the children of Israel had their camp while Moses went up into the Mount of God and came down again. And all the way along the valley the holy men were showing us the different places.

[1] Exod. 3.5; cf. Acts 7.33.

2 Right at the head of the valley, where we had spent the night and seen the Burning Bush out of which God spoke to holy Moses, we saw also the place where Moses was standing before the Bush, when God said to him, "Undo the fastening of thy shoes: for the
3 place whereon thou standest is holy ground." And now that we were leaving the Bush[n] they showed us the rest of the places. They pointed out the place where the children of Israel had their camp during the time Moses was in the Mount. They showed us where the calf had been made, where a large stone was set in the ground
4 and still stands. As we went along, we saw facing us a mountain peak, overlooking the whole valley, from which holy Moses saw the children of Israel holding their dances after they had made the calf.[1] And they showed us an enormous rock, the place where holy Moses and Joshua the son of Nun[2] were bringing the tables of stone down from the mountain when Moses became angry and broke them.

5 All along the valley they showed us how each Israelite had a house, and they were round stone houses, as you can still see from the foundations. They showed us where holy Moses ordered the children of Israel to run "from gate to gate"[3] when he had come
6 back from the Mount. They also showed us where holy Moses ordered them to burn the calf which Aaron had made for them; and the bed of the stream from which, as you read in Exodus,
7 holy Moses made the children of Israel drink.[4] And they pointed out the place where a portion of Moses' spirit was given to the seventy men,[5] and where the children of Israel had their craving for food.[6] They showed us also the place called "The Fire",[7] a part of the camp which was burning, where the fire stopped when
8 holy Moses prayed. And they showed us where the manna and the quails[n] descended on the people.[8]

So we were shown everything which the Books of Moses tell us took place in that valley beneath holy Sinai, the Mount of God. I know it has been rather a long business writing down all these places one after the other, and it makes far too much to remember.

[1] Exod. 32.19.
[2] Egeria writes "Jesus the son of Naue" throughout.
[3] Exod. 32.27.   [4] Exod. 32.20.   [5] Num. 11.25.
[6] Num.11.4.   [7] Taberah, Num. 11.3.   [8] Num. 11.6,31.

But it may help you, loving sisters, the better to picture what happened in these places when you read the holy Books of Moses.

9 Then again this is the valley where the children of Israel kept the Passover a year after they left Egypt,[1] because they stayed in it quite a time. In fact they lived there until Moses had gone up into the Mount of God and returned for the first and second times, and they had to stay on there till the tabernacle had been made, and all the other things which were revealed on the Mount. We were shown the actual place where Moses constructed the original tabernacle, and finished everything which God had told him to

10 make when he was in the Mount.[2] Right at the end of the valley we saw the Graves of Craving,[3] [n] and there we left the great valley, and rejoined the road between the mountains by which, as I have told you, we had come in.

That day we came across some more of the monks. They had not been with us when we made the Offering on the Mount, not because they were irreligious, but simply through being too old or too weak. They were most kind and courteous in the reception

11 they gave us when we came to their cells. By this time, either coming in or on our return journey, we had seen all the holy places we had hoped to visit, and all the places where the children of Israel had been on their way to the Mount of God and back,[4] and we had visited all the holy men who lived there. So, in the

12 name of the Lord, we went back to Paran. I know I should never cease to give thanks to God, but I thank him specially for this wonderful experience he has given me, beyond anything I could expect or deserve. I am far from worthy to have visited all these holy places. And I cannot do enough to express my gratitude to all the holy men who so kindly and willingly welcomed so unimportant a person as me to their cells and, what is more, took me round all the biblical sites I kept asking to see. And most of the holy men who lived at the Mount of God or near it—at least the ones who were strong enough—were good enough to escort us all the way to Paran.

6.1   It is thirty-five miles from the Mount of God to Paran, and,

---

[1] Num. 9.1–5.   [2] Exod. 40.17   [3] Cf. 1.1.
[4] For this journey back to Clysma compare the outward journey, PD, Y12–14.

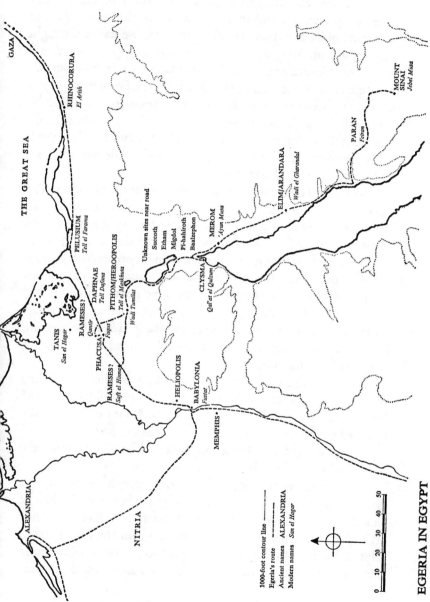

EGERIA IN EGYPT

THE GREAT SEA

GAZA

RHINOCORURA
El Arish

PELUSIUM
Tell el Farana

TANIS
San el Hagar

RAMESES?
Qantir

DAPHNAE
Tell Defana

PHACUSA
Faqus

RAMESES?
Saft el Hinna

PITHOM/HEROOPOLIS
Tell el Maskhuta

Wadi Tumilat

Unknown sites near road
Succoth
Etham
Migdol
Pi-hahiroth
Baalzephon

MEROM
'Ayun Musa

CLYSMA
Qal'at el Qulzum

ELIM/ARANDARA
Wadi el Gharandal

PARAN
Feiran

MOUNT
SINAI
Jebel Musa

HELIOPOLIS

BABYLONIA
Fustat

MEMPHIS

NITRIA

ALEXANDRIA

1000-foot contour line —·—·—·—
Egeria's route - - - - - - -
Ancient names ALEXANDRIA
Modern names *San el Hagar*

0 10 20 30 40 50

when we arrived there, we needed two days' rest. On the day
after, we pressed on and reached once more the staging-post in
the desert of Paran where, as I have told you, we stayed the night
on our way in. Next day we renewed our supply of water, and
after a short journey through the mountains we left the mountain
road and came to the staging-post beside the sea. From there on you
stop going between mountains and once again you are going by
the sea all the way. At one time you are so close that the animals'
feet are in the water, then you are a hundred or two hundred yards
from the shore, and sometimes you are half a mile from the sea
and going through desert.

2   It is all sandy desert there, and there is no road whatsoever. The
Paranites travel on their camels, and here and there are the direc-
tion-marks they have put there to follow by day. But the camels
know how to make for them by night, and this means that the
Paranites can travel by night even faster and more safely than any-
3 one else can when the way is visible. So now on our return
journey we left the mountains at the same point where we had
entered them, and turned to go along beside the sea; this is just
what the children of Israel did, rejoining the Red Sea after coming
back here from Sinai, the Mount of God, to the point where we
emerged from the mountains.

From this point we "went our way" back by the way we had
come, and it was from the same point that the children of Israel
"went their way",[1] as we are told in the Books of Moses. We
returned by the same route and the same staging-posts to Clysma,[2]
and there we had to have a long rest, as the way through the
desert had been so sandy.

7.1   I already knew the land of Goshen[n] from my first visit to
Egypt.[3] But I wanted to see all the places where the children of
Israel had been on their way from Rameses to the Red Sea. They
arrived there at the place now known (from the fort there) as
Clysma,[4] and from Clysma we wanted to go on into Goshen to
the so-called "City of Arabia".[n] It gets its name from the region,

---

[1] See Num. 10.12; 33.16ff.   [2] For this journey see PD, Y9–12.
[3] Traces of this first journey appear in PD, V7b—Y3.
[4] On Clysma and its surroundings see PD, Y5–8.

which is called "the land of Arabia, the land of Goshen",[1] a region which, while it is part of Egypt, is a great deal better than
2 any of the rest. From Clysma and the Red Sea it is four desert staging-posts[n] before you reach the City of Arabia, and the desert is of a kind where they have to have quarters at each staging-post[n] for soldiers and their officers, who escorted us from one fort to the next. All the way I kept asking to see the different places mentioned in the Bible, and they were all pointed out to me by the holy men, the clergy and monks with us. Some of the places were to the right and others to the left of our route, some a long way off
3 and others close by. So, as far as I can see, loving sisters, you must take it that the children of Israel zigzagged their way to the Red Sea, first right, then back left again, now forwards, and now back.
4 Pi-hahiroth[2][n] was pointed out facing us, and we went to Migdol, today a fort with an officer and men representing the Roman authorities. As usual they escorted us to the next fort. Baalzephon too was pointed out to us—in fact we went there; it is the plain by the Red Sea beside the mountain of which I have told you, the one where the children of Israel "cried out"[3] when they saw the
5 Egyptians coming after them. We were also shown Etham, "on the edge of the wilderness" as it says in the Bible, and also Succoth.[4] Succoth is a gentle rise in the middle of a valley, and it was next to this rise that the children of Israel pitched their camp.
6 This is where they received the Law of the Passover.[5] Pithom too was pointed out to us, the city built by the children of Israel; it was the point at which our route took us across the frontier of Egypt and we left the land of the Saracens, and it is now a fort.
7 The Heroes' City[6] was a real city when Joseph went up there to meet his father Jacob when he came, as it says in the Book of Genesis, but now it is a village, one of the big ones[n] we call a township. It contains a church, some martyria, and a great many cells, and we visited each one of them to see the holy monks in
8 our usual way. Today this township is called Hero, and it is on the

---

[1] Cf. Gen. 46.34,LXX.
[2] Exod. 14.2. Egeria's name for it is Epauleum; cf. LXX.
[3] Exod. 14.10; see also PD, Y9.
[4] Exod. 13.20; cf. 12.37.   [5] Exod. 12.43.
[6] Heroöpolis, the name added in Gen. 46.29,LXX, see p. 6 above.

frontier of Egypt sixteen miles[n] from the land of Goshen, a very attractive place with an arm of the Nile[n] flowing through it.

9 Then, leaving Hero we reached what is called the "City of Arabia", a city of the land which the Bible mentions as Goshen when Pharaoh tells Joseph, "Settle your father and your brothers in the best of the land, in the land of Goshen, the land of Arabia."[1]

8.1 Four miles from the City of Arabia is Rameses,[n] and on our way to stay in "Arabia" we travelled right through it. The city Rameses[n] is now a level site without a single dwelling, but it is still visible, and once it had many buildings and covered a huge

2 area. Even though it is ruined, its remains are still vast. The only thing there now is a great Theban stone,[n] a single piece out of which rise two huge statues. They are said to represent holy men, Moses and Aaron, and the people tell you that the children of

3 Israel set them up in their honour. There is also a sycamore tree there, which is said to have been planted by the patriarchs. Though it is now extremely old, and thus small, it still bears fruit, and people who have something wrong with them pick its

4 twigs, which do them good. We learned this from the holy Bishop of Arabia,[n] and it was he who told us that the Greek name for this tree is *Dendros Aletheias* or, in our language, "The Tree of Truth". This holy bishop was kind enough to meet us at Rameses. He is now a man of some age, of a godly life since the time he became a monk, and an approachable man, who is very good at welcoming pilgrims and also very knowledgeable about God's

5 Scriptures. He very kindly took the trouble to meet us there, showed us everything, and told us about the statues of which I have told you, and the sycamore tree. And this holy bishop told

* us that, when Pharaoh saw that the children of Israel had deserted him, he went to Rameses and burned it all down before he set out in pursuit.

9.1 By the happiest coincidence we arrived at the staging-post of Arabia on the day before the most blessed Epiphany, the very day when they were going to hold the vigil service in the church; so the bishop kept us with him for two days. I knew him quite well

[1] Gen. 47.6,LXX.

from the time I visited the Thebaid, and he is a holy man, a true
2 man of God. This holy bishop had been a monk, brought up in a cell since boyhood, and this is how he came to know so much about the Bible, and to live the faultless life I have mentioned.
3 At this point we dismissed the soldiers who had provided us with an escort on behalf of the Roman authorities when we went through the danger areas. We no longer needed military protection, since we were on the state highway from the Thebaid to Pelusium, which passed through the City of Arabia.
4 Our whole journey on from there led through the land of Goshen, past vineyards (of grapes as well as balsam), orchards, well-kept fields, and many gardens. All the way the road followed the bank of the Nile past the extremely fertile farms which had once been the estates of the children of Israel, and really I do not
5 think I have ever seen a landscape better kept than Goshen. From the City of Arabia we travelled for two days through the land of Goshen, and then we arrived at Tathnis,[1][n] the city which was once Pharaoh's capital, in which holy Moses was born.
6 This district, as I have told you, was already known to me from the time when I visited Alexandria and the Thebaid, but we had to go back to the land of Goshen and on to Tathnis because I wanted to learn more about the places which the children of Israel visited on the way from Rameses to Sinai, the Mount of God. From Tathnis we went by the way I already knew, and arrived at
7 Pelusium. And from there we went on through all the Egyptian staging-posts of our outward journey till we reached the frontier of Palestine. And from there, in the name of Christ our God, I returned after several staging-posts in Palestine to Aelia,[n] which is Jerusalem.
10.1 Some time went by. Then, impelled by God, I conceived the desire to go once more into Arabia,[n] to Mount Nebo. It is the mountain which God told Moses to climb, in the words "Ascend this mountain Araboth,[n] Mount Nebo, which is in the land of Moab over against Jericho; and view the land of Canaan, which I give to the people of Israel for a possession; and die on the

---

[1] See PD, V9.

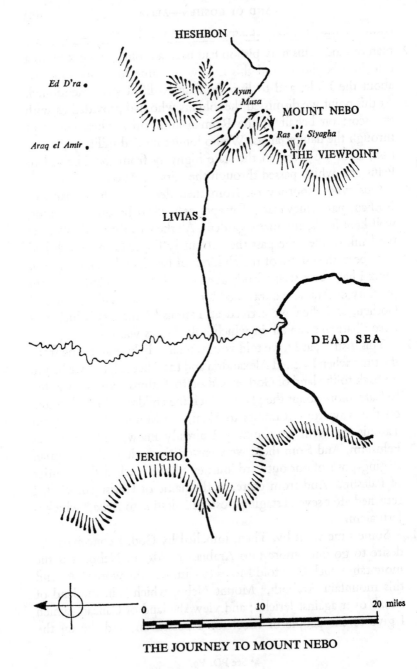

HESHBON

Ed D'ra •

Ayun Musa

MOUNT NEBO

Ras el Siyagha

THE VIEWPOINT

Araq el Amir •

LIVIAS

DEAD SEA

JERICHO

0   10   20 miles

THE JOURNEY TO MOUNT NEBO

10.2 mountain which you ascend."[1] And Jesus our God, who never fails those who hope in him, saw fit to grant[n] my desire.

3 　　With us came some holy men from Jerusalem, a presbyter and deacons, and several brothers (monks), and we reached the place on the Jordan where holy Joshua the son of Nun sent the children of Israel across, and they passed over, as we are told in the Book of Joshua the son of Nun.[2] We were also shown a slightly raised place on the Jericho stretch of the river, where the children of ✻ Reuben and Gad and the half tribe of Manasseh made an altar.[3]

4 After crossing the river we came to the city of Livias,[n] in the plain where the children of Israel encamped in those days. The foundations of the camp and dwellings of the Israelites are still to be seen there today.

　　It is a vast plain stretching from the foot of the Arabian mountains to the Jordan, where the Bible says that "the children of Israel wept for Moses in Araboth Moab at Jordan over against

5 Jericho forty[n] days".[4] It is where Joshua the son of Nun "was filled with the spirit of wisdom" when Moses died, "for Moses

6 had laid his hands upon him",[5] as it is written. It is where Moses wrote the Book of Deuteronomy,[6] and where he "spoke the words of this song until they were finished, in the ears of all the assembly of Israel",[7] the song written in the Book of Deuteronomy.[8] And it is where holy Moses the man of God blessed each of

7 the children of Israel in order before his death.[9] When we reached this plain, we went on to the very spot, and there we had a prayer, and from Deuteronomy we read not only the song, but also the blessings he pronounced over the children of Israel. At the end of the reading we had another prayer, and set off again, with thanksgiving to God.

　　And it was always our practice when we managed to reach one of the places we wanted to see to have first a prayer, then a reading from the book, then to say an appropriate psalm and

---

[1] Deut. 32.49–50. Egeria gives *Arabot* instead of "Abarim".
[2] Josh. 3 and 4.　　　[3] Josh. 22.10.
[4] Deut. 34.8, which has "Araboth," but "thirty", not forty days.
[5] Deut. 34.9.　　　[6] Deut. 31.24.
[7] Deut. 31.30.　　　[8] Deut. 32.1–43.
[9] Deut. 33.1: "in order" seems to come from Gen. 49.28, Jacob's blessing.

another prayer. By God's grace we always followed this practice whenever we were able to reach a place we wanted to see.

8   Now we had to hurry to carry out our intention of reaching Mount Nebo. As we travelled along, the local presbyter from Livias (we had asked him to leave his home and accompany us because he knew the area so well) asked us, "Would you like to see the water that flows from the rock, which Moses[n] gave to the children of Israel when they were thirsty?[1] You can if you have the energy to turn off the road at about the sixth milestone."[n]

9   At this we were eager to go. We turned off the road at once, the presbyter led the way, and we followed him. It is a place with a tiny church under a mountain—not Nebo, but another one not very far from Nebo but further in. A great many monks[n] lived there, truly holy men of the kind known here as ascetics.

11.1   The holy monks were good enough to receive us very hospitably, and welcomed us indoors. Going in with them we joined them in prayer, and they then very kindly gave us the "blessings" which it is normal for them to give to those whom they entertain.

2   Between the church and the cells was a plentiful spring which flowed from the rock, beautifully clear and with an excellent taste, and we asked the holy monks who lived there about this water which tasted so remarkably good. "This", they told us, "is the water which holy Moses gave the children of Israel in this

3   desert." As usual we had there a prayer, a reading from the Books of Moses, and one psalm.

Then we set off for the mountain, and with us came the holy clergy and monks who had accompanied us, and many of the holy monks who lived near the spring were kind enough to come too, or at least the ones who had the energy to ascend Mount

4   Nebo. So we set out and came to the foot of Mount Nebo; it was very high, but mostly possible to ascend on the donkeys, though there were some steeper parts where we had to dismount, and it was hard going.

12.1   On reaching the mountain-top we came to a church,[n] not a very big one, right on the summit of Mount Nebo, and inside, in the

---

[1] Cf. Exod. 17.6 and Num. 20.8.

position of the pulpit, I saw a slightly raised place about the size
2 of a normal tomb. I asked about it, and the holy men replied,
"Holy Moses was buried here—by angels, since the Bible tells us
'No human being knoweth his burial'.[1] [n] And there is no doubt
that it was angels who buried him, since the actual tomb where he
was buried can be seen today.[n] Our predecessors here pointed out
this place to us, and now we point it out to you. They told us that
this tradition came from their predecessors."

3   Soon we had had the prayer and the other things which were
usual in a holy place, and we were about to leave the church. Then
the presbyters and holy monks who were familiar with the place
asked us, "Would you like to see the places which are described
in the Books of Moses? If so, go out of the church door to the
actual summit,[n] the place which has the view, and spend a little
time looking at it. We will tell you which places you can see."
4 This delighted us, and we went straight out. From the church
door itself we saw where the Jordan runs into the Dead Sea, and
the place was down below where we were standing. Then,
facing us, we saw Livias on our side of the Jordan, and Jericho on
the far side, since the height in front of the church door, where we
5 were standing, jutted out over the valley. In fact from there you
can see most of Palestine, the Promised Land[2] and everything in
the area of Jordan as far as the eye can see.

To our left was the whole country of the Sodomites, including
6 Zoar,[3] [n] the only one of the five cities which remains today. There
is still something left of it, but all that is left of the others is heaps
of ruins, because they were burned to ashes.[4] We were also shown
the place where Lot's wife[n] had her memorial, as you read in the
7 Bible.[5] But what we saw, reverend ladies, was not the actual pillar,
but only the place where it had once been. The pillar itself, they
say, has been submerged in the Dead Sea—at any rate we did not
see it, and I cannot pretend we did. In fact it was the bishop there,
the Bishop of Zoar, who told us that it was now a good many years
since the pillar had been visible. It used to stand near the sixth

---

[1] Deut. 34.6.; cf. Jude 9.   [2] Cf. Heb. 11.9.
[3] Gen. 19.22. Egeria uses the LXX and Latin name *Segor*.
[4] Gen. 19.24.   [5] Gen. 19.26.

milestone from Zoar, but was now completely submerged by
8 water. Then we went round outside to the right of the church,
and they showed us two cities facing us. One was Heshbon,[n] now
called Exebon, the city of Sehon, king of the Amorites,[1] and the
other the city of Og, king of Bashan, which is now called Safdra.[2]
* Also from this point they pointed out facing us Peor,[3] [n] a city of
9 the kingdom of Edom. All these cities we saw were perched in the
mountains, but just below us was a flatter tract of land; there, we
were told, Moses and the children of Israel had their camp when
they were fighting the cities, and we could see traces of the camp.
10 From what I call the left side of the mountain, the side nearest the
Dead Sea, we were shown a very abrupt mountain which was
once called the Viewpoint.[4] [n] This is the mountain where Balak
the son of Beor[n] put Balaam the Seer so that he should curse the
children of Israel, and God would not allow it, as we are told in the
11 Bible. So when we had seen all we wanted, we returned in the
name of God, by way of Jericho and the same road by which we
had come, to Jerusalem.

13.1   Some time later I decided to visit the land of Uz[5] on pilgrimage[n]
to the tomb of holy Job. I saw many holy monks from those parts
when they came to Jerusalem on pilgrimage to the holy places,
and all they told me about Uz made me eager to take the trouble
to make a further journey to visit it—if one can really speak of
2 trouble when one sees one's wishes fulfilled. So I set off from
* Jerusalem with some holy men who were kind enough to keep me
company on the journey, and wanted to make the pilgrimage.
Jerusalem is eight staging-posts from Carneas,[n] which is the
present name of the city of Job, though formerly its name was
Dinhaba[6] in the land of Uz, on the borders of Idumaea and
Arabia.

On the way I saw a valley[n] running down to the river Jordan,
remarkably beautiful and very well kept, and it was full of vines
3 and trees because there was plenty of good water there. In it was a
big village called Sedima;[n] it is in the middle of a plain, and in the

[1] Num. 21.26.   [2] Edrei (Num. 21.33).
[3] Num. 23.28; Josh. 13.20.   [4] See Num. 23.14,LXX; Josh. 13.20.
[5] Ausitis; cf. Job 1.1,LXX.
[6] See LXX appendix to the Book of Job = 42.17d; cf. Gen. 36.32; I Chron. 1.43.

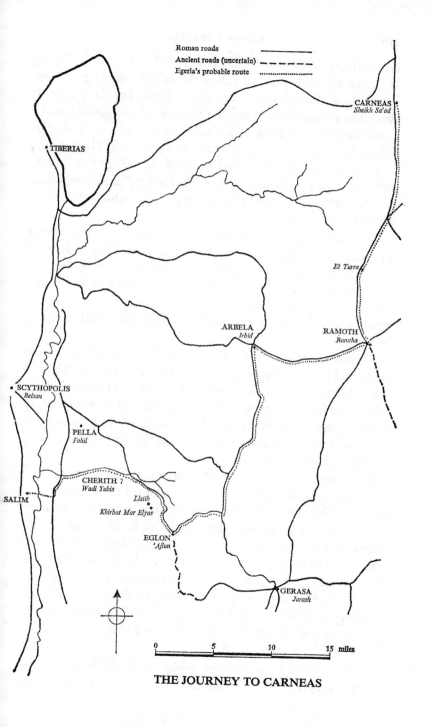

Roman roads
Ancient roads (uncertain)
Egeria's probable route

TIBERIAS

CARNEAS
Sheikh Sa'ad

Et Tiara

ARBELA
Irbid

RAMOTH
Ramtha

SCYTHOPOLIS
Beisan

PELLA
Fahil

CHERITH ?
Wadi Yabis

SALIM

Listib

Khirbat Mar Elyas

EGLON
'Ajlun

GERASA
Jarash

0   5   10   15 miles

THE JOURNEY TO CARNEAS

centre it has a fairly small hillock shaped like a big tomb. On top
is a church, and below, all round the hillock, are huge ancient
4 foundations,[n] though only a few communities live there now. It
was all so attractive that I asked "What is this delightful place?"
I was told, "This is King Melchizedek's city. Its name used to be
Salem, but it has now been corrupted into Sedima. The building
you see on that hillock in the middle of the village is a church,
and its present Greek name is *Opu Melchisedech*,[n] since it is 'where
Melchizedek' offered God pure offerings of bread and wine, as we
are told in the Bible."[1]

14.1   On hearing this we dismounted, and at once the holy presbyter
and clergy of the place kindly came to meet us. They welcomed
us, and took us up to the church. When we got there, we had our
usual prayer, an appropriate reading from the Book of Moses, and
a psalm appropriate to the place. After another prayer we came
2 down. And when we got to the bottom, we had a talk with the
holy presbyter.

He was an oldish man with an excellent knowledge of the
Bible, and had been in charge of the place from the time when he
was a monk. Later on we came to know a good many bishops
who spoke highly of his way of life, and said that he was certainly
the right man to be in charge of this place, where holy Melchizedek met Abraham returning, and was the first of the two to
offer pure offerings to God.[2]

When we had got down to the bottom, as I have already told
you, this holy presbyter said to us, "You see these foundations
round the hillock. They were part of Melchizedek's palace, and
to this day any time some one decides to build a house in the
neighbourhood, and comes here to get foundation-stones, he is
likely to find little fragments of silver and bronze among them.
3 You see that road which runs between this village and the river
Jordan. That is the road by which holy Abraham returned from
the slaughter of Chedorlaomer,[n] king of the Nations,[3] on his way
back from Sodom, and it was on that road that he was met by
holy Melchizedek, king of Salem."

15.1   Then I remembered that according to the Bible it was near

[1] Cf. Gen. 14.18.   [2] Cf. Heb. 7.1.   [3] Cf. Gen. 14.17–18.

Salim that holy John baptized at Aenon.[1] So I asked if it was far away. "There it is", said the holy presbyter, "two hundred yards away. If you like we can walk over there. It is from that spring that the village has this excellent supply of clean water you
2 see." Thanking him I asked him to take us, and we set off. He led us along a well-kept valley to a very neat apple-orchard, and there in the middle of it he showed us a good clean spring of water which flowed in a single stream. There was a kind of pool in front of the spring at which it appears holy John Baptist administered
3 baptism.[n] "This garden", said the holy presbyter, "is still known in Greek as *Cepos tu Agiu Iohanni*, or in your language, Latin, 'St John's Garden'." A great many brothers, holy monks from *
4 different parts, travel here to wash at this place. So once more we had a prayer and a reading at this spring as we did in the other places. We said a suitable psalm, and did everything which was usual when arriving at a holy place.
5   The holy presbyter also told us that nowadays at Easter the candidates who are to be baptized in the village, in the church called *Opu Melchisedech*, receive their actual baptism in the spring itself. Then, directly afterwards, they go off by torchlight[n] singing psalms and antiphons, and accompanied by the clergy and monks. In this way they are taken after their baptism from the
6 spring to the church of holy Melchizedek. Then the presbyter gave us apples from St John Baptist's orchard as "blessings", and so did the holy monks who had cells inside the orchard. So then we set out[n] to continue our journey, not without thanksgiving to God.
1   We travelled through the Jordan valley for a little, and at times the road took us along the river-bank itself. Then Tishbe[n] came in sight, the city from which the holy prophet Elijah gets his name "the Tishbite".[2] To this day they have there the cave in which he lived, and also the tomb of holy Jephtha of whom we read in the
2 Book of Judges.[3] So we gave thanks to God there in our usual way, and set off once more. As we went on we saw a very well-kept valley[n] coming down towards us on the left. It was very large, and had a good-sized stream in it which ran down into the Jordan.
3   In this valley was the cell of a brother, a monk. You know how

---

[1] John 3.23.   [2] 1 Kings 17.1.   [3] Judg. 11,12; cf. 12.7.

inquisitive I am, and I asked what there was about this valley to
make this holy monk build his cell there. I knew there must be
some special reason, and this is what I was told by the holy men
with us who knew the district: "This is the valley of Cherith.[1] The
holy prophet Elijah the Tishbite stayed here in the reign of King
Ahab; and at the time of the famine, when God sent a raven to
bring him food, he drank water from this brook. For the watercourse you can see running down the valley to the Jordan is
4 Cherith." So we set off again—as indeed we did every single day—
giving renewed thanks to God for his goodness in showing us all
the things we wanted to see, and so much more than we deserved.
From day to day we continued our journey, and the next thing
we saw was an enormous high mountain[n] which came in sight on
our left, the side on which we looked across at part of Phoenicia.
The mountain stretched out into the distance . . .[2]

5 . . . after so many years of living in the desert this holy man,
monk and ascetic, had to set off and enter the city of Carneas. He
asked the bishop of those days and the clergy to do as had been
revealed to him, and to dig at the spot which he had been shown.
6 As they dug they at first discovered a cave, then, following it in
for about a hundred yards they suddenly came upon a stone.
When they had thoroughly uncovered it, they found carved on its
cover the name JOB.[n] So at once they built this church[n] which you
can see in Job's honour. They did not remove[n] the stone coffin
with the body, but left them where the body had been found, and
so arranged things that the body should rest beneath the altar. I
believe that this church was built by some tribune or other, and it

---

[1] I Kings 17.3–6. Egeria uses the form *Corra* for Cherith.
[2] At this point a leaf (two pages) is missing from the manuscript, depriving us
of as much text as there is between this point and the middle of section 19.5.
Fortunately the following passage from the Madrid manuscript (De Bruyne,
lines 20–5) is based on what Egeria wrote in the missing passage:

> The dunghill[n] where Job sat is now a clean place surrounded by an iron
> screen, where a great lantern burns each night. And where he scraped his
> sores with a potsherd there is a spring which four times in the year changes
> its colour, becoming first the colour of pus, then of blood, then of gall,
> and then it is clear.

Cf. Job 2.8.

7 stands today, though till now it remains unfinished. The next day in the morning we asked the bishop[n] if he would make the Offering. He kindly did so, and, when he had blessed us, we went on our way. So, receiving Communion, and continually giving thanks to God, we returned to Jerusalem by the same staging-posts through which we had passed on our outward journey.[n]

1 Some time after that, since it was already three full years since my arrival in Jerusalem, and I had seen all the places which were the object of my pilgrimage, I felt that the time had come to return in God's name to my own country. But God also moved me with a desire to go to Syrian Mesopotamia.[1] [n] The holy monks there are said to be numerous and of so indescribably excellent a life that I wanted to pay them a visit; I also wanted to make a pilgrimage to the martyrium of the holy apostle Thomas,[n] where his entire body is buried. It is at Edessa, to which Jesus, our God, was sending Thomas after his ascension into heaven, as he tells us in the letter he sent to King Abgar by the messenger Ananias.[2] This letter has been most reverently preserved at Edessa where

2 they have this martyrium. And, believe me, loving sisters, no Christian who has achieved the journey to the holy places and Jerusalem misses going also on the pilgrimage to Edessa. It is

3 twenty-five staging-posts away from Jerusalem. But Mesopotamia is not as far from Antioch. So, since my route back to Constantinople took me back that way, it was very convenient for me at God's bidding to go from Antioch to Mesopotamia, and that, under God, is what I did.

4 Thus in the name of Christ our God I set out from Antioch to Mesopotamia. I passed through a number of different staging-posts and cities belonging to the province of Coele-Syria,[n] which has Antioch as its capital. From there I crossed the frontier into the province of Augustophratensis, and reached the city of Hierapolis; it is the capital of this province Augustophratensis, a city of great plenty, rich and very beautiful, and it was where I had to stay, since it was not very far from there to the frontier of

5 Mesopotamia. Fifteen miles after leaving Hierapolis I arrived in

---

[1] This expression renders the Paddan-Aram of Gen. 28.12.

[2] See pp. 151–2 below.

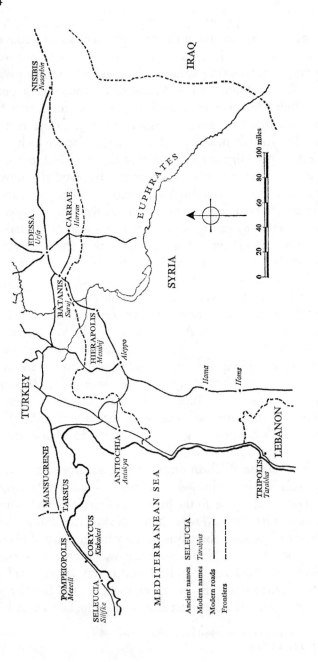

THE JOURNEYS TO EDESSA AND SELEUCIA

God's name at the river Euphrates, and the Bible is right to call it "the great river Euphrates".[1] It is very big, and really rather frightening since it flows very fast like the Rhône,[n] but the
3 Euphrates is much bigger. We had to cross in ships, big ones, and that meant I spent maybe more than half a day there. So, after crossing the river Euphrates, I went on in God's name into the region of Syrian Mesopotamia.

9.1 After several more staging-posts I came to Batanis,[n] a city mentioned in the Bible,[2] and still there to this day. It has a church with a really godly bishop who is both monk and confessor. There are several martyria. And the city has a vast population, and
2 a garrison with a tribune in charge. From there we set out again, and came, in the name of Christ our God, to Edessa.

As soon as we arrived, we went straight to the church and martyrium of holy Thomas;[n] there we had our usual prayers[n] and everything which was our custom in holy places. And we read
3 also from the writings of holy Thomas[n] himself.[3] The church there is large and beautiful, and built in the new way—just right, in fact, to be a house of God. In this city there was so much I
4 wanted to see that I had to stay there three days. I saw a great many martyria[n] and visited the holy monks, some of whom lived among the martyria, whilst others had their cells further away from the city where it was more private.

5 The holy bishop of the city was a truly devout man, both monk and confessor.[n] He welcomed me and said, "My daughter, I can see what a long journey this is on which your faith has brought you—right from the other end of the earth. So now please let us show you all the places Christians should visit here." I gave thanks to God, and eagerly accepted the bishop's invitation.
6 So first of all he took me to the palace of King Abgar,[n] and showed me a huge marble portrait of him. People said it was an excellent likeness, and it shone as if it was made of pearl. The look on Abgar's face showed me, as I looked straight at it, what a wise and noble man he had been,[n] and the holy bishop told me, "That is King

---

[1] Gen. 15.18.
[2] This Batanis is neither Beten (Josh 19.25) nor Batanaea (= Basan).
[3] Perhaps the reading was Acts of Thomas 170; see Hennecke 2, p. 530.

Abgar. Before he saw the Lord he believed in him as the true Son of God".[1] Next to this portrait was another of the same marble; he told me it was the king's son Magnus,[n] and he too had a wonderful face.

7   Then we went inside the palace, and saw the pools with the fish[n] in them. I have never seen fish like them, they were so big, so brightly coloured, and tasted so good.

The only water-supply which the city has inside its walls at the present day is this one which comes from the palace, and it is like a

8 great river of silver. The holy bishop told me this about it: "King Abgar wrote a letter to the Lord, and the Lord sent his answer by the messenger Ananias; then, quite a time after, the Persians

9 descended on this city and encircled it. So at once Abgar, with his whole army, took the Lord's letter to the gate,[n] and prayed aloud: 'Lord Jesus,' he said, 'You promised us that no enemy would enter this city.[2] Look now how the Persians are attacking us.' With that the king held up the letter, open in his hands, and immediately a darkness fell over the Persians, who were by then close outside the city walls. It made them retire three miles away, and the darkness was so confusing to the Persians that they found it difficult to pitch camp and carry out patrols even at three miles'

10 distance from the city. They were too confused to discover how to enter the city, so for the next few months they stayed at a distance of three miles from the walls, leaving it with the gates shut, and

11 besieging it. Then, since they could find no way of breaking into the city, they decided to kill the inhabitants by thirst.

"At the time, my daughter, the city had its water from the small hill you see up there. The Persians realized this, so they cut a channel to divert the water away from the city to the side where

12 they had their camp. On the very day, and at the very moment they diverted the water, God brought water flowing out of the springs you can see here; and by God's grace it has continued to flow ever since. But at that same moment the water in the channel which had been made by the Persian besiegers dried up. They had not even enough water left for one day. And it is like that today,

---

[1] Cf. John 20.29.
[2] This promise is not in the Eusebian version; see p. 152 below.

as you can see, for since then there has never been any water
13 running in it.[1] So, by God's will, they had to go home to Persis,[n] as
he had promised. And ever afterwards,[n] if any enemy has come
here and tried to overthrow the city, the letter is produced and
read in the gate; and at once, by God's favour, he is driven away."
14 According to the holy bishop the springs had appeared lower
down than Abgar's palace in a field[n] which was inside the city.
"Abgar's palace,[n] as you can see, had been on higher ground, like
15 the other palaces of those days. But after the springs began to flow,
then Abgar built round them this palace for his son Magnus, the
one whose portrait you saw next to the one of his father."

16 After the holy bishop had told me this, he said, "Now let us
go to the gate where the messenger Ananias came in with the
letter of which I have been telling you." When we got to the
gate, the bishop stopped. He said a prayer and read the actual
17 letters.[n] Then he blessed us, and said another prayer. The holy
man also told us this; from the day when the messenger Ananias
brought in the Lord's letter through this gate[n] until now neither
has any one been allowed to pass through it who is unclean or in
18 mourning, nor has any dead body been taken out through it. The
holy bishop also showed us the tomb of Abgar[n] and all his family
(which was beautiful, but old-fashioned), and he took us up to
Abgar's first palace, and showed us all the other things there were
to see.

19 One thing specially pleased me. I received from this holy man
the copies of Abgar's letter to the Lord, and the Lord's letter to
Abgar, which he had read to us. I have copies of them at home,
but even so it is much better to have been given them there by
him. And it may be that what we have at home is not so complete,[n] because what I was given here is certainly longer. So,
dearest ladies, you yourselves must read them when I come home,
if such is the will of Jesus our God.

1 I spent three days there, and then the next place I had to visit was
Carrae,[n] which is its present name. But in holy Scripture Abraham
lived in a place called Charra, as you find in Genesis when the
Lord says to Abraham, "Get thee out of thy country and from thy

[1] See Additional Note H. pp. 284–7 below.

20.2 father's house, and go unto Charra",[n] and so on.[1] When I reached
Charra I went straight to visit the church inside the city,[n] and was
soon seeing the bishop of the place. He was a very godly man, and
he too was both monk and confessor.[n] He readily agreed to show
us all the places we wanted to see.

3   First he took us to a church outside the city[n] on the site of
Abraham's house. According to the holy bishop it was built of
the same stones and on the same foundations. In the church we
had a prayer and read the passage from the book of Genesis, then
one psalm and a second prayer; the bishop blessed us,[n] and we
4 went outside. Then he kindly took us to the well at which holy
Rebecca[n] used to draw water.[2] "This", said the holy bishop, "is
the well where holy Rebecca drew water for the camels of Eleazar[3]
the servant of holy Abraham", and he was at pains to show us all
there was to see.

5   At this church where originally Abraham's house used to stand,
which, as I have told you, was outside the city, there is also a
martyrium. This, my ladies and reverend sisters, is the tomb of a
certain holy monk called Helpidius,[n] and things turned out very
well for us, since we happened to arrive on the eve of this holy
Helpidius' martyrium day, the twenty-third of April. This is a
day when all the monks of Mesopotamia have to come in to
Charra, including the illustrious ones called ascetics who dwell
in the desert. The feast itself is kept with great solemnity, but
they also come in to commemorate holy Abraham, since it was
his house which stood on the site of the church in which is buried
6 the body of the holy martyr. So we had the unexpected pleasure
of seeing there the holy and truly dedicated monks of Mesopotamia, including some of whose reputation and holy life we had
heard long before we got there. I certainly never thought I would
actually see them, not because God would be unable to grant it—
after all, he has granted me everything else!—but because I had
heard that these monks never come in from the places where they
live, except at Easter and at the feast of this martyr, and also

---

[1] Egeria uses Charris for the modern name and Charra (like LXX Charran)
for the biblical name. English versions of Gen. 12.4 give Haran.
[2] Cf. Gen. 24.15–20.
[3] Eliezer, the name traditionally given to the servant, is from Gen. 15.2.

because these are of the kind who perform many miracles. What is more I had no idea of the month of the martyrium's feast-day, so the fact that I happened to arrive on the very day was providential, and completely unexpected.

7 We stayed there for two days, to keep the festival and meet the holy men, and they were far kinder than I deserved, greeting me warmly, and having conversations. But after the martyrium day there was not a monk to be seen. While it was still night every 8 single one of them made off for his cell in the desert. Absolutely no Christians[n] live in this city, apart from a few clergy, and any holy monks who happen to be living there. The whole city is heathen,[n] and just as we venerate the place which was originally the house of holy Abraham, and honour his memory, so they venerate the tombs of Nahor and Bethuel,[1][n] which are about a mile outside the city.

9 The bishop of the city knew a great deal about the Bible,[n] so I asked him, "Sir, I wonder if you would tell me something I am anxious to know." "Tell me what it is, my daughter," he said, "and if I know I will tell you." "I know from the Bible", I said, "that holy Abraham came here with his father Terah and his wife Sarah and his nephew Lot.[2] But I have not read of any occasion when Nahor or Bethuel passed this way. The only other person I know to have come here was Abraham's servant, who came to Charra later on to seek Rebecca, the daughter of Bethuel son of 10 Nahor, for Isaac the son of his master Abraham".[3] The holy bishop replied, "Genesis certainly tells us, as you say, my daughter, that holy Abraham moved here with his family. But, though the canonical scriptures[n] do not tell us when Nahor and Bethuel passed this way, it is clear that they did come here later on, since we actually have their tombs here, about a mile from the city. In fact Scripture tells us that the servant of holy Abraham came here to be given holy Rebecca, and also that holy Jacob came here when he was given the daughters of Laban the Syrian."[4]

11 There was a well from which Jacob watered the animals which were being fed by Rachel, the daughter of Laban the Syrian, and I

---

[1] Cf., for example, Gen. 24.24.   [2] Gen. 11.31.
[3] Gen. 22.23; 24.1f.   [4] Gen. 28.2.

asked where it was. The bishop told me, "The place is six miles
from here. It is beside a village which was originally the property
of Laban the Syrian, and when you want to go there we will
come with you. There is a holy church there and a great many
12 monks, ascetics and very godly men." I also asked the bishop
whereabouts Terah and his family lived when they were among
the Chaldees, and the holy bishop replied, "My daughter, the
place you ask about is ten staging-posts from here, inside the
frontiers of Persis. From here to Nisibis[n] is five staging-posts, and
it is five more from there to Ur, the city of the Chaldees; but at
present Romans are not allowed to go there, since that whole
area belongs to the Persians. In fact this region is specially called
the "Eastern" province because it lies on the Roman frontier
13 with Persia and Chaldea." He was kind enough to tell us much
else besides, as indeed did the other holy bishops and holy monks,
always about God's Scriptures, or the deeds of holy monks,
whether it was miracles done by those who had already passed
away, or the deeds done today by those "still in the body",[1]
especially the ascetics. For I want you to realize, loving sisters, that
the monks' conversation is always either about God's Scriptures
or the deeds of the great monks.

21.1   We stayed there two days. Then the bishop took us to the well,
where holy Jacob[n] watered the animals of holy Rachel,[2] which is
six miles from Carrae. A holy church has been built near the well,
as a mark of honour, and it is very large and beautiful. When we
reached the well, the bishop said a prayer, the passage was read
from Genesis, we had one psalm suitable to the place, and then
2 after another prayer the bishop gave us his blessing. Beside the
well was the enormous stone which Jacob rolled away from it,
3 and it is still to be seen today. The only people who lived near the
well were the clergy of the church, and some monks who had cells
near by. The bishop told me some amazing things about their
way of life, so, after we had had our prayer in the church, I went
round with the bishop and visited the holy monks in their cells.
I gave thanks to God, and to them too, since they were so kind
and welcoming when I entered their cells, and entertained me

[1] Cf. 2 Cor. 12.3.   [2] Gen. 29.2.

with the kind of conversation which befits monks. Those who welcomed me into their cells kindly gave "blessings" to me and the people with me, as is their custom.

4 The place where we were was in a large plain, so the holy bishop was able to point out to me a big village[n] facing us, about half a mile from the well, and our road went past it. According to the bishop this village was once the property of Laban[n] the Syrian.[1] Its name is Fadana,[2][n] and in it I was shown the tomb of Laban the Syrian, Jacob's father-in-law, and also the place from which

5 Rachel stole her father's images.[3] So when we had seen all this, we said goodbye to the holy bishop and the holy monks who had kindly escorted us to this point. And in God's name we returned by the same road[n] and the same staging-posts by which we had come from Antioch.

2.1 When I got back to Antioch, I spent a week there, till we had all we needed for the journey. Then, leaving Antioch,[n] we went on by several staging-posts[n] and reached the province called Cilicia; Tarsus[n] is its capital city, and I had already been there on my way

2 out to Jerusalem. But in Isauria, only three staging-posts on from Tarsus, is the martyrium of holy Thecla,[n] and, since it was so close, we were very glad to be able to make the extra journey there.

.1 Leaving Tarsus, but still in Cilicia, I reached Pompeiopolis,[n] a city by the sea, and from there I crossed into Isauria, and spent the night in a city called Corycus.[n] On the third day I arrived at a city called Seleucia of Isauria,[n] and, when I got there, I called on the bishop, a very godly man who had been a monk, and saw a

2 very beautiful church in the city. Holy Thecla's is on a small hill about a mile and a half[n] from the city, so, as I had to stay somewhere, it was best to go straight on and spend the night there.

Round the holy church[n] there is a tremendous number of cells

3 for men and women. And that was where I found one of my dearest friends, a holy deaconess[n] called Marthana.[n] I had come to know her in Jerusalem when she was up there on pilgrimage. She was the superior of some cells of apotactites or virgins,[n] and I

[1] Laban is "the Syrian" in Gen. 25.20,LXX.
[2] Paddan-Aram (Gen. 25.20; 28.2, etc.).   [3] Gen. 31.19.

simply cannot tell you how pleased we were to see each other
4 again. But I must get back to the point.

There are a great many cells on that hill, and in the middle a
great wall[n] round the martyrium[n] itself, which is very beautiful.
The wall was built to protect the church against the Isaurians,[n]
who are hostile, and always committing robberies, to prevent
them trying to damage the monastery which has been established
5 there. In God's name I arrived at the martyrium, and we had a
prayer there, and read the whole Acts of holy Thecla; and I gave
heartfelt thanks to God for his mercy in letting me fulfil all my
6 desires so completely, despite all my unworthiness. For two days I
stayed there, visiting all the holy monks and apotactites, the men as
well as the women; then, after praying and receiving Communion,
I went back to Tarsus to rejoin my route.

I stayed there three days before setting off to continue my
journey, and then, after a day's travelling, arrived at a staging-post
called Mansucrene below Mount Taurus. We stayed the night
7 there, and the next day we climbed Mount Taurus, and continued
along a road we already knew, since our outward journey had
brought us along it. Passing through the same provinces of
Cappadocia, Galatia, and Bithynia, I reached Chalcedon, and I
stayed there because it contains the renowned martyrium of holy
8 Euphemia,[n] long known to me. Next day I crossed the sea and
reached Constantinople, giving thanks to Christ our God for
seeing fit, through no deserving of mine, to grant me the desire
to go on this journey, and the strength to visit everything I wanted
and now to return again to Constantinople.

9 And in all the churches[n] at Constantinople, in the tombs of the
apostles, and at many martyria, I never ceased to give thanks to
Jesus our God for his grace in showing me such mercy.

10 So, loving ladies, light of my heart, this is where I am writing to
you. My present plan is, in the name of Christ our God, to travel
to Asia,[n] since I want to make a pilgrimage to Ephesus, and the
martyrium of the holy and blessed Apostle John.[n] If after that I
am still alive, and able to visit further places, I will either tell you
about them face to face (if God so wills), or at any rate write to
you about them if my plans change. In any case, ladies, light of

my heart, whether I am "in the body" or "out of the body", please do not forget me.[n]

4.1   Loving sisters, I am sure it will interest you to know about the daily services they have in the holy places, and I must tell you about them. All the doors of the Anastasis are opened before cock-crow each day, and the "*monazontes* and *parthenae*",[n] as they call them here, come in, and also some lay men and women, at least those who are willing to wake at such an early hour. From then until daybreak they join in singing the refrains to the hymns, psalms, and antiphons. There is a prayer between each of the hymns, since there are two or three presbyters and deacons each day by rota, who are there with the monazontes and say the prayers between all the hymns and antiphons.

2   As soon as dawn comes, they start the Morning Hymns, and the bishop with his clergy comes and joins them. He goes straight into the cave, and inside the screen he first says the Prayer for All (mentioning any names he wishes) and blesses the catechumens, and then another prayer and blesses the faithful. Then he comes outside the screen, and everyone comes up to kiss his hand. He ✱ blesses them one by one, and goes out, and by the time the dismissal[1] takes places it is already day.

3   Again at midday everyone comes into the Anastasis and says psalms and antiphons until a message is sent to the bishop. Again he enters, and, without taking his seat, goes straight inside the screen in the Anastasis (which is to say into the cave where he went in the early morning), and again, after a prayer, he blesses the faithful and comes outside the screen, and again they come to kiss ✱ his hand.

4   At three o'clock they do once more what they did at midday, but at four o'clock they have *Lychnicon*, as they call it, or in our language, Lucernare. All the people congregate once more in the Anastasis, and the lamps and candles are all lit, which makes it very bright. The fire is brought not from outside, but from the cave—inside the screen—where a lamp is always burning night and day. For some time they have the Lucernare psalms and antiphons; then they send for the bishop, who enters and sits in

[1] Dismissal = *missa*, see p. 57 above.

the chief seat. The presbyters also come and sit in their places,
5 and the hymns and antiphons go on. Then, when they have
finished singing everything which is appointed, the bishop rises
and goes in front of the screen (i.e. the cave). One of the deacons
make the normal commemoration of individuals, and each time
he mentions a name a large group of boys responds *Kyrie eleison*
(in our language, "Lord, have mercy"). Their voices are very
6 loud. As soon as the deacon has done his part, the bishop says a
prayer and prays the Prayer for All. Up to this point the faithful
and the catechumens are praying together, but now the deacon
calls every catechumen to stand where he is and bow his head,
and the bishop says the blessing over the catechumens from his
place. There is another prayer, after which the deacon calls for all
the faithful to bow their head, and the bishop says the blessing
over the faithful from his place. Thus the dismissal takes place at
** 7 the Anastasis, and they all come up one by one to kiss the bishop's
hand.

Then, singing hymns, they take the bishop from the Anastasis
to the Cross,[n] and everyone goes with him. On arrival he says one
prayer and blesses the catechumens, then another and blesses the
faithful. Then again the bishop and all the people go Behind the
Cross, and do there what they did Before the Cross; and in both
* places they come to kiss the bishop's hand, as they did in the
Anastasis. Great glass lanterns are burning everywhere, and there
are many candles in front of the Anastasis, and also Before and
Behind the Cross. By the end of all this it is dusk. So these are the
services held every weekday at the Cross and at the Anastasis.

8   But on the seventh day, the Lord's Day, there gather in the courtyard before cock-crow all the people, as many as can get in, as if
it was Easter. The courtyard is the "basilica"[n] beside the Anastasis,
that is to say, out of doors, and lamps have been hung there for
them. Those who are afraid they may not arrive in time for
cock-crow come early, and sit waiting there singing hymns and
antiphons, and they have prayers between, since there are always
presbyters and deacons there ready for the vigil, because so many
people collect there, and it is not usual to open the holy places
before cock-crow.

9   Soon the first cock crows, and at that the bishop enters, and goes into the cave in the Anastasis. The doors are all opened, and all the people come into the Anastasis, which is already ablaze with lamps. When they are inside, a psalm is said by one of the presbyters, with everyone responding, and it is followed by a prayer; then a psalm is said by one of the deacons, and another prayer; then a third psalm is said by one of the clergy, a third prayer, and the Commemoration of All. After these three psalms and prayers they take censers into the cave of the Anastasis, so that the whole Anastasis basilica[n] is filled with the smell. Then the bishop, standing inside the screen, takes the Gospel book and goes to the door, where he himself reads the account of the Lord's resurrection. At the beginning of the reading the whole assembly groans and laments at all that the Lord underwent for us, and the way they weep would move even the hardest heart to tears. When the Gospel is finished, the bishop comes out, and is taken with singing to the Cross, and they all go with him. They have one psalm there and a prayer, then he blesses the people, and that is the dismissal. As the bishop goes out, everyone comes to kiss his hand. *

2   Then straight away the bishop retires to his house,[n] and all the monazontes go back into the Anastasis to sing psalms and antiphons until daybreak. There are prayers between all these psalms and antiphons, and presbyters and deacons take their turn every day at the Anastasis to keep vigil with the people. Some lay men and women like to stay on there till daybreak, but others prefer to go home again to bed for some sleep.

1   At daybreak the people assemble in the Great Church built by Constantine on Golgotha Behind the Cross.[n] It is the Lord's Day, and they do what is everywhere the custom on the Lord's Day.[n] *
But you should note that here it is usual for any presbyter who has taken his seat to preach, if he so wishes, and when they have finished there is a sermon from the bishop. The object of having this preaching every Sunday is to make sure that the people will continually be learning about the Bible and the love of God.

2   Because of all the preaching it is a long time before the dismissal, which takes place not before[1] ten or even eleven o'clock. And

---

[1] "Not before" is Gamurrini's conjecture; the Ms. reads "before".

when the dismissal has taken place in the church—in the way which is usual everywhere—the monazontes lead the bishop with singing to the Anastasis. While they are singing and the bishop approaches, all the doors of the Anastasis basilica are opened, and the people (not the catechumens, only the faithful) all go in.

25.3 When they are all inside, the bishop enters, and passes straight inside the screen of the tomb, the cave itself.[1] [n] They have a thanksgiving[n] to God and the Prayer for All; then the deacon calls every single person to bow his head, and the bishop blesses them

4 from his place inside the screen. Then he comes out, and, as he does so, everyone comes to kiss his hand. Thus the dismissal is delayed till almost eleven or twelve o'clock.

Lucernare is held in the same way as on other days.

Except on the special days, which we shall be describing below,

5 this order is observed on every day of the year. What I found most impressive about all this was that the psalms and antiphons they use are always appropriate, whether at night, in the early morning, at the day prayers at midday or three o'clock, or at Lucernare. Everything is suitable, appropriate, and relevant to what is being done.

6 Every Sunday in the year except one they assemble in the Great Church which Constantine built on Golgotha Behind the Cross; the exception is Pentecost, the Fiftieth Day after Easter, when they assemble on Sion. You will find this mentioned below,[2] but what they do is to go to Sion before nine o'clock after their dismissal in the Great Church . . .[3]

. . . "Blessed is he that cometh in the name of the Lord",[4] and so on. They have to go slowly for the sake of the monazontes who are on foot, so they arrive in Jerusalem almost at daybreak, but just before it is light, at the moment when people can first recognize each other. When they arrive, the bishop goes straight

7 into the Anastasis, and everybody goes with him. Extra lamps

---

[1] Latin *martyrii speluncae*.   [2] See 43.

[3] Here a further leaf is missing from the manuscript, as in 16.4. In the course of the missing passage Egeria begins to describe the celebration of the Epiphany in Bethlehem; cf. *AL*, Nos. 1–2.

[4] Matt. 21.9.

have been lighted there. Then they have one psalm and a prayer, and the bishop blesses first the catechumens, and then the faithful. He then retires, and all the people return to the places where they are staying to have a rest, but the monazontes stay there to sing hymns till daybreak.

8   Just after seven in the morning, when the people have rested, they all assemble in the Great Church on Golgotha.[1] And on this day in this church, and at the Anastasis and the Cross and Bethlehem, the decorations really are too marvellous for words. All you can see is gold and jewels and silk; the hangings are entirely silk with gold stripes, the curtains the same, and everything they use for services at the festival is made of gold and jewels. You simply cannot imagine the number, and the sheer weight of the candles and the tapers and lamps and everything else they use for the services.

9   They are beyond description, and so is the magnificent building itself. It was built by Constantine, and under the supervision of his mother[n] it was decorated with gold, mosaic, and precious marble, as much as his empire could provide, and this not only at the Great Church, but at the Anastasis and the Cross, and the other
0 Jerusalem holy places as well. But I must get back to the point.

On the first day they have the service in the Great Church on Golgotha, and all the preaching and all that they read or sing is appropriate to the day. Then, after their dismissal in the church, they go with singing to the Anastasis in the usual way, and the
1 dismissal there takes place at about noon. Lucernare that day takes place in the way which is usual every day.

On the second day they assemble in the church on Golgotha, and also on the third, and their rejoicing lasts until noon in Constantine's church on all those three days. On the fourth day they decorate everything and celebrate in the same way on the Eleona[n] (the very beautiful church on the Mount of Olives), on the fifth at the Lazarium,[n] about a mile and a half from Jerusalem, on the sixth on Sion, on the seventh at the Anastasis, and on the eighth At the Cross.[2] The decorations and rejoicing continue for eight days in all these places I have mentioned.

[1] *AL*, No. 2.   [2] For this list cf. *AL*, Nos. 1–8.

12   But in Bethlehem they go on for eight days continuously. All the
presbyters and clergy of the place, and the monazontes who reside
there, take part, but during that season the bishop must celebrate
the festival in Jerusalem. So at night everyone goes back with him
to Jerusalem; but all the Bethlehem monks keep vigil in the
church at Bethlehem, and sing hymns and antiphons till it is day.
For this feast day and the celebrations great crowds come to Jerusalem from all parts, not only monks, but lay men and women as
well.

26.   Note that the Fortieth Day[n] after Epiphany[1] is observed here
with special magnificence. On this day they assemble in the
Anastasis. Everyone gathers, and things are done with the same
solemnity as at the feast of Easter. All the presbyters preach first,
then the bishop, and they interpret the passage from the Gospel
about Joseph and Mary taking the Lord to the Temple, and about
Simeon and the prophetess Anna, daughter of Phanuel, seeing the
Lord, and what they said to him, and about the sacrifice offered by
his parents.[2] When all the rest has been done in the proper way,
they celebrate the sacrament and have their dismissal.

27.1   Then comes the Easter season, and this is how it is kept. In our
part of the world we observe forty days before Easter, but here
they keep eight weeks. It makes eight weeks because there is no
fasting on the Sundays or the Saturdays (except one of them,
which is a fast because it is the Easter vigil—but apart from that
the people here never fast on any Saturday in the year). So the
eight weeks, less eight Sundays and seven Saturdays—one being a
fasting Saturday—make forty-one fast days. The local name for
Lent is *Heortae*.[3]

2   Here is what is done on each day of these weeks. On Sundays
the bishop reads the Gospel of the Lord's resurrection at first cock-
crow, as he does on every Sunday throughout the year. Then, till
daybreak, they do everything as they would on an ordinary
3 Sunday at the Anastasis and the Cross. In the morning they
assemble (as they do every Sunday) in the Great Church called the

[1] *AL*, No. 13.
[2] *AL*, No. 13 confirms this Gospel as Luke 2.22–40.
[3] Meaning "Feasts"; see p. 72 above.

Martyrium on Golgotha Behind the Cross, and do what it is usual to do on a Sunday. After the dismissal in this church they go singing, as they do every Sunday, to the Anastasis, and it is after eleven o'clock by the time they have finished. Lucernare is at the normal time when it always takes place in the Anastasis and At the Cross and in all the other holy places; for on Sundays there 4 is no service[1] at three o'clock. At first cock-crow on Monday people go to the Anastasis, and till morning they do what is normal during the rest of the year. Then at nine o'clock they go to the Anastasis and do what during the rest of the year would be done at noon, since this service at nine o'clock is added during Lent. The services at noon and three o'clock, and Lucernare, are 5 held as is usual in the holy places all the year round. On Tuesday everything is done as on Monday, and on Wednesday they again go on to the Anastasis while it is still night, and follow the usual order till morning, and so at nine o'clock and at midday. But at three o'clock they assemble on Sion, because all through the year they regularly assemble on Sion at three o'clock on Wednesdays and Fridays. On those days there is fasting even for catechumens, unless they coincide with a martyrs' day, and this is their reason for assembling on Sion at three o'clock. But even on a martyrs' day they still assemble on Sion at three o'clock if it also happens to be a Wednesday or Friday in Lent.

6   On Wednesdays in Lent, then, they assemble, as during the rest of the year, at three o'clock on Sion, and have all the things usual for that hour,[2] except the Offering. The bishop and the presbyter are at pains to preach, to ensure that the people will continue to learn God's Law. And after the dismissal the people conduct the bishop with singing to the Anastasis, starting out in time to arrive at the Anastasis for Lucernare. They have the hymns and antiphons, and the Lucernare dismissal takes place at the Anastasis 7 and the Cross, though during Lent it is later than at other times of the year.

Thursday is exactly like Monday and Tuesday, and Friday like Wednesday since they again go to Sion at three o'clock and from

[1] "No service" is Duchesne's conjecture; the Ms. reads "there is a service".
[2] See *AL*, Nos. 18–32.

there conduct the bishop with singing to the Anastasis. But from the time of their procession from Sion on Friday there is a vigil service in the Anastasis until the early morning. It lasts from the time of Lucernare till the morning of the next day (Saturday) and they make the Offering in the Anastasis so early that the dismissal

8 takes place before sunrise. Throughout the night they have psalms with refrains or antiphons, or various readings, and this goes on till morning. So the Saturday service, the Offering, in the Anastasis is before sunrise, by which I mean that at the time when the sun begins to rise the dismissal has already taken place in the Anastasis. That is how they keep each week of Lent.

9   They have the Saturday service as early as this, before sunrise, so that the people here called hebdomadaries can break their fast as soon as possible. The Lenten fasting rule for these hebdomadaries (people who "keep a week") is that they may eat on a Sunday—when the dismissal is at eleven in the morning. And since their Sunday meal is the last they will have had, and they cannot eat till Saturday morning, they receive Communion early on the Saturday. So the Saturday service at the Anastasis takes place before sunrise for the sake of these people, so that they can break their fast all the sooner. But when I say that the service is early because of them, it is not that I mean that they are the only ones to receive Communion. Anyone who wishes may make his Communion in the Anastasis on Saturdays.

28.1   These are their customs of fasting in Lent. There are some who eat nothing during the whole week between their meal after the Sunday service, and the one they have after the service on Saturday

2 in the Anastasis. They are the ones who "keep a week". And, though they eat on Saturday morning, they do not eat again in the evening, but only on the next day, Sunday, after the dismissal at eleven o'clock (or later), and then nothing more till the following

3 Saturday, as I have described. The people known here as apotactites as a rule have only one meal a day not only during Lent, but also during the rest of the year. Apotactites who cannot fast for a whole week in the way I have described eat a dinner half way through Thursday, those who in Lent cannot manage this eat on two days of the week, and those who cannot manage this have a

4 meal every evening. No one lays down how much is to be done, but each person does what he can; those who keep the full rule are not praised, and those who do less are not criticized. That is how things are done here.

And this is what they eat during the Lenten season. They are not so much as to taste[1] a crumb of bread, nor oil either, or anything which grows on trees; only water and a little gruel. Lent is kept in the way I have described.

9.1 During Lent they have a vigil service at the Anastasis from Lucernare on Friday (when they have come singing psalms from Sion) to the morning of Saturday when they make the Offering in the Anastasis, and they do this from the second to the sixth 2 week as they do in the first. But in the seventh week when, counting this week, there are two left before Easter, they do the same as in the other weeks, but the vigil service they have been holding in the Anastasis is, on the Friday of the seventh week, held on Sion, though they follow the same order as they did during the previous six weeks in the Anastasis. At each of these occasions the psalms and antiphons they have are appropriate to the place 3 and the day. At dawn on the morning of Saturday the bishop makes the usual Offering of a Saturday morning. Then, for the dismissal, the archdeacon makes this announcement: "At one o'clock today let us all be ready at the Lazarium."

Just on one o'clock everyone arrives at the Lazarium, which is 4 Bethany, at about two miles from the city. About half a mile before you get to the Lazarium from Jerusalem there is a church by the road. It is the spot where Lazarus' sister Mary met the Lord.[2] All the monks meet the bishop when he arrives there, and the people go into the church. They have one hymn and an antiphon, and a reading from the Gospel about Lazarus' sister meeting the Lord. Then, after a prayer, everyone is blessed, and they go on with singing to the Lazarium.

5 By the time they arrive there so many people have collected that they fill not only the Lazarium itself, but all the fields around.

[1] Reading *quid libari*, the conjecture of Chr. Mohrmann and R. Weber, for the words *quid liberari* which appear in the Ms.; see *VC* 12 (1958), pp. 93–7.
[2] John 11.29.

They have hymns and antiphons which—like all the readings—are suitable to the day and the place. Then at the dismissal a presbyter announces Easter. He mounts a platform, and reads the Gospel passage which begins "When Jesus came to Bethany six days before the Passover".[1] After this reading, with its announce-

6 ment of Easter,[2] comes the dismissal. They do it on this day because the Gospel describes what took place in Bethany "six days before the Passover", and it is six days from this Saturday to the Thursday night on which the Lord was arrested after the Supper. Thus they all return to the Anastasis and have Lucernare in the usual way.

30.1 The next day, Sunday, is the beginning of the Easter week or, as they call it here, "The Great Week". On this Sunday they do everything as usual at the Anastasis and the Cross from cock-crow to daybreak, and then as usual assemble in the Great Church known as the Martyrium[3] because it is on Golgotha behind the

2 Cross, where the Lord was put to death. When the service in the Great Church has taken place in the usual way, before the dismissal, the archdeacon makes this announcement: "During this week, starting tomorrow, let us meet at three in the afternoon at the Martyrium" (that is, in the Great Church). And he makes another announcement: "At one o'clock today let us be ready on

3 the Eleona." After the dismissal in the Great Church, the Martyrium, the bishop is taken with singing to the Anastasis. They do in the Anastasis the things which usually follow the Sunday dismissal in the Martyrium, and then everyone goes home and eats a quick meal, so as to be ready by one o'clock at the Eleona church on the Mount of Olives, the place of the cave where the Lord used to teach.

31.1 At one o'clock all the people go up to the Eleona Church on the Mount of Olives. The bishop takes his seat, and they have hymns and antiphons suitable to the place and the day, and readings too. When three o'clock comes, they go up with hymns and sit down at the Imbomon, the place from which the Lord ascended into

[1] *AL*, No. 33 confirms the Gospel as John 11.55—12.11.
[2] *Pascha*, the word here used, means both "Passover" and "Easter".
[3] *AL*, No. 34.

heaven. (For when the bishop is present everyone is told to sit down, except for the deacons, who remain standing the whole time.) And there too they have hymns and antiphons suitable to
2 the place and the day, with readings and prayers between them. At five o'clock the passage is read from the Gospel about the children[1] who met the Lord with palm branches, saying, "Blessed is he that cometh in the name of the Lord."

At this the bishop and all the people rise from their places, and start off on foot down from the summit of the Mount of Olives. All the people go before him with psalms and antiphons,[2] all the time repeating, "Blessed is he that cometh in the name of the
3 Lord." The babies and the ones too young to walk are carried on their parents' shoulders. Everyone is carrying branches, either palm or olive, and they accompany the bishop in the very way the
4 people did when once they went down with the Lord. They go on foot all down the Mount to the city, and all through the city to the Anastasis, but they have to go pretty gently on account of the older women and men among them who might get tired. So it is already late when they reach the Anastasis; but even though it is late they hold Lucernare when they get there, then have a prayer At the Cross, and the people are dismissed.

2.1   On Monday, the next day, they do the same as in the rest of Lent from cock-crow till morning, at nine o'clock, and at midday. But at three o'clock everyone meets in the Great Church, the Martyrium, and there they spend some time singing hymns and antiphons, with readings appropriate to the place and the day[3] and
2 prayers in between. This goes on till seven in the evening, and at seven Lucernare is held there. The dismissal at the Martyrium thus takes place in the night, and then the bishop is taken with hymns to the Anastasis. When they have entered, they have one hymn and a prayer, then the catechumens are blessed, and the faithful, and they have the dismissal.

3.1   Tuesday is the same as Monday, but with one addition. Late at night, after the dismissal in the Martyrium, when they have gone

---

[1] Matt. 21.9; but note that children are not mentioned in any of the Gospel accounts of the triumphal entry; cf., however, Matt. 21.15f.
[2] For the psalm see *AL*, No. 34.   [3] See *AL*, No. 35.

to the Anastasis and had their second dismissal there, everyone goes out, late though it is, to the church which is on Mount
2 Eleona. When they are inside the church, the bishop enters the cave where the Lord used to teach his disciples, and, taking the Gospel book, he stands and reads the passage from the Gospel according to Matthew where the Lord says, "See that no man lead you astray."[1] The bishop reads the whole of that discourse, and, when he finishes it, there is a prayer. The catechumens are blessed and then the faithful, and the dismissal takes place. At last everyone returns from the Mount and they go home very late indeed.

34.   Wednesday is exactly like Monday and Tuesday from cock-crow and through the day, but at night, after the dismissal in the Martyrium,[2] the bishop, when he is taken with singing to the Anastasis, goes straight into the cave of the Anastasis and stands inside the screen. A presbyter stands in front of the screen, and he takes the Gospel book, and reads the passage about Judas Iscariot going to the Jews and fixing what they must pay him to betray the Lord.[3] The people groan and lament at this reading in a way that would make you weep to hear them. After a prayer the catechumens are blessed, then the faithful, and they have the dismissal.

35.1   Thursday is like the other days from cock-crow till morning in the Anastasis, at nine o'clock, and at midday. But it is the custom to assemble earlier than on ordinary days in the afternoon at the Martyrium,[4] in fact at two o'clock, since the dismissal has to take place sooner. The assembled people have the service; on that day the Offering is made in the Martyrium, and the dismissal takes place at about four in the afternoon. Before the dismissal the archdeacon makes this announcement: "Let us meet tonight at seven o'clock in the church on the Eleona. There is a great effort
2 ahead of us tonight!" After the dismissal at the Martyrium they go Behind the Cross, where they have one hymn and a prayer; then

[1] *AL*, No. 36 confirms the Gospel as Matt. 24.1—26.2.
[2] *AL*, No. 37.
[3] *AL*, No. 37 confirms the Gospel as Matt. 26.3–16.
[4] *AL*, No. 38.

the bishop makes the Offering there,[1] and everyone receives Communion. On this one day the Offering is made Behind the Cross, but on no other day in the whole year. After the dismissal there they go to the Anastasis, where they have a prayer, the usual blessings of catechumens and faithful, and the dismissal.

Then everybody hurries home for a meal, so that, as soon as they have finished it, they can go to the church on Eleona[2] which contains the cave which on this very day the Lord visited with the
3 apostles. There they continue to sing hymns and antiphons suitable to the place and the day, with readings and prayers between, until about eleven o'clock at night.[3] They read the passages from the Gospel about what the Lord said to his disciples
4 when he sat in the very cave which is in the church.[4] At about midnight they leave and go up with hymns to the Imbomon,[5] the place from which the Lord ascended into heaven. And there they again have readings and hymns and antiphons suitable to the day, and the prayers which the bishop says are all appropriate to the day and to the place.

5.1   When the cocks begin to crow, everyone leaves the Imbomon, and comes down with singing to the place where the Lord prayed,[6] as the Gospels describe in the passage which begins, "And he was parted from them about a stone's cast, and prayed."[7] The bishop and all the people go into a graceful church which has been built there, and have a prayer appropriate to the place and the day, and one suitable hymn. Then the Gospel passage is read where he said to his disciples, "Watch, lest ye enter into temptation",[8] and, when the whole passage has been read, there is another prayer.
2 From there all of them, including the smallest children, now go down with singing and conduct the bishop to Gethsemane.[n] There are a great many people and they have been crowded together, tired by their vigil, and weakened by their daily fasting—and they have had a very big hill to come down—so they go very slowly

---

[1] Cf. AL, No. 39.   [2] Cf. Mark 14.26.
[3] See AL, No. 39.
[4] AL, No. 39 confirms this Gospel as John 13.16—18.1.
[5] AL, No. 40.   [6] Cf. AL, No. 40.
[7] Luke 22.41; contrast AL, No. 40.
[8] AL, No. 40 confirms this Gospel as Matt. 26.31-56.

on their way to Gethsemane. So that they can all see, they are
3 provided with hundreds of church candles.[n] When everyone
arrives at Gethsemane, they have an appropriate prayer, a hymn,
and then a reading from the Gospel about the Lord's arrest. By
the time it has been read everyone is groaning and lamenting and
weeping so loud that people even across in the city can probably
hear it all.

Next they go with singing to the city, and walking they reach
the gate at the time when people can first recognize each other.
And from there every single one of them, old and young, rich
and poor, goes on through the centre of the city to be present at
the next service—for this above all others is the day when no one
leaves the vigil till morning comes. Thus the bishop is conducted
from Gethsemane to the gate, and from there through the whole
4 city[1] as far as the Cross. By the time they arrive Before the Cross[2]
it is pretty well full day, and they have another Gospel reading,
the whole passage about the Lord being led away to Pilate, and
all the recorded words of Pilate to the Lord or to the Jews.[3]

5 Then the bishop speaks a word of encouragement to the people.
They have been hard at it all night, and there is further effort in
store for them in the day ahead. So he tells them not to be weary,
but to put their hope in God, who will give them a reward out of
all proportion to the effort they have made. When he has given
them as much encouragement as he can, he speaks to them as
follows: "Now off you go home till the next service, and sit
down for a bit. Then all be back here at about eight o'clock so
that till midday you can see the holy Wood of the Cross, that, as
every one of us believes, helps us attain salvation. And from
midday onwards we must assemble here Before the Cross again,
and give our minds to readings and prayers till nightfall."

37.1 Before the sun is up, the dismissal takes place At the Cross, and
those with the energy then go to Sion to pray at the column[n] at
which the Lord was scourged, before going on home for a short
rest. But it is not long before everyone is assembled for the next
service.[4] The bishop's chair is placed on Golgotha Behind the

---

[1] Contrast *AL*, No. 41.　　　　　[2] As *AL*, No. 42.
[3] *AL*, No. 42 confirms this Gospel as John 18.28—19.16.　　　[4] *AL*, No. 43.

Cross (the cross there now), and he takes his seat. A table is placed before him with a cloth on it, the deacons stand round, and there is brought to him a gold and silver box containing the holy Wood of the Cross.[n] It is opened, and the Wood of the Cross and the Title are taken out and placed on the table.

2 As long as the holy Wood is on the table, the bishop sits with his hands resting on either end of it and holds it down, and the deacons round him keep watch over it. They guard it like this because what happens now is that all the people, catechumens as well as faithful, come up one by one to the table. They stoop down over it, kiss the Wood, and move on. But on one occasion (I don't know when) one of them bit off a piece[n] of the holy Wood and stole it away, and for this reason the deacons stand round and keep watch in case anyone dares to do the same again.

3 Thus all the people go past one by one. They stoop down, touch the holy Wood first with their forehead and then with their eyes, and then kiss it, but no one puts out his hand to touch it. Then they go on to a deacon who stands holding the Ring of Solomon,[n] and the Horn[n] with which the kings were anointed. These they venerate by kissing them, and they start round about eight o'clock[1] with everybody going by, entering by one door and going out through the other, till midday. All this takes place where on the previous day, Thursday, they made the Offering.

4 At midday they go Before the Cross—whether it is rain or fine, for the place is out of doors—into the very spacious and beautiful courtyard between the Cross and the Anastasis, and there is not even room to open a door, the place is so crammed with people.

5 They place the bishop's chair Before the Cross, and the whole time between midday and three o'clock is taken up with readings.[2] They are all about the things Jesus suffered: first the psalms on this subject, then the Apostles (the Epistles or Acts) which concern it, then passages from the Gospels. Thus they read the prophecies about what the Lord would suffer, and the Gospels about what he

6 did suffer. And in this way they continue the readings and hymns from midday till three o'clock, demonstrating to all the people by the testimony of the Gospels and the writings of the Apostles

---

[1] Accepting Franceschini's second conjecture. [2] See *AL*, No. 43.

that the Lord actually suffered everything the prophets had fore-told. For those three hours, then, they are teaching the people that nothing which took place had not been foretold, and all that was foretold was completely fulfilled; and between all the readings are prayers, all of them appropriate to the day.

7   It is impressive to see the way all the people are moved by these readings, and how they mourn. You could hardly believe how every single one of them weeps during the three hours, old and young alike, because of the manner in which the Lord suffered for us. Then, when three o'clock comes, they have the reading from St John's Gospel about Jesus giving up the ghost,[1] and, when that has been read, there is a prayer, and the dismissal.

8   After the dismissal Before the Cross, they go directly into the Great Church, the Martyrium, and do what is usual during this week between three o'clock and evening.[2] After the dismissal they leave the Martyrium for the Anastasis where, once inside, they read the Gospel passage about Joseph asking Pilate for the Lord's body and placing it in a new tomb.[3] After the reading there is a prayer, the blessings of the catechumens and faithful, and the dismissal.

9   On this day there is no announcement that people are to keep vigil in the Anastasis. Obviously they are tired. But none the less it is the custom to watch there, and all who wish—I should have said, all who can—keep the vigil there. Some cannot watch till morning, and they do not stay, but the vigil is kept by the clergy, or at any rate by the ones young enough to have the energy. All the night through they sing hymns and antiphons till morning comes.[4] Most of the people watch, but some only come later on, and some at midnight, doing whatever they can manage.

38.1   The following day is the Saturday, and they have normal services at nine o'clock and midday. But at three they stop keeping Saturday because they are preparing for the paschal vigil in the Great Church, the Martyrium, They keep their paschal vigil[5] like us, but there is one addition. As soon as the "infants" have been

---

[1] *AL*, No. 43 confirms this Gospel as John 19.17–37.
[2] See *AL*, No. 43.
[3] *AL*, No. 43 confirms this Gospel as Matt. 27.57–61.
[4] See *AL*, No. 44.   [5] See *AL*, No. 44.

baptized and clothed, and left the font, they are led with the
2 bishop straight to the Anastasis. The bishop goes inside the screen
and after one hymn says a prayer for them. Then he returns with
them to the church, where all the people are keeping the vigil in
the usual way.[1]

They do all the things to which we are accustomed, and, when
the Offering has been made, they have the dismissal. After their
dismissal in the Great Church they at once go with singing to the
Anastasis, where the resurrection Gospel is read,[2] and once more
the bishop makes the Offering. They waste no time during these
services, so as not to detain the people too long; in fact they are
dismissed from their vigil at the same time as us.

39.1 The eight days of Easter they celebrate till a late hour, like us,
and up to the eighth day of Easter they follow the same order as
people do everywhere else. The arrangements and decorations for
the eight days of Easter are like those for the season of Epiphany
in the Great Church, and also in the Anastasis, At the Cross, on the
2 Eleona, at Bethlehem, the Lazarium, and elsewhere. On the first
Sunday, Easter Day itself, they assemble in the Great Church,
the Martyrium,[3] and similarly on the Monday and Tuesday; and
when they have had the dismissal, there they always go with
singing from the Martyrium to the Anastasis. But on the Wednesday they assemble on the Eleona, on the Thursday in the Anastasis,
on the Friday on Sion, on the Saturday Before the Cross, and on
the eighth day, the Sunday, they assemble once more in the
Great Church, the Martyrium.

3 On each of the eight days of Easter the bishop, with all the
clergy, the "infants" who have been baptized, all the apotactites
both men and women, and any of the people who wish, go up to
the Eleona[4] after their meal (the Eleona contains the cave where
Jesus used to teach his disciples) and in that church they have
hymns and prayers, and also at the Imbomon (the place from which
4 the Lord ascended into heaven). When the psalms and prayer are
finished, they go down with singing to the Anastasis in time for
Lucernare. And this happens on each of the eight days; but on a

[1] See *AL*, No. 44.   [2] See *AL*, No. 44.
[3] As *AL*, Nos. 45–6; contrast Nos. 47–52.   [4] *AL*, No. 45.

Sunday at Easter time, after the people have been dismissed from Lucernare at the Anastasis, they all lead the bishop with singing to

5 Sion.[1] When they get there, they have hymns suitable to the day and the place, a prayer, and the Gospel reading which describes the Lord coming to this place on this day, "when the doors were

* shut";[2] for this happened in the very place where the church of Sion now stands. That was when one disciple, Thomas, was not present; and when he returned and the disciples told him that they had seen the Lord, he said, "Unless I see I do not believe." After this reading and another prayer, the catechumens are blessed, and the faithful, and everyone goes home late, at about eight at night.

40.1   On the eighth day of Easter, the Sunday, all the people go up with the bishop immediately after midday to the Eleona.[3] They start in this church, taking their places for a time and having hymns and antiphons, and prayers appropriate to the day and place. Then they go up to the Imbomon and do as on the Eleona. Then the time comes for all the people and apotactites to take the bishop with singing to the Anastasis,[4] and they arrive there for

2 Lucernare at the usual time. Lucernare is held at the Anastasis and At the Cross, and from there all the people, every single one, conduct the bishop with singing to Sion. When they get there, they have hymns (also suitable to the place and day), and again read the Gospel passage about the Lord coming on the eighth day of Easter to the place where the disciples were, and rebuking Thomas for his unbelief.[5] When they have had the whole passage, and a prayer, the catechumens and the faithful are blessed in the usual way, and everybody goes home, as on Easter Sunday, at eight at night.

41.   From Easter till Pentecost (the Fiftieth Day after) not a single person fasts,[n] even if he is an apotactite. Throughout the season they have the usual services from cock-crow to morning at the Anastasis, and also at midday and Lucernare, assembling on Sundays in the Great Church, the Martyrium, and afterwards going with

---

[1] AL, No. 45.
[2] AL, No. 45 confirms this Gospel as John 20.19–25.
[3] AL, No. 52.   [4] AL, No. 52.
[5] AL, No. 52 confirms the Gospel as John 20.26–31.

singing to the Anastasis. No one is fasting on Wednesdays or Fridays, so on those days they assemble on Sion, but in the morning, and the service takes place in the usual way.

The Fortieth Day after Easter[1] is a Thursday. On the previous day, Wednesday, everyone goes in the afternoon for the vigil service to Bethlehem, where it is held in the church containing the cave where the Lord was born. On the next day, the Thursday which is the Fortieth Day, they have the usual service, with the presbyters and the bishop preaching sermons suitable to the place and the day; and in the evening everyone returns to Jerusalem.

The Fiftieth Day is a Sunday, and a great effort for the people. At cock-crow they have the usual service, a vigil at the Anastasis with the bishop reading the regular Sunday Gospel about the Lord's resurrection, and what follows in the Anastasis is what they do during the rest of the year.

In the morning the people all assemble in their usual way in the Great Church, the Martyrium,[2] and have sermons from the presbyters and then the bishop, and the Offering is duly made in the way which is usual on a Sunday, except that the dismissal at the Martyrium is earlier, taking place before nine o'clock, and straight after the dismissal in the Martyrium all the people, every single one, take the bishop with singing to Sion, where they arrive in time for nine o'clock.[3] When they arrive, they have a reading of the passage from the Acts of the Apostles about the descent of the Spirit[n], and how all the languages spoken were understood, after which the service proceeds as usual.

The presbyters concern themselves with this reading because Sion (though it has now been altered into a church) is the very spot where what I have just mentioned was done by the multitude who were assembled with the apostles after the Lord's passion.

They have the reading there from the Acts of the Apostles, and afterwards the service proceeds as usual, and they make the Offering there. Then as the people are dismissed the archdeacon makes this announcement: "Let us all be ready today on the Mount of Eleona at the Imbomon immediately after midday."

---

[1] Cf. *AL*, No. 57. [2] *AL*, No. 58.
[3] *AL*, No. 58; cf. Acts 2.15.

4   So all the people go home for a rest, and, as soon as they have
     had their meal, they go up Eleona, the Mount of Olives, each at
5   his own pace, till there is not a Christian left in the city. Once they
     have climbed Eleona, the Mount of Olives, they go to the Imbo-
     mon[1] (the place from which the Lord ascended into heaven),
     where the bishop takes his seat, and also the presbyters and all the
     people. They have readings, and between them hymns and
     antiphons suitable to this day and to the place. Also the prayers
     which come between are concerned with subjects appropriate to
     the day and the place. They have the Gospel reading about the
     Lord's ascension, and then the reading from the Acts of the
     Apostles about the Lord ascending into heaven after the
6   resurrection. When this is over, the catechumens are blessed, then
     the faithful.
        It is already three o'clock, and they go down with singing from
     there to the other church on Eleona,[2] containing the cave where
     the Lord used to sit and teach the apostles. By the time they get
     there it is after four, and they have Lucernare. The prayer is said,
     the catechumens are blessed, and then the faithful, and they go out.
        All the people, every single one of them, go down with their
     bishop, singing hymns and antiphons suitable to that day, and so,
7   very gradually, they make their way to the Martyrium. Even
     when they arrive at the city gate, it is already night, and the
     people are brought hundreds of church lamps to help them. It is
     quite a way from the gate to the Great Church, the Martyrium,
     and they arrive there at about eight at night, going very slowly
     all the way so that the walk does not make the people tired. The
*   great doors which face the market are opened, and the bishop and
     all the people enter the Martyrium singing.
        Inside the church they have hymns and a prayer, and the
     catechumens are blessed, then the faithful. Then they set off once
8   more with singing to the Anastasis. Again in the Anastasis they
     have hymns and antiphons and a prayer, and the catechumens are
     blessed, and then the faithful. Then the same is done again At the
     Cross, and once more every single member of the Christian
9   community conducts the bishop with singing to Sion. On arrival

     ------

     [1] AL, No. 58.   [2] See AL, No. 58.

they have suitable readings, psalms and antiphons, a prayer, the blessing of the catechumens, and then the faithful, and then the dismissal. After the dismissal everyone goes to kiss the bishop's * hand, and at about midnight everybody goes home. Thus this is a very hard day for them, for they have never stopped all day since they kept the vigil in the Anastasis, and the services have taken so long that it is midnight by the time they are dismissed on Sion, and all go home.

4.1   From the day after the Fiftieth they fast in the way which is usual during the rest of the year. Everyone does what fasting he can, except on Saturdays and Sundays, when no one here ever fasts. And on the days which follow they have the usual services which are held all the year round. There is is always a vigil in the 2 Anastasis from cock-crow. At cock-crow on a Sunday the bishop reads the usual passage about the Lord's resurrection in the Anastasis, the normal Sunday passage, and then hymns and antiphons are said there. From cock-crow to daybreak on days other 3 than Sunday they have only hymns and antiphons. All the apotactites are present, and any of the people who can be there, and clergy take it in turn to be there at cock-crow. When it begins to get light, the bishop always comes with his clergy to give the morning dismissal, but he has to come at cock-crow on a Sunday to read the Gospel in the Anastasis. Similarly, they have the usual services at midday and three o'clock in the Anastasis, and Lucernare follows the order which is normal for the rest of the year. But on Wednesdays and Fridays it is the custom that the three o'clock service is always held on Sion.

1   I feel I should add something about the way they instruct those who are to be baptized at Easter. Names must be given in before the first day of Lent, which means that a presbyter takes down all the names before the start of the eight weeks for which Lent lasts 2 here, as I have told you. Once the priest has all the names, on the second day of Lent at the start of the eight weeks, the bishop's chair is placed in the middle of the Great Church, the Martyrium, the presbyters sit in chairs on either side of him, and all the clergy stand. Then one by one those seeking baptism are brought up, men coming with their fathers and women with their mothers.

3 As they come in one by one, the bishop asks their neighbours questions about them: "Is this person leading a good life? Does he respect his parents? Is he a drunkard or a boaster?" He asks about
4 all the serious human vices. And if his inquiries show him that someone has not committed any of these misdeeds, he himself puts down his name; but if someone is guilty he is told to go away, and the bishop tells him that he is to amend his ways before he may come to the font. He asks the men and the women the same questions. But it is not too easy for a visitor to come to baptism if he has no witnesses who are acquainted with him.

46.1 Now, ladies and sisters, I want to write something which will save you from thinking all this is done without due explanation. They have here the custom that those who are preparing for baptism during the season of the Lenten fast go to be exorcized by the clergy first thing in the morning, directly after the morning dismissal in the Anastasis. As soon as that has taken place, the bishop's chair is placed in the Great Church, the Martyrium, and all those to be baptized, the men and the women, sit round him in a circle. There is a place where the fathers and mothers stand, and any of the people who want to listen (the faithful, of course)
2 can come in and sit down, though not catechumens, who do not come in while the bishop is teaching.

His subject is God's Law; during the forty days he goes through the whole Bible, beginning with Genesis,[1] and first relating the literal meaning of each passage, then interpreting its spiritual meaning. He also teaches them at this time all about the resurrec-
3 tion and the faith. And this is called *catechesis*. After five weeks' teaching they receive the Creed, whose content he explains article by article in the same way as he explained the Scriptures, first literally and then spiritually. Thus all the people in these parts are able to follow the Scriptures when they are read in church, since there has been teaching on all the Scriptures from six to nine in
4 the morning all through Lent, three hours' catechesis a day. At ordinary services when the bishop sits and preaches, ladies and sisters, the faithful utter exclamations, but when they come and hear him explaining the catechesis, their exclamations are far

[1] Cf. *AL*, No. 17 (List C, pp. 276–7 below).

louder, God is my witness; and when it is related and interpreted like this they ask questions on each point.

At nine o'clock they are dismissed from Catechesis, and the bishop is taken with singing straight to the Anastasis. So the dismissal is at nine, which makes three hours' teaching a day for seven weeks. But in the eighth, known as the Great Week, there is no time for them to have their teaching if they are to carry out 5 all the services I have described. So when seven weeks have gone by, and only the week of Easter remains, the one which people here call the Great Week, the bishop comes early into the Great Church, the Martyrium. His chair is placed at the back of the apse, behind the altar, and one by one the candidates go up to the bishop, men with their fathers and women with their mothers, 6 and repeat the Creed to him. When they have done so, the bishop speaks to them all as follows: "During these seven weeks you have received instruction in the whole biblical Law. You have heard about the faith, and the resurrection of the body. You have also learned all you can as catechumens of the content of the Creed. But the teaching about baptism itself is a deeper mystery, and you have not the right to hear it while you remain catechumens. Do not think it will never be explained; you will hear it all during the eight days of Easter after you have been baptized. But so long as you are catechumens you cannot be told God's deep mysteries."

.1   Then Easter comes, and during the eight days from Easter Day to the eighth day, after the dismissal has taken place in the church and they have come with singing into the Anastasis, it does not take long to say the prayer and bless the faithful; then the bishop stands leaning against the inner screen in the cave of the Anastasis, 2 and interprets all that takes place in Baptism.[1] The newly-baptized come into the Anastasis, and any of the faithful who wish to hear the Mysteries; but, while the bishop is teaching, no catechumen comes in, and the doors are kept shut in case any try to enter. The bishop relates what has been done, and interprets it, and, as he does so, the applause is so loud that it can be heard

---

[1] For the readings see *AL*, No. 52 and List D, p. 277 below.

outside the church. Indeed the way he expounds the mysteries and interprets them cannot fail to move his hearers.

3   In this province there are some people who know both Greek and Syriac, but others know only one or the other. The bishop may know Syriac,[n] but he never uses it. He always speaks in Greek, and has a presbyter beside him who translates the Greek into Syriac, so that everyone can understand what he means.

4 Similarly the lessons read in church have to be read in Greek, but there is always someone in attendance to translate into Syriac so that the people understand. Of course there are also people here who speak neither Greek nor Syriac, but Latin. But there is no need for them to be discouraged, since some of the brothers or sisters who speak Latin as well as Greek will explain things to

5 them. And what I admire and value most is that all the hymns and antiphons and readings they have, and all the prayers the bishop says, are always relevant to the day which is being observed and to the place in which they are used. They never fail to be appropriate.

48.1   The date when the Church on Golgotha (called the Martyrium) was consecrated to God is called Encaenia,[1] and on the same day the holy church of the Anastasis[n] was also consecrated, the place where the Lord rose again after his passion. The Encaenia of these holy churches is a feast of special magnificence, since it is on the

2 very date when the cross of the Lord was discovered. So they arranged that this day should be observed with all possible joy by making the original dedication of these holy churches coincide with the very day when the cross had been found. You will find in the Bible that the day of Encaenia was when the House of God

* was consecrated, and Solomon stood in prayer before God's altar, as we read in the Books of Chronicles.[2]

49.1   At the time of Encaenia they keep festival for eight days,[3] and for many days beforehand the crowds begin to assemble. Monks and apotactites come not only from the provinces having large numbers of them, such as Mesopotamia, Syria, Egypt, and the Thebaid, but from every region and province. Not one of them

[1] Cf. 2 Chron. 7.5,9; John 10.22.
[2] 2 Chron. 6.12.   [3] Cf. AL, No. 68.

fails to make for Jerusalem to share the celebrations of this solemn feast. There are also lay men and women from every province
2 gathering in Jerusalem at this time for the holy day. And although bishops are few and far between, they never have less than forty or fifty in Jerusalem at this time, accompanied by many of their clergy. In fact I should say that people regard it as a grave sin to miss taking part in this solemn feast, unless anyone had been prevented from coming by an emergency.
3   The feast ranks with Easter or Epiphany, and during Encaenia they decorate the churches in the same way, and assemble each day in different holy places, as at Easter and Epiphany. On the first and second days they assemble in the Great Church, the Martyrium, on the third day in the Eleona Church on the Mount from which the Lord ascended into heaven after his passion (I mean the church which contains the cave where the Lord taught the apostles on the Mount of Olives). On the fourth day . . .[1]

[1] The remaining pages are lost from the manuscript.

Extracts
from other
Authors

The Letter of King Abgar (after 250)
The Pilgrim of Bordeaux (333)
Eusebius on the Buildings on Golgotha (*c.* 337)
Pseudo-Cyril on the Eucharist (*c.* 390)
The Letter of Valerius (*c.* 650)
Peter the Deacon (compiled 1137)

The Letter of King Abgar to Christ

It seems that the legend of Abgar took shape in about A.D. 250 under Abgar IX, the first Christian king of Osrhoëne. It is known in two principal versions, that of Eusebius,[1] which was in Greek, and that which appears in the *Didascalia Addai*, a Syriac document which in the form in which we know it dates from about 400.

In chapter 17.1 Egeria speaks as if St Thomas were the apostle sent by Christ to Edessa, whereas both the main sources have it that the apostle Christ was going to send was "a disciple" (whose name occurs later in the narrative as Addai or Thaddaeus), and tell us that "Judas Thomas" sent him after the resurrection.[2]

In 19.19 she is glad to be given a copy of the letters, since she suspects that the copies she has at home may perhaps be shorter. It is known that Rufinus translated the letters soon after Egeria's time, and no doubt the earlier translations which had reached the West were made from the Greek. Egeria's suspicion was justified, since the Syriac version is in fact longer and contains the final promise that the "fortress shall be blessed and no enemy shall rule over it for ever". Eusebius seems to ✱ have omitted this, and several other passages from the documents he used.[3]

Copy of a letter[4] written by Abgar the Toparch to Jesus, and sent to him at Jerusalem by the hand of Ananias, a courier.[5]

Abgar Ukhama, toparch, to Jesus, gracious Saviour, who has appeared in the region of Jerusalem, greeting. I have heard of thee and of thy cures as having been wrought by thee without medicines or herbs. For by a word[6] thou dost make the blind to receive their sight, the lame to walk, and dost cleanse the lepers, cast out unclean spirits and devils, heal[7] them that are tormented[8] with long sickness, and raise up the dead.[7] And when I heard all this

[1] Eusebius, *HE* 1.13.5–10, *PG* 20.121–4. The translation given here is that of H. J. Lawlor and J. E. L. Oulton in their valuable work *Eusebius, Bishop of Caesarea, The Ecclesiastical History and the Martyrs of Palestine*, 2 vols. (London 1927), see vol. 1, pp. 29–31, and vol. 2. pp. 56–8.

[2] Compare Eusebius, *HE* 1.13.6, *PG* 20.124.

[3] See Lawlor and Oulton, vol 2, p. 57, and P. Devos, "Egérie à Edesse", *A.B.* 85 (1967), p. 396.

[4] Except where otherwise noted this is Lawlor and Oulton's translation of Eusebius' version of the letters.

[5] Cf. Egeria 17.1.

[6] This meaning comes from the Syriac version.

[7] Based on Luke 7.21–2.   [8] Probably from Matt. 8.6.

concerning thee, I was convinced of one of two things: either that thou art God, and doest these things, having come down from heaven; or that, because thou doest them, thou art the Son of God. Therefore for this cause I write and beseech thee to trouble thyself to come to me and heal the disorder which I have. For verily I have heard that even the Jews are murmuring at thee and wish to do thee harm. But I have a very small city, yet a stately one; which will suffice us both.

The written reply of Jesus to the Toparch Abgar sent by the hand of the courier Ananias.

Blessed art thou who didst believe in me, not having seen me.[1] For it is written of me that they who have seen me will not believe in me, even that they who have not seen me may themselves believe and live.[2] But as to that which thou didst write to me, that I should come to thee, I must fulfil all things for the which I was sent hither; and having fulfilled them, be received up[3] immediately to him that sent me.[4] And when I am received up, I will send thee one of my disciples, to heal thy disorder and bestow life on thee and those with thee. And thy fortress shall be blessed, and no enemy shall rule over it for ever.[5]

[1] Cf. John 20.29.
[2] Cf. Isa. 7.9ff; Matt. 13.14ff; John 12.39ff.
[3] Acts 1.2,11,22; 1 Tim. 3.16.   [4] Cf. John 16.5.
[5] This is the sentence omitted from the Greek version, but present in the Syriac.

The Pilgrim of Bordeaux

The earliest of all the pilgrims who have described their visit to the Holy Land in any detail arrived from Bordeaux in 333, a date which he fixes by naming the consuls in office.[1] Though the larger part of his work is in the form of a list of the staging-posts by which he made the journey, he occasionally notes points of interest such as:

Change of horses at Peripidis (10 miles). There the poet Euripides is buried.[2]

The pilgrim (whose name is not recorded) travelled from Bordeaux to Constantinople through Arles, Aosta, Milan, Aquileia, Mitrowicz (Sirmium), and Sofia (Serdica). Then he crossed to Chalcedon and went on via Ankara and Mansucrinae[3] to Paul's city of Tarsus; then to Antioch, Laodicea, Beirut, and Sidon

And from there to Sarepta (8 miles). Elijah went up there and asked the widow to give him food.[4]

For Haifa (Sycaminos) he notes:

Mount Carmel is there. There Elijah did his sacrifice.[5]

He goes on to Caesarea Palaestinae; at this point the list of staging-posts changes into the prose text which follows, which describes the holy places. When his visits are completed, he returns from Jerusalem to Constantinople, and makes detours through Macedonia and to Rome before returning to Milan (where the account ends) and presumably to Bordeaux.

7 There [that is, at Caesarea] is the Bath of Cornelius the centurion,[6] who gave much alms. At the third milestone from there is Mount ✳ Syna,[7] where there is a spring, and women who wash in it become pregnant.

[1] The edition used for this translation is *Itinerarium Burdigalense* (ed. P. Geyer and O. Cuntz) in *Corpus Christianorum, Series Latina* 175 (Turnhout 1965). The page numbers are those of the fully annotated edition of P. Wesseling in his *Vetera Romanorum Itinera* (Amsterdam 1735), pp. 535–617: for the consuls see p. 571.
[2] 604. [3] 579.
[4] 583; cf. 1 Kings 17.10ff. Sarepta is the modern Sarafand.
[5] 584; cf. 1 Kings 18.19ff. El Muhraqa, the traditional place of the sacrifice, is on the south-eastern brow of the mountain, and it thus seems clear that the pilgrim did not visit it.
[6] Jerome, *Ep.* 108.8, *PL* 22.882, mentions not the Bath, but the centurion's ✳ House.
[7] M. Avi-Yonah places this "Syna" north-west of Caesarea on the road by

City of Maximianopolis[1] (18 miles).

City of Jezreel[2] (10 miles); it was there that King Ahab lived and Elijah prophesied; there also is the plain where David killed Goliath.[3]

City of Scythopolis[4] (12 miles).

* 586   Aser;[5] there was the estate of Job (16 miles).

City of Neapolis[6] (15 miles). Mount Gerizim[7] is there, where

* 587   according to the Samaritans, Abraham offered his sacrifice.[8] There are 1,300 steps leading to the top of the mountain.[9] Near by, at the foot of the mountain, is the place called Shechem,[10] which

588   is the site of the tomb in which Joseph[11] is buried, in the estate

---

which the pilgrim approached from Haifa, rather than that by which he left for Legio Maximianopolis. See his *Map of Roman Palestine* in *Israel Exploration Journal* 1 (1950), pp. 54ff.

[1] The full name, Legio Maximianopolis, was usually abbreviated to Legio, and this name survived in Arabic as el Lajjūn, which until recent times was a village one mile south-south-west of Tell Megiddo.

[2] Jezreel (*Isdrahela*) is now called Yizre'el or Zer'īn; cf. PD, V5.

[3] The plain was where Deborah defeated Sisera, and not far from Mount Gilboa where Saul and Jonathan were killed; but for the correct location of Goliath's death see PD, V7.

*   [4] The pilgrim makes no mention of the tombs of the martyrs Basil and Procopius which were in this city. It is now called Bet She'an or Beisān.

[5] The connection of this village with Job is otherwise unknown. It is now called Tayāsīr, and the sixteenth Roman milestone has survived.

[6] Vespasian founded this city, then Flavia Neapolis, now Nāblūs, as a colony for veterans in A.D. 72. He placed them there to control the Samaritans.

[7] The mountains on either side of the valley containing Neapolis were correctly identified both by Jews and Samaritans with Mounts Gerizim and Ebal (Josh. 8.33; see *Soṭa* 32a, Soncino edn, p. 158). But Jews later reacted against the Samaritans, and came to hold that they were near to Jericho; cf. *Siphre Deut.* 56. The Christians received both traditions; so Eusebius (*Gebal, Golgol*) places them near Jericho on the grounds those near Neapolis were too far

*   apart for the ceremony described in Joshua. But Jerome (*Ep.* 108.13) places them near Neapolis; and the sixth-century Madaba map names them in both localities.

*   [8] This was the Samaritans' Mount Moriah (Gen. 22.2). For Jews Mount Moriah was the Rock in the Temple at Jerusalem: thus Josephus (*Ant.* 7.13.4) says that the threshing-floor of Araunah "happened to be" the place where Abraham went to offer his sacrifice. See further M. Avi-Yonah, *The Madaba Map* (Jerusalem 1954), p. 33.

[9] These steps were a feature of which Neapolis was so proud that they appeared on its coins; they led to the Temple of Jupiter which Hadrian had built on Mount Gerizim, and led up from the present shrine called Rijāl el Amūd. Epiphanius *XII Gem.* 258 reported 1,500 steps. The most recent archæological examination is reported by R. J. Bull in *P.E.Q.*, July–December 1970, p. 110.

[10] Shechem itself was a ruined site in the fourth century (Eusebius, *On, Sichem*); cf. PD, T.

[11] Josh. 24.32. The site near Shechem was supported by Jewish as well as by

given him by his father Jacob. That too was where Dinah, Jacob's daughter, was seized by the sons of the Amorites.[1]

A mile from there is the place called Sychar,[2] where the Samaritan woman went down to draw water, at the very place where Jacob dug the well, and our Lord Jesus Christ spoke with her. Some plane trees are there, planted by Jacob, and there is a bath which takes its water from this well.   *

Twenty-eight miles from there on the left of the road to Jerusalem is the village called Bethar,[3] and a mile from there is the place where Jacob slept on his way from Mesopotamia,[4] and the almond-tree[5] is there, and he saw a vision, and an angel wrestled with him.[6] King Jeroboam was there, and a prophet was

89 sent to convert him to God the Most High; and the prophet was commanded not to eat with the false prophet who was with the king; and because he was led astray by the false prophet, and ate with him when he was returning, a lion met him in the way and killed him.[7]

Jerusalem is twelve miles further on. In Jerusalem beside the Temple are two large pools, one to the right and the other to the

---

Samaritan tradition, as in *Gen. Rabbah* 79.7, and this site was accepted by Christians. But another tradition seems to have placed Joseph's tomb in Judah at Hebron. The first Christian pilgrim to be shown the tomb there is Antoninus   *
of Piacenza (*Itin.* 30) in about A.D. 570, who found it with the tombs of Abraham, Isaac, and Jacob, i.e. at the present Ḥaram el Khalīl. Jeremias, *Hg*, p. 32, n. 3, regards this statement of Antoninus as "a plain error"; it is certainly unsupported except by later Muslim tradition.

[1] Gen 34.2.

[2] Eusebius, *On, Sychar* describes the well, and by 390 when Jerome translated the description he added that a church had then been built there. Compare PD, R, which shows that the church was already built by Egeria's time if, as is likely, the passage is hers.   *

[3] Bethar, otherwise Bethaun (Bethaven, Josh. 7.2; 18.12), and Epiphanius *PM* 73, Dean, p. 75.

[4] Bethel (Gen. 28.12; 32.24). Jerome adds a note that a church had been built there to his translation of Eusebius, *On, Agai,* and also mentions it in *Ep.* 46.12, Compare PD, V7, which, if from Egeria, antedates *Ep.* 46 by three years.

[5] The Luza of Gen. 28.19 can be translated "almond-tree". It was the name of the place before Jacob gave it the name Bethel (cf. Gen. 13.3).

[6] The commemoration of Peniel (Gen. 32.30) was also made at Bethel at this   *
time by this pilgrim, but this commemoration is not mentioned in the *On*.

[7] See 1 Sam. 13, esp. vv. 11 and 29–31. Doubtless this pilgrim, like Egeria (see PD, V7) was shown the prophet's tomb. In later tradition this prophet received the name Joad (*Hg*, p. 51).

* left, built by Solomon,[1] and inside the city are the twin pools with five porches called Bethsaida.[2] People who had been sick for many years used to be cured there. The water of these pools is turbid and its colour is scarlet.

There is also a vault there[3] where Solomon used to torture
590 demons,[4] and the corner of a very lofty tower,[5] which was where the Lord climbed and said to the Tempter, "Thou shalt not tempt the Lord thy God, but him only shalt thou serve." And there also is the great corner-stone of which it was said, "The stone which the builders rejected has become the head of the corner."[6]

Below the pinnacle of this tower are very many chambers where Solomon had his palace. There too is the chamber where he was when he wrote of Wisdom, and it is roofed with a single stone.[7] Below ground there are some great water-cisterns and pools built with enormous labour.

591   And in the sanctuary itself, where the Temple stood which

[1] One of these pools was probably Birkat Israel, now filled with earth, to the south of the road immediately inside St Stephen's Gate, and the other may have been outside the gate; but see C. Kopp, *The Holy Places of the Gospels* (London 1962), p. 373, and Josephus, *War* 5.11.4.

* [2] Bethesda (John 5.2) was filled by water brought by aqueduct from beyond Bethlehem. Eusebius, *On, Bezatha/Bethsaida*, mentions the colour, and the fact that it was rain-water. But the size of the pools has been revealed by the long series of excavations which have been carried out there, and it seems unlikely that rain-water can have been the only supply. No sign of the five porches has yet been revealed by the excavations, for which see R. de Vaux and J. M. Rousée, *R.B.* 64 (1957), pp. 226–8 and 69 (1962), pp. 108–9. No
* church is mentioned there in the fourth century.

[3] I.e. somewhere in the area of the Temple ruins.

[4] According to the graphic account in Talmud, *Giṭṭin* 7.68a (Soncino edn (London 1936), pp. 323ff) Solomon tied a male and female demon together to make them tell him where to find Ashmedai, the prince of the demons. When he was found, he came to stay with Solomon and helped him to build the Temple. Josephus simply said that Solomon had "learned that skill which expels demons" (*Ant.* 8.2.5).

* [5] Mark 4.7,10. PD, E mentions two pinnacles. Eusebius records the tradition that James the Just was killed by being thrown from this tower (*HE* 2.23.12, *PG* 20.201f, quoting Hegesippus). This pinnacle was at the south-eastern corner of the Temple area, above what is now called the "Tomb of James" in the Kidron valley.

[6] Some of the corner-stones in the outer wall are as much as six metres in length. The one here mentioned (Ps. 118.22 = Matt. 21.42) may have been the capstone;
* the capstone of the corner to the west was discovered in 1970 by B. Mazar.

* [7] The chamber roofed with a single stone later received from the Muslims the name "Cradle of Christ", which it still bears. It forms the way down to the substructures of the great platform built by Herod the Great, now known as Solomon's Stables.

Solomon built,[1] there is marble in front of the altar which has on it the blood of Zacharias[2]—you would think it had only been shed today. All around you can see the marks of the hobnails of the soldiers who killed him, as plainly as if they had been pressed into wax.[3] Two statues of Hadrian stand there,[4] and, not far from them, a pierced stone which the Jews come and anoint each year.[5] They mourn and rend their garments, and then depart. There too is the house of Hezekiah, king of Judah.[6]

92   Moreover, as you leave Jerusalem to climb Sion, you see down in the valley on your left, beside the wall, the pool called Siloam.[7] It has four porches and a second pool outside,[8] and it flows for six days and six nights; but the seventh day is the Sabbath, and then it does not flow at all, either by night or day.

Climbing Sion from there you can see the place where once the house of Caiaphas used to stand,[9] and the column at which they fell on Christ and scourged him still remains there.[10]

Inside Sion, within the wall, you can see where David had his

[1] See Introduction, p. 36 above. The Temple remained in ruins till the clearing and re-use of the site by the Muslims in the seventh century. See also PD, E.

[2] Matt. 23.35; 2 Chron. 24.20–2; cf. PD, E.

[3] Zachariah the son of Barachiah was soon confused with Zacharias the father of St John Baptist who, it was believed, was killed by a crowd of assassins incited by Herod, who was angry that he had failed to kill John among the Innocents. See PD, E, n. 9.

[4] Jerome, Com. in Matt. (4) 24.15, PL 26.177, says that there was an equestrian statue of Hadrian there. It may be that the other statue represented Antoninus, Hadrian's heir and successor.

[5] It is hard to avoid identifying the pierced stone with the central outcrop of rock now enclosed within the Dome of the Rock. But Avi-Yonah, MM, p. 59, produces some evidence that Jews were not allowed to go there. See also Milik in MUJ 37 (1961), p. 175.

[6] The text suggests that this was shown inside the Temple perimeter.

[7] As the pilgrim saw it, the Pool of Siloam was surrounded by the cloister which Hadrian added there to transform it into the Tetranymphon. It stood inside the city wall built by Herod Agrippa, as confirmed by recent examinations; see K. Kenyon, Jerusalem (London 1967), p. 156. The pilgrim leaves Jerusalem near the present Dung Gate. The water which reaches Siloam is erratic, flowing at best three or four times a day.

[8] Now known as Birkat el Ḥamra.

[9] Cyril, Cat. 13.38, PG 33.817, also speaks of this site as desolate, but some building was probably erected by the time of the Armenian Lectionary, since it was used for a station on the night of the Thursday before Easter (see No. 41). Its location is first mentioned by the mid sixth-century pilgrim Theodosius (7 C.C.S.L., p. 118) about fifty paces from Sion Church, and Kopp, pp. 352–7, says that it was to the north.

[10] Egeria (37.1) says people go on to Sion to venerate this column. Jerome (Ep. 108.9) says that it was a support of the portico of Sion Church.

palace.[1] Seven synagogues were there, but only one is left—the rest have been "ploughed and sown" as was said by the prophet
593 Isaiah.[2] As you leave there and pass through the wall of Sion[3] towards the Gate of Neapolis,[4] down in the valley on your right you have some walls where Pontius Pilate had his house, the Praetorium[5] where the Lord's case was heard before he suffered. On your left is the hillock Golgotha[6] where the Lord was crucified,
594 and about a stone's throw from it the vault[7] where they laid his body, and he rose again on the third day. By order of the Emperor Constantine there has now been built there a "basilica"—I mean a "place for the Lord"[8]—which has beside it cisterns of remark-
* able beauty,[9] and beside them a bath where children are baptized.[10]

* [1] David would be associated with Sion simply by its name. But it is possible that his traditional Jerusalem tomb was there (see Josephus, *Ant.* 7.15.3 and 16.7.1). Another tomb of David was in Bethlehem, as in 598 below. See also Acts 2.29, and Jeremias, *Hg*, pp. 57–60.

* [2] See Isa. 1.8. Sion was the Christians' traditional centre in Jerusalem (see Intro., p. 38 above). The pilgrim mentions no church—only the wall (cf. PD,E) and the palace—but there is a church by 348, since Cyril, *Cat.* 16.4, PG 33.924 calls it "The Upper Church of the Apostles" recalling the descent of the Holy Spirit at Pentecost.

* [3] This was the north wall of Sion, the original southern wall of Jerusalem built by Herod the Great (compare figs. 14 and 15 in K. Kenyon, *Jerusalem* (London 1967), pp. 145, 157), but there may also have been a wall above the eastern slopes. The pilgrim presumably passed through not far from the present Sion Gate.

[4] The present Damascus Gate, which was known as St Stephen's Gate after Eudocia had built St Stephen's Church to the north of it in 455–60.

* [5] Perhaps near the present Gate of the Chain; see *MM*, p. 57, and Milik, *MUJ* 37 (1961), p. 151. Cyril (*Cat.* 13.39, PG 33.820) speaks of the desolation of the "Hall of Pilate" in A.D. 348, but the site was later chosen for the Church of St Sophia.

* [6] The rock outcrop called Golgotha or the whole raised area with the basilica?
[7] The stone tomb. Thus it seems that the Anastasis had not yet been built, and that the tomb was still in the open air, since it is unlikely that the pilgrim would praise the cisterns if he had also seen the Anastasis itself.

[8] "Basilica" is a word not yet apparently in current use as a Christian technical term, as is also deducible from Eusebius' way of using it; see G. Downey, "Constantine's Churches at Antioch, Tyre, and Jerusalem" in *MUJ* 38 (1960–1), p. 191. The Latin word for basilica (*dominicum*) is also used by Jerome (*Chron.* anno. 331, PL 27.677). Cf. Egeria 24.8.

* [9] The pilgrim was evidently taken down to visit the cisterns (see above, 589 and p. 158, n. 1); they have been thoroughly examined, see *R.B.* 69 (1962), pp. 100–7.

[10] The baptistery is later reported (Ps-Cyril *Myst.* 1.2, PG 33.1068) to have had an outer hall where the candidates renounced Satan before going in to the "bath" itself; cf. Egeria 38.1.

Arriving at the gate of Jerusalem which faces the east,[1] on your way to go up the Mount of Olives, you come to what is called the Valley of Jehoshaphat.[2] On the left is a vineyard where is also the rock where Judas Iscariot betrayed Christ;[3] and on the right ₅95 is the palm-tree[4] from which the children[5] took branches and strewed them in Christ's path. Near by, about a stone's throw away, are two memorial tombs of beautiful workmanship.[6] One

[1] This description may possibly echo the "East Gate" of Neh. 3.29. The present name "St Stephen's Gate" was that used by the Crusaders, since their principal sanctuary of St Stephen was on the Mount of Olives, but the Arabs still know it by the older name "My Lady Mary's Gate", since it was also the gate next to St Anne's Church and leading out to the Tomb of the Virgin.   *

[2] Jehoshaphat signifies "Yahwe judges", and Joel (3.2,12) makes a Valley of Jehoshaphat the scene of the Last Judgement; this was identified by Jews and Christians alike with the Kidron valley. Christians, following Zech. 14.4, placed the Lord's Second Coming on the Mount of Olives (see, for example, Cyril, *Cat.* 12.11, *PG* 33.737, and PD, I below).   *

[3] Neither here nor in other fourth-century accounts is there mention of the Cave of Gethsemane, despite the fact that recent examination has shown it to have been used from early times as a burial chapel (see V. Corbo in *La Terra Santa* 33 (1957), pp. 167-71). Gethsemane implies both the place of Christ's arrest and (a stone's throw away; cf. Luke 22.41) his agony, and the two spots in the Gethsemane area were distinct.   *

The evidence seems to favour the present site of the Church of All Nations for the arrest and somewhere a good deal higher up for the agony. But there are two difficulties. The first is the evidence of Jerome, who in the *On.* says that the place of the prayer was "at the foot of" the Mount of Olives, thus changing what Eusebius wrote, and speaks of a church then (sc. in 390) built over it. This is most likely to be the church first built on the site of the present Church of All Nations and the rock mentioned by Bord., and Jerome was perhaps combining the place of the arrest with the place of the prayer.

The second difficulty arises through the words of Peter the Deacon (I): "Across the Brook Kidron is a cave, and above it a church where, on the Thursday after supper, the Jews arrested the Saviour." Most of the rest of this passage seems to come from Egeria, but there is a certain interpolation later on (see p. 185 below), and the same is almost certainly the case here, since no church has ever been built over the Gethsemane cave (see Milik in *R.B.* 67 (1960), p. 550). Peter seems to be confusing the cave (certainly believed to be the place of the arrest in the sixth century) with the church over the rock.

[4] The palm tree was still visible in 348 (Cyril, *Cat.* 10.19, *PG* 33.688), but there is no mention of it in Egeria's account of Palm Sunday (see 31), and only its site is shown in PD, I.

[5] On the connection of children with the Triumphal Entry, cf. Egeria 31.2, and see above, p. 133, n. 1.

[6] These two monuments were rock pillars outside the entrance of tomb-systems, and shaped from solid rock; they are known today as the Tombs of "Absalom" and "Zechariah". The "Tomb of Absalom" has had this name only since the twelfth century (contrast Josephus, *Ant.* 7.10.3).

The pilgrim's identification of one of these monuments with that of Isaiah reflects a tradition known from the *Vitae Prophetarum*, resting on a source

of them, formed from a single rock, is where the prophet Isaiah was laid, and in the other lies Hezekiah, king of the Jews.

On the Mount of Olives, where the Lord taught before his passion, a basilica has been built by command of Constantine.[1] And not far off is the hillock[2] where the Lord went up to pray, and where there appeared Moses and Elijah, when he took Peter 596 and John apart with him. A mile and a half eastwards from there is the village called Bethany, and in it is the vault in which was laid Lazarus,[3] whom the Lord raised.

Eighteen miles from Jerusalem is Jericho. Coming down the mountain range you reach a tomb on the right,[4] and behind it is the sycamore tree which Zacchaeus climbed[5] in order that he could see Christ. A mile and a half from the city is the spring of the prophet Elisha;[6] at one time any woman who drank from it would never have children. Then Elisha brought a cruse with

---

* anterior to Hadrian's time, that the prophet was buried near Siloam (see Jeremias, *Hg*, pp. 61-6), but the tomb itself had long been lost, owing to a systematic destruction of monuments in the course of Hadrian's alterations to Jerusalem. Similarly the name of Hezekiah was associated with the tombs of the kings, south of Jerusalem (cf. 2 Chron. 32.33), but its identification here is merely a memory of the old tradition transferred to a visible monument.

* The present "Tomb of Zechariah" and the neighbouring "Tomb of James the Less" were the family tombs of the Beni Ḥezir, a priestly family, and were probably constructed in the second century B.C.

* [1] The Eleona here seems already to have been finished by the time of the pilgrim's visit in 333; but see p. 162, n. 2 below, and Intro., p. 49 above.

[2] By the time of Cyril the commemoration of the Transfiguration (Matt. 17.2) had been located on Mount Tabor, where it became fixed for good (Cyril, *Cat.* 12.16, PG 33.744; cf. Jerome, Epp. 46.12; 108.13), and a church was built there by the mid-sixth century. For the "Hillock" see Intro., p. 49 above.

[3] A church had been built there by the time of Egeria; see 25.11; 29.3; and Intro., pp. 52-3 above.

[4] This tomb has not been identified. Eusebius, *On.*, speaks of three cities of Jericho. The first was the one overthrown by Joshua, which contained Elisha's spring (excavated, though all remains of the city of Joshua's time had already disappeared; see K. M. Kenyon, *Jericho* (London 1961)). The second was built to replace the first (1 Kings 16.34), and to it Christ came and spoke to Zacchaeus and cured the blind. Near by was the winter palace which Herod the Great built, and in which he died (excavated; see BASOR 120 (1950) and 123 (1951)). Its inhabitants were driven out by Titus in A.D. 69 (Josephus, *War* 4.8.2), and a new city was built on the present site, a mile to the north-east.

[5] Jerome also speaks of the sycamore in *Ep.* 108.12. See also PD, P2.

* [6] Next to the ancient Jericho, the present Tell es Sulṭān. Justinian built a church over the spring (*MM*, p. 44). Note that, like Syna (585 above) this spring and its miracle (2 Kings 2.19ff) are interpreted in connection with human fertility; cf. Josephus, *War* 4.8.3.

salt in it, and came and stood over the spring, saying, "Thus saith the Lord, he hath cleansed these waters." Now if a woman drinks from it she will have children. And above the spring is the house of Rahab the harlot,[1] which is the house where the spies came and she hid them, at the time when Jericho was overthrown, and she was the only one to escape. That was where the city of Jericho used to stand at the time when the children of Israel marched round it with the ark of the covenant, and the walls fell down.[2] From this point you have a view of the very place where the children of Israel set down the ark of the covenant, and placed the twelve stones which they brought up out of the Jordan.[3] It is also the place where Joshua the Son of Nun circumcised the children of Israel and buried their foreskins.[4]

It is nine miles from Jericho to the Dead Sea. Its water is extremely bitter, fish are nowhere to be found in it, and no ships sail there. If anyone goes to swim in it, the water turns him upside down.[5] Five miles from there in the Jordan is the place where the Lord was baptized by John,[6] and above the far bank at the same place is the hillock from which Elijah was taken up to heaven.[7]

[1] Despite Jerome's silence this house was regularly visited by later pilgrims.
[2] Cf. PD, P2.
[3] The rabbinic tradition of the mid-second century (see *Sota* 32a, Soncino edn, p. 159 and 36a, p. 177) speaks of these stones (see Josh. 4.20). They were venerated not only by Jews but also, in Eusebius' time, by Gentiles (*On, Golgol*); Jerome simply says "by the mortals" of the district. The stones were later incorporated into a Christian church (*MM*, pp. 36f), and it may be from this church that the columns come which were incorporated into the central court of the Islamic palace at Khirbat al Mafjar, since this site was in the neighbourhood; see Milik *R.B.* 66 (1959), p. 566, and on the palace see R. W. Hamilton, "Who built Khirbat al Mafjar?" in *Levant* 1 (1969), pp. 61–7.
[4] Josh. 5.3,10.
[5] Vespasian verified what he was told about the Dead Sea by finding men who could not swim, tying their hands behind their backs, and throwing them in (Josephus, *War* 4.8.4).
[6] The pilgrim, like most others, approached from the west bank, and Bethabara is shown on the west bank on the Madaba Map (cf. Origen, *in Ioan.* 6.24, *PG* 14.269). But the hillock of Elijah's ascension (2 Kings 2.11) is necessarily on the other side; cf. *MM*, pp. 38f, and Kopp, p. 115. Jerome speaks of the Place of Baptism and the crossing of the river (*Ep.* 108.12). Eusebius (*On, Bethabara*) says that "many brothers esteem it as a place of baptism", and it was no doubt at this place that Constantine on his death-bed wished he had been baptized (cf. Eusebius, *VC* 4.62, *PG* 20.1216).
[7] The site is probably Jebel Mar Elyas, beside Wadi el Kharrar, a mile and a half to the east of the Place of Baptism.

Four miles from Jerusalem, on the right of the highway to Bethlehem, is the tomb in which was laid Jacob's wife Rachel.[1] Two miles further on, on the left, is Bethlehem, where the Lord Jesus Christ was born, and where a basilica has been built by command of Constantine.[2] Not far away is the tomb of Ezekiel, Asaph, Job, Jesse, David, and Solomon.[3] Their names are written in Hebrew characters low down on the wall as you go down into the vault.

599   Fourteen miles away is Bethsur, at which is the spring where Philip baptized the eunuch.[4] It is nine miles to Terebinthus,[5]

[1] Ephrath and Rama (see Gen. 35.19; 48.7; cf. 1 Sam. 10.2) were originally north of Jerusalem, but by the time the text of Genesis was established it already included an explanatory note that Ephrath was Bethlehem. Since then the grave of Rachel has in both Jewish (see, for example, Tos. Soṭa 11.11) and Christian tradition (see Justin, Dial. c. Tryph. 78, PG 6.657–60) been shown in its present position near Bethlehem. See Jeremias, Hg, p. 75.

* [2] Like the Eleona above (595) this basilica is described as if it was already finished; but it was not dedicated till 31 May 339; see J. T. Milik, R.B. 67 (1960), p. 572.

[3] The first three names are presumably the three sons of Zeruiah (2 Sam. 2.18), Joab, Abishai, and Asahel, Jesse's grandchildren and David's nephews, as was first suggested by L. Heidet, Das Heilige Land, N.F. 3 (1898), pp. 105ff, 143ff. Eusebius, On, Bethleem, mentions David and Jesse, and Jerome speaks of the "mausoleum" of David in Bethlehem (Ep. 46.13; cf. PD, LI). The sixth-
* century pilgrim Antoninus of Piacenza says that a church had been built over the tomb, and that it was half a mile from Bethlehem, (29, C.C.S.L., p. 144), and Arculf in the seventh century says that it lay to the north (4.4, C.C.S.L., p. 207). David's tomb in Jerusalem was probably destroyed by Hadrian (see Jeremias, Hg, p. 79), but both locations rested on ancient traditions; cf. 1 Kings 2.10 and Neh. 3.16. This site has not yet been identified.

[4] This spring (Ain edh Dhirwe) according to Eusebius (On, Bethsur) was "said to be" where the eunuch was baptized; but the road on which it lies is not the most direct route from Jerusalem to Gaza, which may explain Jerome's explanatory phrase that it was "the ancient road leading to Gaza" (Ep. 108.11). An alternative spring (Ain Hanniye) on the principal road was shown in 570 to Antoninus of Piacenza (32, C.C.S.L., p. 145). Cf. Acts 8.38.

[5] This site is the Mamre of Gen. 18.1, the present Rāmat el Khalīl, which
* excavations show to have been an early Israelite holy place rebuilt before Herod's time (see E. Mader, Mamre (Freiburg 1957), p. 48). The tree was known to Josephus, who reports that it was very large, and had continued alive since the creation of the world (War 4.9.7). Eusebius said that it was to be seen in his day, and that the Gentiles worshipped it (On, Chebron), and tells how Eutropia in reaction persuaded her son-in-law Constantine to build a Christian basilica there, which he did (VC 3.51–3, PG 20.1112–17), on the grounds that it was fitting that Christians should pay due honour to the place where Abraham entertained "two angels and the Saviour". According to Jerome the tree died in about A.D. 350, but local people continued to worship its site (On, Arboch; cf. Ep. 108.11); but it still had some life in it in A.D. 680, according to the report of Bishop Arculf (2.11.3, C.C.S.L. 175, p. 211).

where Abraham lived and dug a well beneath the terebinth tree, and spoke and ate with the angels; an exceptionally beautiful basilica has been built there by command of Constantine. Two miles on from there is Hebron,[1] where there is a remarkably beautiful tomb, square and made of stone, in which are laid Abraham, Isaac, and Jacob, and Sarah, Rebecca, and Leah.[2]

[1] Gen. 49.31 is the first mention of these graves in Hebron, but it is disputable whether the tomb-building existed until Herod built it (see Jeremias, *Hg*, pp. 91–2). It is first recorded by Josephus (*War* 4.9.7) who says that it was elegantly made of marble. Bord. is the next witness. See also PD, N.2.

[2] At this point the pilgrim's manuscript reverts to the form of a list of staging-posts and the distances between them, and provides no further information about holy places, except the negative indications that he passed through (600) Nicopolis, Lydda, Antipatris, Bethar, and Caesarea without mentioning any holy places they may have contained.

Eusebius on the Buildings on Golgotha

The first and only systematic description of Constantine's buildings on Golgotha is the one which Eusebius included in his *Life of Constantine*. Precious as it is to the student, it is long, wordy, and ambiguous, and only some salient extracts are provided below;[1] even so it is a description which shows a number of emphases different from those of Egeria. The most important is that nowhere does the description of Eusebius necessarily imply the existence of any building over the holy Cave which contained Christ's Tomb.[2]

VC

3.25 *Constantine's Aim*

He realized that he ought to display the most blessed place of the Saviour's Resurrection[3] in Jerusalem in a worthy and conspicuous manner. So, without delay, he gave orders that a house[4] of prayer should be erected.

26 *The Temple of Aphrodite*

Godless people ... had gone to great pains to cover up this divine memorial of immortality so that it should be forgotten. With much labour they brought in soil from elsewhere and covered the whole site, and by raising the level[5] and laying a stone pavement they concealed the divine cave under a heap of earth. And, as though this were not enough, they built above ground ... a gloomy shrine of lifeless idols dedicated to the impure

[1] The text is translated from Eusebius' *Life of Constantine* 3.25–39, PG 20.1085–1100. The chapter-headings there included are a later addition, and not from Eusebius' hand, and no attempt has been made here to reproduce them. They have been replaced with sub-headings supplied by the present translator.

[2] The classic exposition of this point is that of E. Wistrand, *Konstantins Kirche am heiligen Grab in Jerusalem nach den ältesten literarischen Zeugnissen* (Göteborgs Högskolas Årsskrift 58). Göteborg 1952.

[3] On Constantine's policy for the Holy Land see Introduction, p. 10 above. Note that here the whole emphasis is on the resurrection, and that no mention is made of the crucifixion as a separate event with a separate location. Contrast Bord. 593–4, p. 158 above.

[4] The word "house" is constantly used to mean "church" or some part of a church by Eusebius; see G. Downey, "Constantine's Churches at Antioch, Tyre, and Jerusalem", in *MUJ* 38, (1961), fasc. 8.

[5] Recent examination suggests that a great part of the site was used as a quarry, which meant that any use for building entailed a great deal of filling. Note that Eusebius here ascribes to the "godless people" (i.e. to the Emperor Hadrian) the same motive of obliteration which in the next extract he ascribes to Constantine.

demon Aphrodite,[1] where they poured foul libations on profane and accursed altars . . .

—its destruction

27 As soon as he had issued his orders, this false device was cast to the ground . . . with its images and gods. The Emperor also commanded that the stone and timber of the ruins should be removed and dumped as far away as possible, and that a large area of the foundation soil, defiled as it was by devil-worship, should be dug away to a considerable depth, and removed to some distance.[2]

28 *The Holy Cave Revealed*

At once the work was carried out, and, as layer after layer of the subsoil came into view, the venerable and most holy memorial of the Saviour's resurrection,[3] beyond all our hopes, came into view; the holy of holies, the Cave,[4] was, like our Saviour, "restored to life" . . . by its very existence bearing clearer testimony to the resurrection of the Saviour than any words.[5]

[1] Jerome says that "From the days of Hadrian until the reign of Constantine, a period of about 180 years, a likeness of Jupiter was set up in the place of the resurrection, and a statue of Venus on the rock of the cross, which were worshipped by the heathen. The authors of persecution calculated that thus they might take away our faith in the resurrection and the cross if they defiled the holy places with their idols" (*Ep.* 58.3, *PL* 22.581, which goes on to mention the grove of Thammuz or Adonis which overshadowed the Bethlehem cave). The mention of the statue of Jupiter is a valuable supplement to what we are told by Eusebius. We know from Bord. 591, p. 157, n. 4 above, that a statue of Hadrian stood among the ruins of the Temple. We may thus have in the two halves of Jerusalem statues of the two figures who provided the pagan name of Jerusalem, Aelia Capitolina: Publius Aelius Hadrianus, and Jupiter Capitolinus.

[2] The clearing of the site produced an uneven rock slope which stretched westwards from the street of shops for about 150 yards. It seems that the forum immediately to the south of the site was left virtually untouched, but it is not this forum which Egeria describes (43.7), but more probably the street of shops.

[3] The Greek words for memorial and resurrection are *martyrion and anastasis.*

[4] The Cave receives attention, but there is no mention of the outcrop of rock which Bord. 593–4 may call "Golgotha". The description of the Cave as the "Holy of Holies" emphasizes its importance, and seems to have become a commonplace (see Ps-Cyril *Myst.* 1.11, *PG* 33.1076 and Jerome *Ep.* 46.5). The phrase combines with the name "New Jerusalem" in 33 below to contrast the new architectural creation on Jerusalem's western hill with the ruins of the Jewish Temple on the east of the Tyropoeon valley.

[5] An enduring testimony to the resurrection, as Cyril, *Cat.* 10.19, 14.22, *PG* 33.688, 853; but contrast the later understanding recorded by Egeria (30.1).

29 *Instructions to Build*

Thereupon the Emperor . . . gave orders that a house of prayer should be built in the precincts of the saving Cave,[1] rich, royal, and magnificent. It was as though he had long foreseen all this, and had by some superior acumen known what was going to happen. He ordered the governors of the eastern provinces to provide lavish supplies in order that the work should be extremely great and magnificent, and to the bishop then presiding over the Church in Jerusalem he wrote this letter:

30 THE VICTOR CONSTANTINE, MAXIMUS, AUGUSTUS TO MACARIUS[2] . . .

31 You are an able man, and it is your task to make all the arrangements and plans for the construction of a basilica[3] finer than any other. Moreover, the rest of the buildings must also be made finer than those in any other city.

—*responsibilities of imperial officers*

Know that to our friend, the Illustrious Dracilianus, Deputy of the Praetorian Prefects, and to the Governor of the Province, we have entrusted the planning and decoration of the walls. It is ordered, in My Piety, that they are to dispatch at once whatever in your judgement you may tell them is requisite in the way of craftsmen, labourers, and anything else for the building.

—*the columns and marble*

When the plans have been drawn up[4] see that you write and inform us of the quantity of columns and marble you judge to be

---

1 "In the precincts of" can also mean "round". It is not clear whether the Emperor intends a building like the Anastasis of Egeria's time, or simply buildings in the area of the Cave, but the following notes assume the latter, since Eusebius mentions no church except the one which Egeria calls "The Great Church, the Martyrium".

2 Macarius, bishop of Jerusalem, was already an old man by the time he received the letter, and did not in fact live to see the buildings completed.

3 The word *basilica* has not become a technical word here in its ecclesiastical sense (see Downey, op. cit., p. 191 and Bord. 594, n. 8) nor had it by the time of Egeria (see p. 158 above).

4 Jerome's *Chronicle* for the year 326 mentions a priest Eustathius sent from Constantinople who earned recognition for his zealous part in the work, and other chroniclers mention as well an architect called Zenobius; see, for example, Philostorgius, ed. J. Bidez, G.C.S. (Leipzig 1913), p. 208.

required to ensure that the building is as splendid as it should be. When we receive your estimate of the requirements, they can be supplied from all sources. The most wonderful place on earth deserves to be made also the most splendid.

2 —*the ceiling*

I desire to know from you how the roof of the basilica is to be made. Is it to be coffered? If so, it may be gilded as well.

God preserve you, dear Brother.[1]

3 *A New Jerusalem*

Once the Emperor had written this letter the work began to take shape, and over the true memorial of salvation was built the New Jerusalem, facing the far-famed Jerusalem of old time . . .[2]

THE BUILDINGS

The Holy Cave

First of all (since it was the principal feature) he adorned the holy Cave where the bright angel once announced good news of a new birth for all men, revealed through the Saviour. This principal feature the munificent Emperor adorned with choice columns and much ornament, sparing no art to make it beautiful.[3]

---

[1] Egeria believed that the Martyrium and Anastasis were built "in the presence of" the Emperor's mother Helena; see 25.9. Helena must have visited the site when she came and dedicated the churches on the Mount of Olives and at Bethlehem (Eusebius describes the visit in chapters 42–6, which come just after the extracts here printed; see *PG* 20.1102–5). But Eusebius mentions no special connection between the Empress and the buildings on Golgotha, even though her visit later became so renowned. See Note C, The Finding of the Cross, pp. 240–1 below.

[2] The Golgotha site looks across the Tyropoeon valley (Josephus' name for it; see *War* 5.4.1) to the Temple site.

[3] When Eusebius speaks of "adorning" the caves on the Mount of Olives and at Bethlehem (*VC* 3.41) he means in both cases the building of a complete church to enclose them, as well as garnishing the caves themselves. But here the Cave, according to the earliest representations, was itself adorned with columns (see Note D, p. 249 below); and Eusebius' omission of any mention of a building surrounding it combines with the description in Bord. 593–4 (see p. 158 above), and the evidence of Cyril (e.g. *Cat.* 14.22) to suggest that there was in their time one church building properly so called (what Egeria calls the Martyrium; cf. 46.1) and to the west of it the Cave, standing in an open cloister. Cf. Wistrand, op. cit., p. 24 and *VC* 4.46.

A Court

35 He passed on[1] to a vast area open to the sky. The Emperor paved it with polished stone, and surrounded it with long colonnades on three sides.

36 *A Church*

To the side opposite the cave (on the east) was attached a basilical church, a masterpiece.[2] It was enormously lofty, and of generous proportions.[3]

—its decoration

The inner surfaces of the building were finished with polychrome

---

[1] "Passed on" could equally mean "passed through", and has been thus interpreted by those who believe that the Anastasis had already been built. But recent excavation has revealed a preliminary stage of the layout of the Anastasis site before the building now there was begun, a rectangular space round the tomb, which seems to be what Eusebius is here describing (see Plan on p. 45 above). Although such an arrangement would well fit the words Eusebius uses, the great difficulty is that there is no record of the benefactor who

* added the Anastasis between the time of Eusebius and that of Egeria. It is conceivable that it was an Arian emperor, perhaps Valens, whose association with the site was submerged in the glorious memory of the orthodox Helena and the apostolic Constantine, but this cannot be more than pure speculation.

Eusebius himself provides evidence that the tomb could be regarded as an isolated feature in a wide space when, in the *Theophania* 3, PG 24.619, he describes the tomb (as the disciples saw it at the time of Christ's resurrection): "The tomb was a cave recently cut in the rock. . . . It was a marvellous sight that rock, the only thing standing in a wide space. And it contained but a single tomb . . . and a huge stone closed him in." This passage no doubt reflects the appearance of the site as Eusebius witnessed it, but whether it refers to its state on the discovery of the tomb, or after the site had received its architectural development, it is impossible to say (see Intro., p. 42 above). It may be to the open court that Cyril refers when he says that a garden used to be there, and that traces remained of it in his time (*Cat.* 14.5, PG 33.829).

Note also that one of the outstanding features of this court (whether or not the Anastasis was built) was the outcrop of rock, projecting about twelve feet high above the level of the pavement, which Cyril calls Golgotha (*Cat.* 10.19; 13.4; 13.39, PG 33.688,776,820), despite the fact that he also used the name Golgotha for the whole site of the Martyrium Church (e.g. *Cat.* 1.1; 13.22; 16.4, PG 33.372,800,924). Eusebius passes over this rock in silence, and makes no mention of any cross on it. But Egeria (whether or not she mentioned a cross) certainly treats it as the place where Christ's Cross was erected.

* [2] Little of this church has so far been excavated, but in 1967 the foundation of its apse was revealed, protruding westwards towards the holy Cave, in contrast to most other churches of the period which, like the Constantinian churches in Bethlehem and on the Mount of Olives, had their sanctuary at the east.

[3] Though not enormous by modern standards of judgement, this church was, as pointed out by Wistrand, op. cit., pp. 16–18, large in comparison with any churches built before Constantine's time. Cf. *VC* 2.46.1–3.

marble panels, and the outer surface of the walls was veneered with polished stones[1] which gave them a superb finish quite equal to marble.

—the roof

The outer covering of the roof was lead, a reliable protection against winter rain. The inside was carved and coffered, making a pattern of connected coffers which stretched over the whole basilica like a great sea.[2] It was all brightly gilded, and made the whole church shine and sparkle.

—double colonnades

Around the two sides were two rows of double colonnades, at ground level and above,[3] which stretched the whole length of the church. They had gilded roofs.

—the colonnade of the façade

The ones on the façade of the building[4] bear on huge columns, and those inside the façade are carried on pillars with heavy surface decoration.

—three doors

And three well-spaced doors[5] facing east receive the crowds going inside.

---

[1] One of the walls of the area known today as the Russian Excavation clearly shows the keying for this veneer; it is in fact an earlier wall (perhaps Hadrian's) which was incorporated into the Constantinian plan. *

[2] The coffered ceiling was presumably attached to cross-beams of the kind visible today in the Bethlehem church. Wooden roofs were used in early Palestinian churches, to judge from the thickness of their walls, and vaulted stone roofs were not usual until the time of the Crusaders in ecclesiastical buildings, though they are often found in the Roman secular buildings of Palestine.

[3] It is not clear whether these double rows of columns were inside the building * (thus making it a five-aisled church like the one at Bethlehem) or outside, as suggested by Telfer, *Cyril*, pp. 48–51 (thus giving the exterior appearance of a two-storeyed building). There are several passages which would support the view that the floor of this church was raised above the level of the surrounding courts; Cyril, *Cat.* 10.19, speaks of Golgotha as "this holy place which is raised above all others", and *AL* (Nos. 37, 43, 52) speaks of "descending from the Martyrium to the Anastasis", which is clearly a deliberate expression, since going in the other direction is described as "ascending" (No. 44).

[4] I.e. on the church; for "on the façade of" compare the description of the position of the fountains in the church at Tyre (Eusebius, *HE* 10.4.40, *PG* 20.865).

[5] I.e. the church doors, not those of the court, described in section 39 below.

38 —the hemisphere

At the end opposite to these doors was the principal feature, a hemisphere[1] which reached the full height of the basilica. It was crowned with columns, twelve of them, like the Saviour's holy apostles; their capitals were adorned with great silver bowls,[2] a splendid gift from the Emperor to his God.

39 The Entry Court

Going on towards the entries in front of the church he introduced a court. This was the entry court,[3] and it had colonnades on either side, and doors[4] at the far side.

The Entrance

And beyond, right in the middle of the street of shops[5] of the forum, was a marvellously ornate entrance, which allowed a breath-taking view of the interior to those passing by.[6]

[1] Since the word "hemisphere" is in itself ambiguous, it could mean a dome-shaped ciborium over the altar: another interesting suggestion is made by J. G. Davies in "Eusebius' Description of the Martyrium", *American Journal of Archaeology* (1957), pp. 171–3, who maintains that hemisphere usually means "dome". More probably the word refers to the semi-circular ground-plan of the apse, with a semi-circle of columns standing round the inner surface. They would thus form the "principal feature" of the basilica, as the holy Cave forms the principal feature of the whole complex of buildings (compare sections 33–4 above). This latter meaning is confirmed by the use of "hemisphere" in one of the fourth-century Mss. in the British Museum (Pap. London 755).

[2] These may have been free-standing columns surmounted by bowls (compare the pair of columns surmounted by statues on the Arch of Constantine (M. Gough, *The Early Christians* (London 1961), pl. 32)); or columns supporting an architrave, with their bowl-shaped capitals plated with silver; or the bowls may have been mosaics above the capitals (compare the design above the windows of the Orthodox Baptistery at Ravenna (Gough, op. cit., pl. 75) and for the use of mosaic in the decoration see Egeria 25.9).

[3] None of the sources mentions any provision of water in the entry court; but the one at Tyre is explicitly mentioned in Eusebius, *HE* 10.4.39, *PG* 20.865.

[4] These are the great doors of Egeria 43.7, and have been identified since the nineteenth century.

[5] The Jerusalem forum was in the conventional position (see Hyginus, *Munit. Castr.* 11.17.19, written shortly before the time of Hadrian), and remains of it are visible to the south of, and adjacent to, the church site. The Greek word for "street of shops" is *plateia*, lit. "avenue of colonnades" (see Milik in *MUJ* 37, fasc. 7 (1961), p. 161). But Eusebius is speaking of an entrance leading on to the street, not out of the side into the forum, though some such side-entrances may well have existed.

*   [6] The position of the ornate entrance was no doubt distinguished by colossal

) *Magnificence*

Such then was the church which the Emperor founded, an illustrious memorial of the saving resurrection, bright with rich and and royal splendour. And he adorned it with untold wealth of gifts—gold, silver, and many kinds of precious stone. But this is not the place for a detailed description of its craftsmanship, materials, dimensions, and decorations.[1]

---

columns breaking into the sequence of smaller columns which decorated the main streets, in the manner still visible at Jerash. Eusebius makes a point of mentioning the view from outside the precincts looking in; as in his description of the church at Tyre (*HE* 10.4.38–9).

[1] Eusebius in fact promises the Emperor a detailed description (see *VC* 4.4.6). But, if he ever wrote it, it has not survived.

Pseudo-Cyril's Mystagogical Lecture on the Eucharist

* In teaching the candidates for baptism Cyril (*c.* 350) or possibly his successor John (*c.* 390) gave an explanation of the Eucharist which describes what happens from before the prayer of consecration until after receiving Communion. This passage (*Cat.* 23.2–22, *PG* 33.1109–25) establishes an outline which Egeria seems to have accepted as normal, since she mentions very little in the service (apparently nothing in this part of it) which is different from what is done everywhere else (25.1). But it is probable that she did not wish to describe "the mysteries" in writing, and it is not certain that she was good enough at Greek to follow all that was said by the bishop (Cyril himself) who presided (see 47.3). The outline of the Eucharist described by Cyril is as follows:

2 *Washing the hands of the presbyters* (not because they were dirty, but as a symbol showing that you ought to be clean).

4 *The kiss:* "The deacon cries, Receive ye one another, and let us kiss one another" . . . (this kiss means reconciliation).

The Thanksgiving or prayer of consecration

Presbyter: Lift up your hearts.
People: We lift them up unto the Lord.
5 Presbyter: Let us give thanks to the Lord.
People: It is meet and right.

6 After this we make mention of heaven and earth and sea . . . angels . . . seraphim, who cried, "Holy holy holy".

7 Then . . . we call upon the merciful God to send forth his Holy Spirit upon the gifts lying before him, that he may make the bread the Body of Christ, and the wine the Blood of Christ. For whatever the Holy Spirit has touched is sanctified and changed.

8 Then, when the spiritual sacrifice is made perfect . . . we entreat God for the common peace of the Church, for the tranquillity of the world, for kings, for soldiers and allies, for the sick, for the afflicted, and in fact for everyone who needs help we all supplicate and offer this sacrifice.

9 Then we commemorate also those who have fallen asleep before us: first, the patriarchs, prophets, apostles, and martyrs, that at their prayers and intervention God would receive our prayer; and then on behalf of the holy fathers and bishops who have fallen asleep among us, believing that it will be of the greatest advantage to the souls for whom we offer prayer while that holy and most awesome sacrifice is being offered.

11 *The Lord's Prayer.*

20 Presbyter: Holy things to holy people!
   People: One is holy, One is the Lord Jesus Christ!

After this a singer invites you to the communion of the holy mysteries with a holy song, saying, "O taste and see that the Lord is good" (Ps. 34.9).

22 *The Communion*

(The communicants approach, and receive the consecrated bread and wine. Cyril instructs them to "make your left hand like a throne for your right, which is about to receive the King". On receiving they say Amen, and before consuming the bread they are to "hallow their eyes and forehead by the touch of the holy Body" [cf. Egeria 37.3 where the same thing is done with the Wood of the Cross]. They make a similar gesture with the wine from their lips when they have received from the cup.)

A prayer: Then wait for the prayer, and give thanks to God, who has accounted you worthy of such great mysteries.

The Letter in Praise of
the Life of the Most Blessed Egeria
written to his Brethren
Monks of the Vierzo by Valerius[1]

393 [1a] Holy brethren, beloved of God, I beseech you to consider with attention the vigour with which we must perform the various tasks which fall to us, if we are to obtain the reward of the kingdom of heaven. We revere the valorous achievements of the mighty saints who were men, but we are amazed when still more courageous deeds are achieved by weak womanhood, such deeds as are indeed described in the remarkable history of the most blessed Egeria, who by her courage outdid the men of any age whatever.

[1b] At that point of time when at length the gracious dawn of the catholic faith was seen, and after long delay our holy religion arrived with its bright and endless light at this part of the furthest West, a longing for God's grace set on fire the heart of this most
394 blessed nun Egeria. In the strength of the glorious Lord she fearlessly set out on an immense journey to the other side of the world. *Guided by God she pressed on until after a time she reached what she had longed for, the most holy places of the birth,[2] passion, and resurrection of the Lord, and of the bodies of countless holy martyrs*[3]

---

[1] Valerius was a monk in Galicia in the seventh century. The *Letter* was published with an introduction by Z. Garcia, "La Lettre de Valérius aux moines du Vierzo sur la bienheureuse Aetheria" in *A.B.* 29 (1910), pp. 377-99, to which the marginal numbers refer. The letters added to the section-numbers belong to the present translation.

The virgin's name appears in the manuscripts examined by Garcia in a variety of forms: Egeria (adopted in this translation), Echeria, Eiheria, Etheria, Heteria, and (Garcia's choice) Aetheria. See Note A, p. 235 below. Passages in italics refer to parts of Egeria's text now lost.

[2] Compare Peter the Deacon L1, p. 155 below.

[3] Many tombs of patriarchs and Old Testament worthies are mentioned by Egeria. Among the prophets (also considered as martyrs) are Habakkuk (PD, V.8), Obadiah (V.6), Amos (L.2), Elisha (V.6), Micah (V.8), and the prophet who attacked Jeroboam (V.7).

The New Testament saints are John Baptist (PD, V.6), James the Just (E), John the Evangelist (23.10), Thomas (17.1). The tombs of martyrs of later times are those at Batanis (19.1), Constantinople (23.9), and Heroöpolis (7.9); and those of Helpidius (20.5), Euphemia (23.7), and Thecla (22.2; 23.1).

in many different provinces and cities. Her purpose was to pray and to find edification; for the more she had advanced in holy doctrine, the more insatiably her holy longing burned in her heart.

[IC] *First with great industry she perused all the books of the Old and New Testaments, and discovered all its descriptions of the holy wonders of the world; and its regions, provinces, cities, mountains, and deserts.* Then in eager haste (though it was to take many years) she set out, with God's help, to explore them. *At length she penetrated the East, and there, according to her earnest desire, she visited the coenobia of the glorious congregations of holy monks in the Thebaid, and likewise the holy cells of the anachoretae.*[1] *Much fortified by the blessings of so many saints, and refreshed by the sweet nourishment of their charity, she left them, and went on to visit all the provinces of Egypt. With the greatest application she sought out, and then elegantly described, all the places where the children of Israel had lived during their ancient wanderings, the extent of each province, the marvellous fertility of the land,*[2] *and the remarkable buildings and other sights in the cities.*[3]

[2a] *Then at length, moved by the longing for a pilgrimage to pray at the most sacred Mount of the Lord, she followed in the footsteps of the children of Israel when they went forth from Egypt.*[4] *She travelled into each of the vast wildernesses and tracts of desert which are set forth in the Book of Exodus.*[5] *The children of Israel marched for three days, thirsty and without water; and when they murmured, and the Lord made Moses bring abundance of water out of the hard rock,*[6] *the hearts of those men remained ungrateful. She at that place thirsted for the Lord, and in her heart a fount of living water sprang up unto life eternal. That multitude hungered, and by God's dispensation received the holy manna coming down from heaven.*[7] *But even then they despised it, and longed for the accursed food of Egypt. She at that very place was refreshed by the Word of God, and, giving him unwearying thanks, went on her way without fear. They, many times hearing God's voice, could see his grace going before them by day and night in the pillar of*

---

[1] Compare Egeria's own reference to this journey (9.1,3).
[2] Compare 9.4, and PD, Y3.
[3] PD, Y1,6. [4] PD, Y5,8,9. [5] PD, Y11–12.
[6] PD, Y15. [7] PD, Y13.

cloud and fire; yet still they doubted, and thought to retrace their steps. But this woman, once having heard the voice of the gospel,[1] hastened to the Mount of the Lord, and went, you may be sure, joyfully and without the slightest delay. They, while Moses was receiving the Law of the Lord, could not wait forty days, and made themselves a graven image to take God's place[2]; but she awaiting the Lord's coming as though she could perceive it already, forgot her

396 female weakness, and went on to the holy Mount Sinai[3] (from which, in his time, we hope for him to come in the clouds of heaven). With unflagging steps, and upheld by the right hand of God, she hastened to that beetling summit with its top almost in the clouds; and thus, borne onwards by the power of her holy zeal, she arrived at the rocky mountain-top where the divine glory itself, God Almighty, condescended to abide whilst Moses was given the holy Law.[4] There her joyful exultation burst forth in paeans of prayer, and she offered to God the sacrifices of salvation,[5] and giving heartfelt thanks to his glorious Majesty, went forward again to see what lay beyond.[6]

[2b]   At length, not content with travelling to the bounds of almost the whole earth, she exerted herself to climb to the top of other great mountains. One was Mount Nebo (as lofty as the afore-mentioned Sinai) from whose summit blessed Moses looked across into the Promised Land, and on which he died,[7] and, they say, was buried by angels.[8] *Another was the mountain towering above Faran, extremely high, on the top of which Moses prayed with outstretched arms while the people fought until they had gained victory.*[9] *There was the dread eminence of Tabor, where the Lord appeared in his glory with Moses and Elijah;*[10] *an equally vast mountain called Hermon in which the Lord used to rest with his disciples;*[11] *and a third called Eremus, very lofty, on which he taught the disciples the Beatitudes.*[12]

397 *There was a very high mountain called the Mount of Elijah on which the Prophet himself dwelt, and the hundred prophets were hidden;*[13]

---

[1] At this point the manuscript of Egeria opens.
[2] Cf. 2.2; 5.1.   [3] Cf. 2.4.   [4] Cf. 3.2.
[5] Cf. 3.5.   [6] Cf. 4.1.   [7] Cf. 10.1 and PD, P2.
[8] Cf. 12.2.   [9] PD, Y15.
[10] PD, V1.   [11] PD, P3; V1.
[12] PD, V3.   [13] PD, V6.

and another like it which overhangs Jericho,[1] *sanctified, like the others, by the Lord.* All these different mountains she climbed under the guidance of One alone, and on each of them she offered her prayers to Almighty God with exultant joy and thanksgiving (for each of them had been provided with its altar and holy church).

[3] Thus, as we may clearly perceive, her heart and her whole being were on fire with an earnest longing to seek the kingdom of heaven on high, the joyful company of holy virgins in paradise, and the rewards of grace; so that she did not weary, and, even when she reached the summits of the most inaccessible mountains, the weakness of her body gave way, by God's help, before the burning desire in her heart, and she bore the effort lightly.[2] None can measure how her heart was chilled by her dread of the judgement to come, how warmly she was suffused by the devotion of her love for him who is Love, or how brightly her heart blazed with hope and faith in God. Nothing could hold her back, whether it was the labour of travelling the whole world, the perils of seas and rivers, the dread crags and fearsome mountains, or the savage menaces of the heathen tribes,[3] until, with God's help and her own unconquerable bravery, she had fulfilled all her faithful desires.

[4a] We cannot but blush at this woman, dearest brothers—we in the full enjoyment of our bodily health and strength. Embracing the example of the holy Patriarch Abraham, she transformed the weakness of her sex into an iron strength, that she might win the reward of eternal life; and while, compassed about with her weakness, she trod this earth, she was obtaining paradise in calm and exultant glory. Though a native of Ocean's western shore,[4] she became familiar with the East. While she sought healing for her own soul, she gave us an example of following God which is marvellously profitable for many. Here she refused rest, that she might with constancy attain to eternal glory and bear the palm of

---

[1] Cf. PD, P2 which does not mention this mountain (presumably Jebel 'Uruntul).
[2] Cf. 3.2 and PD.
[3] Cf. the Saracens (7.2) and the Isaurians (23.4).
[4] See 19.5 and cf. PD, Y10.

victory. Here she inflicted material burdens on her earthly body, that she might present herself irreproachable, a lover of heaven to heaven's Lord. Here, by her own will and choice she accepted the labours of pilgrimage, that she might, in the choir of holy virgins with the glorious queen of heaven, Mary the Lord's mother, inherit a heavenly[1] kingdom.

[4b] Thus, my beloved brethren, though we can scarcely deserve to merit God's grace in a measure equal to this exemplary woman, great beyond description, yet we have by our own choice promised to serve God faithfully in the religious life. And since there are many paths of righteousness, but all lead to our single native land, the kingdom of heaven; since also with God's help there remains virtue in labours, in watchings, in fastings, in frequent prayers, and all the observances which go to make up our obedience to our Rule, so we must be ready, and day and night without wearying abstain from all forbidden pleasures, and the snares of this world with its manifold wickedness. Otherwise, if we should spend this short time of ours in neglect, then we should know this: she will return to that very place where in this life she walked as a pilgrim, and there with the holy virgins and saints she will meet the Lord in the air at his coming. Her lamp will be alight with the oil of bright holiness, but we then (which God forbid!) shall be locked out, with the doors closed and our lamps gone out. Miserably cast out, we shall beg to be admitted to life, we who have awaited the Lord's coming with such sloth and idleness.

[4c] Remember then the words spoken by our Lord: "Walk while you have the light, lest the darkness overtake you", and "He who perseveres to the end, the same will be saved". For as each of us is when he departs this life, so he will be presented in the Judgement: that each may receive according to his works.

HERE ENDS THE LETTER IN PRAISE OF THE VIRGIN EGERIA

[1] "Heavenly" = *aetherea*.

Peter the Deacon's Book on the Holy Places

Peter the Deacon, a monk of Monte Cassino, and its librarian, wrote a work on the holy places, to which in 1137 he added a prologue and dedicated it to the newly elected Abbot Guibald. In the course of it he reveals two important facts: the first, that he collected what he had written from "I might say, all the books", and the second, that he expected the contents of the book to be generally familiar to Guibald because of what he had already learned by meeting people who had been to see the Sepulchre of the Lord, or by his own reading.

The books which Guibald had read would doubtless include the travels of pilgrims to the Latin Kingdom, which had by 1137 been established in Jerusalem for nearly forty years, and it is clear that Peter used at least one of these in writing his own compilation. Peter himself used two others which can be identified, and possibly more.

The most important source is Bede's work on the Holy Places,[1] which provides the majority of Peter's material. His procedure was to reproduce one of Bede's chapters, and then to add to it information from other sources. He tends to follow his sources fairly closely as far as vocabulary is concerned, only occasionally giving a modern word where an old one might be misunderstood,[2] and he makes no attempt to harmonize the information given in the different books he uses.[3] Thus, Bede provides the framework for his book, but it is not known how it ended, since Peter's manuscript is incomplete.

Next in importance to Bede comes Egeria, and Peter may have used the very manuscript which later found its way to Arezzo. He abbreviates and modifies her account more than Bede's since Bede, like Peter, was writing an impersonal account compiled from books, and his text could almost be copied, while Egeria was writing about her own daily experiences. But there are many traces of her style even in Peter's condensed version.[4] Here is an example of the way he handles his original:

EGERIA 3.8.

... from beside the church where we were standing, on the summit of the central mountain, the mountains round us, which had been almost too much for us to climb, were down below. They only looked like little hillocks beside us

PETER Z.15

From the summit of the central mountain the other very lofty mountains below look like little hillocks.

[1] The latest edition is that of I. Fraipont, C.C.S.L. 175, pp. 252-80, which includes the parallel passages of Peter the Deacon.
[2] E.g. sepulchrum (Y17) for memoria (Egeria 1.1)
[3] The Temple of the Lord stands in C3, but is destroyed in E.
[4] See especially section Y.

when we stood on the central mountain, but in fact I do not think I have
ever seen any that were bigger.

This passage is taken from the last part of Peter's manuscript, which
overlaps the first part of Egeria's.[1]

In the translation which follows, the parts printed in italics are those
which seem to come from the twelfth-century source, while those in
roman may come from Egeria. Peter, however, has a practice of slip-
ping short passages of one source into longer passages from another,
and it is by no means possible to guarantee that all the passages here
shown in roman are from Egeria in all their details.

The surest guide to the passages which belonged to her original text
is the *Letter* of Valerius,[2] since all the places he mentions occur somewhere in Peter's work, even though for some of them Peter has taken
his descriptions from some source later than Egeria.

Peter the Deacon's treatise was first edited in 1729,[3] and several
editions were made in the nineteenth century.[4] The text has been most
conveniently arranged in *Corpus Christianorum*, vol. 175, pp. 94–103,
where the sections which reproduce Bede or the existing manuscript
of Egeria are printed with their originals, and those which have no
parallels are collected in an appendix to Egeria (op. cit., pp. 93–103).
These sections are distinguished by letters in the *Corpus Christianorum*
and the same letters are used in the extracts printed here. All the passages
which may have been extracted from Egeria are included, below, but
the prologue and sections which come directly from Bede, have been
omitted.

A (Prologue)

B JERUSALEM AND ITS HOLY PLACES
(≑ Bede sections 1–2a)

C1 *The Sepulchre of the Lord,*[5] *of which we have spoken above, has been*

---

[1] They are set out together in *C.C.S.L.* 175, pp. 37–47, and the overlap extends
as far as Egeria's chapter 7.3.

[2] See pp. 174–8 above.

[3] This edition contained only the prologue; it formed part of E. Martène and
U. Durand, *Veterum scriptorum et monumentorum . . . amplissima collectio*, vol. 6
(Paris 1729), col. 789–91.

[4] E.g. D. Tosti's of 1842, which was reprinted in Migne, *PL* 173. 1115–34, and
P. Geyer's in *C.S.E.L.* 38 (Vienna 1898), pp. 105–21.

[5] This name is in common use in the twelfth century, but never used by Egeria,
who speaks of "the screen" and "the cave".

constructed in the middle of a temple,[1] and the temple is in the city centre towards the north, not far from David's Gate.[2] Behind the Resurrection is a garden in which holy Mary spoke with the Lord.[3] Behind the church and outside it is the Centre of the World,[4] the place of which David said, "Thou hast worked salvation in the midst of the earth." Also another prophet says, "This is Jerusalem: I have set her in the midst of the nations".[5]

2   And on Golgotha is part of the Wood of the Saving[6] Cross to which the Lord was fastened, and the Title, which is placed in a silver box. Also in that place is the Horn with which the kings were anointed, and the Ring of Solomon. *Not far from the Centre of the World is the Prison;[7] and there is his binding and scourging, and near there is his robbing and the division of his garments.[8]*

On Calvary,[9] where the Lord was crucified, the mountain is cleft,[10] and one goes up on to this Mount Calvary by seventeen steps, and nine lamps hang there, each with a silver cloth. Below is Golgotha, where Christ's blood fell on the cleft stone.

3   *To the east, below Mount Calvary, is the Temple of the Lord, in*

---

[1] I.e. the "circular" church which represented the twelfth-century development of Constantine's Anastasis; see Daniel 10, *IRO*, p. 12 (1106, i.e. before the Latin restoration of the church) and Ernoul 9, *IJ*, p. 36 (1200, when the restoration had been done; compare p. 44 above).

[2] This name is first found in Adamnan 1.3 (*C.C.S.L.* 175, p. 185) (c. 680).

[3] The garden is mentioned in John 19.41, and also by Cyril (*Cat.* 14.5). But no fourth-century pilgrims mention it, and it reappears as the place "where he first appeared after his Resurrection to Mary Magdalene" in Cont. Wm of Tyre 9, *IJ*, p. 164 (1261).

[4] Cyril (*Cat.* 13.28) puts forward the idea that Golgotha is the centre of the earth, also quoting Ps. 74.12, but the idea does not appear again till Adamnan 11, *C.C.S.L.* 175, p. 195. It was then marked by a column, and the mark in 1231 was called the *Compas* (*Les Pèlerinages* 6, *IJ*, p. 93). Since it was also mentioned by Daniel 10, *IRO*, p. 14, the tradition was apparently continuous.

[5] Ezek. 5.5.

[6] Not one of Egeria's words; otherwise cf. 37.1,3.

[7] The first witness to the prison here is the ninth-century Greek *Typicon*.

[8] The abstract nouns (apart from the "robbing", *dispoliatio*) might be relics as in G below, but are more likely the names of two chapels, the Flagellation and Parting of the Garments, both mentioned by Saewulf (1102).

[9] Egeria does not use the word "Calvary", still less distinguish between Calvary and Golgotha. This is like the arrangement described by Daniel 11–12, *IRO*, pp. 14–15.

[10] The cleft is noticed by Cyril (*Cat.* 13.39, *PG* 33.820), and by Rufinus (*Hist.* 9.6, *G.C.S. Eus.* 2.2, p. 815), but is not mentioned by pilgrims till the Latin Kingdom.

another part of the city, which was built by Solomon. It has four doors, the first on the east, the second on the west, the third on the south, and the fourth on the north, which signify the four quarters of the world, and outside it has eight corners, each one turning a corner of twelve paces. In the middle of the Temple is a great mount surrounded by walls, in which is the Tabernacle; there also was the Ark of the Covenant which after the destruction of the Temple was taken away to Rome by the Emperor Vespasian.[1]

On the left side of the Tabernacle the Lord Jesus Christ placed his foot, on the occasion when Symeon took him in his arms, and his footprint remains there exactly as if it had been made in wax. And on the other side of the rock is the opening of the Tabernacle, into which people go down by twenty-two steps. There the Lord prayed, and there also Zacharias offered sacrifice. Outside the Temple is the place where Zacharias the son of Barachias was killed.[2] Above the rock in the middle of the Temple is a golden lamp containing the blood of Christ which fell down through the cleft rock.

C4   *And not far away to the south has been built the Temple of Solomon,[3] in which he lived, which has twenty-five doors. There are 362 columns inside it, and not far away the Cradle of Christ[4] and his Bath, and the bed of the Holy Mother of God. Below the Temple of the Lord to the east is the Gate Beautiful, by which the Lord came in, sitting on the foal of an ass. It was there also that Peter healed the lame man. To the north is the Church of Saint Anne,[5] where Blessed Mary was nurtured for three years. And near it is the Sheep Pool,[6] which has five porches.*

---

*   [1] Cf. the mention of Tiberius in another late passage, G below. This passage describes the Dome of the Rock in the way common among French pilgrims of the twelfth century, though they seem to take the building to be the Temple itself, while the Russian Daniel clearly says it was built by "Amor", a Saracen leader (17, IRO, p. 20). Compare *Les Pèlerinages* 7, IJ, pp. 94–5.

*   [2] This is an ancient commemoration; cf. Bord 591, p. 157, n. 2 above, but the mention taken from Egeria is probably that at the end of E below.

*   [3] I.e. the Mosque el 'Aqsā; for the architectural history see K. A. C. Creswell *A Short Account of Early Muslim Architecture* (Harmondsworth 1958), pp. 204–213.

[4] This name originated with the Muslims; cf. Bord. 590, p. 156, n. 7 above.

[5] This name was first recorded by Saewulf (1102).

[6] *Piscina Probatica*, the name preserved in association with the churches near by; cf. John 5.2. But Eusebius *On, Bethsaida*, already speaks of the five porches as if they had disappeared.

D JERUSALEM: SION AND OTHER HOLY PLACES
(≑ Bede 2b)

E   And in the church called Holy Sion[1] is the Throne of James,[2] the Lord's brother, who is buried near the Temple.[3] It has been built in the place where after his passion the Lord appeared to the disciples as they were at supper, "the doors being shut".[4] Near there is the door by which the angel led Peter out.[5] And of the Temple which Solomon built there have survived two pinnacles: one, much the higher, is where the Lord was tempted by the Devil.[6] But the rest of the Temple has been destroyed.[7] The Temple had been built on the threshing-floor of Araunah the Jebusite.[8] Near its gate was shed the blood of Zacharias the son of Barachias.[9]

[1] Nothing in section E need be later than Egeria's time. Though note that the phrase "Holy Sion" does not appear in her text as we have it, and "Holy" is probably an addition by Peter. Otherwise what he writes about the Lord's resurrection appearance here agrees well with Egeria 39.5 and 43.3, and probably derives from her main description of the church.

[2] Eusebius frequently mentions a throne in connection with James (e.g. *HE* 2.11.1,2; 2.23.1) and in *HE* 7.19 he writes: "Now the Throne of James, who was the first to receive from the Saviour and the apostles the throne of the episcopate of the Church at Jerusalem (who also, as the Divine Books show, was called a brother of Christ) has been preserved to this day; and by the honour paid to it by the brethren in succession there, they show clearly to all the reverence in which the holy men were and still are held." A throne of James is shown in the present-day Armenian Cathedral not far from Sion.

[3] Eusebius (*HE* 2.23.18) also says that "they buried him at the place beside the Temple", and that his monument remains there. In this passage he is quoting Hegesippus, who wrote in the second century. Its exact position in early tradition is uncertain, but it may well have been pointed out in the place assigned to it today, i.e. between the tombs of "Absalom" and "Zechariah".

[4] John 20.19,26; cf. above, n. 1.

[5] The "Iron gate that leadeth into the city" of Acts 12.10 seems here to be in a position near the modern Sion Gate. It linked Jerusalem proper to the walled area called Sion, which contained the disciples' house to which Peter went.

[6] Cf. Matt. 4.5. Bord. 590 mentions only one pinnacle.

[7] Cf. C4 (or 3 ?) above. Peter gives no explanation to account for this discrepancy.   *

[8] See 2 Sam. 24.18, and cf. Bord. 587 and p. 154, n. 8 above, and 591.

[9] Three Zachariahs come to be confused: there is the son of Berechiah, the prophet (Zech. 1.1), there is the son of Jehoiada who prophesied against Joash, and was stoned "in the court of the house of the Lord" (2 Chron. 24. 20-2), and there is Zacharias the father of St John Baptist. J. Jeremias, *Hg*, p. 67, shows that the two Zachariahs of the Old Testament were already seen as one by the time Matt. 23.35 was written, and cites a story from a *Chronicle* by the seventh or eighth-century writer, Hippolytus of Thebes,

F ACELDAMA: THE HEADCLOTH OF CHRIST
(≑ Bede 3–4a)

G   *And the Headcloth with which Christ wiped his face, otherwise
known as the Veronica,*[1] *was taken away to Rome in the time of
Tiberius Caesar. And the Reed with which his head was struck, his
Sandals and the Bonds with which he was bound, his Circumcision and
his Blood are reverently honoured in Rome.*[2]

H VALLEY OF JEHOSHAPHAT
MOUNT OF OLIVES AND BETHANY
(≑ Bede 4b–6)

* I   *Across the Brook Kidron is a cave, and above it a church, where on the
Thursday after supper, the Jews arrested the Saviour.*[3] This place is at
the head of the Valley of Jehoshaphat. In this valley stood the
palm from which the children[4] took branches when they cried
Hosanna.[5] Also on the Mount of Olives is a splendid cave with an
altar in it, where the Lord used to teach his disciples,[6] and over the

---

which confuses the resulting character with the Zacharias of the New Testament; compare also Kopp, p. 88, who shows that even Origen followed this
*   opinion, and *Protev. James* 23.1–3, Hennecke I, p. 387, which is later than
Origen.

[1] The whole of this section is from Peter's twelfth-century source, for, though
the Veronica legend began to take shape early (see the fourth-century *Acts of
Pilate*, Hennecke I, p. 457, cf. p. 484, the cloth did not come to be called the
Veronica till the twelfth century (the first witness is Giraldus Cambrensis,
Speculum Ecclesiae 6).

[2] These relics, if in Rome by Egeria's time, would certainly have deserved a
mention in the *Liber Pontificalis* (sixth century), but it does not speak of them.

* [3] The cave of Gethsemane is not mentioned in the fourth century, and, when it
came to be used, it seems that it was simply a tomb-chamber, with arrangements for worship. See V. Corbo *Ricerche Archeologici al Monte degli Ulivi*
(= Pubblicazioni dello Studium Biblicum Franciscanum No. 16) (Jerusalem
1965), pp. 1–57. Corbo produces no evidence of its use before the fifth century.
Neither Bord. 594, p. 159, n. 3 above, nor Egeria 36.2–3 speaks of a church at
the place of Christ's arrest, still less of a church above a cave.

[4] Cf. Bord. 595, p. 159, n. 5 above on the mention of children, and Matt. 21.4–9.

[5] Cyril (*Cat.* 10.19, *PG* 33.688) is the last witness to speak of this tree as standing.
It may well have died not long before Egeria's visit.

* [6] Cf. Mark 13.3ff. All that was left of the Eleona after its destruction by the
Persian invaders in 614 was part of the substructure of the courtyard, and this
became connected specifically with Christ's teaching of the Lord's prayer;
cf. Daniel 24, *IRO*, p. 24, or Ernoul 25, *IJ*, p. 51. If, as is likely, the *Acts of John*
(Bonnet 97, Hennecke 2, p. 232) provide the earliest evidence for the veneration
*   of the cave at the Eleona, it is interesting that even at this early stage the teach-

cave a large holy church. *Not far away is the martyrium of holy Stephen,*[1] and not far from that is the place where the Lord prayed, when his sweat became like drops of blood.[2] And on the road to Bethany is the village from which the ass was brought.[3]

K BETHLEHEM
(≑ Bede 7)

1   *Near Bethlehem*[4] is the pool where the Rabshakeh uttered his reproaches.[5] The well from which David wanted water is next to the mouth of a cave,[6] and in a valley in Bethlehem are the tombs of the kings of Judah.[7] Not far from there is the church called At the Shepherds.[8] A big garden is there now, protected by a neat

---

ing was intimately connected with the passion. The description given here accords well with Egeria 33.2. Note the words a "splendid" (*lucida*) cave "with an altar in it", which recur, for example, in V6 below, a passage almost certainly Egeria's, and are probably both a regular part of her vocabulary; the words of Valerius (2b, end, p. 177 above) suggest that Egeria's descriptions contained more mentions of altars than remain in the existing manuscript.

[1] The Martyrium of St Stephen, built by Melania the Younger, and dedicated in 439, was inside the colonnade of the Imbomon; see Milik, *R.B.* 67 (1960), pp. 558-9. The later basilica built by Eudocia was little visited, owing to its association with lepers, and the Martyrium on the Mount of Olives was ✳ probably the principal sanctuary of St Stephen; cf. Milik, *R.B.* 67 (1960), p. 567 whose evidence rests on a ninth-century document.

[2] Luke 22.44; this site seems to be near the summit rather than at the foot of the ✳ Mount of Olives; cf. Egeria 36.2 and *AL*, 40, also Bord. 594, p. 159. n. 3 above.

[3] Egeria 29.4 describes this in different words, but the words in Peter's text rest on Luke 19.30: it is therefore impossible to ascribe this or "the place where the Lord prayed" with certainty either to Egeria or to a twelfth-century source.

[4] This site was in fact in Jerusalem, see following note. But Egeria certainly described Bethlehem; see Valerius 1b, p. 174 above.

[5] 2 Kings 18.17 makes it clear that this event took place at "the conduit of the upper pool" (cf. also Isa. 7.3), at the north end of Hezekiah's tunnel. The ✳ event is not mentioned by other pilgrims, and probably depends on Egeria, though the mistake is probably introduced by Peter in the course of his transcription.

[6] See 2 Sam. 23.14-16. The well and tomb-caves are probably Biyar Da'ūd, half a mile north-north-west of the Church of the Nativity, on a spur of the hill on which Bethlehem stands. See B. Bagatti, "Recenti scavi a Betlemme" in *LA* 18 (1968), pp. 181-237.

[7] See Bord. 598, p. 162, n. 3 above. The tombs have not been identified.

[8] Luke 2.9. The name is formed in the same way as "On Horeb" (Egeria 4.1), or "Where Melchizedek" (13.4). Jerome, *Ep.* 46.12 (cf. 108.10) speaks of this site as "the Folds of the Shepherds", but, assuming that the text above is to be attributed to Egeria, it would be the earliest mention of a church on the site. The place is Deir er Ru'āt, as argued by Kopp, pp. 36-47.

wall all round, and also there is a very splendid cave with an altar. It is the place where the angels appeared to the shepherds as they kept watch, and brought them the news of Christ's birth.

L2   In Anathoth is the tower where the prophet Jeremiah uttered his Lamentations.[1] It is four miles[2] from Jerusalem. Twelve miles from Jerusalem is the tomb of the holy prophet Amos, at the place called Tekoa.[3] On the way there you can see across to the mountain which was constructed by Herod, where he made himself a palace above the desert which goes down to the Dead Sea.[4] In Timnath-serah is the tomb of holy Joshua the son of Nun, and in it are stone swords which were used for circumcising the children of Israel for the second time.[5] A church has been built there, and it is twenty miles from Jerusalem.[6] On another mountain two miles away[7] is the church in which rest the bodies of holy Eleazar and Phinees.[8] Nine miles from Jerusalem there is a church at

[1] See Jer. 1.1. The tower is not mentioned by other pilgrims, nor in *On*, *Anathoth*, and its location is unknown.

[2] Various distances are mentioned in this section, none of which agree with those given in the *Onomasticon*. Indeed, in all the sections which may be attributed to Egeria there is only one such agreement, which suggests that she did not know it. In any case there is no indication that she knew enough Greek to read it.

[3] Cf. Amos 1.1. Only one tomb of Amos was ever shown in Jewish and Christian tradition; see, for example, Eusebius, *On*, *Theco*, *Elthece*, and Jeremias, *Hg*, p. 87. Tekoa is today a large area of ruins called Khirbat Tequ', five miles south of Bethlehem. When the present excavations are completed there, it may be possible to find some relation between the church (of which the font has long been visible) and the tomb of Amos, which is probably a near-by cave.

[4] For the Herodium cf. Josephus, *Ant.* 15.9.4; 17.8.3.

[5] Timnath-heres (Judg. 2.9) or Timnath-serah (Josh. 24.30) was in Jewish tradition located at Thamna, as in Josephus, *Ant.* 1.29. But the Samaritans may have believed in an alternative site at Kefr Ḥaras; see Jeremias, *Hg*, pp. 40-2. On a hill immediately to the south of the ruins of Thamna (Khirbat Tibneh) M. V. Guérin found an impressive group of cave-tombs, and in Qubbat el Andiah, the largest, many flint knives (cf. Josh. 5.2). Its fine pillared entrance is now destroyed, but can still be identified by the many niches in its walls, which were probably intended for lamps. See Guérin's *Description géographique, historique, et archéologique de la Palestine* 2 (La Samarie) (Paris 1875), pp. 89-104, and F. de Saulcy, *Voyage en Terre Sainte* 2 (Paris 1865), pp. 227-30.

[6] Jerome mentions the place three times in the *Onomasticon* (*Thamnathsara*, *Aenam*, *Gaas*) and again in his Letter about Paula (108.13), but never says that there is a church there; cf. note on P4 below.

[7] Gaash; see Josh. 24.(30),33.

[8] Josephus, like the Hebrew text of Josh. 24.33, speaks of Gibeah of Phinees as the burial place of the Eleazar who, as Aaron's son, succeeded him in the high-

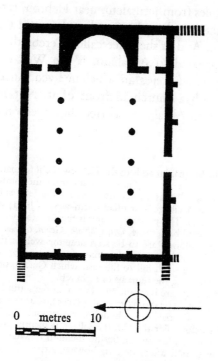

0 metres 10

AN EARLY CHURCH BUILDING AT DEIR EL AZAR
(Kiriath Jearim)

Kiriath-Jearim, the place where the Ark of the Lord used to be.[1]

M HEBRON AND MAMRE
(≑ Bede 8)

N1   Twenty-four miles from Jerusalem, near Hebron, is the spring in which Philip, the apostle and evangelist,[2] baptized the eunuch of Queen Candace. And at the place called Terebinthus, where the three angels appeared to Abraham, is the Well of Abraham,[3] *and the two very splendid caves*[4] in which he lived. An altar has been erected there with a church in front of it. Not far off is the mountain to which Abraham escorted the angels on their way to Sodom.[5]

---

    priesthood. The Septuagint adds to the Hebrew the information that Phinees also was buried there. In the Samaritan tradition the tomb of Eleazar and Phinees (and Ithamar) was at 'Awarta, but for the Jews and Christians the tomb was at Jībia, a village four miles north-west of Jifnā; see Jeremias, *Hg*, pp. 38–40 and 48–9. The present passage is the first to mention a church at Jībia (not mentioned by Jerome, *On, Gabiath, Gebin,* or *Gaas*; cf. note on P4 below). Ancient columns are to be seen near the well in the village, Nebi Bayāzīd el Bastānī, and there are the ruins of some large ancient buildings at Khirbat es Siyā on a small hill to the east, which Guérin, op. cit., pp. 106–9 identified as containing the remains of a church.

*

[1] See 1 Sam. 7.1–2. There is an ancient church on the summit of Deir el Āzar above the village of Abu Ghosh (see *R.B.* 4 (1907), p. 415) which may already have been built in Egeria's time, though not mentioned in *On, Cariathiarim*; cf. note on P4 below. For the *On.* the village is mentioned as the home of Uriah the prophet (cf. Jer. 26.22), but no mention is made of the ark of the covenant. The second association is, however, the one celebrated in the Armenian Lectionary (see No. 61).

[2] Philip the apostle (Mark 3.18) was commonly identified in early times with Philip the Deacon (Acts 6.5); see Acts 8.38, and cf. Bord 599, who describes the site at Bethsur also described here.

[3] The Well is also mentioned by Bord 599, pp. 162–3 above; for the site see E. Mader, *Mambre: die Ergebnisse der Ausgrabungen im Heiligen Bezirk Rāmet el-Halīl in Südpalästina 1926–28* (Freiburg im Breisgau 1957), esp. p. 110, Zeichnung 40, and Plan 1.

[4] Macpelah (Gen. 23.9) is rendered "double cave" by LXX, and this reference to "two caves" is probably a confusion between Hebron and Terebinthus. Indeed, it may well be that the two caves are mentioned here because section N1 above is a violent abridgement of what Egeria wrote, and this suspicion is strengthened by the fact that N1 ends at Kefr Barucha (beyond Hebron). In this case the whole of N2 can be assigned to a twelfth-century source.

[5] See Gen. 18.16; this is the Kefr Barucha mentioned by Jerome, *Ep.* 108.11, now Bani Na'īm.

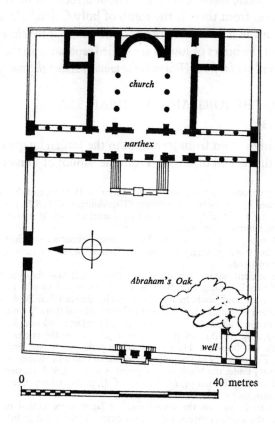

church

narthex

Abraham's Oak

well

0   40 metres

THE SANCTUARY AT TEREBINTHUS

2   *In Hebron itself stands the House of David.*[1] *Part of it remains, and to this day people still go to pray in the chamber where he lived. Not far out of Hebron—three hundred yards off, at the place called Abramiri—is the House of Jacob, where a church without a roof has been built.*[2] *Fifty yards on from there is the tomb of holy Caleb.*[3] *Abramiri is a vineyard, and in it is the cave where rest the bodies of the eleven Sons of Jacob*[4] *(but the bones of Joseph are buried separately in their own church*[5]*). And not far from Hebron is the tomb of Abner the son of Ner.*[6]

O   JERICHO, THE JORDAN, THE DEAD SEA
     (≑ Bede 9–13)

* P1 If a man wishes to go from Jerusalem to the Jordan he goes down by way of the Mount of Olives. From the Mount of Olives Christ

[1] 2 Sam. 2.3 witnesses to the fact that David lived in Hebron, and the same fact is mentioned by sixth-century pilgrims (Theodosius 5, C.C.S.L. 175, p. 117; Adamnan 2.8.1, C.C.S.L., p. 209) and by Daniel in 1106. But none of these mention the house as an oratory.

[2] Cf. Bord. 599, p. 163, n. 1 above. The "church without a roof" is the Ḥaram el Khalīl, but it is here strangely called the "house" when it actually contained the tomb of Jacob.

[3] Hebron's ancient name "Kiriath-Arba" (Gen. 23.2) was thought to mean "City of Four"; thus a fourth name had to be found to add to those of Abraham, Isaac, and Jacob. In about A.D. 200 R. Banna'a (b.B.B.58a) gave the interpretation of Josh. 14.15 "Adam the Great is placed there", which Jerome included in the Vulgate (cf. Q. in Gen. 32.2, PL 23.972 and com. Matt. 27.33, PL 26.209; Epp. 108.11; 46.3). But Jerome also knew the ancient tradition that Caleb was buried in Hebron (based on Josh. 14.13); see Jeremias, Hg, pp. 96–8. The memory of Joseph replaced that of Caleb in Hebron only in the tenth century under the Muslims (Hg, pp. 96–8 and 100), and was then adopted by Christians (e.g. Daniel 54, IRO, p. 45; cf. IJ, p. 70), which means that this sentence probably comes from Egeria.

[4] Despite a tradition that the eleven sons of Jacob were buried in Hebron attested in the second century B.C. by, for example, the Book of Jubilees 46.9 (cf. Josephus, Ant 2.8.2), the early Christian location was in Shechem, following Acts 7.15–16. The earliest pilgrim to say that they were buried in Hebron is Daniel 53, IRO, p. 45. See Jeremias, Hg, pp. 95–6, who is surely correct in assuming that Antoninus (30, C.C.S.L. 175, p. 144) said that Joseph's tomb was at Mamre simply through a misunderstanding.

[5] This probably refers to Joseph's tomb near Nablus; see section R below, and Exod. 19.13; Josh 24.32. But it might equally well refer to a church near the "church without a roof", the very building described above as the tomb of Caleb (N2, n. 3). The second supposition is the more probable, since it would mean less interlocking of the two sources.

[6] 2 Sam. 3.32 (cf. Josephus, Ant. 7.1.6). This is the only Christian reference to Abner's tomb, but since it agrees with the medieval Jewish location, it most probably comes from Peter's late source. See Jeremias, Hg, pp. 99–100.

ascended to heaven, *and it was there that he made the Pater Noster.*[1]

Mount Sion is to the south; there holy Mary died, and there the Lord had the Supper with the disciples.[2] There too he sent the Holy Spirit on the disciples.

And in the church which is in Bethlehem is the table at which Holy Mary ate with the three kings[3] *who came seeking Christ the Son of God. Inside this church are sixty-four columns.*[4] There rest the children killed for Christ by Herod.[5]

It is still possible to see part of the foundations of the walls of the city of Jericho, the ones which were overthrown by Joshua the son of Nun.[6] And *next to*[7] the house of Rahab is the sycamore tree into which Zacchaeus climbed. Not far from Jericho is the place where Elijah was caught up into heaven;[8] and across the Jordan are some very high mountains, among them a specially lofty one called Nebo.[9] This is the one which Moses climbed when he surveyed the Promised Land, and then died. *Not far from Jerusalem is Gibeon, which was captured by*[10] *Joshua, and sixty stades from Jerusalem is Emmaus,*[11] *where the Lord had the supper with his*

---

[1] The final phrase cannot be Egeria's; see p. 184, n. 6 above.

[2] The Dormition of the Blessed Virgin Mary was not definitely attached to Mount Sion till the seventh century (cf. B. Meistermann, *Guide de Terre Sainte* ✱ (Paris 1936), p. 186), and the Last Supper not till the sixth (cf. Kopp, pp. 326–331); neither is mentioned by Jerome when he describes St Paula's visit to Sion in *Ep.* 108.9.

[3] Jerome's descriptions of Bethlehem are sufficiently detailed to have included this table, even if it had been omitted by other writers merely visiting Bethlehem. We may safely assume that it was not yet there in his time, and that this passage comes from Peter's late source.

[4] The (inaccurate) counting of pillars is also a characteristic of the late passage C4 above.

[5] Though no fourth-century sources mention the burial-place of the Innocents, they have a feast-day in the fifth century (*AL*, No. 55), and a church was built in the fifth or sixth century beside the south wall of the basilica in their honour; see Milik *R.B.* 67 (1960), p. 573.

[6] Josh. 6.20; see Bord 597, p. 161, n. 2 above.

[7] "Next to" seems to be a careless transcription by Peter, since Bord 596, p. 160, n. 5, shows that the two sites were some way apart.

[8] See Bord 598, p. 161, n. 7.

[9] Cf. Egeria 12.5.

[10] "Captured" seems to be another misunderstanding which is more likely to be Peter's than Egeria's; see Josh. 9.18.

[11] Christians of Palestine all believed from the fourth century onwards that the Emmaus of Luke 24.13 was Nicopolis, seventeen miles away from Jerusalem. This opinion is reflected not only by Eusebius (*On, Emmaus*) and Jerome (*Ep.* 108.8) but also in those manuscripts of the Gospel which give "160" for "60"

disciples after the resurrection. In the Tower Cades was the house of Jacob, and its foundations can still be seen today.[1]

3   In Galilee is Shunem, the village of Abishag the Shunammite[2] and of the woman in whose house Elisha stayed—and the house is still there today.[3] Mount Hermon[4] is very lofty, and from it there is a view over the whole of Galilee, unequalled for beauty, since the whole vast plain is vineyards and olive-groves. The field is there in which the Lord ate with his disciples,[5] and you can still see the stone on which he rested his arm. Not far from this mountain is a spring which the Saviour blessed, and it does good to sick people of all kinds.[6]

4   In the village of Nain is the house of the widow whose son was brought back to life, which is now a church, and the burial-place where they were going to lay him is still there to this day.[7]

---

stades. Western Christians living in Jerusalem during the twelfth century began to use places nearer Jerusalem to commemorate Emmaus (see L. H. Vincent and F. M. Abel, *Emmaüs, sa Basilique et son Histoire* (Paris 1932), pp. 358–61), and PD may thus be quoting from his later source here.

[1] Cades (for Gader, Gen. 35.21) was closely associated with the Place of the Shepherds (see L1 below, *On, Bethlehem,* and Jerome, *Ep.* 108.10, who speaks as if the tower was still standing).

[2] 1 Kings 1.3.

*   [3] 2 Kings 4.8–10. *On, Sonam* agrees with the description above.

[4] Psalm 89.12 speaks of "Tabor and Hermon", and, probably through the familiarity of the association, a hill in the neighbourhood of Tabor acquired the name Hermon, Hermoniim, or Little Hermon (see Jerome, *Epp.* 46.12; 108.13). The hill which was pointed out in the fourth century was Jebel Duḥī, five miles south of Tabor, which has Shunem (P3) on its southern flank and Nain (P4) on the northern. It was certainly visited by Egeria (see Valerius 2b, p. 176, n. 11 above). The field may be on the summit where there is now the large Weli of Nebi Duḥī, and from which there is a remarkable view of Tabor, Gilboa, and the plain of Jezreel.

*   [5] This vague description may refer to the occasion when the disciples plucked corn on the Sabbath (Mark 2.23).

[6] The spring may be the ancient Bir esh Sheikh, just below the summit to the north. It contains sulphurous water to which curative properties might well be ascribed. But Kopp (p. 239) prefers to connect the spring here mentioned with the following sentence, and to place it in Nain. The title "Saviour" nowhere appears in Egeria's manuscript, and Peter sometimes uses it when transcribing later passages (like I above). But it is quite possible that he imported it into Egeria's description here.

[7] Luke 7.11. Here and elsewhere in Galilee Egeria (assuming that the description comes from her) mentions churches which do not appear in other fourth-century sources. Jerome, for instance, merely points out Nain from Mount Tabor without visiting it (*Epp.* 46.12; 108.13): but he shows no sign of familiarity with the region as a whole, and probably depended on Eusebius for most

In Nazareth is a garden in which the Lord used to be after his return from Egypt.[1]

Q NEAPOLIS: JACOB'S WELL
($\dot{=}$ Bede 14)

R This church [that is, the one containing Jacob's Well] is two miles away from the village which was once called Shechem. Fifty yards from this church is another in which rests Holy Joseph.[2]

S TIBERIAS, CAPERNAUM, NAZARETH
($\dot{=}$ Bede 15)

T There is a big and very splendid cave in which she [that is, Holy Mary] lived.[3] An altar has been placed there, *and there, within the actual cave, is the place from which she drew water.*[4] *Inside the city the synagogue where the Lord read the book of Isaiah is now a church,*[5] *but*

---

of his knowledge of it. On church building in Galilee see Kopp, pp. 53–5 and Jeremias, *Hg*, p. 15. Both comment on the proposals of Joseph of Tiberias, who had been authorized to build by Constantine. He complained about his difficulties to Epiphanius in 359 (*Adv. Haer.* 30.11.9f, PG 41.425). The present church (1895) is said to have been built over the ruins of a previous sanctuary.

[1] This mention of Nazareth seems to belong to the same description as the opening words of section T below. Peter no doubt continued abbreviating his source, here probably Egeria, then recognized that Bede's text demanded a mention of Neapolis next, before he could resume his description of Nazareth. This would be the garden of "Joseph's house"; cf. Matt. 1.18,24.

[2] See Bord 588, p. 154, n. 11 above. The church over the well is mentioned by Jerome (but not Eusebius), *On, Sychar* and *Ep.* 108.13, but the mention of a church over the Tomb of Joseph (assuming that the one above is Egeria's) is unsupported by the Madaba Map (see *MM*, p. 46 and compare Jeremias (*Hg*, pp. 34–5) who identified some columns there which appear to have belonged to this church. They are no longer to be seen). It may well be that the "churches" often recorded by Peter the Deacon were sometimes small martyria or cenotaphs, rather than full-blown buildings for congregational worship.

[3] This seems to describe the cave now included within the Church of the Annunciation (not yet built in the fourth century, see Kopp, p. 62).   *

[4] This, however, is clearly the crypt and spring which form part of the present Church of St Gabriel. Peter appears to have confused the two, if we are right to assume that the opening sentence of the section comes from Egeria.

[5] A synagogue was shown to pilgrims in 570 (Antoninus 5, C.C.S.L., pp. 130–1)   *
and in 1285 (Burchard, cited by Meistermann, *Guide*, p. 543, who mentions that it is transformed into a church); the later date is to be preferred owing to the mention of the church, and the context. Cf. Luke 4.17.

the spring from which Holy Mary used to take water is outside the village.[1]

U MOUNT TABOR
(≑ Bede 16)

V1   [Mount Tabor][2] is much higher and loftier than Hermon,[3] and from it can be seen the whole of Galilee and the Sea of Tiberias. These two mountains face each other.

In Endor is the house of the witch whom Saul visited by night,
2 and its foundations are still to be seen.[4] In Tiberias there is now a church on the spot where once stood the house of the apostles James and John.[5] Near there is the Sea of Tiberias on which the Lord walked.[6]

Moreover, in Capernaum the house of the *prince of the apostles* has been made into a church, with its original walls still standing.[7]

---

[1] This site was still inside the city in the time of Arculf (Adamnan 2.26.2, which was copied by Bede, and from Bede by Peter; see *C.C.S.L.*, pp. 219,276). But the boundary had moved by 1106, and Daniel describes it as outside the city (94, *IRO*, p. 72), which identifies this phrase as coming from Peter's later source.

[2] These words, following on from Bede's description of Mount Tabor, are probably Egeria's. She certainly visited Mount Tabor (see Valerius 2b, p. 176, n. 10 above).

[3] Cf. P3 above.

[4] 1 Sam. 28.7; *On, Aendor* mentions the commemoration but not the house.

[5] Cf. Mark 1.19. In A.D. 359 Joseph of Tiberias wished to build a church in Tiberias (see above, P4, n. 11). It is not known whether he succeeded.

[6] Matt. 14.25.

[7] Beneath the foundations of the fifth-century octagonal church at Capernaum recent excavations have revealed the remains of a modest house. One of its rooms, which corresponds with the centre of the octagon, shows signs that it was treated in a way which distinguished it from any of the rooms surrounding it, since the walls were plastered, and decorated with painted patterns. Among the graffiti on the plaster are the names of the "Lord Jesus Christ" and "Peter", and Fr V. Corbo, who excavated this room, finds signs of veneration dating back to the first century A.D.; see his preliminary report, *The House of St Peter at Capernaum*, tr. S. Saller (Jerusalem 1969), esp. pp. 54f. This holy room was shown to Egeria, and Peter the Deacon must here be quoting her, since the "house of the prince of the apostles" was already obliterated by the octagonal church in A.D. 450 (Corbo, op. cit., p. 18). It is true that the phrase "the prince of the apostles" in unlikely to have been used by Egeria, and probably comes from the pen of Peter the Deacon. But it is unlikely that he is here citing a contemporary source, since in his time Capernaum (Tell Ḥum) was deserted (cf. Daniel in *IRO*, pp. 53–4) and in the later Middle Ages pilgrims were shown a "House of Peter" in Tiberias rather than Capernaum (see Kopp, 226).

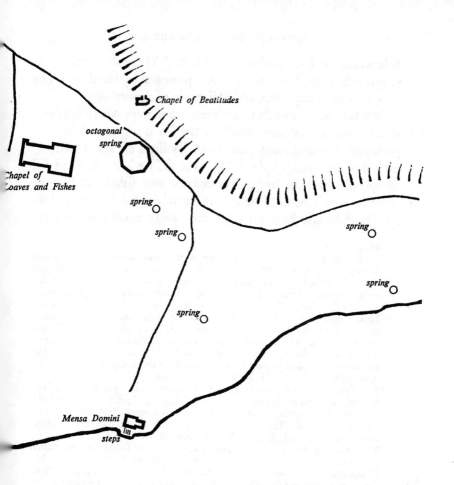

Chapel of Beatitudes

octagonal
spring

Chapel of
Loaves and Fishes

spring

spring

spring

spring

spring

Mensa Domini
steps

SEA OF GALILEE

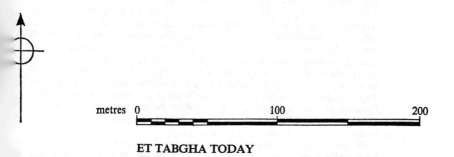

metres 0   100   200

ET TABGHA TODAY

It is where the Lord healed the paralytic.[1] There also is the synagogue where the Lord cured a man possessed by the devil.[2] The way in is up many stairs, and it is made of dressed stone.

Not far away from there are some stone steps where the Lord
V3   stood.[3] And in the same place by the sea is a grassy field with plenty of hay and many palm trees. By them are seven springs,[4] each flowing strongly. And this is the field where the Lord fed the people with the five loaves and the two fishes.[5] In fact the stone on which the Lord placed the bread has now been made into an altar.[6] People who go there take away small pieces of the

[1] Mark 2.1–12.

[2] Mark 1.23. The synagogue seen by Egeria may have been the predecessor of the large synagogue visible today, which the most recent excavations suggest was built in the fourth or early fifth century A.D. The site of the earlier synagogue is not known; see V. Corbo, S. Loffreda, and A. Spijkerman, *La Sinagoga di Carfarnao dopo gli scavi del 1969* (Jerusalem 1970), esp. pp. 58–60.

* [3] Now begins a description of Eṭ Ṭabgha. The four steps still exist beside a chapel on the lake shore. Just inside the chapel is a higher outcrop of rock, much worn, but with a roughly rectangular base. It therefore seems likely that the occasion commemorated was when the Lord "stood" by the shore after the resurrection, and prepared fish and bread for the disciples when they had been fishing (John 21.4, etc.). See Kopp, pp. 224f.

* [4] Six of the seven springs can be seen today; see the plan (p. 195) is adapted from S. Loffreda, *Scavi di Tabgha* (Jerusalem 1970), p. 17. Egeria here records the fact that seven springs existed. But later documents show that the area came to be called "The Seven Springs". The Greek version of this name,
* *Heptapegon*, is the origin of the Arabic name Ṭabgha.

[5] Mark 6.37–44. For the small chapel ascribed to the fourth century which commemorated this miracle see the plan (p. 198) and A. M. Schneider, *The Church of the Multiplying of the Loaves and Fishes* (London 1937), pp. 20–3. Note
* that, though this and the other two small religious buildings described in this passage are all assigned by archaeologists to the fourth century, Egeria only certainly mentions one (the "church" connected with the stone on which the Lord placed the bread, about to be mentioned).

[6] Loffreda, op. cit., pp. 27–30 and 104f, describes the worn rock with the rectangular base now in the lake-shore chapel of the Primacy of Peter. He shows that the foundations at the west end of this chapel go back to the fourth century, but is unable to say that they were the foundations of a church, on the basis of what is left on the site. Schneider, however, (op. cit., pp. 14–15 and 41–2) believes that the stone made into an altar, and subsequently chipped away by pilgrims, was the one under the fifth-century altar in the Church of The Multiplying. It is hard to be certain whether the stone was connected in the mind of Peter the Deacon (or Egeria) with the resurrection appearance, or with the feeding of the five thousand, since both Gospel narratives mention bread and fish (see Mark 6.41; John 21.9,13).

On the whole, it is more probable that this altar was connected with the resurrection appearance. The outcrop beside the lake from which both the steps and this altar were fashioned was in a dramatically appropriate position

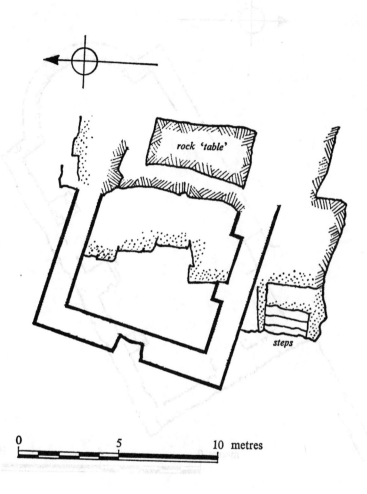

rock 'table'

steps

0   5   10 metres

ET TABGHA
REMAINS OF THE FIRST MENSA DOMINI CHAPEL

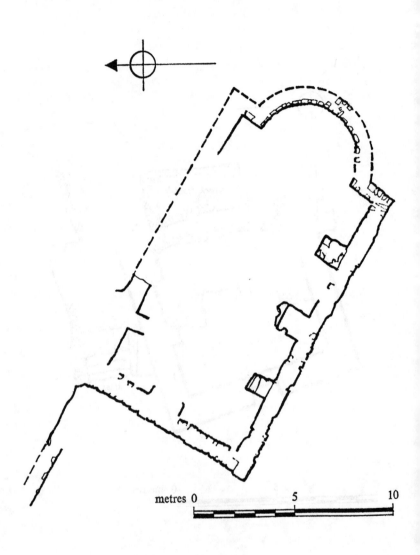

ET TABGHA
FOUNDATIONS OF THE FIRST CHAPEL
OF THE LOAVES AND FISHES

metres 0   5   10

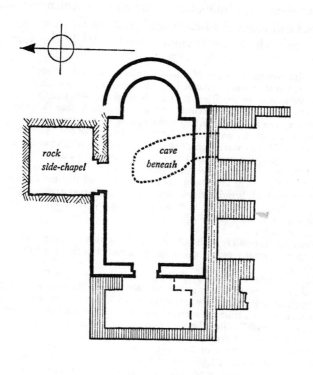

rock
side-chapel

cave
beneath

0   5   10   metres

**ET TABGHA
THE FIRST CHAPEL OF THE BEATITUDES**

stone to bring them prosperity, and they are very effective.[1] Past the walls of this church[2] goes the public highway on which the Apostle Matthew had his place of custom.[3]

V 4 Near there on a mountain is the cave to which the Saviour climbed and spoke the Beatitudes.[4] And not far from there is the synagogue which the Saviour cursed.[5] While the Jews were

---

for the commemoration of Christ's appearance to the disciples, especially before the altar was surrounded by a building. And it is highly unlikely that the stone now in the Church of the Multiplying was in exactly its present position before the fifth century. Such a suggestion raises the difficulty that the text would thus revert to a description of the resurrection appearance after an interpretation concerned with the feeding of the five thousand. But Peter the Deacon was capable of a process of editing which produced this kind of result (see his interrupted account of Nazareth in P4 and T above).

If this guess is correct, we may further guess that the resurrection appearance was the first event commemorated at Ṭabgha, and that the fact that it was connected with bread and fish, and that the place was grassy, suggested this as a suitable site for the commemoration also of the feeding of the five thousand (cf. Mark 6.39).

[1] Cf. Egeria 8.3.

[2] The church, possibly built before 350, was smaller than the one now shown, with its famous mosaic, which was constructed in the first half of the fifth century.

[3] Matt. 9.9; the location may well be accurate, as argued by Kopp, p. 171.

[4] Valerius 2b, p. 176. n. 12 above says that Egeria called the Mountain of the Beatitudes "Eremus". It was not necessarily the site shown to pilgrims today, and in Jerome's time the location was uncertain—"on Tabor or some other lofty mountain" as he believed, or according to some of the simpler brethren on the Mount of Olives (Comm. in Matt. 5.1). To locate the Sermon in a cave seems strange in view of the multitudes who were its cause (Matt. 5.1), but the commentators of Egeria's time believed that this teaching was addressed to the disciples, and that he deliberately avoided the crowds (for a selection of such interpretations see St Thomas Aquinas' Catena Aurea in IV Evang. ad loc. (Rome 1953), vol. I, p. 71). There is thus no reason to suspect that the word "cave" is an error (as Gamurrini and Kopp, pp. 205–7).

Since Jerome does not seem to have had any deep familiarity with Galilee, his uncertainty is no argument against the possibility that Egeria was shown a place venerated as that of the preaching of the Beatitudes. Indeed, the cave she mentions may well be the one among the ruins of a chapel and monastery on the hillside immediately above the present Church of the Multiplying. B. Bagatti assigns this chapel to the fourth century in "La Cappella sul Monte delle Beatitudini" in Rivista di Archeologia Cristiana 14 (1937), pp. 43–91. His plan I is reproduced in Loffreda, op. cit., p. 43.

[5] It has been suggested that this was the ruined synagogue at Chorazin (see E. L. Sukenik, Synagogues, pp. 21–4). Chorazin was "cursed" by Christ in Matt. 11.20–4, and the present story may well have had its origins in such a passage. But the Chorazin synagogue (Khirbat Kerāzeh, two miles to the north) is still relatively complete, and its condition in Egeria's time is unlikely to have given rise to such a story. The story itself is unknown apart from this passage.

building it, he went by and asked them this question, "What are you doing?" "Nothing", they said, and he replied, "If it is nothing you are doing, then what you are doing will for ever be nothing!" And till this day it remains so. For after that, whenever the Jews decided to build, the work they did in the day used to fall down in the night, and in the morning their building was at just the height it had been at the moment when it was cursed.

5   Not far away are the mountains of Gilboa,[1] and also the village of Gebus, where Saul and Jonathan died.[2] In Jezreel there is nothing left of Naboth's vineyard but its well, and the foundations of a tower.[3] The tomb of Jezebel is stoned by everyone to this very day.[4] And not far from the city is the mountain where Elijah hid himself when Jezebel was pursuing him.[5]

6   Some way away is part of Mount Carmel, and the place where Elijah dedicated the altar to God.[6]

Sebastia, once called Samaria, has in its church the resting-place of the body of holy John Baptist,[7] and also of Elisha and Obadiah.[8] Two miles away is a very lofty mountain on which are two most splendid caves. In one of them the prophets were hidden in the time of Jezebel, and Elijah lived in the other.[9]

[1] 1 Sam. 31.1. The present name is Jebel Fukū'a.
[2] 1 Sam. 31.13. The place (Jalbūn), which seems to have been pointed out rather than visited, is mentioned in *On*, *Gelboe, Gelbus*.
[3] 1 Kings 21.1; cf. Bord 585, p. 154, n. 2 above.
[4] 2 Kings 9.35. At the end of the nineteenth century the Jews in Jerusalem still stoned the Tomb of Absalom because he had been disobedient to his father. The next witnesses to Jezebel's tomb are both of the twelfth century, but this does not mean that Egeria is not the source here. See Jeremias, *Hg*, pp. 28–9.
[5] See 1 Kings 19.2–4, which clearly refers to Horeb, forty days' journey south of Beer-Sheba, which is itself 100 miles south of Jezreel. This mention could be a confused recollection of Egeria 4.2.
[6] 1 Kings 18.19,32. The place of sacrifice, El Muhraqa, was the principal holy place on Mount Carmel, and was only eclipsed by the cave of Elijah at the other end of the mountain when the Carmelite convent was built there in 1767.
[7] Matt. 14.2; cf. *On*, *Someron*.
[8] Late Jewish tradition located the tomb of Elisha in Sebastia, and Christians accepted the location, Egeria being here the first Christian witness to it. 2 Kings 13.20–1 (and Ecclus. 48.13) record a miracle which gave rise to a strange cult described by Jerome (*Ep.* 108.13). Obadiah (the prophet, identified with Obadiah who was Ahab's steward; see 1 Kings 18.3f; cf. Siphre Num. 133 on 27.1) became the third to be venerated at the tomb in the cathedral. The tomb is second or third-century Roman; see R. W. Hamilton, *Guide to Samaria-Sebaste* (Amman 1953), p. 40, and Jeremias, *Hg*, pp. 30–1.
[9] 1 Kings 18.4. Egeria visited this mountain according to Valerius 2b, p. 176, n. 13 above. The caves have not been identified.

V7   At the twentieth milestone from Shechem[1] is the temple of Shiloh, now destroyed,[2] and also in that place is the tomb of Eli the priest.[3]

Moreover, in Bethel there is a church which has been built at the place where Jacob, on his way to Mesopotamia, saw the ladder which reached up to heaven.[4] In that place there is also the tomb of the prophet who prophesied against Jeroboam.[5]

*   And twenty-two miles from Jerusalem, between Socoh of Judah and Zecara Mahel, David slew Goliath the Philistine.[6]

8   At Bycoyca in[7] Eleutheropolis is the tomb of the prophet Habakkuk.[8] Fifteen miles from Eleutheropolis, at the place called Asoa,

---

[1] I.e. at the twentieth milestone from Jerusalem, which the traveller from Sebastia reached via Shechem.

[2] 1 Sam. 1.3. Jerome knew the ruins (*Ep.* 108.13), which have since been excavated by H. Kjaer; see "The Danish Excavation of Shiloh", *P.E.Q.S.* (1927), pp. 202–13 and *J.P.O.S.* 10 (1930), and also M. L. Buhl and S. H. Nielsen, *Shiloh: the Danish Excavations at Tell Sailūn, Palestine, in 1926, 1929, 1932, and 1963: The Pre-Hellenistic Remains* (= *Publications of the National Museum, Archaeological-Historical Series* I, vol. 12) (Copenhagen 1969).

[3] 1 Sam. 4.18. This notice, if from Egeria, is the only early Christian testimony to the tomb, which was recorded only in the thirteenth and fourteenth centuries by Jewish pilgrims (Jeremias, *Hg*, p. 43). For the excavation see H. Kjaer in *P.E.F.Q.S.* (1931), pp. 71–88, who suggests that of the two welis there, the southern one (Weli Sittīn) is the site of this tomb of Eli. The other weli (Weli Yetim) also appears to comprise much ancient material.

[4] Gen. 28.1–22; Eusebius, *On, Agai* and Bord 588 mention no church, but it was built by the time Jerome wrote *Ep.* 46.12, as witnessed here.

[5] 1 Kings (11.29),13.1: cf. Bord 588, p. 155, n. 7 above.

[6] 1 Sam. 17.1 places the battle at Ephesdammim "between Socoh and Azekah"; i.e. the traveller has finished the journey to Jerusalem from the north, and now describes this battlefield (the valley of Elah) and a variety of tombs to the south and west of Jerusalem. They are not presented in the order of a journey. Zecara Mahel (The Place of Zechariah) is a mile and a half north-east of Azekah, and is where the prophet's bones were unearthed in 415 (Sozomen *EH* 9.17, *PG* 67. 1628–9). The modern name of this village is Zakhariya. Goliath was slain in this neighbourhood, rather than that of Bord 585, p. 154, n. 3. See Jeremias, *Hg*, p. 73 and n. 4.

[7] "In" here means "in the toparchy" of which Eleutheropolis was the capital. *Bycoyca* means "Habakkuk's Place" as *Lazarium* means "Lazarus' Place".

[8] Two sites for Habakkuk's tomb are mentioned by Eusebius. They seem both to have existed in late Jewish tradition (see Jeremias, *Hg*, pp. 81f), and there are ancient ruins to be seen at both. They are Khirbat Beit Sikariya (*On*, s.v. *Gabatha*) and Khirbat Qīla (*On*, s.v. *Cela, Eccela*). The second is probably intended here, since, unlike the first, it was in the toparchy of Eleutheropolis. Just after Egeria's visit, in A.D. 385, Khirbat Qīla conclusively gained the approval of Christians by becoming the scene of the discovery of the bones of

*   Habakkuk (Sozomen, *EH* 7.29.2, *PG* 67.1505).

is the tomb of the holy prophet Ezra,[1] and three miles away, at the place now called Chariasati but once Morasthi, is the tomb of the holy prophet Micah.[2]

9   Taphnis is on the bank of the River Nile.[3] The palace of Pharaoh is there, where Moses was when they took him to be the son of Pharaoh's daughter. Also in that place is the headquarters where holy Moses worked his wonders before Pharaoh.

X ALEXANDRIA
(÷ Bede 18)

Y1   Also Memphis still contains the palace where holy Joseph so often used to go.[4] Six miles from there, facing the bank of the River

---

[1] Josephus records a tradition that Ezra was magnificently buried in Jerusalem (*Ant.* 11.5.5), and this indication of his tomb in Asoa, fifteen miles northwards of Eleutheropolis, stands on its own. Asoa may well, in view of its name, and its distance from Eleutheropolis, be Ishwa' (or Eshtaol), and Egeria's Tomb of Ezra may be the present "Tomb of Samson". It stands on the south side of the road to Tel Aviv 1.4 km. from "Samson's road junction", and is surrounded by apparently ancient masonry.

[2] Mic. 1.1 and Jer. 26.18 refer to the prophet, but Judg. 17—18 is the account of another Micah from Mount Ephraim, to the north of Jerusalem. Owing to an identification between the two Micahs the late Jewish tradition is ambiguous, implying a tomb in Ephraim (though not giving it any exact location; see Jeremias, *Hg*, p. 82), but also placing it next to the Graveyard of the Anakim, or Giants, who were associated with the region south of Jerusalem (see Deut. 1.28). The local name of the city which the Romans refounded as Eleutheropolis was Beth Gubhrin (its Arabic name is still Beit Jibrīn), which can mean "House of the Giants".

Eusebius, *On, Morasthi*, places Moresheth-Gath, Micah's native city "to the east of Eleutheropolis", and in 385 Micah's bones were discovered at a place Sozomen calls Berath (= castle) Satia, clearly the Charia-(= village) sati of our text (cf. Sozomen, *EH* 7.29.2, *PG* 67.1505—8). This site, including the remains of the church mentioned by Jerome (*Ep.* 108.13) and the Graveyard of the Giants was discovered by Jeremias in 1932 (see *Hg*, p. 86) at Khirbat el Baṣal, two miles north-east of Beit Jibrīn.

[3] Now begins a fragment of a journey to Egypt, coming in by Taphnis, which is the biblical Tahpanhes (Jer. 49.3). In Greek it was called Daphnae (Herodotus 2.30) or Taphnae (LXX), and it stood on the Pelusiac arm of the Nile, which has since dried up (see Ball, p. 176). It was also on the main road from Pelusium to Memphis (see Y1 below). The Hebrew of Jer. 43.9 informs us that it was the site of a "government house", which corresponds well with the "headquarters" (*capitaney*) of the present text. The building has been excavated, by W. Flinders Petrie in 1886, and he gives a plan in his *Tanis*, vol. 2 (London 1888), plate XLIV.

[4] The area of ancient Memphis covers a number of small villages linked by ground full of ruins, but there has so far been very little excavation. If the monument here described was in fact a palace, it may have been that of Apries, immediately to the north of El Gebu, or that of Merenptah near Kōm el Gala. See Gen. 41.14.

Nile, is the throne of Moses and Aaron.[1] These thrones are on a lofty mountain where there are two turrets with many steps leading to the top. One of them has a roof, but it was to the top of the other one (which has no roof) that Moses used to climb when he encouraged the children of Israel during their oppression.[2] The other one he used for prayer. All round is the plain where the children of Israel made bricks,[3] and a mile away on the river bank is the village where holy Mary stayed with the Lord when she went to Egypt.[4]

Y2 In the twelve-mile stretch between Memphis and Babylonia[5] are many pyramids, which Joseph made in order to store corn.[6] Heliopolis[7] is twelve miles from Babylonia, and has in the centre a large piece of ground which contains the Temple of the Sun. Potiphar's house is there, and between this and the Temple is Asenath's house.[8] The inner wall of the city is of a considerable age, as old as the Temple, or the houses of Asenath and Potiphar, and like them it is made of stone. In the same place is the Garden of the Sun, with the great column called the Bomon,[9] where the Phoenix used to settle after five hundred years.

[1] Despite the details of this description the throne cannot at present be identified, since there seems to be no "lofty mountain" with the plain surrounding it.

[2] Exod. 4.29.

[3] Exod. 1.14. The plain between Memphis and Gizeh is full of the remains of ancient and more recent brick buildings, and of modern brick factories.

[4] If Egeria here means the far side of the river, she may be referring to Deir Adhra, Maadi (see O. Meinardus, *Atlas of Christian sites in Egypt* (Publications de la Société d'Archéologie Copte) (Cairo 1962), Map 2).

[5] *Babylonia* was the name of the Roman fort which was later surrounded by Old Cairo. The district is still known by the name Fusṭāṭ (from *fossatum*, "moated"). The name Babylonia is not found in literature before Strabo (*Geography* 17.1.35), who visited Egypt *c*. 20 B.C.; see A. J. Butler, *The Coptic Churches of Egypt* (Oxford 1884), pp. 171–2, for ancient theories about the origin of the name.

[6] This became the regular Christian explanation of the pyramids. The first witness usually quoted is Julius Honorius, a Roman orator of the fourth or fifth century; see his *Cosmographia* in Riese, *Geographi Latini Minores* (Heilbronn 1878), p. 51. But Egeria may well have been the first to have recorded it. It was no doubt the standard explanation given by Christian guides. For its persistence see E. Iversen, *The Myth of Egypt and its Hieroglyphs* (Copenhagen 1961), p. 59, and I. E. S. Edwards, *The Pyramids of Egypt* (Harmondsworth 1961), p. 295.

[7] Gen. 41.45, *On* (Hebrew) is changed to *Heliopolis* in the Septuagint.

[8] Gen. 39.1; 41.45.

[9] *Bomon* is the Greek rendering of the Egyptian *Benben*, described, for example,

3   Egypt is very fertile, but even so the places where the children of Israel lived are better still.[1] The part of Arabia which joins up with Palestine has a road, but it is impassable, since its fifteen staging-posts are in waterless areas.[2]

4   From Jerusalem to the holy Mount Sinai it is twenty-two staging-posts.[3] Pelusium is the capital of the province Augustamnica (a province of Egypt), and from Pelusium to Mount Sinai it is twelve staging-posts.[4]

5   Before you reach the holy Mount Sinai you come to the fort of Clysma[5] on the Red Sea, the place where the children of Israel crossed the sea dryshod.[6] And the tracks of Pharaoh's chariot are permanently marked across the sand; its wheels were a good deal further apart than the chariots of today that we have in the Roman Empire, since it measured twenty-four feet from wheel to wheel, and its tracks are two feet broad. Pharaoh's chariot-tracks reach right down to the sea-shore at the point where he entered the sea in his efforts to catch the children of Israel.[7] And at the point where

---

by Herodotus (2.73). Of the monuments at Heliopolis which are described here, one large (but minor) obelisk alone remains visible above ground; for a modern plan of what has been revealed by excavation see E. P. Uphill, "Pithom and Raamses: their location and significance", in the *Journal of Near Eastern Studies* 27 (1968), p. 295.

[1] Gen. 47.6. See Valerius, 1c, p. 175, n. 2 above. Valerius, like Peter, may here be referring to Egeria 7.1, since section 3 is independent of the Taphnis–Memphis journey, and also of section 4, which starts afresh from Jerusalem.

[2] "Arabia" is here used to refer to the desert beyond the bounds of Egyptian cultivation. Cultivation at this time extended a little east of the Pelusiac arm of the Nile, but not far, and a salient of desert divided this cultivated area from the Wādī Ṭumīlāt. The usual way to travel from Palestine to the Red Sea via the Mediterranean was to follow the coast to Pelusium (Tell Farāma) and then turn south; but Pliny (*Nat. Hist.* 5.11; 6.29) comments on the difficulty of finding the way across the desert, south of Pelusium. See Ball, p. 82. Egeria is not here speaking of the road south from Pelusium, but a road running south-west, perhaps the one from Gerrum (el Maḥamdīya).

[3] At this point Egeria's journey to Sinai begins, in the course of which her own manuscript becomes available.

[4] Egeria here goes directly south from Pelusium. Hence her explanation of the detour she made on the return journey; see 7.1.

[5] Suez, which still retains the name Kōm Qulzum near by. Clysma is the Greek for "shore". The fort was built by the Romans on a site occupied since the time of Rameses III; see B. Bruyère, *Fouilles de Clysma-Qoulzoum (Suez) 1930–32 (Fouilles de l'Institut d'Archéologie Orientale du Caire*, vol. 27) (Cairo 1966).

[6] Exod. 14.29. See Valerius 2a, p. 175, n. 4 above.

[7] Exod. 14.9: Antoninus (41, *C.C.S.L.* 175, pp. 150–1) saw the same stone ✱

they entered, where his tracks finish, two marks like small columns stand to right and left.[1] This spot is not far from Clysma fort.

Y6   Clysma itself is on the shore, right by the sea. It has an enclosed harbour which makes the sea come right inside the fort,[2] and it is the port for India, which is to say that it receives the ships from India, for ships from India can come to no other port but this in Roman territory.[3] And the ships there are numerous and great, since it is a port renowned for the Indian merchants who come to it. Also the official known as the logothete[4] has his residence there, the one who goes on embassy each year to India by order of the Roman emperor, and his ships lie there. The children of Israel came to this place on their way out of Egypt when they were escaping from Pharaoh, and the fort was built later on, to be a defence and deterrent against Saracen raids.[5]

7   Apart from one mountain by the sea[6] this is entirely an area of flat sandy deserts. From the far side of the mountain they quarry purple marble, and the Red Sea gets its name from the fact that this mountain stretches beside it for a great distance, and it is made of red or purple stone and has a reddish appearance. This mountain is on your right as you come from Egypt, and it was on the right of the children of Israel as they fled from Egypt and began to approach the sea. It is very high and lofty, and as sheer as a wall cut by a mason. The area of the mountain is completely arid, and not even shrubs grow there.

8   Thus, when the children of Israel left Rameses[7] on their march, they went wandering across the sands.[8] Then, as they neared the

---

remains in 570, and describes them as "the arms of Pharaoh, or the tracks of his chariot-wheels: but all the arms have been turned into marble".

[1] The original purpose of the "chariot-tracks" seems to have been to drag up ships on rollers for careening. The marks may have been bollards.

[2] Port Suez today contains two enclosed harbours, but neither corresponds to the one mentioned here.

[3] Clysma was famous as the port for India; cf. Pliny, *Nat. Hist.* 6.26–7.

[4] Literally "Auditor"; the title was later used for the Chancellor of the Eastern Roman Empire, but the official in Suez was well known at this earlier time.

[5] Clysma was part of a chain of forts stretching north along the frontier, which were strengthened or rebuilt by the Romans for the reason here given.

[6] Jebel 'Ataqa; cf. Egeria 7.4.

[7] See Exod. 12.37.   [8] Cf. Egeria 7.3.

Red Sea, this mountain came into sight on their right. Following along the mountain they arrived at the sea, with the flank of this lofty mountain on their right and the sea on the left. Then, still going on, there suddenly appeared ahead of them the place where the mountain joins the sea or, rather, where it juts out into it and 9 forms a promontory.[1] Here, in a vast plain of enormous dimensions, the children of Israel stayed that night with Moses.[2]

The mountain begins to overhang the sea half a mile from Clysma fort,[3] and between the fort and the mountain is an open space leading to the promontory of the mountain, where the children of Israel entered the sea, and Pharaoh after them. The distance across the sea at the place where they went over dryshod is eight miles.[4]

10   This sea has the name "Red" not because the water is red or muddy. Indeed, it is quite as sparkling clear and cold as the Ocean.[5] Its shellfish[6] are excellent, and unusually sweet, and all types of fish from this sea taste as good as the fish in the Italian Sea.[7] You have all the sea-food you could want: there are trumpet-shells and oysters of various kinds, white-shells, and several kinds of large snail. And the different things you find along the shore are bigger and prettier than by any other sea. Also there is a great deal of coral on this shore. The Red Sea is a part of the Ocean.[8]

1   Shur, the desert where they went for three days without water,[9] is of an enormous size. No one has ever seen a bigger desert, and no one could guess the quantities of sand. Between the Desert of Shur and Marah[10] there is one staging-post next to the sea, and at

[1] Rās 'Adabiya.
[2] This seems to be the large plain between Jebel 'Ataqa and Suez.
[3] This measurement is probably incorrect.
[4] This agrees well with the distance across from Ras 'Adabiya.
[5] Cf. Egeria 19.5; Valerius 4a, p. 177, n. 4 above. Ocean may here mean the Atlantic part of it.
[6] *Elecesse* would mean "shellfish" if its root were *helix*; but the word may rather be connected with *alac* and mean simply "fish".
[7] An unusual expression for the Mediterranean.
[8] The Ocean was (rightly) believed to surround the world; hence the Red Sea is as much part of it as the Atlantic.
[9] Exod. 15.22.
[10] Exod. 15.23; Marah is to be identified a good way to the north of Elim, and the traditional site shown to Egeria is therefore right opposite Ras 'Adabiya. This supposition is confirmed by the present name 'Uyūn Mūsa, Springs of

Marah itself there are some palm-trees (very few), and the two springs which holy Moses made sweet.

Y12   From there on for three days' journey there is an endless desert to the left. Then you reach Arandara, the Arandara which was called Elim.[1] There is a stream there, and, though it dries up from time to time, there is water to be had from its bed or from near the bank. In that place there is plenty of grass and a great many palm trees, and all the way from Shur where we crossed the Red Sea there is no place as pleasant as this, or with such good plentiful water. The next staging-post from there is beside the sea, and it is halfway.[2]

13   Next, two mountains come into sight on the left, and, before you reach them, there is the place where the Lord rained manna[3] on the children of Israel. They are lofty mountains, and very steep. On one side of the mountains the valley is perfectly flat and like a colonnade about two hundred yards wide, with the steep high mountains on either side. But where the mountains open out the valley is six miles wide and a good deal longer.

14   All around the mountains caves[4] have been carved out, and, if you just took the trouble to put up some curtains, they would make marvellous bedrooms. Each bedroom is inscribed with Hebrew letters. At the far end of the valley there is good water in plenty, but it is not the equal of Elim. This is called the Desert of Paran, and it was from here that Moses sent out spies to explore

---

Moses, even though this location makes it hard to understand how "they went for three days without water" before reaching the springs. It would not have seemed so strange to Egeria, who presumably travelled round the head of the Gulf by road.

*   [1] Antoninus (41, *C.C.S.L.* 175, p. 150) returned from Sinai this way in 570, and mentions a small village at this place called *Surandela*. The modern name of the valley is the Wādī al Gharandal. Cf. Exod. 15.27.

      [2] This staging-post is presumably the modern Abu Zenima. Cf. Egeria 6.1.

*   [3] Exod. 16.14. See Valerius 2a, p. 175, n. 7 above, and cf. Egeria 5.8. The mountains are perhaps Jebel Nakhal and Jebel Ṣamrah, seen from Wādī Nakhal before the coastal strip widens by Rās Abū Rodeis.

      [4] Cf. Num. 12.16; *Paran* means "full of caves", but there are remarkably few obvious caves on the way up to Mount Sinai, except in the mountains immediately east of Rās Abu Rodeis, through which Egeria now passes to enter Wādī Mukattib ("The valley which has writing all over it"). Here the mountains are honeycombed with caves, and the rocks covered with graffiti in a wide variety of languages.

the land.[1] It is protected by mountains on both sides, but it has no fields or vineyards, and there is nothing there but the water and some palm trees.

Close to the village of Paran—a mile and a half away—the mountains converge to make a valley not quite thirty feet wide. It is the place called Rephidim, and it is where Amalek[2] met the children of Israel,[3] where the people murmured for water,[4] and where Moses was met by Jethro, his father-in-law.[5] The very lofty steep mountain which overhangs Paran is the place where Moses prayed while Joshua defeated Amalek; a church has now been built at the spot where Moses prayed,[6] and you can still see the place where he sat, and how he had the stones under his couch. When Amalek was defeated, Moses built an altar there to the Lord.[7] And for half a mile there it is all so steep that you would think you were going up a wall.

From Paran there is a thirty-five mile journey before you reach the holy Mount Sinai.[8] In Hazeroth you can still see how stony it is in the valley where the children of Israel lived when they returned from the Mount of God.[9] And on a raised spot there stand three stone seats, one of which was for Moses, and the other two for Aaron and Jethro. You can still see the cell in which Moses' sister Miriam was separated for seven days.[10] It projects two feet out of the ground.

All the way from Hazeroth to the holy Mount Sinai the valley running between the mountains is full of monuments to the right

---

[1] From Wadi Mukattib Egeria joins Wadi Feiran. See Num. 13.1. She continues, to mount the same valley till she reaches Feiran (Paran).

[2] A quotation from the Madrid manuscript (see Egeria 16.4) may refer to a remark made to Egeria by local monks here: "They lived together peacefully like the monks, not in the least like Amalekites. In fact they so disliked the name Amalekite that this was the oath they used: 'May my body never rest among the Amalekites'" (De Bruyne 11.1–5).

[3] Exod. 17.8.

[4] Exod. 17.2; 18.5; see Valerius 2a, p. 175, n. 6 above.

[5] Exod. 17.8–13.

[6] The remains of several churches are visible today; for the mountain see Valerius 2b, p. 176, n. 9 above, and see Meinardus, op. cit., Map 6.

[7] Exod. 17.15.

[8] Cf. Exod. 19.2. Egeria turns up the Wadi Solāf to approach Sinai by Naqb al Hawa and Wadi er Raha.

[9] Num. 11.35.

[10] Num. 12.15.

and left, and near the holy Mount the place called The Graves of Craving is all full of tombs.[1]

[1] The Arabic name for these tombs is *nawāmīs*, which resembles the plural of the word for mosquitoes, and thus led to the local story that the tombs had been built to protect the Israelites from these insects.

Egeria's own account of her travels begins at the Graves of Craving; see p. 91 above. Peter the Deacon's rendering of her text continues in parallel until her chapter 7.3, but at that point ends, since it is incomplete.

Notes
on the text of
Egeria

1—9 MOUNT SINAI

1-3 SINAI: THE APPROACH AND ASCENT

1.1 Travel in the Sinai peninsula is along the gravel surface of dry torrent-beds which run between the mountains. The account of this journey begins at PD, Y4. At the point where her own manuscript begins Egeria has come through Naqb el Hawa, a pass three hundred yards wide, leading through the vast wall of mountains which runs north-eastward from this pass to Jebel Banat and the Waṭia pass, and then onwards for several miles. On either side of the pass are lofty granite mountains from which she now emerges.

1 *an endless valley:* The Wadi er Rāha (Valley of Rest) leading to Jebel Mūsā (Egeria's Mount Sinai).

1 *the "Graves of Craving"* stretch half a mile behind her at the entry to the pass. "These remains ... consist of several *nawāmīs* (see PD, Y17, n. 1) or stone houses, and immense stone-circles that present the appearance of a gigantic cemetery" (Sir C. W. Wilson in his topographical appendix to J. H. Bernard, *The Pilgrimage of St Silvia of Aquitania* (London 1891), p. 137). They are ancient beehive tombs, according to C. T. Currelly in W. Flinders Petrie, *Researches in Sinai* (London 1906), pp. 260-1, 243-4.

*

2 *usual ... to say a prayer:* The local monks (and elsewhere often the local bishops) regularly lead the pilgrim in prayer; cf. 10.7; 14.1; 19.16. "Holy men" is Egeria's general term for monks and clergy. Though it is possible to obtain glimpses of the massif of Jebel Mūsā before passing through Naqb el Hawa, a clearer view is now visible: Egeria could see the ridge of Ras Sufsafeh, which is only four hundred feet lower than the main summit, and thus hides it from view.

2 *four miles:* This, like most of Egeria's estimates of distance, is tolerably accurate (as at PD, Y9).

1 *sixteen miles long:* The valley by which Egeria approached turns east under Jebel Mūsā, and then turns back to the north to emerge from the mountain wall at the Waṭia pass. The total distance from Naqb el Hawa to Waṭia is about fifteen miles, and Egeria may have heard this measurement mentioned by her guides, and misunderstood it.

4 *four miles wide:* This measurement is hard to fit with the site. It may be that Egeria is referring to the length of the east–west part of Wadi ed Deir, which crosses the valley up which she came, and which is nearly four miles from end to end.

2 *were waiting:* Hence the name "Valley of Rest". Egeria mentions the particular sites again in chapter 5 below.

the head of this very valley: The continuation of Wadi er Rāha goes past the place of the Bush (the present Monastery of St Katherine) and the view is closed by Jebel Muneija. Egeria now goes on to say how her approach took her round to the right of the massif, up Wadi el Lejā. St Katherine's was surrounded with its present fortress-like wall of granite by the Emperor Justinian (Eutychius,

Ann. 2.61, *PG* 111.1071) in order to guard the passes under Mount Sinai from the attacks of the desert-dwellers to the north. But this was done a century and a half later than Egeria's visit.

4 *Paran:* The modern Feirān; see PD, Y15.

5 *It looks like a single mountain:* The massif has, as Egeria says, a number of subsidiary peaks, but the summit of Jebel Mūsā is at the southern end.

7 *you cannot see it:* Modern travellers go up a path from the place of the Bush, and can see the summit from far below, but Egeria accurately describes the ascent by the ancient path from Wadi el Lejā.

7 *facing you* = Latin *de contra.* In one instance (19.6 "as I looked straight at it") *de contra* can only have the meaning "facing". But Gingras usually translates the phrase "at a distance" following the suggestion of Erkell (see Gingras, p. 166, n. 20). Gingras may well be right to take the phrase as patient of both meanings, and it might mean either in most of its occurrences (e.g. 5.4; 7.4; 12.4; 16.4). In this translation the meaning "facing" is used consistently.

3.1 *cells:* Egeria regularly uses the word *monasteria* to mean "cells". Of the several convents whose remains are visible in the Wadi el Lejā, Egeria probably went to that of El Arba'īn (The Forty), which is nearest the ascent. These were Forty Martyrs massacred by their Bedouin neighbours.

1 *received us most hospitably:* Egeria uses the phrase *humane suscipere,* a technical Christian expression for fulfilling the duty of hospitality.

1 *a church with a presbyter:* The monks were for the most part lay people, one of whom might be ordained (see 14.2 below), and most of the bishops Egeria meets had been monks (see 8.4; 19.1,5; 20.2). In 19.1 she uses the phrase "a church with a bishop".

1 *Straight at each one:* Being the shortest way up the mountain this path is extremely abrupt.

3 *The church:* The present church has been rebuilt with the masonry of its predecessors, and the foundations of a larger building can be seen, which is more likely to have been that erected by Justinian than the chapel seen by Egeria.

5 *The cave:* Ten yards from the present church is the cave, which has the present mosque built over it.

6 *the Offering:* The fact that so many people had climbed to the summit for this Eucharist suggests that their regular Sunday celebration was held in their holiest place.

6 *"blessings":* see Introduction, p. 24 above. Most of the "blessings" she was given were outside the context of a Eucharist.

6 *vegetable-beds,* reading *arationes* with Heraeus and Löfstedt for *orationes* in the manuscript.

6 *cells:* Many remains are visible today.

3 *Egypt and Palestine:* Both the Red Sea (the Gulf of Suez, and therefore the
Egyptian mountains on the far shore) and the Gulf of Aqaba are sometimes
visible from the summit of Jebel Mūsā, and Egeria may have seen them in the
clear winter air. But usually they are hidden by a blue haze, which is more
probably what she saw, and Palestine and the Parthenian Sea are never visible.

3 *the Saracens:* Egeria seems to be the first writer to use this word, which derives
from the Arabic *sharqiyīn*, "easterners", and is applied to those who lived in
Arabia Felix and Arabia Petraea, i.e. the Sinai peninsula and El Hisma with the
region of Petra between.

4–5 HOREB, THE BUSH, AND THE ISRAELITES' CAMP:

the church called "On Horeb": In the sixth century Antoninus of Piacenza was
shown Jebel ed Deir (not Jebel Mūsā) as Horeb (37–9, *C.C.S.L.* 147–9). Perhaps
this chapel had been abandoned at that time, since the present church of Elijah is
the successor to the one seen by Egeria. It stands in a slight depression among the
peaks, and is close to the path leading down the mountain towards the place of
the Bush. The cave is below the present church. Gingras, p. 173, n. 51, points
out that the Bible does not mention Elijah as building an altar on Horeb.

Eusebius in his *Onomasticon, Choreb,* gives a vague account of the position of
Horeb, saying that "it lies near Mount Sinai beyond Arabia in the desert"; but
Jerome, in translating the passage, added "But it seems to me that it is a single
mountain which has two names, now Sinai, now Horeb."

The Books of the Kingdoms: The Books of Samuel and Kings are called "Kingdoms" in the Greek Old Testament, and the Old Latin versions which followed
it. Jerome's new Vulgate version returned to the Hebrew literally and called
them the Books of the Kings. Egeria was accustomed to an Old Latin version,
since Jerome had not finished translating the Gospels at the time of her visit, and
only finished the whole Bible in 404.

the Offering: This is the second celebration of the Sunday. Note that it is in a
different church from the first, and that on this occasion Egeria does not mention that she received Holy Communion.

where Aaron: The place is still shown today a little to the north of the chapel of
Elijah.

an appropriate psalm: For the form of these pilgrimage prayers see Introduction
p. 64 above.

the Bush: The Bush is shown outside the east end of the monastery church of
St Katherine, and the shrub is no doubt a lineal descendant of that shown to
Egeria. The St. Katherine traditionally buried at Sinai is the Katherine of Alexandria who died as a virgin in the course of Maxentius' visit to Alexandria in
307, as described by Eusebius (*HE* 8.14.15, *PG* 20.785). But the belief that angels
brought her body to Sinai for burial is not recorded before the end of the eighth
century, and was clearly unknown to Egeria.

excellent water: A "Well of Moses" forms the present water-supply of the
monastery, and is to the south of the church.

8 *where holy Moses was standing:* This is today a chapel to the east of the sanctuary of the church, and thus close to the Bush.

5.3–9 *we were leaving the Bush:* The only one of these places which is now identifiable is the Mould of the Calf.

8 *the manna and the quails:* Cf. PD, Y13, n. 3, p. 208 above, which refers to the version of the miracle of manna and quails, recounted in Exodus 16.13–15, as the Israelites left Elim. The miracle recorded in Numbers (and recalled here) took place near Taberah (Num. 11.26) before they went on to Hazeroth (Num. 11.35).

10 *Graves of Craving:* Here it seems that the monuments are at the southern end of the pass (cf. 1.1). It may well be that these were *nawāmīs* and that the whole group near the pass were known as the Graves of Craving.

6 FROM PARAN TO CLYSMA

See the more detailed description of this stage in Egeria's outward journey in PD, Y11–14.

7–8 CITIES OF THE LAND OF GOSHEN

7.1 *the land of Goshen:* Egypt was still divided into nomes in Egeria's time, and it seems that Egeria followed the Septuagint's identification of Goshen with Arabia, taking Arabia to mean the nome of that name. For her it therefore begins at a frontier sixteen miles from Heroöpolis (Tell el Maskhūṭa) going west
* along the Wadi Ṭumīlat (i.e. Gezīrat al Khadra); see 7.9.

1 *the "City of Arabia":* The phrase suggests the capital of the Arabian nome, which according to Ptolemy (writing in A.D. 150) was Phacusa. Being the civil capital it was also in the fourth century the seat of a Christian bishop (see *PG* 25.376–7 and H. Munier, *Receuil des listes episcopales de l'église copte, Textes et documents* (Cairo 1943), p. 2). The name has been preserved as Faqūs, and the identification of this modern town with Phacusa should be accepted (as, for example, in the nineteenth-century "Oxford List of Bishoprics" described by W. E. Crum, *Catalogue of the Coptic Mss. in the John Rylands Library* (Manchester 1909), p. 226).

2 *four desert staging-posts:* Taken as a measure of progress this information suggests that Egeria here took five days for a journey of about ninety miles, travelling an average of eighteen miles a day.

2 *quarters at each staging-post:* The manuscript strangely gives the word *manasteria* for "quarters". Either this is a misspelling of the usual word for "cells", or else possibly a scribal error for *castra*, "forts"; if the latter, it is hard to explain except by comparison with 7.4. For a discussion of this passage, see Vermeer, *Obs.*, p. 130.

4 *Pi-hahiroth*, like Migdol and Baalzephon (7.4), Etham and Succoth (7.5), are here described as Egeria passed them (i.e. in the opposite order to that in which they occur in Exodus). To satisfy the biblical account all should be visible at

once, and they are probably all near Suez. At Migdol and Baalzephon were frontier-forts used by the Romans, of which an ancient example is to be seen five miles west of the southern tip of the Little Bitter Lake between Wadi Sālyāl and Wadi Abu Hassan (see J. Clédat, "Notes sur l'Isthme de Suez", in *Bulletin de l'Institut français au Caire* 16, p. 204). The camel track which leads past it towards Clysma may have been the route taken by Egeria.

7 *a village, one of the big ones:* "Large village" was a technical administrative term in the eastern empire and occurs frequently in Eusebius' *Onomasticon*; though Egeria may not here intend it in its technical sense. Heroöpolis was the capital of its nome, and Pithom its near-by ancient fort, now called Tell el Maskhūta. See Introduction, p. 6 above.

8 *sixteen miles:* Heroöpolis is sixteen miles east of Tell el Kebir, which was the   *
border of the Arabian nome, Egeria's "land of Goshen". Heroöpolis itself was on the frontier between Egypt as a whole and the "lands of the Saracens". See Gingras, p. 184, n. 109.

8 *an arm of the Nile:* The main waterway through the Wadi Ṭumilat was a canal which originated in the days of Pharaoh Necho (609–594 B.C.). Trajan (A.D. 98–117) improved it by making it run from the Pelusiac arm of the Nile at Phacusa. See also Herodotus 2.158.

8.1 *Rameses:* Qanṭir is an important ruined site four miles beyond Faqūs in a northerly direction. It is probable that Egeria arrived in the neighbourhood of Faqūs with enough time to go on to Qanṭir before turning back for a night's lodging in Faqūs. Ṣaft el Ḥinna is another ruined site which has been proposed as the "Rameses" she visited (see, for example, Wilson in Bernard, pp. 143–4), but it is impossible to find a convincing "City of Arabia" at four miles distance from it. Qanṭir has also been proposed as the probable site of the biblical Pi-Ramses; see M. Hamza, *Annales du Service des Antiquités de l'Egypte*, tome 30 (1930), pp. 31ff; but see also L. Habachi, "Khatá'na—Qanṭir—Importance" ibid., tome 52 (1954), pp. 444–8. Dr Habachi points out that much of the masonry from Qanṭir was taken away to build Tanis, which may explain why Egeria saw only fallen ruins.

2 *Theban stone:* Red granite was brought by water from the Thebaid. What Egeria was probably shown was a double statue of a king beside a god, of a type which is by no means rare in Egypt.

4 *Bishop of Arabia:* This expression means rather Bishop of (the city of) Arabia, than of the province. The other bishops mentioned by Egeria (like those of today) are all named after cities and not provinces.

9 THE CITY OF ARABIA

9.5 *Tathnis* (which the manuscript here spells with a gap for one letter in the middle, i.e. Tat nis; cf. 9.6 where it is spelt in full) is clearly on the main road to Pelusium, which Egeria had joined at Faqūs (compare 9.7). It is therefore the same as the Taphnis of PD, V9, q.v.

7 *Aelia*, Hadrian's new name for Jerusalem, was the one in normal use in the Roman empire, see Eusebius, *VC* 26, n. 1 (p. 165); indeed the name Jerusalem was sometimes forgotten except by Jews and Christians. See Introduction, p. 10 above.

10—12 MOUNT NEBO

10.1 *Arabia* here describes not the Egyptian nome (see 7.1 above), but the large provincial area to the east and south of Palestine (see Map, p. 11).

1 *Araboth* means plains, and Araboth Moab has the traditional associations described in 10.4-7 below (cf. Eusebius, *On, Araboth, Dysme Moab*). The mountain where Moses died is Abarim (Deut. 32.49-50).

2 *saw fit to grant:* Egeria here, as on several other occasions, seems to be borrowing the language of formal prayers.

4 *Livias:* So named to flatter Augustus (Herod chose the name of his wife). But in A.D. 14 her name was changed, by the Will of Augustus, from Livia to Julia. The town's name was officially changed to Julias, but by the second century the change had been forgotten, and Livias was the only name used. Er Rameh is the present name of the site.

4 *forty:* Both the Hebrew and the Greek texts of the Bible give "thirty".

8 *Moses:* Cf. PD, Y11 (Merom). Any local memory of Moses attracts the memory of one of his water-miracles to a neighbouring spring. There is today a similar name given to the spring in the Wadi Mūsā outside Petra.

8 *the sixth milestone* has been found at el Maḥatta.

9 *many monks:* There are remains of buildings here, but the church has not been identified by excavation. The place is known as el Meshhed; see F. M. Abel in *R.B.* 40 (1931), pp. 375-6, and S. J. Saller, *The Memorial of Moses on Mount Nebo* (Jerusalem 1941), pp. 335-6.

12.1 *a church:* Saller excavated this, and his report shows the remains of the small chapel here mentioned. The present part of this site which Saller has identified with "Moses' tomb" is, however, outside the area of the early chapel. See plan. A further chapel ascribed to the fourth century has recently been discovered; see V. Corbo, "Nuovi scavi archeologici nella cappella del Battistero della Basilica del Nebo", in *LA* 17 (1967), pp. 241-58.

2 *his burial:* "No man knows his tomb" is the meaning of the Hebrew of Deut. 34.6. Egeria's informants, however, use the word *sepultura* which (like the LXX word here, ταφή) has the primary meaning of "act of burial". Only if the word can be taken in the latter sense is it then possible for the guides to go immediately on and point out the tomb.

2 *can be seen today:* The manuscript gives the meaning "cannot be seen to this day", which is in line both with Deut. 34.6 and with the late Jewish tradition set out by Jeremias, *Hg*, p. 102 (see, for example, 2 Macc. 2.7). But the editors are divided, and it seems impossible to maintain Jeremias' preference for the

manuscript reading without doing violence to the context, which demands an explanation of the "slightly raised place" as the place where Moses was buried. Christians were sadly ready to do violence to Jewish tradition, and the excavations, as Jeremias admits, make it certain that at a later date "Moses' Tomb" was located on Mount Nebo.

3 *the actual summit:* There is a viewing platform eighty metres north-west of the door of the chapel visited by Egeria, and, although it belongs to the later arrangement of the site, it would in any case have commanded the best view to the east, and was probably where she stood.

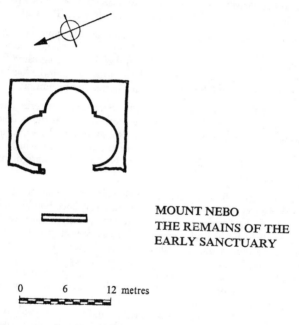

MOUNT NEBO
THE REMAINS OF THE
EARLY SANCTUARY

0   6   12 metres

5 *Zoar,* or Segor, is usually believed to have been some ruins south of the Dead Sea in the Ghor eṣ Ṣafi which would not be visible from the viewing platform at Nebo (Rās el Siyāgha). See *MM*, pp. 42–3. But the places her guides pointed out to her from here (as from the summit of Sinai in 3.8 above) are rather what they fancy than what could be seen. Some are obvious (Livias, Jericho, Heshbon) but others seem impossible, as will appear in the notes below. What Egeria was here shown can hardly be the present Shaghūr, since it is too close to Er Rameh, and probably formed part of Livias.

Lot's Wife: Josephus writes: "I have seen the pillar of salt, and it remains at this day" (*Ant* 1.11.4), and in early Christian tradition it is a commonplace that the pillar is still to be seen (cf. Wisd. 10.7; Clement R., *I ad Cor* 11.4; Irenaeus, *Haer.* 4.31.3). Yet Ps-Cyril (*Myst.* 1.8, PG 33.1073) speaks of Lot's wife, but not of the pillar. Egeria thinks that it has been submerged in the Dead Sea, but

* Theodosius and Antoninus of Piacenza both saw it, apparently at the northern end of the Dead Sea, in the sixth century (Theodosius 20, Antoninus 15, C.C.S.L. 122, 137). The pillar was no doubt one of the strange formations of the friable white marl which appears in the area near the river bank. These alter rapidly, and would explain the constant variations in the tradition.

8 *Heshbon*, Ḥisbān, or at least its direction, is visible from Rās el Siyāgha; but the city of Og, Edrei (which is presumably what is meant by "Safdra"), is a good forty miles away, and Egeria was probably shown the ruin Eḍ Ḍra'a on the high ground four miles east of 'Arak al Amir. The association of Og with Sehon (see Pss. 135.11; 136.20) leads to the identification of a place in the same neighbourhood, as with Tabor and Hermon (see PD, P3, n. 4).

9 *Peor*, or, as Egeria spelt it, Fogor, is the name usually applied to a mountain, and Beth-peor to the city on its slopes (Josh. 13.20). There is no need to assume with J. Ziegler (see Introduction, p. 6 above) that this reference came from Eusebius' *Onomasticon*. It might equally well have come through the local monks' study of Josh. 13.20 in combination with the narrative of Num. 23.

10 *the Viewpoint* is Pisgah or Phasga, in the Septuagint rendering, and Saller (op. cit., fig. 2) has identified it with the southern end of the double spur which forms Rās el Siyāgha. But it might also, as C. Conder suggested to Wilson (Bernard, op. cit., p. 145) be "one of the high rocks which rise from the
* plateau Nebo, probably Khazeikat an Nasābah, 'the upright stakes', a conspicuous point".

10 *Balak the son of Beor*: Egeria here makes an error, since Num. 22.2, etc., call Balak the son of Zippor. It is a significant error, since Eusebius makes the same mistake in the *Onomasticon* (76.9; cf. Jerome 77.14), and it is probable that the monks of Nebo had referred to the *Onomasticon* in working out the account they gave their visitors. Further signs of the use of the *Onomasticon* in this section may be the description of Peor as "a city of the kingdom of Edom" (cf. *On* 170.13), and the occurrence of "Safdra" (assuming it to mean Adra) immediately before the "Viewpoint", which come next to each other and in this order in *On* 12.13–19.

J. Ziegler, "Die Peregrinatio Aetheriae und das Onomastikon des Eusebius" in *Biblica* 12 (1931), pp. 70–84, followed by Gingras, p. 195, n. 164, suggests that Egeria herself used Jerome's translation of the *Onomasticon* when she was writing this passage, which would mean that she could not have written before 390. But if she had had personal access to the work, either in Greek or Latin, it is hard to see why she neither quotes it *verbatim* nor uses it in any other known or probable parts of her work.

13—16 THE LAND OF UZ

13—14 SALEM AND MELCHIZEDEK

13.1 *on pilgrimage*: Egeria's words are "go to a place for the sake of prayer" (*orationis gratia*).

2 *Carneas*: Ashtaroth (Tell 'Ashtarah) gave way to Carnaim (Sheikh Sa'ad) as the

principal city of Bashan, and Eusebius (*On, Carnaim*) reports that "by some tradition they show there the House of Job". It is clear that the Book of Job is concerned with some southern region (which is supported by the LXX, which states in the additional passage 42.17ᵈ translated from "the Syriac book" that he lived "in the land of Ausitis, on the borders of Idumaea and Arabia", that "his name before was Jobab" (cf. Gen. 36.32), and that "the name of his city was Dennaba", a city of Edom in the south). Both the memory of Job and the name Dennaba (Dinhaba) were artificially transported to Carnaim in the north, and there may be the echo of an anterior tradition of a northern Land of Uz in Josephus, who in *Ant.* 1.6.4 says that Uz, son of Aram (cf. Gen. 10.23) "founded Trachonitis and Damascus", though there is no other early Jewish evidence for the northern location. The miracle described in 16.5–6 may thus be the result of an attempt to establish the credentials of the northern site, and it is interesting to note the emphasis with which Jerome rejects the possibility (*On. Dannaba*, ✳
disputing the identity of Job with Jobab). Compare Jeremias, *Hg*, pp. 101–2, and see also the note on 16.6 *this church* below.

2 *a valley:* Probably the Wadi Shubbash.

3 *Sedima:* 13.4 tells us, probably correctly, that "its name used to be Salem". ✳
F. M. Abel, *Géographie de la Palestine* (Paris 1938), p. 441, says that Salim became Sedima just as Arbela became Irbid. 15.1 tells us that this small hill is two hundred yards from the spring with a pool which is identified with Aenon. The location is discussed at length by Kopp, pp. 129–37, but it can probably be identified with Tell Ridgha. The main objection to this identification was W. F. Albright's report of an "absence of Roman pottery" there (A.A.S.O.R. 19 (1925), p. 18); but since then plenty has been found, mainly of the fourth and sixth centuries, round the pool and south of the antiquities site. The site was first identified by E. Robinson in 1852 (see his *Biblical Researches in Palestine*, vol. 3 (London 1867), p. 315, and agrees well with Eusebius, *On, Aenon, Salim*, ✳
which indicates a place eight miles south of Scythopolis (Beisān). It is interesting that the Muslim worthy whose tomb is there is called Sheikh Sālim, and not by a name reflecting Egeria's corrupt form. Jerome, writing shortly after the time of Egeria's visit calls this Salim by another name, that is, Salumias. J. T. Milik's suggestion that Sedima may be Tell Ḥusn at Scythopolis (*R.B.* 66 (1959), pp. 562–6) is unlikely to be correct. It is hardly possible that she would pass by Scythopolis without mentioning it. She would have to retrace her steps to reach Tishbe (16.1). And Tell Ḥusn is surrounded not by a plain, but by steep hills and valleys.

3 *huge ancient foundations:* The associated pottery begins in the seventeenth century B.C. (Middle Bronze 2), but there is nothing earlier; see N. Suri in *Israel Archaeological Survey, Bet She'an* (Hebrew) (Jerusalem 1962), No. 66, pp. 163–4.

4 *Opu* is Greek for "where"; cf. the form "On Horeb" as a church title and see Additional Note J, p. 293 below.

3 *Chedorlaomer* seems here to be confused with "Tidal, king of the nations".

15 AENON AND JOHN THE BAPTIST

15.2 *administered baptism:* Egeria uses the word *operari*, which in Christian usage meant "exercised his ministry"; see Bastiaensen, *Obs*, p. 56.

5 *by torchlight:* This procession should be compared with the entry of the Jerusalem candidates from the baptistery (38.1).

6 *we set out:* Egeria now crosses the Jordan, though she does not mention the fact, any more than she mentions the far more formidable crossing of the Nile at Pelusium (9.7 above), which was on the west bank of the Pelusiac arm (Josephus, *War* 5.11.5). It may be presumed that she went much the same way to the ford as E. Robinson: "over a long narrow island . . . we got over very well . . . and soon came out upon the more elevated Ghor above, which is here narrow, and at first dry and desert. We struck across it obliquely, about East by North, towards the mouth of the Wadi Yābis as it issues from the mountains" (op. cit., p. 316). This is the route favoured by A. Augustinović and B. Bagatti "Escursioni nei Dintorni di 'Aglun", *LA* 2 (1951–2) pp. 22–8.

16 THE VALLEY OF CHERITH

16.1 *Tishbe* is Listib, on the way up the hill to 'Ajlūn, with Khirbat Mar Elias near by, the remains of a monastery of Saint Elijah. Egeria gives no description, and it should be assumed that the place was simply pointed out to her, while she and her party went up the Wadi Yābis. See Jeremias, *Hg*, pp. 105–6, who argues for an original tradition in Judg. 12.7 that Jephtha was buried at "Zaphon in the Land of Gilead" (cf. Judg. 12.1, *R.V.* mg), supported by Josephus' *Sebee* (*Ant.* 5.7.12).

2 *a very well-kept valley:* Wadi Yābis divides below Judeidah, and the road follows round to the right. Egeria may have gone on by Arbela (Irbid) and Ramoth (Ramthā).

4 *an enormous high mountain:* Probably Egeria's first view of Hermon, from some point just beyond Eṭ Ṭurra.
(Note 2) *The dunghill:* St John Chrysostom preaches about the meaning of pilgrimage to Job's dunghill in 387 (*Hom. ad pop. Ant. de Statuis* 5.1–3, *PG* 49.69), but does not mention the tomb. This has been taken as an argument for dating Egeria's visit later than the sermon (see Jeremias, *Hg*, p. 102, n. 1, and M. le Cour Grandmaison and B. Billet, "Le Pèlerinage au Fumier de Job et la date de l'Itinerarium Egeriae", in *R.S.R.* 48 (1960), pp. 460–5). But Chrysostom is not describing the area—indeed he had probably never been there—but preaching on one aspect which he judged appropriate. This reference need therefore have no more bearing on the dating of Egeria than Jerome's comparable silence about the tomb in the *Onomasticon*.

6 *the name* JOB: See Note G, "The Finding of Job", pp. 281–3 below.

6 *they built this church:* The tomb of Job and his wife is in an ancient buildingcomplex, once a monastery, at el Merkez, three-quarters of a mile south of Sheikh Sa'ad. The building in which these cenotaphs stand is not ancient. At

Sheikh Sa'ad itself are the Rock of Job "on which he sat and received his friends" according to the account given to G. Schumacher (*Across the Jordan* (London 1886), p. 191) which stands in what appears to be a late medieval shrine. The rock itself is an Egyptian stele from the reign of Rameses II (1304–1237 B.C.). Job's Bath mentioned in the Madrid fragment (cf. Holy Qur'ān, s. 38 Ṣad) is to the east of the Maqam Sh. Sa'ad near by. See Schumacher, op. cit., pp. 186–196, and W. F. Albright in BASOR 19, p. 15 and 89, pp. 12–13. There has been one excavation at Sh. Sa'ad, by Professor Hrozny in 1920 ("The First Czechoslovak Excavations in the Near-East", in *Central European Observer* 4 (1926), pp. 511ff and 527–9), and the site is still little known.

6 *They did not remove:* Since this was an exclusively Christian site, there was no reason to remove the bones.

7 *we asked the bishop*: For another celebration of the Eucharist at Egeria's request compare 4.8. Egeria's is the only surviving evidence for the existence of a bishop at Carneas.

7 *on our outward journey:* The manuscript adds the words "for three years", which seem to have been introduced from the next sentence; they are here ignored, following the suggestion of Wistrand.

17—23 THROUGH MESOPOTAMIA TO CONSTANTINOPLE

17–18 THE EUPHRATES

7.1 *Syrian Mesopotamia* is used here by Egeria as the biblical name for the region known as Osrhoene in the Roman Empire, of which Edessa was the capital.

1 *the holy apostle Thomas:* The apostle Thomas has traditionally had two types of connection with Edessa. From some time before the middle of the third century A.D. it was believed that his body had been brought to the city from India, since this is the date of compilation of the Syriac original of the Acts of Thomas (sec. 170, Hennecke 2.530), and this belief is still maintained in the tradition of the Jacobite Syrians of Malabar. And from about the time of Egeria it came to be accepted that he was the apostle sent to Edessa by Christ. The early tradition of the conversion of Edessa in the Syriac language names the apostle as Addai (see Segal, p. 65), but the earliest account in Greek, which happens also to be the earliest now available to us, names him as Thaddaeus. This name seems to have been chosen because it was the best available approximation to Addai actually to appear in the New Testament, but the name Thomas also appears, since this apostle was dispatched to Edessa by "Judas, who was also Thomas" (see p. 151 above). Segal, p. 66, also mentions a Greek inscription, only slightly later than the time of Egeria which gives a version of the *Letter of Jesus*. It was found at Kırk Magara close to Edessa, and gives the name of the apostle sent to the city as "Thaddaeus, that is, Thomas". Thus Egeria seems here to be recording faithfully the stage which the story had reached in her time. Segal, pp. 67–9, adds the interesting suggestion that the form of the story of the conversion of

Edessa may have arisen out of the very similar account of the conversion of the royal house of Adiabene to Judaism, which is told in Josephus, *Ant.* 20.2.

18.1 *Coele-Syria*, with Antioch as the capital, was from the end of the second century A.D. the name of the northern part of what had formerly been the province of Syria. This was in about 341 further divided into Coele-Syria and Augusta Euphratensis (which had its capital at Hierapolis (Membij)), an important military centre. At the end of the fourth century, soon after Egeria's visit, Coele-Syria was further divided into Syria Iᵃ and IIᵃ.

  2 *the Rhône*, over which Egeria must have crossed on any overland route from the Atlantic coast of Spain or south-western France. She may even have crossed it from Nîmes to Arles, like the Bordeaux pilgrim (552, *C.C.S.L.* 175, p. 2). It is therefore most likely that her remark on its speed is a personal recollection, since her Latin style does not suggest any familiarity with the works of the authors who provide it with epithets (Ausonius—*praeceps*; Lucan and Claudian —*velox*; or Silius—*ferox*).

  3 *more than half a day:* It is notable that this and 10.3 are the only places—both exceptional—where Egeria troubles to record crossing rivers. Delays at ferries and fords were perhaps taken for granted.

19 EDESSA: TOMBS OF SAINT THOMAS AND KING ABGAR

19.1 *Batanis*, or Batnae (Sürüj), in Osrhoene was a town where important annual fairs were held, which were given strong military protection. Egeria perhaps
  ✳ thought that Josh. 19.25 referred to it.

  1 *Bishop, confessor.* The word confessor (ὁμολογητής) is a term reserved for Christian heroes who have suffered for the faith without actually being put to death. This bishop may well be the Abraham to whom St Basil wrote; see Note B, p. 237 below.

  2 *to the church and martyrium of holy Thomas:* It seems to have been Egeria's normal practice to make straight for the principal church when she first arrived in a new city (cf. 14.1; 20.2; 23.1) so as to meet the bishop or priest who would conduct her prayer. But the phrase "church and martyrium" raises a teasing question: does it refer to one building or two? If a certain answer could be given, it might provide evidence for the date of Egeria's visit, since the *Chronicle of Edessa* (c. 540) states that "on 22 August 394 they took the coffin of Mar Thomas the Apostle into his own great church". But certainty cannot be gained on this subject for three reasons. First, Egeria's text here (*ad ecclesiam et ad martyrium sancti Thomae*) inclines only slightly in favour of two buildings, and could mean only one. Secondly, our knowledge about the churches of Edessa at the end of the fourth century is far from exhaustive (see Segal, p. 181, n. 4). Before 373 there was certainly a martyrium of St Thomas outside the city to the west, and there may possibly have been a church of St Thomas inside the city as well (Segal, p. 175 and n. 5). And thirdly, the information in 19.3 that the church visited by Egeria was "built in the new way" cannot be associated with any archaeological evidence. Not only has there been no excavation of the

churches of Edessa, but it is probable that excavation would be useless in view of the frequency of violent floods in the city. We know that the principal church was rebuilt in 313 and extended in 327–8 (Segal, p. 181). And since at these dates there was not as yet any standard plan for a church building, Egeria, in using the phrase "built in a new way", may simply mean that she found the arrangement of this church unfamiliar.

2 *our usual prayers:* The plural "prayers" need not indicate two acts of prayer, one in the "church" and one in the "martyrium", but may equally apply to a single act of prayer at the place of St Thomas' burial, since, as indicated in 10.7 above, the standard scheme of worship used in a holy place had a prayer both at the beginning and at the end.

2 *the writings of holy Thomas:* Probably the Acts of Thomas (cf. Baumstark, *CL*, p. 14). The Gospel of Thomas, though it had a wide circulation in the West, had regularly been condemned as a Gnostic work since the time of Origen, *Hom. 1 in Luc.*, PG, 13.1803 (Latin). Cyril tells his catechumens: "Let no one read the Gospel according to Thomas, for it is the work not of one of the Twelve apostles, but of one of the three evil followers of Manes" (*Cat.* 6.31, PG 33.593).

4 *many martyria:* Segal, p. 174, points out that until about A.D. 350 the remains of martyrs, like those of other citizens, were buried in cemeteries outside the city walls. Thus by 345 there was a martyrium erected at the burial place of the Edessan martyrs Guria, Shmona, and Habbib (Segal, p. 182) and St Ephraim Syrus was buried nearby in 373 (Segal, p. 182, n. 1). Their tombs are probably those beneath the ruins of a church on the west side of what is now the playground of the Yakup Kalfa School; see also P. Peeters on "La basilique des Confesseurs à Edesse" in "Glanures Martyrologiques", *AB* 58 (1940), pp. 110–23. The monasteries further away cannot certainly be located, but there must have been many, since by A.D. 449 there were 90,000 monks in the hills of Edessa (Segal, p. 191, n. 6).

5 *The holy bishop . . . confessor:* Eulogios is recorded in the *Chronicle* of Edessa (C.S.C.O., Scr. Syr. ser. 3. tom. 4, pp. 5–6, art. 34) as bishop 379–78, and had ✳ been exiled to the Thebaid by Valens (Emperor 364–78). thus earning the title "confessor". See Note B, p. 237 below.

6 *the palace of King Abgar:* Section 15 below shows that this was a later palace built below one which occupied the site of the present citadel. A king called Abgar Uchama reigned over Osrhoene from 4 B.C. to A.D. 50. But Abgar IX (179–214) was converted to Christianity, and it was probably later in the third century that the story came to be told of Abgar's letter to Christ (see p. 151 above and Segal, pp. 17, 26).

6 *wise and noble:* For another estimate of Abgar Uchama see Tacitus, *Ann.* 12.12.14. A few possibly contemporary statues have been found in Edessa, see Segal, p. 33, and plates 12 and 15. Note that Egeria does not describe any portrait of Christ at Edessa, though such a portrait is already mentioned by about A.D. 400 by *The Doctrine of Addai* in recounting its version of the Abgar legend, and the portrait became one of the city's most prized possessions.

6 *Magnus* (Ma'nou) was also an Edessene dynastic name.

7 *the pools with the fish:* These, like the fishpools at Hierapolis, had in all probability been sacred to the Syrian Goddess Atargatis or Hera (Segal, pp. 6, 8, 46-9, and 54). The two pools still exist with their great shoals of fish, under the names of Birkat Ibrahim and Ain Zilhah, "Zilhah" being probably not the traditional name of Potiphar's wife in this case, but a version of "Sulkha", the name given by Muslims to Nimrod's mother (Segal, p. 2). Muslims continue to treat the fish with reverence. On the evidence of this section for the development of Edessa's water-supply see Note H below, pp. 284-7.

9 *the gate:* see below, note on 19.17.

13 *Persis* is the province of Persia today called Fars (the same name) or Farsistan.

13 *ever afterwards:* Edessa had in fact been taken by the Persian King Sapor I in A.D. 259-60, but the bishop was possibly unaware of the fact.

14 *in a field:* The two pools occupy a low level which seems in fact to have been the river-bed before it was adorned with the later palace.

14 *Abgar's palace:* Segal (p. 17) dates the building of the upper palace as probably 205-6. Its commanding position had the additional advantage of securing it against any possible floods, like that of 201, which had entirely destroyed an earlier palace on the site of the fishpools. See also R. Duval, *Histoire politique, religieuse, et littéraire d'Edesse* (Paris 1892), p. 12.

16 *the letters* were condemned as spurious by a Roman synod of 494-5, but were accepted as genuine for much longer in the Eastern part of the Church.

17 *through this gate:* The main route from the eastern coast of the Mediterranean, and the one through which Egeria most probably entered the city, was the one on the west. It is therefore through this gate that the messenger was most probably thought to have entered (cf. Segal, p. 186). Egeria's report that "no dead body has been taken out through it" may well refer, as Segal suggests, to the fact that one of the main cemeteries which used to lie outside it had recently been closed.

18 *the tomb of Abgar:* The most notable tomb which is visible from the citadel is on the hill immediately to the south, and has a large arched door cut in the rock face (see E. Sachau, *Reise in Syrien und Mesopotamien* (Leipzig 1883), p. 201; its name is Apker Takavor = King Abgar). But Egeria seems rather to be referring to some monument she was shown before she reached the citadel, or "first palace".

19 *not so complete:* Egeria's suspicion was correct; see p. 152, n. 5 above, and Segal, pp. 62-76.

20 CARRAE: HOLY ABRAHAM AND SAINT HELPIDIUS

20.1 *Carrae* is spelt Charris in the manuscript, and its biblical name is Haran (LXX, Charran) here spelt Charra; it is thus often hard to know which name Egeria means to use. This city was the site of Crassus' famous defeat by the Parthians in 63 B.C.

1 *go unto Charra:* God's call comes to Abraham in Haran (see Gen. 12.4) in the Old Testament, but Egeria is here recalling the New Testament version (see Acts 7.2–3) where the call comes in Ur.

2 *the church inside the city:* Two have been discovered in modern times; see Sachau, op. cit., p. 219 and compare S. Lloyd and W. Brice, "Harran" in *A.S.* 1 (1951), p. 86, and Lloyd and Brice, op. cit., pp. 105–8, but it may well be that neither was yet in existence at the time of Egeria's visit. Note that there were few Christians there, and that she speaks of "the church".

2 *the bishop . . . confessor:* Until 381, when he signed the decrees of the First Council of Constantinople, the Bishop of Carrae was Vitus (Bitos). See C. H. Turner in *Journal of Theological Studies* 15 (1914), p. 168. Soon afterwards he was succeeded by Protogenes, who as a presbyter had accompanied Eulogios of Edessa into exile in the Thebaid. See Theodoret, *HE* 4.18.14; 5.4.7, *PG* 82. 1157–60, 1204.

3 *a church outside the city:* Immediately outside the city walls to the north-west is the shrine of Sheikh Hayat al Harrani (see Lloyd and Brice, op. cit., p. 86). Muslims believe this to be the tomb of Aran, Haran's founder, and it is therefore *a priori* likely that Christians had identified the same spot with Abraham's house. This tradition would be likely to have been lost in Muslim tradition since for them Urfa (Edessa) is the ancient Ur of the Chaldees, where they now venerate Maqam Ibrahim as Abraham's House. Christians of Egeria's time believed that Ur of the Chaldees was in Persia as is shown by section 5 below. "Abraham's House" contained, or was beside, a martyr's tomb, as also appears from section 5. But for the later condition of this "House" see D. S. Rice, *A.S.* 2 (1952), p. 42.

the bishop blessed us: The blessing is only added to the pilgrimage prayers by bishops; cf. 16.7.

the well at which holy Rebecca: This well seems to be the one used as the main water-supply by those who live in Haran, which is now called "Jacob's Well". But the name clearly belongs to Muslim rather than to Christian tradition. Egeria here connects the well with Isaac's bride, not Jacob's, and identifies a Jacob's Well elsewhere in section 11 below.

Helpidius is otherwise unknown, and it is uncertain whether the 23 April was his holy day, or its eve.

Absolutely no Christians: This feature of Carrae is confirmed by Theodoret; see references in note on 20.2 above.

The whole city is heathen: Apart from her mention of the people of Paran (6.2) this is Egeria's only other mention of contemporary non-Christians.

the tombs of Nahor and Bethuel: It is impossible to suggest a location for any such tombs (see Lloyd and Brice, op. cit., pp. 96–7); it is interesting to hear that Nahor and Bethuel were in fact held in special honour. Many of those in the district were Sabians who venerated the moon and the heavenly bodies (see Lloyd and Brice, op. cit., pp. 87–96, and J. B. Segal, "Pagan Syriac Monuments in the Vilayet of Urfa", *A.S.* 3 (1953), esp. pp. 107–12). In section 9 Egeria herself seems courteously to show surprise at what the bishop has told her.

9 *knew . . . about the Bible:* Though this is a conventional way of praising clerics (cf. 8.4; 14.2), it was perhaps obviously true of Protogenes, who had spent his time in exile at Antinoe holding a bible school; see Theodoret, *HE* 4.18.8–9.

10 *canonical Scriptures* (scriptura canonis): Egeria is probably here using a relatively new word, since only in the mid-fourth century did *canon* acquire the meaning of the list of recognized biblical books.

12 *Nisibis* had been in the Roman Empire, but Jovian had to abandon it to the Persians in 363.

21 FADANA: LABAN'S VILLAGE AND JACOB'S WELL

21.1 *the well where holy Jacob:* Six miles from Haran is the northern of the two hills called Telfidan (=Fadana). It contains many wells and cisterns, and the one reputed to be the oldest, which is to the north-east of the hill, is surrounded by masonry scattered over a considerable area. This masonry may well have belonged to the church of which Egeria here speaks.

4 *a big village:* Probably the southern Telfidan, though it is more than half a mile away.

4 *Laban* is "the Aramean" in the Hebrew and "the Syrian" in the Greek of Gen. 25.20. The Old Latin version follows the Greek; see Gingras, p. 210, n. 234.

4 *Fadana*, like "Syrian Mesopotamia" (see note on 17.1 above) is a version of the name "Paddan-Aram" (Gen. 25.20; 28.2).

5 *we returned by the same road:* Since in section 4 Egeria says that her road went past Telfidan and she has come from Haran, she is not returning to Edessa, but taking the main road running west to Sürüj (Batanis); it was therefore at Sürüj that she rejoined the road to Antioch.

22–3 SELEUCIA IN ISAURIA: SAINT THECLA

22.1 *Antioch:* No doubt its holy places, for example, the tomb of the Maccabees which Jerome suspects as spurious (*On, Modeim*), were described by Egeria in her account of her outward journey.

1 *several staging-posts:* The Bordeaux pilgrim mentions only one: 581, *C.C.S.L.* 175, p. 11.

1 *Tarsus:* Little remains of what Egeria may have seen apart from the battered but massive Roman "Sea Gate" and perhaps "St Paul's Well".

2 *Holy Thecla:* The Acts of Paul and Thecla, part of the late second-century Acts of Paul, was extremely popular, as is shown by the large number of early

translations which have survived. It describes Thecla as converted at Iconium, working with St Paul, and suffering as the first woman confessor. She ended her life at Seleucia, and her martyrium is at what is now Meriamlik (see Note I, p. 288 below).

23.1 *Pompeiopolis:* One kilometre south of the town of Mezetli, among the houses of Viranşehir and next to the sea, are the ruins of Pompeiopolis. The Roman remains include a street of which many pillars are still standing, and the concrete *
core of the west gate, through which Egeria probably left the city.

1 *Corycus:* Now Kizkalesi, contains the remains of a flourishing Christian city, though the Christian remains are all later than Egeria's time.

1 *Seleucia of Isauria* is still named Silifke. It has not been explored in a way which would suggest the position of the church here mentioned, but the main mosque, though itself a medieval building, stands on an ancient site well below the level of the surrounding streets.

2 *a mile and a half:* The distance is greater by the modern road, but Egeria's estimate corresponds with the old one, which still exists as a track running southwestwards from Silifke.

2 *Round the holy church:* Egeria speaks as if there were a single church in the late fourth century, though the site today contains three of the fifth century. For the Martyrium of St Thecla see Note I, p. 288 below.

3 *deaconess:* Marthana, like Macrina, sister of St Basil of Caesarea and St Gregory of Nyssa, was probably made a deaconess through the episcopal laying on of hands.

3 *Marthana* is praised by a fifth-century Bishop Basil of Seleucia in his *Life of St Thecla,* 2.30 PG 85. 618. See H. Delehaye in *A.B.* 43 (1925), pp. 49–57.

3 *apotactites or virgins:* This is the first mention of women who lead the religious life in the manuscript, but apotactites and virgins are frequently mentioned in the later part of the text where Egeria speaks of Jerusalem. See Introduction, pp. 34–5 above.

4 *a great wall* of which remains are still visible in places.

4 *the martyrium* is a crypt in the rock under the church. See Note I, p. 288 below.

4 *the Isaurians:* Their raids eventually brought about the decline of Silifke.

7 *the holy Euphemia:* St Euphemia was martyred at Chalcedon in 303–4, and in 451 the Council of Chalcedon took place in the basilica dedicated in her name.

9 *all the churches:* See the description in Eusebius, *VC* 4.58, *PG* 20.1209, and F. van der Meer and C. Mohrmann, *Atlas of the Early Christian World* (Eng. tr. M. F. Hedlund and H. H. Rowley) (London 1958), Map. 37.

10 *Asia,* i.e. the province on the west coast of Asia Minor.

10 *the martyrium of the . . . Apostle John:* On which see H. Plommer in *A.S.* 12 (1962) pp. 119–29.

10 *do not forget me:* This phrase has a final ring about it, as if Egeria has now come to the end of her letter from Constantinople. It is possible that she despatched what she had written to her sisters independently of writing the rest of the text.

24—25 THE WEEKLY SERVICES

24. 1–7 ON WEEKDAYS

24.1 *monazontes and parthenai:* See Introduction, p. 35 above.

7 *the Cross:* Egeria no doubt described this in her account of her first arrival in Jerusalem, which may account for its abrupt introduction here.

24.7–12—25. 1–6a ON SUNDAY (INCOMPLETE)

8 *basilica* seems to be a word unfamiliar to Egeria, who uses it of the Anastasis and of the courtyard (as here; cf. 24.10; 25.2; and Vermeer, *Obs*, pp. 100–5). But her regular word for the Martyrium building is *ecclesia*, compare Bord. 594, p. 158, n. 8 above, and Eusebius, *VC* 3.31, p. 166 above.

10 *basilica:* This expression makes it clear that by the time of Egeria the Anastasis was a building, and not a place in the open air; but the same fact is clear from the regularity of the services which are held in it.

12 *his house:* The bishop probably lived in one of the houses surrounding the buildings on Golgotha, like those which have been discovered to the north-west of the present rotunda: see V. Corbo, *La Basilica del Santo Sepolcro* (*Quaderni de "La Terra Santa"*) (Jerusalem 1969), top right corner of Plate 1.

25.1 *on Golgotha Behind the Cross:* "Golgotha" must here be a word which applies to the whole Martyrium site; cf. Bord 593, p. 158, n. 6, above, which may be using the name in the same way.

* 3 *the tomb, the cave itself:* Latin *martyrii speluncae*, "of the 'testimony', the cave"; cf. Eusebius, *VC* 3.28, p. 165, n. 5, above, and Vermeer, *Obs*, p. 118.

3 *a thanksgiving:* It has been suggested that this expression implies a second celebration of the Eucharist, as by Bastiaensen, *Obs*, pp. 85–8; but see Introduction, pp. 60–1 above.

9 *under the supervision of his mother:* but see p. 46, n. 1 above.

25.6b—49 THE LITURGICAL YEAR

25.6b–12 EPIPHANY (INCOMPLETE)

11 *Eleona* is the name both of the Mount of Olives and of the church which Constantine built on its summit. The word is formed of the Greek (elaiōn) "of olives" with the addition of a semitic ending. See *VA, Jérusalem* 2, p. 382, and Introduction, p. 49 above: also note J, p. 293 below.

11 *the Lazarium:* See Introduction, p. 53 above.

26 THE FORTIETH DAY AFTER EPIPHANY

5. *the Fortieth Day:* Gingras, p. 225, n. 317, points out that this is the calculation prescribed in Lev. 12.2–5.

27 THE FORTY DAYS BEFORE EASTER—THE SERVICES

28 THE FORTY DAYS BEFORE EASTER—FASTING

29 SATURDAY IN THE SEVENTH WEEK

30—38 THE GREAT WEEK

30–31 THE SUNDAY

32–35 MONDAY—THURSDAY

36–37 FRIDAY

2 *Gethsemane:* Wherever Gethsemane was, the name implied first and foremost the place of arrest; thus Cyril, *Cat.* 10.19, *PG* 33.688, "Gethsemane is his witness, which to the eyes of our imagination almost shows Judas still", and 13.38, *PG* 33.817.

2 *hundreds of church candles:* Cf. 43.7.

1 *the column:* Jerome, *Ep.* 108.9 (written in 404, twenty years after Egeria's visit), ＊ speaks of this column as "holding up the porch of the church [at Sion]; it is stained with the Lord's blood".

1 *the holy Wood of the Cross:* See Note C, pp. 240–1 below.

2 *bit off a piece:* Procopius, *Bell. Pers.* 2 (see Gingras, p. 239, n. 384), records the theft of a large piece of the cross by a Syrian. He took it to Apamea, where it was long venerated.

3 *the Ring of Solomon:* See Bord 589, p. 156, n. 4 above. The ring plays a vital part in the tale of Solomon's building of the Temple.

3 *the Horn:* This relic is not mentioned in earlier tradition as far as we know it.

38 SATURDAY

39—41 THE DAYS OF EASTER

not a single person fasts: Gingras, p. 244, n. 418, quotes Tertullian, *de Corona* 3, "Fasting on Sunday, or kneeling for prayer, we regard as a crime, and we enjoy exemption from both from Easter Day through till Pentecost."

42 THE FORTIETH DAY AFTER EASTER

43 THE FIFTIETH DAY AFTER EASTER

43.3 *the descent of the Spirit:* See 37.1; 39.5 for the other commemorations of Sion.

44 THE REST OF THE YEAR

45—47 THE PREPARATION OF THE CATECHUMENS

45-46 BEFORE EASTER

47 DURING THE DAYS OF EASTER

47.3 *Syriac,* according to Telfer, *Cyril,* p. 35, is, strictly speaking, Palestinian Aramaic.

48-49 THE DAYS OF ENCAENIA (INCOMPLETE)

48.1 *on the same day . . . the Anastasis:* Egeria at least believed that the Anastasis as she knew it was dedicated at the same time as the Martyrium. But it is hard to sustain this opinion in view of Eusebius' descriptions; see p. 40 above.

Additional
Notes

A *The Name of the Pilgrim*

The manuscript of the *Travels* has lost its opening and final pages, where it would be reasonable to expect her name to appear. Hence, when the first edition appeared in 1887, J. F. Gamurrini, its editor, had to supply a name, and chose that of a pilgrim from Aquitaine who was mentioned by Palladius. Her name was Silvia,[1] and until 1903 this conjecture was not questioned. But in 1903 Dom M. Férotin recognized that a seventh-century *Letter in praise of the Blessed Aetheria* was in fact about the *Travels*. It was written by a monk of Galicia called Valerius.

Following Dom Férotin most scholars adopted the name Aetheria. But this version of the name was in fact only one among many offered by different manuscripts of Valerius' *Letter*, which included also Egeria, Echeria, Etheria, Heteria, and Eiheria. Egeria was the name of one of the Latin goddesses,[2] and Dom Férotin thought that a literary scribe had mistakenly substituted this familiar name for the less familiar Aetheria, which he preferred.

Other evidence has since been assembled which makes it more probable that Egeria is in fact the correct name. The *Liber Glossarum*, quoting the *Travels* Ch. 15.3 gives the source as "Egeria" in two of its chief manuscripts,[3] written before the eleventh century. This spelling might arguably be based on a manuscript of the *Travels* which in three successive catalogues of the library of St Martial at Limoges is listed as *Itinerarium Egerie abbatisse*. The first of these catalogues was written in the twelfth century. The abbey of Celanova in Galicia in the twelfth century listed one of its books as *Ingerarium Geriae*.[4] Indeed the entries at Limoges and Celanova may even refer to one and the same manuscript.

---

[1] Silvia or Silvania; *Hist. Laus.* 142, *PL* 73.1210; cf. Ps-Heraclides, *Paradisus* 42, *PL* 74.328.

[2] See Vergil, *Aeneid* 7.762–3.

[3] W. M. Lindsay and J. F. Mountford, *Glossaria latina iussu Academiae Britannicae edita*, vol. I (Paris 1926), p. 110, CE 379. The third manuscript reads *egene*.

[4] See J. F. Mountford, "Silvia, Aetheria, or Egeria?", in *The Classical Quarterly*, vol. XVII (January 1923) pp. 40–41, and A. Lambert, "Egeria. Notes critiques sur la tradition de son nom et celle de l'Itinerarium", in *Revue Mabillon*, vol. XXVI (1936), pp. 71–94.

What little evidence there is thus points to Egeria as the most probable of the variants which exist in Valerius' *Letter* in its different manuscripts; but it is hardly conclusive.

B *The Date of the Pilgrimage*

From the time when the manuscript of the *Travels* was discovered it was seen that its date was somewhere between 363 and 540. The first is the date when Nisibis became inaccessible to Romans,[1] and the second the date when Chosroes destroyed Antioch, but the latitude was very great, and many attempts have been made to provide a more definite date for the extremely important evidence which Egeria provides. In recent years it was generally ✳ agreed that Egeria saw the Holy Land in about A.D. 400.

In 1911 A. Baumstark[2] had once again drawn attention to the importance of the title "confessor" which Egeria applies to the Bishops of Batanis, Edessa, and Carrae.[3] He took the word to mean a Christian who has undergone heroic sufferings in time of persecution, without being martyred, and identified Eulogios of Edessa as the only confessor to occupy the see during the period when Egeria might have visited the city. Eulogios and Protogenes, who became Bishop of Carrae, had been sentenced to exile in the Thebaid by the Arian Emperor Valens (A.D. 364–78), and after Eulogios' return to his see, and the Council of Constantinople (381), he consecrated Protogenes Bishop of the needy city of Carrae.[4] Egeria's third "confessor" bishop may have been Abraham. He was Bishop of Batanis in 373 (though we know from St Basil of Caesarea's *Letter 132* that at that time he was a wanderer) and attended the Council of Constantinople in this capacity.

Since Bishop Eulogios died on 23 April 387, Egeria must have visited him, at the latest, in that year. It was in fact on this date in the year that she travelled from Edessa to Carrae for the eve of St Helpidius. The latest date for her visit to Edessa is therefore 386, and the earliest is 382, since Protogenes' predecessor Bitos signed his name on behalf of the see of Carrae at the Council of

[1] Cf. 20.12; Jovian was driven back by the Persians.
[2] Cf. 19.1; 19.5; 20.2. ✳
[3] "Das Alter der *Peregrinatio Aetheriae*" in *Oriens Christianus*, n.s., vol. 1 (1911), pp. 32–76. The argument was first put forward by Gamurrini (1887), pp. XXVIII–XXIX.
[4] See Theodoret, *Hist. Eccl.* IV.17,18, PG 82.1156.

Constantinople (which ended in July 381), and the spring of 382 was thus the first when Egeria could have visited Carrae and found Protogenes as bishop.

Baumstark's argument was contested by Dom A. Lambert[1] in 1938, who held that in the West, and specially in Spain, *confessor* meant a monk whose particular work was the celebration of the divine office, or, in other words the same as the Eastern word *aputactita*. But, if this were so, it is hard to see why Egeria could not have used *aputactita* in this context, since she uses it freely elsewhere—indeed ten times in the *Travels* as we have it.

In 1967 P. Devos arrived independently at the same conclusion as Baumstark,[2] and showed not only that it was well-founded, but that only one of the years 382–86 was a possibility.

Egeria says that she spent "three full years" in Jerusalem (17.1), then on her way back to Constantinople made her journey to Carrae, where she arrived on 23 April. In fact she seems to have intended no more than a visit to Edessa (17.1) and was delighted to find that the day of her arrival at Carrae was the eve of an important feast. Egeria seems to have had plenty of time at her disposal,[3] and it is incredible that she should choose to leave the Holy City in the spring without waiting to celebrate Easter there.

But from Jerusalem to Edessa was a considerable journey—twenty-five staging-posts (17.2)—and, since Egeria normally travelled a stage a day, and says that she spent one complete day in Hierapolis (18.1) and three in Edessa (19.3), besides the day travelling on from Edessa to Carrae, we must reconstruct her journey as follows, working back from Carrae:

23 April	arrival at Carrae after journey from Edessa
20–22 April	stay in Edessa
19 April	arrival in Edessa
	twenty-four days of travel and one staying in Hierapolis
25 March	departure from Jerusalem.

[1] "*L'Itinerarium Egeriae* vers 414–416", in *Revue Mabillon*, vol. 28 (1938), pp. 49–69.

[2] See the important article "La Date du Voyage d'Égérie" in *A.B.*, vol. 85 (1967), pp. 165–94.

[3] E.g. she was able to consider visiting Ephesus (23.10).

Between 382 and 386 the dates of Easter were:

382	17 April
383	9 April
384	24 March
385	13 April
386	5 April

Devos holds that Egeria visited the three confessor bishops in Syrian Mesopotamia in 384, and that her stay in Jerusalem lasted from Easter 381 to Easter 384. This is the dating here accepted. *

C   *The Finding of the Cross*

The wood of the holy cross was kept in Jerusalem in Egeria's time and exposed for veneration on Good Friday (37.1–2), and she notes that the Jerusalem dedication festival was arranged to co-incide with the day when the Lord's cross had been found (48.2). But, although she speaks of the Empress Helena as present during Constantine's works at the Martyrium, (25.9), she does not so much as hint that it was Helena who found the cross.

Eusebius' *Life of Constantine* lays surprisingly little emphasis on the crucifixion, though he is well aware of the general position of Golgotha,[1] and, although he mentions Helena as closely connected with the churches at Bethlehem and on the Mount of Olives,[2] he clearly knew nothing of her having found the cross.[3]

In 347, however, twelve years after the dedication of the Martyrium, Cyril of Jerusalem preached his catechetical lectures there. In contrast with Eusebius he makes constant mention of Golgotha, and also of "the holy wood of the Cross . . . which is seen among us to this day, and because of those who have in faith taken thereof, has from this place now almost filled the whole world".[4] No wonder he took such pains to see that no more pieces were removed when Egeria witnessed his precautions at the Good Friday veneration. No doubt what was "seen among us" was the relic in its silver box seen by Egeria, and it is certain that in the second half of the fourth century relics of the cross were relatively common.[5] St Macrina, who died in 379, used to wear one in a locket,[6] and Chrysostom in the nineties speaks as if this was a widespread practice.[7]

Chrysostom is the last major author who seems to be ignorant

---

[1] Cf. his *Onomasticon* s.v. *Golgotha*, 248 and *De Laud. Const.* 9, PG 20.1372.

[2] Vit. Const. 3.41ff.

[3] He could hardly have omitted so important a detail from both the *Life of Constantine* and from the panegyric *De Laudibus Constantini* if it had been familiar to his contemporaries.

[4] *Cat.* 10.19. There is no clear reason to doubt the authenticity of these words.

[5] An inscription dated 359 and mentioning a relic DE LIGNO CRUCIS was found at Tixter, near Sétif in Algeria.

[6] Gregory of Nyssa, *Vita St Macr.*, PG 46.989.

[7] Chrysostom, *Contra Jud. et Gent.* 9, PG 47. 826.

of the story of Helena's finding the cross, for, though he describes its discovery,[1] he says nothing of Helena. The first mention of her as the one who found it comes in St Ambrose's sermon on the death of Theodosius in 395.[2] He tells how the Empress found three crosses, the title (cf. Egeria 37.3), and two nails.[3] Rufinus, writing six years later, mentions a similar story which is clearly an attempt to combine Eusebius' account of the clearing of the Martyrium site with new material.[4] But, whereas the versions of Chrysostom and Ambrose are content with the identification of Christ's cross by the title, it has become detached in Rufinus' version, and the ✻ cross is distinguished from those of the robbers by its efficacy in curing a sick woman; and this version appears in subsequent church histories.[5] But other versions were also in circulation. In 403 St Paulinus of Nola describes Helena's discovery of the cross in a letter accompanying a relic of the cross which he sent to a friend,[6] and substitutes the revival of a corpse for the recovery of a sick woman.

Since Egeria's main description of the Jerusalem holy places must have occupied pages of her manuscript now lost, we cannot know in what form she knew of the finding of the cross. But she says enough about the cross to make it extremely improbable that she thought Helena discovered it, and is likely to witness to an earlier and less developed stage in the evolution of the story.

[1] Chrysostom, *In Joh. Hom.* 85.1, *PG* 59.461.
[2] Ambrose, *In Ob. Theod.* 46, *PL* 16.1399.
[3] One of which she made into a crown and the other into a bridle for Constantine. The bridle is carefully explained.
[4] Rufinus, *Hist. Eccl.* 1.7, *PL* 21.475ff.
[5] E.g. Socrates I.17; Sozomen II.1; Theodoret. I.18.
[6] Paulinus, *Ep.* XXXI, *PL* 61.325f.

D *The Cave of the Anastasis*

In her description of the liturgy in Jerusalem Egeria often mentions the Cave of the Anastasis; every morning the bishop "goes straight into the Cave, and inside the screen he first says the Prayer for All" (24.2), and at Lucernare every afternoon "the fire is brought not from outside, but from the cave—inside the screen—where a lamp is always burning night and day" (24.4). What Egeria says is definite enough, but she leaves so much unsaid that it is impossible to visualize the Cave unless we supplement her description from other sources.

Eusebius hints that the cave was "the only thing standing in a wide space" (cf. *VC* 35, p. 168, n. 1) and says that the Emperor "adorned" it with "choice columns and much ornament, sparing no art to make it beautiful" (*VC.* 34, p. 167, n. 3). Cyril recalls
* (*Cant* 2.14) "the cleft in the rock", and explains that this means "the shelter which was then at the door of the saving tomb, and was hewn out of the rock, as is normally done here in front of tombs. You cannot see it now, because the outer cave has been hewn away for the sake of the present decoration, but before His Majesty zealously decorated the tomb there used to be a cave in

**JERUSALEM:
"ABSALOM'S TOMB'**

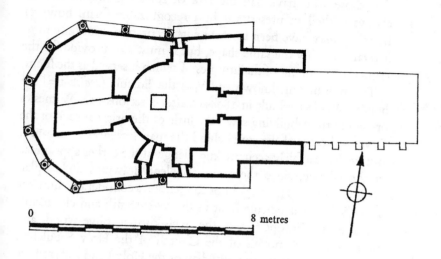

THE EDICULE IN 1609

the face of the rock" (*Cat.* 14.9). Cyril also tells us that the stone which closed the mouth of the tomb is "lying there to this day" (*Cat.* 14.22) and indeed part of the same stone is in all probability visible today.[1]

These scraps of evidence enable us to form some picture of the type of monument Egeria saw. It had been a cave with a porch-like opening in front of it, but only the cave was left after it had been adorned with columns and other decoration. This was still rock, and thus possibly comparable in general type with the so-called "Tomb of Absalom" or the Tomb of the Virgin, both of which are rock monuments artificially isolated from their original surroundings, round which the rock has been levelled to form a floor.

In view of the ambiguous and scanty early evidence for the form of the tomb the wisest procedure is to work back from the known

---

[1] It forms the *mensa* of the very small altar in the Chapel of the Angel.

to the unknown. In adopting this procedure it is safe to assume that those who have had the task of restoring the monument always wished to preserve it in a recognizable form, however free they may have been to change its decoration. Not only must it retain roughly the same shape, but it must also provide for the regular functioning of the liturgies of which it served as the focus.

The monument, known today as the Edicule (*aedicula* = little house), was last rebuilt in 1808–10 after a serious fire. Witnesses present at the rebuilding saw very little of the original rock of the Cave, and most of the core behind the marble veneer is masonry. But we have a fairly accurate knowledge of the earlier appearance of the edicule, since there are excellent drawings and a plan published in 1609 (p. 243),[1] not to mention a considerable number of replicas of the edicule built in the seventeenth and eighteenth centuries in Europe,[2] and the well-known olive-wood and mother-of-pearl models of the Church of the Holy Sepulchre.

In 1555 the Franciscan Custodian of the Holy Land restored the edicule, but whatever alterations he made were slight. Jan Van Scorel, who made a careful study of the holy places in about 1520, left a painting[3] which agrees in all essentials with the evidence later than 1555. There is also evidence provided by other replicas,[4] of which one of the earliest and most important is that at Eich-stätt (see facing page),[5] erected in the time of the Latin Kingdom. The replica shows only slight variations from the form known in the sixteenth century, and is probably very faithful to its prototype in Jerusalem, lacking only the cupola which is known from other sources to have surmounted the tomb-chamber.[6]

The full descriptions and other evidence for the edicule take us back with some confidence to its state at the time of the Crusaders'

[1] Bernardino Amico, *Trattato delle Piante ed Imagini dei Sacri Edifici* (Rome 1609).
[2] For those in Germany see G. A. Dalman, *Das Grab Christi in Deutschland* (Leipzig 1922); there are also replicas at Troyes (S. Nicolas), in Prague, and near Cracow, which belong to this period.
[3] *Jeruzalem-Broederschap te Haarlem*, painted 1527–9, in the Frans Halsmuseum, Haarlem, cat. no. 263. Compare the engravings in Amico, op. cit., and Cornelis de Bruyn, *Reizen* (Delft 1698), pl. 146 (facing p. 284).
[4] For the interior especially that of the Sacro Monte, Varallo, Val de Sezia, and for the exterior the one at Hilfikon, Switzerland.
[5] Dalman, op. cit., pp. 56ff (modifying the conjecture in *VA*, fig. 125, p. 265).
* [6] These sources can be consulted most conveniently in *VA*, esp. pp. 181–300.

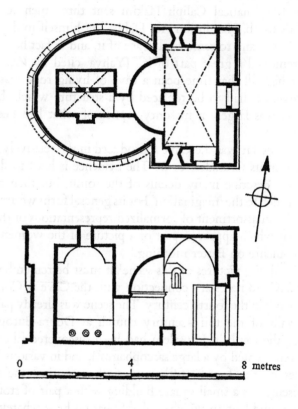

0   4   8 metres

THE EICHSTÄTT REPLICA

kingdom. But for its earlier state there is less evidence. We know
that it was restored by the Emperor Monomachos in 1048, and
that there had been a serious earthquake in 1034. But the chief
turning-point in the history of the edicule had come in 1009,
when the fanatical Caliph Ḥakim sent three men to destroy
Christ's tomb. Ḥusain ibn Abī Ḍāhir "set himself to destroy the
holy Tomb and to remove all trace of it, and in fact he cut down
and removed a great part of it" (Yaḥya, cited by *VA*, p. 246).
What had till that time been a cave of living rock was largely
destroyed. It had to be replaced by a structure which, however
similar, was largely a masonry replica of what had been there
before.

But how far was the Cave reproduced in the relatively familiar
edicule in its Crusader form? The evidence is hard to decipher.
Pilgrims describe many details of the tomb, but their accounts
leave much to the imagination. For its general form we are thrown
back on an assortment of formalized representations of the tomb,
most of which appear as part of a picture of the women visiting
the sepulchre on Easter morning.

In studying pictures of this scene[1] it must be remembered that
they have no necessary connection with the Cave as Constantine
adorned it in the fourth century. The scene was already painted on
the walls of the third-century church at Doura-Europos long
before the tomb in Jerusalem had been discovered (the tomb is
here represented by a large sarcophagus[2]), and in various Western
ivories of the fourth, fifth, and sixth centuries[3] the tomb is
represented as a small square building with a pair of stone doors
and a round lantern which probably has nothing whatever to do
with the buildings in Jerusalem.

A more probable source of information about the Cave is the
pair of collections of *ampullae* now in Bobbio and Monza, which
were made in Palestine in about A.D. 600.[4] We know from the

---

[1] J. Villette (*La Résurrection du Christ dans l'Art Chrétien du II au VII Siècle*
(Paris 1957)) discusses the evidence and provides an excellent selection of
plates.

[2] Villette, op. cit., pp. 62–72, and Pl. xxxii.

[3] Villette, op. cit., Pl. xxxviii (Munich), xxxix (Milan), xl (British Museum).

[4] These ampullae can most conveniently be studied in A. Grabar's excellent
work, *Ampoules de Terre Sainte* (Paris 1958). The numbers and page-references

Monza 3, ix   Monza 5, xi   Monza 9: xiv   Bobbio 6, xxxvii

(a) DETAILED REPRESENTATIONS ON THE FLASKS

Monza 10, xvi

(b) SUMMARY VERSION ON A FLASK

Monza 12, xxii   Bobbio 15, xlv

(c) SUMMARY VERSIONS WITH ADDITIONAL DETAILS

evidence of an almost contemporary Italian pilgrim that flasks of oil were blessed and were given to pilgrims[1] in the Holy Land, and nearly half the surviving flasks include pictures of the holy Cave among the elements in their decoration. The Cave appears in two versions: the first is an independent form which shows a considerable amount of detail (p. 247 (a)), and the second is a summary form normally used when it has to be embossed as a small element in a crowded composition[2] (p. 247 (b)) which is often some version of a pillared canopy which seems to represent the rotunda.[3] The summary form is also found on some other metalwork from the eastern shores of the Mediterranean.[4]

The different sizes of the two forms of decoration broadly determine the amount of detail they can include. In the summary form we see a simple rectangular façade surmounted by a triangular pediment. Within the rectangle are two grilled gates (presumably part of Egeria's "screen"), and within the triangle of the pediment, springing up from the middle of the base-line, there is always a fan-shaped ornament.[5] On the apex of the roof stands a cross.[6] Two of the summary versions show additional details: one has what seem to be candles on the roof, and the other shows a small arch between the open gates (p. 247 (c)).

The more detailed version of the picture supplements this information. The arch is again shown (Monza 3 and 5), but a rectangular object appears below it. One of the flasks clearly shows a cloth hanging from the pediment (Bobbio 6, compare Monza 3 and 9; also Egeria 25.8), and two show hanging lamps (Monza 3, Bobbio 9; see Egeria 24.4). Although one flask shows only the façade of the monument, the rest of it is shown in the three others,

---

in the following notes refer to that publication; in each case the plate-number is bracketed.

* [1] See Antoninus of Piacenza 20, *C.C.S.L.*, p. 139. Piacenza is near Bobbio.

[2] Monza 2(v), 6(xii), 8(xiii), 10(xvi), 11(xviii), and Bobbio 18(xlvii).

[3] Monza 12(xxii), 13(xxiv), 14(xxvi), Bobbio 3(xxiv), 4(xxxv), 5(xxxvi), 15 and 16(xlv).

[4] E.g. the Coptic censers discussed by Villette, op. cit., p. 79 and Pl. 35.

[5] Note that this appears even in the extremely small version on flask Bobbio 18(xlvii).

[6] First mentioned in the seventh century; see Adamnan, *Loc. Sanct.* 2.7, *C.C.S.L.*, p. 187.

and to modern eyes gives the impression that the plan was at least hexagonal.[1] Whether this was the intention of the designers is doubtful, and Grabar is probably right in suggesting that three of the sides became visible through a special convention of perspective.[2] Diagram (a) on page 247 appears to show considerable variation in the proportions of the façade, but, apart from Monza 9 (which has been reduced in height to fit into the bottom of a full composition) the variations are not as great as they at first appear.

The fan-shaped ornament appears on one (and probably on two) of these flasks, two show a cross on the surface of the roof as well as on its apex, and all have ornamental columns. One flask shows what look like finials and candles on the roof, and another shows six flowers in the air above.

The evidence of these flasks is of great value as far as it goes. But it is limited by the unknown conventions according to which artists were working, by the small scale of the flasks, and by the fact that they all view the monument from the front. Some of these limitations are fortunately overcome in a marble model of the Cave which has been identified in the lapidary Museum at Narbonne.[3] It is a monolith of local Pyrenaean stone, and was built into the wall of the Moors' Tower, which was built in or before the tenth century on the site of a basilica which had been founded by the Bishop Rusticus in the fifth century. On these grounds it is possible that it once belonged to the basilica, and, as the drawings show (p. 250), it has no walls in front of the tomb-chamber. This suggests that it is not only anterior to the Latin Kingdom (compare the walled space with three doors on the Eichstätt replica, p. 245), but also before the ninth century, when a pilgrim[4] informs us that there were walls between the columns of the façade, whereas the model retains just enough of this part

---

[1] Compare the apparently hexagonal canopy which surrounds it on flasks Bobbio 3(xxxiv) and 4(xxxv).

[2] See A. Grabar, *Martyrium*, vol. 1 (Paris 1946), pp. 275–9.

[3] No. 839 (559 in the Tournal catalogue), fully described in J. Lauffray, "La *Memoria Sancti Sepulchri* du Musée de Narbonne et le Temple Rond de Baalbeck" in *MUJ* 38 (1962), fasc. 9, pp. 199–217.

[4] Bernard the Monk (*c.* 870) cited by *VA*, p. 235.

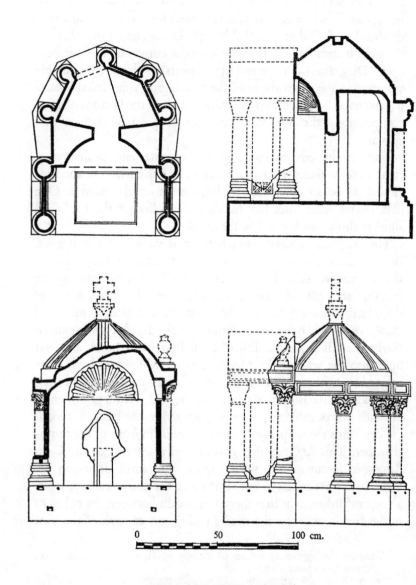

THE NARBONNE MODEL

to show that it had screens of a type which agrees well with Egeria's description.

How far does the evidence of the model agree with that of the oil-flasks? One of the most striking agreements is in the ornament which we have described above as fan-shaped. This, in its many variations, seems to be a representation of the conch above the small entrance to the tomb-chamber. The arch (Monza 3 and 5) between the front gates corresponds to the same feature, assuming that in Bobbio 15 the artist has used both means of portraying it. And at the apex of the roof is a hole which would allow for the attachment of a cross.

Although the front porch has mostly been broken away from the model, we should probably assume that the roof between the pillars was curved. This shape would agree with the curved shape shown in three of the flasks on p. 247 (a); the apex which appears above the curve would then represent the roof behind that of the porch. It is also to be noted that the model has a small hole in the platform of the porch, which touches an incised line forming what is very nearly a square area marked on the floor; this may well have had to do with the stone of the sepulchre, mentioned by Cyril, but now lost from the model. The model has several holes drilled in its surface which presumably formed the keys for veneer or metal decoration, and the shafts of the columns sur-rounding the tomb-chamber, though now lost, were probably inserted in a different coloured stone.

If, as we may reasonably assume, the flasks and the Narbonne model represent the same monument, and it is not substantially different from the one described by Egeria, we may also usefully compare it with the edicule as it was transformed after the disaster of 1009. It would no doubt be unwise to insist too much on the exact dimensions of the model in comparing it with those of the replica at Eichstätt, but two valuable points emerge. The first is that the Eichstätt replica has a front chapel which is as short from east to west as both that of the plan by Amico (p. 243), and also that of the Narbonne model, and the second is the fact that in all these three representations the outer walls of the tomb-chamber converge slightly towards each other as they stretch forward to meet the porch-structure. Closer study of the documents and representations only serves to accentuate that the edicule of modern times is in a far closer structural continuity with the earliest Cave than has usually been imagined.

E *The Old Armenian Lectionary*

Egeria's was the most complete available account of the fourth-century liturgy of Jerusalem when her manuscript was discovered in 1884, but, though she gave a faithful description of the outline of the Christian year, she left a good many gaps, and was often tantalizingly vague. But soon an important supplement came to light, when F. C. Conybeare published a translation of an Armenian manuscript in Paris[1] which we shall call P. It is a lectionary for the services in Jerusalem in the fifth century, and besides providing lessons (and some rubrics) for most of the services described by Egeria, confirming her general accuracy, it gives far fuller indications of the calendar of saints' days and other commemorations.

In 1948 the first part of the *Grand Catalogue of the Armenian Convent of St James in Jerusalem* was published. Since the publication itself was in Armenian, its importance was not at once recognized in the West, but, when Dom Athanase Renoux came to study it, he found that it revealed the existence of another Armenian Lectionary[2] which we shall call J. This manuscript supplies some important information which was missing from P.[3]

The table at the end of this note shows the order of services given in J, as recently published in a full edition by Renoux.[4] It shows much material which simply fills in the picture given by Egeria, but also a good many developments which have taken

[1] F. C. Conybeare, *Rituale Armenorum* (Oxford 1905), pp. 507–27. P is now *ms. Arm. 44* in the Bibliothèque Nationale. It was copied out in the tenth century, but was incomplete at some points, and Conybeare suggested material to fill the gaps from *cod. Arm. d.2* in the Bodleian Library, Oxford; but this represented a considerably later liturgical tradition, and misled Conybeare and some of his readers.

[2] *Cod. Jer. Arm. 121*, copied in 1192. See Dom Renoux' translation of Mgr Artavozd Siwrmēean's catalogue entry, "Un manuscrit du vieux lectionnaire arménien de Jérusalem", in *Le Muséon* 74 (1961), pp. 361–85, and his article of the same title in *Le Muséon* 75 (1962), pp. 385–98 which corrects the first from the manuscript itself. See also his important chapter "Liturgie de Jérusalem et Lectionnaires Arméniens", in *La Prière des Heures* (ed. Cassien and B. Botte = *Lex Orandi*, No. 35) (Paris 1963), pp. 167–99, and his article "Les Catéchèses Mystagogiques dans l'Organisation Liturgique Hiérosolymitaine du IV et V siècles", in *Le Muséon* 78 (1965), pp. 355–9.

[3] See Renoux, *Codex*, p. 183.

[4] See *Patrologia Orientalis*, vol. xxxv, fasc. 3.

place since the end of the fourth century. J must be later than
A.D. 417, since on 29 March[1] it commemorates Bishop John of
Jerusalem who died in that year. But later calendars commemorate John's successors, and it is probably before 438–9, since it
mentions a station but no church at "the Court of the High
Priest, the place of Peter's Repentance".[2] The Lectionary treats
25 December not as the feast of the Nativity, but as the Commemoration of James and David, though it notes that "in other
towns they keep the Birth of Christ".[3] But unfortunately this
provides no indication of date since it is not known precisely when
Christmas Day was introduced into Jerusalem.[4]

Lectionaries J and P therefore represent two stages, closely
related in time, in the development of the Jerusalem liturgy of
the early fifth century, and there is no doubt that they derive
from a Greek original. It is interesting that the Armenian Church
preserved a tradition that its own lectionary originated in Jerusalem, having been prepared by James, the first bishop in Jerusalem, and completed by Cyril, his fourth-century successor.[5]

Whatever the date of manuscript J, the main lines of the Christian year had evolved very little between the date when it was
compiled and that of Egeria's visit. The agreements are frequent,
and provide both a clear view of the readings she found so
appropriate, and many supplementary details which clarify the
structure of the services she describes in general terms.

THE ELEMENTS OF THE SERVICES

PSALMS

The Armenian Lectionary gives two illuminating indications about
the psalms. The first concerns their arrangement at the vigil

---

[1] No. 16. See Renoux, *Codex*, pp. 169–81.
[2] No. 41. The Church was begun there in 438–9, though, as the description is
worded, it does not necessarily imply the existence of a church building. The
church is mentioned in P.
[3] No. 71.
[4] It was again reintroduced in about 495. See B. Botte, "*Les origines de la Fête
de Noël à Jérusalem*" (Louvain 1932), pp. 19–20, and the necessarily inconclusive but valuable discussion by Renoux, *La Prière*, pp. 168–74.
[5] See Renoux, *Codex*, p. 175.

between the Thursday and Friday of the Great Week.[1] The psalms were sung with an antiphon, but in groups of three, each group being called a *gobala*,[2] and consisting of a psalm followed by the next two in numerical order. Only one antiphon is mentioned, and it may have served for all three psalms. The second point of interest which emerges is that the psalms with antiphon which begin the synaxis are far less varied than in later documents. Thus Psalm 116 with the antiphon, "Right dear in the sight of the Lord is the death of his saints", serves not only for martyrs, but also for prophets and confessors.

PRAYERS

Egeria distinguishes ordinary prayers from the "Prayer for All" in which the bishop or a deacon mentioned the names of individuals and the bishop said a concluding collect.[3] The Armenian Lectionary provides a further distinction by its mention of "prayer with kneeling".[4] One fragmentary rubric includes the words "Let us pray to the Lord", which seems to be the ending of a litany-phrase; in the modern Greek liturgies this is a phrase said by the deacon and answered with *Kyrie eleison*—the very response which Egeria mentions in connection with the Prayer for All at Lucernare.[5] Since the Council of Nicaea forbade kneeling on ✻ Sundays and in Eastertide,[6] we should probably conclude that the people knelt during the Prayer for All on ordinary week-days in the time of Egeria, and that its form was first a litanic series of intentions announced by the leader (whether bishop or deacon), for example, "For the holy Church let us pray to the Lord", to which *Kyrie eleison* was the response, and that at the end (if not more frequently) the deacon called the people to kneel for silent prayer for a time before the bishop summed up the petitions in a collect.

---

[1] No. 39.
[2] Conybeare says that this word is derived from the Latin *copula*; see Renoux, *La Prière*, pp. 187–90.
[3] Cf. 24.2 and 5.
[4] See Nos. 43, 44 (= List B) and Renoux, *La Prière*, pp. 179–80.
[5] 24.5.   [6] Council of Nicaea, Canon 20.   ✻

READINGS

The lessons appointed in the Lectionary bear out Egeria's favourable comments; though they vary in length from a single verse[1] to well over a chapter,[2] they appear to be selected almost exclusively with regard to their suitability, and on the same grounds some non-biblical readings are also introduced.[3] When there were a number of Old Testament lessons, those from the Law or the Writings (to use the Jewish distinction) were read before those from the Prophets. The terminology of the Lectionary distinguishes only the Apostles[4] and Gospels from the other readings, using simply the terms "First Reading", "Second Reading", and so on to distinguish the rest. These names have been omitted from the Table below in the interests of brevity. One[5] or two[6] Old Testament lessons may precede the Apostle, and there are sometimes two Apostles;[7] if an account of a martyrdom or miracle is to be read, it follows the Apostle.[8] Further variations, many of which omit the Gospel, appear in the Lenten forms of the synaxis.[9]

Various courses of continuous reading appear, for example, on the Wednesdays of Lent, the Fridays, or the days of Easter Week. And there is an extra course inserted on the remaining week-days of the second week of Lent which may originally have occupied another position.[10]

SPECIAL SERVICES

The Lectionary provides some processional psalms for use on the way from one station to another.[11] For the short acts of worship at

[1] See No. 9.   [2] See, for example, Nos. 3, 36.
[3] See Nos. 10, 14, 54.
[4] I.e. New Testament readings other than the Gospel; see No. 43, where the word "Prophets" is also used, but only in a way which seems compatible with modern usage.
[5] See Nos. 60, 63, 71, also 62, 64.   [6] See Nos. 53, 59, 61.
[7] See Nos. 3, 48–52, 55, 65, 73–4.
[8] As in Nos. 10, 14, 54.
[9] See, for example, Nos. 18, 19, and 35–7.
[10] See p. 264, n. 20[a]. These lessons are not mentioned by Egeria in the course of chapter 27.
[11] See Nos. 34, 41, 42; note that the single psalm provided at 4 p.m. in No. 44 is the first psalm of Lucernare.

the stations either a Gospel on its own,[1] or a psalm and antiphon and Gospel[2] are provided, which, as Egeria shows, were accompanied by prayer.[3]

Two types of vigil are described: that of Easter and Epiphany, which opens with Lucernare and ends at midnight with a celebration of the first Eucharist of the feast. The time between is occupied with a series of psalm-portions and Old Testament readings (eleven at Easter and ten at Epiphany) each followed by prayer with kneeling, which ends with the Song of the Three Children treated as a hymn and provided with special non-biblical responses.[4] But the vigil on the night between the Thursday and Friday of the Great Week[5] has a different structure, and leads up not to a Eucharist but to a procession to various stations. Like the others it follows on Lucernare (which Egeria fails to mention), but consists of five *gobala* (or groups of three psalms) each followed by prayer with kneeling, and a final Gospel.

Though Egeria describes the Three-Hour service on the Friday before Easter,[6] it would hardly have been guessed from her description that its structure was like that of eight consecutive Lenten synaxes, as appears from the Lectionary.

BAPTISMAL READINGS

The Lectionary gives readings[7] to go with both the catechetical lectures for the baptismal candidates and with the mystagogical lectures which were given after Easter. The table shows that these sets of readings were based on the sets already known to us from the works of Cyril, though we learn that he (or the person who took down what he was saying) seems to have used only a short section of the reading prescribed. Cyril complains in the lectures that he is getting behindhand,[8] and in the eighteenth lecture seems

---

[1] See Nos. 1, 39, 40, 41, 42, 44.
[2] See Nos. 40, 42, 44, 45, 52, 58.
[3] See No. 40, and compare Egeria 35.4; 36.1.
[4] See Lists A and B, p. 276 below, and Renoux, *La Prière*, pp. 177–8 and 181–91; cf. Egeria 38.1–2.
[5] No. 39; cf. Egeria 35.2–3. [6] 37.4–7; cf. No. 43.
[7] See Lists C and D, pp. 276–7 below.
[8] Cyril, *Cat.* 17.11, PG 33.981.

to have combined two lectures, since in the course of his lecture as we have it occurs the text which in the Armenian Lectionary appears as a reading to accompany a nineteenth lecture. But five mystagogical lectures appear in the works of Cyril, and only four readings are provided in the Lectionary; yet the evidence of both Cyril and Egeria suggests that there should have been lectures for each of the days of the Easter octave.[1] No doubt this was the original scheme, but it can hardly have been carried out in its entirety, even by Egeria's time. She tells of a daily Eucharist and afternoon service during Easter week,[2] and between the two the people and the bishop broke their fast. The mystagogical lecture was given in the Anastasis after the Eucharist; but such an arrangement would have been impossible on the Wednesday
* described by Egeria,[3] when the morning Eucharist was in the Eleona, and probably impracticable also on the Friday when the service was on Sion.

In recent times the Mystagogical Lectures, which appear among the works of Cyril, have been suspected to be not by him, but
* by John, his successor[4] from 386 to 417, and there is indeed one important manuscript which explicitly states that John was the author.[5] But, if John had inherited an Easter Week in which the daily Eucharists were as Egeria described them, and if he believed that the only suitable place for the mystagogical instruction was the Anastasis, we would have an explanation of the fact that there are only five of the lectures included among the writings of Cyril, and also why the Armenian Lectionary only provides four readings, since by the time of the Lectionary a further eucharistic celebration away from the Anastasis had been introduced into Easter Week.[6]

---

[1] Cyril, *Cat.* 18.33, PG 33.1056; Egeria 47.

[2] 39.2,3.

[3] 39.2.

[4] The argument was put forward by W. Swaans, "A propos des 'Catéchèses Mystagogiques' attribuées à S. Cyrille de Jérusalem", in *Le Muséon* 55 (1942), pp. 1–43.

[5] See F. L. Cross, *St Cyril of Jerusalem's Lectures on the Christian Sacraments* (London 1966), pp. xxxvi–ix.

[6] See No. 47; and for a full statement of this argument Renoux, "Les Catéchèses . . .", in *Le Muséon* 78 (1965), pp. 355–9.

EGERIA'S VOCABULARY AND THE LECTIONARY

The Armenian Lectionary often helps to give precise meanings to words which Egeria leaves ambiguous; an obvious example is the word "hymn" which by comparison is seen to mean "psalm" in most instances.[1] A more puzzling word used by Egeria is *procedere* and its noun *processio*, which in previous translations has often been rendered as if it referred to a procession.[2] Yet, when Egeria refers to processions, her usual expression is "they go with psalms"—*itur cum hymnis*—which is supported by the terminology of the Lectionary, for example, "they go down with psalms".[3] Sometimes the word *procedere* appears in a context which definitely includes the celebration of the Eucharist; so "they 'proceed' in the Great Church, and there takes place what is done everywhere on the Lord's Day".[4] But later in the same section this action is again described in other words: "they all assemble (*colligent se*) in the Great Church".[5] We may therefore take it that the basic meaning of Egeria's *procedere* is "assemble",[6] but is it possible to go further and make the assumption that, when Egeria does not make the word clear by its context, the word is still to be understood as meaning "assemble for the Eucharist"?

To read Egeria alone we might conclude that this was correct, for it might be the exception which proved the rule when she speaks of the Lenten services on Wednesday afternoon and says, "they assemble (*proceditur*) on Sion, and do everything that is customary at that hour, except the Offering".[7] But when we compare her expressions with those of the Armenian Lectionary, we find that it uses the words "assemble at" where she has *procedere*, and not only for the eucharistic assembly, but also for

---

[1] See, for example, 39.4 and *AL*, No. 52.

[2] See, for example, 25.1 in MF, p. 50; Pétré, p. 199.

[3] *AL*, No. 52; cf. No. 41.

[4] 25.1; and see 25.6,10,11; 26; 27.3; 30.1; 39.2; 41; 43.1; 49.3.

[5] 25.8; cf. 25.10. *Se colligere* is again used in the context of the eucharistic assembly in 29.5 and 35.1.

[6] Du Cange (*Glossarium mediae et infimae latinitatis* (Niort 1886), p. 515) shows that the old Latin version of Canon 7 of Laodicea uses *processio* to translate σύναξις; and A. Blaise (*Dictionnaire de Latin Chrétien* (Strasburg 1954), p. 666) cites Gregory the Great (*Hom. Euch.* 19) where *processio* is used in the same sense.

[7] 27.6; cf. 41.

all the Lenten afternoon services,[1] and for the Three Hours' service on the Friday before Easter.[2] Now all these services have a comparable structure, indicated above[3] by the use of the word "synaxis". It must be added that the Lectionary's use of the word "assemble at" also applies in two instances to an assembly for a service of a different pattern, in one instance the Veneration of the Cross, and in the other the station at the Room of the Disciples on the night of Thursday in the Great Week.[4]

Procedere for Egeria was thus the technical word meaning "assemble for a solemn service", in other words for a synaxis which may or may not form the prelude to the eucharistic Offering; and this meaning is confirmed by the Lectionary's "assemble at" and Egeria's own *se colligere*, even though both are used more loosely.[5]

THE SCHEME OF THE LECTIONARY TABLES

The object of the Table below is to provide a ready means of comparing the evidence of the Armenian Lectionary with that of Egeria.

The data are arranged in five columns: the first contains a reference number corresponding with those of Renoux and the Armenian Catalogue, and an abbreviated version of the rubric; words supplied from manuscript P are in square brackets and other additions or cross-references with Egeria in round brackets; the symbol @ indicates the Lectionary's use of the word "assemble" (or "assembly") and Com. means "Commemoration".

The next five columns contain: Psalm with antiphon, Old Testament Lesson, Apostle, Psalmody (either the verse sung for Alleluia or, in penitential seasons, a complete psalm with anti-

---

[1] See *AL*, Nos. 18–32, 35–37.
[2] See *AL*, No. 43; though this is a place where Egeria uses *se colligere* rather than *procedere*. *Se colligere* is an altogether looser word than *procedere*, and is used to describe the assemblies before None (32.1) and Lucernare (24.4), for the informal assembly before the dawn office (24.8), and also for the congregating of monks from elsewhere in Jerusalem at the great feasts (25.12; 43.3; 49.1).
[3] See p. 66 above.
[4] See *AL*, Nos. 43, 40.
[5] On *procedere* see C. Mohrmann, "Missa", in *VC* 12 (1958), pp. 76–7, and Bastiaensen, *Obs.*, pp. 26–39.

phon), and Gospel. In order to maintain the tabular presentation four sets of readings have been removed from the main body of the Table and placed at the end.

Psalms with antiphon are shown thus: 99a5, which indicates that verse 5 of the psalm is used as the antiphon. But the Alleluia-verses in the fourth column are simply shown thus: 15.1. Mtm is sometimes used for "Martyrium" and Acts Mart. means "Acts of the Martyrdom".

References are to *The Holy Bible, and Apocrypha, Revised Standard Version* (London 1959), and to *The Revised Psalter* (London 1964).

#		PS+ANT	O.T. LESSON	APOSTLE	ALL/PS	GOSPEL
1	[THE HOLY EPIPHANY, 6 Jan.: on 5 Jan. @ at the *Place of the Shepherds*]	[23(a1)]			[80]	Luke 2.8-19[-20] / Matt. 1.18-25[a]
—	Vigil in *Church of Bethlehem* (for lessons see List A) and Synaxis[b] at *Bethlehem*	2(a7)		Titus 2.11-15	110.1	Matt. 2.1-12
2	Synaxis in *Martyrium* in Jerusalem (E25.10)	2(a7)		Titus 2.11-15	110.1	Matt. 1.18-25
3	2ND DAY in *Mtm of S. Stephen*[c]	5(a13b)		Acts 6.8—8.2 / Titus 2.11-15	21.1	John 12.24-26
4	SUNDAY in *Martyrium*	[2(a7)]		Heb. 1.1-12	110.1	Matt. 2.13-23
5	4TH DAY @ on *Holy Sion*	110(a3b)		Gal. 4.1-7	132.1	Luke 1.26-38
6	5TH DAY @ on *Eleona*	99(a5)		Heb. 12.18-27	15.1	Luke 1.39-56
7	6TH DAY @ in *Lazarium*	30(a3)		1 Thess. 4.13-18	40.1	John 11.1-46
8	7TH DAY @ at *Golgotha*	96[d](a2b)		Rom. 1.1-7	72.1	Luke 2.1-7
9	8TH DAY, CIRCUMCISION @ at *Anastasis* (E25.11)	98(a3)		Col. 2.8-15	85.1	Luke 2.21
10	End of assemblies of Epiphany					
—	Com. PETER & ABISALOM,[e] 11 Jan. [This set of readings serves for all cons. of Martyrs.]	116(a13b)		Rom. 8.28-39 / Acts Mart.	116.1	Matt. 10.16-22

1[a] This Gospel was read in the Cave of the Nativity; see Renoux, *La Prière*, pp. 186, 192-3.
1[b] Viz. a synaxis followed by the Offering. On 2–8 cf. Egeria 25.11 who gives a different list of places for the Eucharist in the octave.
3[c] See notes on PD, I, p. 185, n. 1 above.

	PS+ANT	O.T. LESSON	APOSTLE	ALL/PS	GOSPEL
11 Com. s. ANTONY, HERMIT, 17 Jan. @ in Anastasis	116(a13b)		Heb. 11.32–40	116.1	Matt. 10.37–42
12 Com. GT. KG. THEODOSIUS[a], 19 Jan. @ in Anastasis	132(a1)		1 Tim. 2.1–7	21.1	Luke 7.1–10
13 40TH DAY FROM BIRTH OF CHRIST, 14 Feb. @ in Martyrium[b] (E26)	98(a4b)		Gal. 3.24–29	98.1	Luke 2.22–40
14 THE FORTY [MARTYRS], 9 [Mar] @ in Mtm S Stephen	116(a13b)		Rom. 8.29–39 Acts Mart.	116.1	Matt. 10.16–22
15 Com. CYRIL,[c] BISHOP OF JERUSALEM, 18 Mar.	116(a13b)		2 Tim. 4.1–8a	116.1	John 10.11–16
16 Com. JOHN,[d] BISHOP OF JERUSALEM, 29 Mar. as for Cyril	116(a13b)		2 Tim. 4.1–8a	116.1	John 10.11–16
17 READINGS AT BAPTISMAL INSTRUCTION (= List C)					
18 READINGS DURING LENT[e] (see E 27.5,7) (4 p.m. is given as the time for each set of readings)					
— 1ST WED. @ on Sion		Exod. 1.1–2.10 Joel 1.14–20		51a1	

12[a] Theodosius, d. 395.
13[b] Egeria 26 places this assembly in the Anastasis.
15[c] Cyril, d. 386.
16[d] John, d. 417.
18[e] Since 32 "ends the Canon of the Sixth Week" and 33 is Lazarus Saturday, there is no doubt that the Lenten period is reckoned as seven weeks rather than the eight mentioned in Egeria 27.1 (cf. 28.2 and Note F, pp. 278–80 below).

	PS+ANT	O.T. LESSON	APOSTLE	ALL/PS	GOSPEL
19	1ST FRI. @ on *Sion*		Deut. 6.4—7.10 / Job 6.2—7.13 / Isa. 40.1-8		41a4
20	2ND MON. @ in *Anastasis*[a]		1 Sam. 1.1—23a / Prov. 1.2—33 / Jer. 1.1—10		130a2
21	2ND TUES. @ in *Anastasis*		1 Sam. 1.23—2.26 / Prov. 2.1—3.10 / Jer. 1.11—2.3		27a9
22	2ND WED. @ on *Sion*		Exod. 2.11—22[b] / Joel 2.1—11 / Mic. 4.1—7		57a1
23	2ND THURS. @ in *Anastasis*		1 Sam. 4.1—18 / Prov. 3.11—4.13 / Jer. 2.31—3.16		39a11b+12a
24	2ND FRI. @ on *Sion*		Deut. 7.11—8.1 / Job 9.2—10.2a / Isa. 40.9—17		65a5
25	3RD WED. @ on *Sion*		Exod. 2.23—3.15 / Joel 2.21—32		71a1

20[a] (also 21,23) These readings of the second week, inserted into the Wednesday and Friday courses once stood at the beginning of Lent in the opinion expressed by A. Baumstark, in *Oriens Christianus* I (1911), p. 68, and cf. A. Rahlfs, "Die alttestamentlichen Lektionen der griechischen Kirche", in *Nachrichten von der kgl. Gesellschaft der Wissenschaften zu Göttingen* (Phil.-Hist. Kl. 1915), pp. 84–92. If they are correct, it is hard to see why there should be three sets, and why they do not fit into the courses of Wednesdays and Fridays.

22[b] This reading ends with the words found in LXX, Cod. Ambrosianus, and the Vulgate.

	PS+ANT	O.T. LESSON	APOSTLE	ALL/PS	GOSPEL
26 3RD FRI. @ on *Sion*		Deut. 8.11—9.10 Job 12.1—13.6 Isa. 42.1—8a		75a1	
27 4TH WED. @ on *Sion*		Exod. 3.16-22 Joel 3.1-8		77a2	
28 4TH FRI. @ on *Sion*		Deut. 9.11-24 Job 16.2—17.16 Isa. 43.22—44.8		83a18	
29 5TH WED. @ on *Sion*		Exod. 4.1-21b Joel 3.9-21		84a5	
30 5TH FRI. @ on *Sion*		Deut. 10.1-15 Job 19.2-29 Isa. 45.1-13		85a7	
31 6TH WED. @ on *Sion*		Exod. 4.21—5.3 Zech. 9.9-16a		86a15 + 16a	
32 6TH FRI. @ on [*Sion*]		Deut. 11.10-25 Job 21.1-34 Isa. 46.3—47.4		88a2	
The canon of the sixth week is finished.					
33 6TH DAY BEFORE THE PASSOVER[a] OF THE LAW, @ at *Lazarium*, 4 p.m.	30(a3)		1 Thess. 4.13—18	40.1	John 11.55—12.11

33[a] The word Passover here refers to the coming Thursday, the day of the Last Supper, but the same word is used for Easter. Egeria (29.**2**,**3**) mentions a previous vigil in Sion, and puts this assembly at 1 p.m., not 4; in 29.5 she confirms John 12.1 as a verse from the Gospel.

	PS+ANT	O.T. LESSON	APOSTLE	ALL/PS	GOSPEL
34 SUNDAY, DAY OF PALMS, @ at Martyrium (E30.1)	98(a9b+10a)		Eph. 1.3–10	99.1[a]	Matt. 20.29—21.17[a]
— At 3 p.m. they ascend the *Mount of Olives* with palm branches, and sing psalms and pray till about 5 p.m.[b]					
— Then they descend to the *Anastasis*, singing	118(a26)[c]				
35 MONDAY FOR EASTER,[d] @ (E32) in Martyrium, 4 p.m.[e]		Gen. 1.1—3.24 Prov. 1.1–9 Isa. 40.1–8		65a5	Matt. 20.17–28
36 TUESDAY, @ at *Eleona* at 4 p.m.[f] (E33.1)		Gen. 6.9—9.17 Prov. 9.1–11 Isa. 40.9–17		25a1	Matt. 24.1—26.2
37 WEDNESDAY, @ at *Martyrium*, 4 p.m. (E34)—		Gen. 18.1—19.30 Prov. 1.10–19 Zech. 11.11–14		41a4	Matt. 26.3–16
— and down to the Anastasis for					

34a J wrongly gives Alleluia as 98.1; P gives Matt. 21.1–11 as the Gospel.
34b Egeria (30.2; 31.1) says they go to the Eleona at 1 p.m. and the Imbomon at 3 p.m.; they have readings in both.
34c P wrongly gives Ps. 106; Egeria confirms the antiphon and the time 5 p.m. (31.2).
35a I.e. the week leading up to Easter; cf. Egeria's *septimana paschale* (30.1).
35e Egeria (32.1) says 3 p.m., not 4.
36f Egeria says not till about 8 p.m. (33.1) but confirms the Gospel (33.2); J wrongly gives the psalm as 23.

	PS+ANT	O.T. LESSON	APOSTLE	ALL/PS	GOSPEL
38 THURSDAY IN THE OLD PASSOVER, of which Jesus said to his disciples, "With desire I have desired to eat this Passover with you"; @ from 1 p.m.[a] in *Martyrium* (E35)		Gen. 22.1–18 Isa. 61.1–6	Acts 1.15–26	55a22	Matt. 26.17–30
— After the psalm they sit down for the commentaries, and the catechumens are dismissed					
39 After the dismissal of the catechumens @ (E35)	23(a5)		1 Cor. 11.23–32		Mark 14.1–26
— then the Offering is made in the *Martyrium* and *Before*[b] *the Cross*	23(a5)		1 Cor. 11.23–32		
— At the same hour they go to *Sion*[c]					
— And at the same hour they ascend the *Mount of Olives* (E35.2), and perform the evening office,					
— to which is added the Vigil, with *gobala*[d] of psalms, three by three, and the prayers are said with kneeling[e]	G1:2(a2) G2:41(a8) G3:59(a1) G4:79(af) G5:109(a2)				

38a Egeria (35.1) says 2 p.m., not 1.
39b Egeria (35.2) says "Behind" the Cross.
39c Egeria mentions no service at Sion in 35.2; the eucharistic readings suggest that this, too, was followed by the Offering.
39d See above, p. 255.
39e On prayer with kneeling see J. Mateos, *Lelya-Sapra*, *Essai d'Interprétation des Matines Chaldéennes* (Rome 1959), p. 367, and *DACL* 6.1017–21.
39f The antiphon is "They are cast away from thy hand; but we are thy people and the sheep of thy pasture" = 88.5 + 79.14.

	PS+ANT	O.T. LESSON	APOSTLE	ALL/PS	GOSPEL
—	And after the 15 psalms (the 5 *gobala*) and the 5 prayers, the same night at midnight they read (E35.3)ᵃ				John 13.16—18.1
40	At the same hour of the night they ascend to the *Hillock*ᵇ (E35.4)	109(a3)			Luke 22.1-65
—	At the same hour of the night @ in the *Room of the Disciples* and readᶜ				Mark 14.27-72
—	At the same hour of the night they descend the *Mount of Olives* and go straight to *Gethsemane*ᵈ (E36.2)				Matt. 26.31-56
41	And at once they go to the *Court of the High Priest*, to the Place of Peter's Repentanceᵉ				Matt. 26.57-75
—	At the same hour of the night they come singing	118(a1)			
42	And, beginning at the gate, they sing with *gobala* till they come *Before Holy Golgotha*ᶠ	G:79			John 18.2-27

39ᵃ If Egeria is speaking of this Gospel (35.3), she indicates that it was read in the Cave.

40ᵇ "Hillock" is the Lectionary's term for the Imbomon. Egeria (35.4) mentions other readings besides this Gospel.

40ᶜ The Room of the Disciples and the "graceful church" mentioned by Egeria (36.1) are not identical; but in both cases the main descent of the Mount of Olives seems to come after this station, which suggests that it is not the present Church of All Nations. Indeed, if it were not for the fact that No. 39 brought the people to the Eleona, the "Room of the Disciples" might be the Eleona cave itself

40ᵈ Egeria confirms the Gospel (36.1); on the site of Gethsemane see p. 53 above and J. T. Milik in *R.B.* 67 (1960), pp. 550–1.

41ᵉ There is no indication of a church at the site of Peter's Repentance (and Denial—see *R.B.* 2 (1905), pp. 154–5) until 438–39. Ms. P, like Egeria, sends the procession directly to Golgotha, but then sends it to the Palace of the Judge (that is, Pilate? Cf. the reading Before the Cross in Egeria 36.4) and then back again to Golgotha. See pp. 39 and 230 above.

42ᶠ Egeria (36.3–4) says Before the Cross. The Lectionary thus seems to treat the rock outcrop as Golgotha. See pp. 39 and 230 above.

	PS+ANT	O.T. LESSON	APOSTLE	ALL/PS	GOSPEL
— At dawn this canon	109(a3)				John 18.28—19.16
43 On FRIDAY, when it is day (E37.1), the precious Wood of the Cross is placed before Golgotha (E37.3f). Those who are assembled @ venerate it till midday					
— At noon @ at Golgotha for 8 psalms, 8 prophets, 8 apostles, and 4 gospels; to each psalm there are two lessons and one single prayer^a (E37.4-7)	35(a11)	Zech. 11.11-14	Gal. 6.14-18		pk
	38(a17)	Isa. 3.9b-15	Phil. 2.5-11		pk
	41(a6)	Isa. 50.4-9	Rom. 5.6-11		pk
	22(a18)	Amos 8.9-12	1 Cor. 1.18-31		pk
	31(a6)	Isa. 52.13—53.12	Heb. 2.11-18		Matt. 27.1-56 pk
	69a]23	Isa. 63.1-6	Heb. 9.11-28		Mark 15.1-41 pk
	88(a^b)	Jer. 11.18-20	Heb. 10.19-31		Luke 22.66—23.49 pk
					John 19.17-37° pk
— Immediately after the Gospel they enter the Martyrium at 4 p.m.^d	102(a1)	Zech. 14.5-11	1 Tim. 6.13-16		
— After the psalm they descend at once to the holy Anastasis^e		Jer. 11.18—12.8 / Isa. 53.1-12		22a18	Matt. 27.57-61

43^a The rubric says "Prayer with singing of psalm: 'Let us pray to the Lord'". The abbreviation pk indicates the rubric "prayer with kneeling".
43^b J wrongly prescribes Ps. 86; the antiphon is "I am become like a man without help: free among the dead" = 88.4b+5a.
43^c Egeria mentions John 19.30 (37.7).
43^d Egeria (37.6) says 3 p.m., not 4. Ms. P gives the first reading as Jer. 11.18-20.
43^e Egeria (37.8) confirms this Gospel, but (37.9) mentions the voluntary vigil service which followed it, not mentioned by the Lectionary.

	PS+ANT	O.T. LESSON	APOSTLE	ALL/PS	GOSPEL
44 SATURDAY dawn, *Anastasis*	88(a6)				Matt. 27.62–66
— On Sat. evening in the holy Easter the bishop sings this psalm in the holy *Anastasis*	113(a2)[a]				
— At the same hour they ascend to the *Martyrium* (E38.1) and the bishop lights a candle; at once the clergy begin the Vigil of holy Easter, and 12 lessons are read. At each lesson there is prayer with kneeling[b] (See List B)					
— And while the hymn is said, at midnight, the throng of the newly-baptized enters with the bishop (see E38.2)	65(a1)		1 Cor. 15.1–11	30.1	Matt. 28.1–20
— And the same hour the Offering is made					
— And after the dismissal at the same hour of the night the Offering is made at the *Anastasis* before Golgotha					
— And immediately there is read at the *Anastasis*					John 19.38—20.18
45 HOLY SUNDAY OF EASTER, dawn @ at *Martyrium* (E39.2)	65(a1)		Acts 1.1–14	147.12	Mark 15.42–16.1

*

44[a] This was the Lucernare psalm. For P a single lamp is lit before the psalm and three afterwards, after which they go to the Anastasis; see Renoux, *La Prière*, p. 182. Note that Conybeare mistranslated P at this point.

44[b] Ms. P adds that there is psalmody with each reading; see List B.

	PS+ANT	O.T. LESSON	APOSTLE	ALL/PS	GOSPEL
— At 3 p.m. they ascend the *Mount of Olives*, and after briefly[a] singing psalms there, they descend to the *Anastasis*					
— And in the evening from there to *Sion*	149(a1)				John 20.19-25[b]
46 MONDAY @ in *Martyrium* (E39.2)	65(a1)		Acts 2.22-41	147.12	Luke 23.50—24.12
47 TUESDAY @ *Mtm S. Stephen*[c]	5(a13b)		Acts 2.42—3.21	21.1	Luke 24.13-35
48 WEDNESDAY @ on *Sion*	147(a12)		Acts 3.22—4.12 / Jas. 1.1-12	65.1	Luke 24.36-40
49 THURSDAY @ on *Eleona*	99(a5)		Acts 4.13-31 / Jas. 1.13-27	15.1	Matt. 5.1-12
50 FRIDAY @ *Before Golgotha*	98(a3)[d]		Acts 4.32—5.11 / Jas. 2.1-13	147.(12)	John 21.1-14
51 SATURDAY @ in *Anastasis*	67(a1)		Acts 5.12-33 / Jas. 2.14-26	81.1	John 21.15-25
52 SUNDAY @ in *Martyrium* (E39.2)	65(a1)		Acts 5.34—6.7 / Jas. 3.1-13	93.1b	John 1.1-17

45[a] Cf. *aliquandiu* (Egeria 40.1).
45[b] Egeria (39.5) confirms this Gospel.
47[c] The places where the Eucharist is celebrated are here given in an order different from Egeria 39.2, and in her day there was no Mtm of S. Stephen.
50[d] Ms. J wrongly gives Ps. 91.

	PS+ANT	O.T. LESSON	APOSTLE	ALL/PS	GOSPEL
— The same Sunday they ascend the *Mount of Olives* at 4 p.m. (E39.3), and when they have sung psalms there for a little they descend with psalms[a] to the holy *Anastasis*					
— from which in the evening they go to holy *Sion* (E40.2)	149(a1)				John 20.26–31[b]
— MYSTAGOGICAL READINGS FOR EASTER (see List D)					
53 Com. JEREMIAH, at *Anatoth*, 1 May	40(a2)	Jer. 1.1–10 Jer. 38.1–28	2 Pet. 2.9–22	30.1	Matt. 2.16–18
54 APPARITION OF THE HOLY CROSS FROM THE HEIGHT OF HEAVEN, @ *Before Golgotha*, 7 May	97(a6)		Gal. 6.14–18 The Letter[c]	98.1	Matt. 24.30–35
55 Com. THE CHILDREN KILLED BY KING HEROD, at *Bethlehem*, 9 May[d]	8(a2)		Acts 12.1–24 Heb. 2.14–18	103.1	Matt. 2.16–18
56 Com. EMP. CONSTANTINE, @ in *Martyrium*, 22 May	132(a1)		1 Tim. 2.1–8	21.1	Luke 7.1–10

52[a] Cf. Egeria's phrase *itur cum hymnis*, "they go with psalms" (e.g. 39.4).
52[b] Egeria (40.2) confirms this Gospel.
54[c] I.e. Cyril's *Letter to Constantius*, PG 33.1165–79, describing the Apparition, which took place in Jerusalem on 7 May 351; J wrongly calls it the Letter to Constantine.
55[d] Ms. P gives 18 May as the date, which is assumed in the argument of P. Devos, "Égérie à Bethléem: Le 40e jour après Pâques à Jérusalem, en 383", in *A.B.* 86 (1968), pp. 87–108.

	PS + ANT	O.T. LESSON	APOSTLE	ALL/PS	GOSPEL
57 At the Assembly @ at the HOLY ASCENSION OF CHRIST[a] after the Forty Days of Easter (See E42)	47(a6)		Acts 1.1-14	24.1	Luke 24.41-53
58 DAY OF PENTECOST, Sunday, @ at Martyrium (E43.2)	143(a11b)		Acts 2.1-21	94.1	John 14.15-24
— Directly after the dismissal from the Martyrium, towards 9 a.m.,[b] they go to *Sion*	143(a11b)			94.1	John 14.25-29
— At 4 p.m.[c] @ on the Mount of Olives at the *Hillock* (E43.4-5)	143(a11b)		Acts 2.1-21	94.1	John 16.5b-15[d]
— And immediately after the Gospel they kneel, and this canon is performed three[e] times—in the same way in all the holy places	143(a11b)				John 14.15-24
59 Deposition of the PROPHET ZACHARIAS, 10 June[f]	26(a8)	Zech. 3.7-4.9	1 Cor. 12.26—13.10	116.1	Matt. 23.34—24.1a
60 PROPHET ELISHA, 14 June	116(a13b)	2 Kings 13.14-21	Heb. 11.32-40	116.1	Luke 4.25-42

57a "The Holy Ascension of Christ" seems to be used here as the title of Poemenia's Church. See pp. 49-53 above and Note J, pp. 293-5 below.

58b See Acts 2.15 for the time, and cf. Egeria 43.2 and 3, which confirms the Acts reading.

58c Egeria 43.3 says "after noon".

58d This Gospel is confirmed by Egeria 43.5, but Egeria's description suggests that the Apostle was Acts 1.1-14. It is possible that, if Ascension Day had for some reason been shifted in the year she made her observations, the lesson was altered on the Day of Pentecost.

58e See Renoux "Un ms", Le Muséon 74 (1961), p. 382, n. 3. Egeria mentions four holy places followed by a fifth station at Sion (43.6-9).

59f P wrongly gives the date as 27 June.

	PS + ANT	O.T. LESSON	APOSTLE	ALL/PS	GOSPEL
61 OF THE ARK OF THE COVENANT, at Kiriath-Jearim, 2 July	132(a8)	1 Sam. 6.19—7.2a / 2 Sam. 6.12b-19	Heb. 9.1-10	98.1	Matt. 5.17-20
62 Deposition of the prophet ISAIAH,[a] 6 July	116(a13b)	Isa. 6.1-10	Eph.[b] 4.7-13	116.1	Luke 4.14-22b
63 Com. THE MACCABEES, 1 August	116(a13b)	2 Macc. 6.18—7.42	Heb. 11.32—12.13	116.1	Matt. 5.17-20
64 Com. MARY THEOTOKOS,[c] at Second Mile from Bethlehem, 15 August	132(a8)	Isa. 7.10-15	Gal. 3.29—4.7	110.1	Luke 2.1-7
65 Com. the APOSTLE THOMAS AND OTHERS, at Bethphage, 23 August[d]	19(a4)		Acts 1.12-14 / 1 Cor. 12.26—13.10	27.1	John 20.24-31
66 Com. JOHN THE BAPTIST, 29 August	116(a13b)		Acts 13.16-42	116.1	Matt. 14.1-12
67 DEDICATION OF THE HOLY PLACES AT JERUSALEM, 1ST DAY, 13 September, at Anastasis (E48.1; 49.3)	65(a1)		1 Tim. 3.14-16	147.12	John 10.22-42

62a The relics of Isaiah were found at Paneas only in 442, but his association with Siloam was much earlier. The tradition passed on in the *Ascension of Isaiah* and the *Vitae Prophetarum* (for which see VA pp. 855-69) spoke of the prophet being tortured near Siloam, and said that the spring burst forth to refresh him; it also said that he was buried there. This was, till 442, the tradition received in the Jerusalem church, since the Bordeaux pilgrim (595, n. 6) was shown his tomb there. When the relics were found at Paneas, they were brought to the Kidron Valley, and placed there on 25 August in the "Foundation of Juvenal" (see Renoux, *Codex*, p. 173).

62b Ms. J wrongly gives Heb.

64c The titl Theotokos was approved by the Council of Ephesus, 431. The site of the Lectionary's commemoration is not Rachel's tomb, but "where the Virgin rested" half way between Jerusalem and Bethlehem (see *Protev. James* 17.2, Hennecke I.383). A church was built there in the time of Juvenal's episcopate, which was later known as τὸ πάλαιον κάθισμα, "the Old Seat"; see J. T. Milik, "Notes", No. 53, in *R.B.* 67 (1960), p. 571.

	PS + ANT	O.T. LESSON	APOSTLE	ALL/PS	GOSPEL
68	2ND DAY^a @ in *Martyrium*, the same canon; and the same day they display the Venerable Cross to the whole congregation	65(a1)		1 Tim. 3.14-16	147.12	John 10.22-42
69	Com the APOSTLE PHILIP, 15 November	19(a4)		Acts. 8.26-40	47.1	John 1.43-51
70	Com, the APOSTLE ANDREW, 30 November	19(a4)		1 Cor. 12.26—14.4	95.1	John 1.35-44
71	Com. JAMES AND DAVID,^b 25 December,^c @ in *Sion* (During this day in other cities they keep the Birth of Christ)	132(a1)	2 Sam. 5.1-10	Acts. 15.1-29	100.1	Matt. 22.41-46
72	Com. ST STEPHEN, 27 December	5(a13b)		Acts. 6.8—7.2	21.1	John 12.24-26
73	Com. the APOSTLES PAUL AND PETER, 28 (Dec.)	19(a4)		2 Pet. 1.12-19 / 2 Tim. 4.1-8	47.1	John 21.15-19
74	Com. APOSTLE JAMES AND EVANGELIST JOHN, 29 (Dec.)	96(a2)		Jas. 1.1-12 / 1 John 1.1-9	85.2?	John 21.20-25

68^a Egeria 49.3 places the first celebration in the Martyrium, and 49.1 speaks of an octave.

71^b "James and David" appear in this order in J, but P gives "David and James", the order which is usual in Eastern Christian calendars. "James and David" seem to be the patriarch Jacob and King David, whose "deposition" was still celebrated on "the day after the Birth of Christ" by the Jews as well as the Christians of Hebron in the early fifth century (*Ant. Plac.* 30, C.C.S.L. 175, p. 144). But in Jerusalem the change of order suggests that in the early fifth century the identity of the saints had been changed to make the feast the great commemoration for Sion, which contained the throne of the first bishop, James the Just, and had been taken by King David to be his capital. This feast would thus be second only to Pentecost for the church on Sion. See Renoux, *Codex*, p. 73.

71^c Egeria does not appear to have celebrated Christmas Day in Egypt, since she must on that day have been in the area of Sinai (see 3.7). This feast was first introduced in Jerusalem (it is not known precisely when) by Bishop Juvenal, and discontinued at his death in 458.

LIST A: VIGIL OF EPIPHANY	LIST B: VIGIL OF EASTER
(see No. 1)	(see No. 44/E38[1])

	LIST A		LIST B	
1	Gen. 1. (1–28) 29—3.20 (=Easter 1)	1	Ps.[a]	Gen. 1.1—3.24 pk
2	Isa. 7.10–18	2	Ps.	Gen. 22.1–18 pk
3	Exod. 14.24—15.12 (=Easter 5)	3	Ps.	Exod. 12.1–24 pk
4	Mic. 5.2–7	4	Ps.	Jonah 1.1—4.11 pk
5	Prov. 1.1–9	5	Ps.	Exod. 14.24—15.21 pk
6	Isa. 9.5b–7	6	Ps.	Isa. 60.1–13 pk
7	Isa. 11.1–9	7	Ps.	Job 38.1–28 pk
8	Isa. 35.4–8	8	Ps.	2 Kings 2.1–22 pk
9	Isa. 40.10–17	9	Ps.	Jer. 31.31–4 pk
10	Isa. 42.1–8a	10	Ps.	Josh. 1.1–9 pk
		11	Ps.	Ezek. 37.1–14 pk

Hymn.
Dan. 3.1–34 (=RSV Dan. 3.1–23 + Song of Three Chil. 1–11)

Lord, send down dew, a dew of mercy, and extinguish the flame of blazing fire; for it is thou only whom we recognize as Saviour.

Dan. 3.35–51=Song of Three Chil. 12–28

Thou hast had pity on our fathers: thou hast visited us and saved us.

Dan. 3.52–90=Song of Three Chil. 29–68

Hymn.
Dan. 3.1–35a (=RSV Dan. 3.1–23 + Song of Three Chil. 1–12a)

(Antiphon as for Epiphany)

Dan. 3.35–51

(As for Epiphany)

(As for Epiphany)

B1[a] Part of Ps. 118a24 is used before each reading. See Renoux, *La Prière*, pp. 182–4, who notes that the Jerusalem Ms. arm. 5 speaks of Ps. 132a1 as the psalm for the Epiphany Vigil.

LIST C: BAPTISMAL INSTRUCTION (No. 17, compare E.45.1)

Instruction of those who are entered in the book for the holy Lent, and of those who are preparing to receive Baptism: Readings:

(*Armenian Lectionary*)	(Cyril, *Cat.* texts)
1 Isa. 1.16–20	=1 Isa. 1.16–19
2 Ezek. 18.20c–23	=2 Ezek. 18.20–23

3	Rom. 6.3–14	=3	Rom. 6.3–4
4	Col. 2.8—3.4	=4	Col. 2.8
5	Heb. 11.1–31	=5	Heb. 11.2
6	Isa. 45.16b–26	=6	Isa. 45.16–17
7	Eph. 3.14—4.13	=7	Eph. 3.14–15
8	Jer. 32.19b–44	≑8	Jer. 32.18–19
9	Job 38.2—39.3c	=9	Job 38.2–3
10	1 Cor. 8.5—9.23	=10	1 Cor. 8.5–6
11	Heb. 1.1—2.1	=11	Heb. 1.1–2
12	Isa. 7.10—8.10	=12	Isa. 7.10–14
13	Isa. 53.1—54.5	=13	Isa. 53.1,7
14	1 Cor. 15.1–28	=14	1 Cor. 15.1–4
15	Dan. 7.2–27	=15	Dan. 7.9–14
16	1 Cor. 12.1–7	=16	1 Cor. 12.1,4
17	1 Cor. 12.8–27	=17	1 Cor. 12.8
18	Ezek. 37.1–14	=18	Ezek. 37.1
19	1 Tim. 3.14–16		(1 Tim. 3.14–16)

The canon of instruction of those who are going to be baptized is ended; nineteen readings.

LIST D: MYSTAGOGICAL READINGS (see No. 52 and E.47.1–2)[a]

Mystagogical Readings for holy Easter in the holy Anastasis after the assembly in the Martyrium:

On the second day: Reading and thereafter he initiates them into the mysteries. 1 Pet. 5.8–14 (⇒Pseudo-Cyril, *Myst.* 1)

On the sixth day: Reading and thereafter (etc) ... 1 John 2.20–27 (=Pseudo-Cyril, *Myst.* 3)

On the seventh day: Reading and thereafter (etc) ... 1 Cor. 11.23–32 (=Pseudo-Cyril, *Myst.* 4)

On the Sunday: Reading and thereafter (etc) ... 1 Pet. 2.1–10 (=Pseudo-Cyril, *Myst.* 5)

[a] Egeria (47.1,2) speaks of mystagogical instruction on every day of Easter week; see ✳ p. 145 above.

278

F *The Duration of Lent*

The period of fasting before Lent was in the fourth century described as "The Fortieth", which is the name of the Sunday which marked its beginning, and this title, or "The Forty Days", is thereafter in regular use. Egeria uses "The Fortieth" (*quadragesimae*) usually where she describes the fasting, and "The Forty Days" for the pre-Lenten period of instruction for the catechumens, but this rule is not invariable.[1]

The Lent which later became familiar in the West[2] was arranged to contain exactly forty days of fasting by omitting Sundays and running through six weeks of the six week-days, making thirty-six, and adding four to the beginning, which made Lent start on a Wednesday. But it is more difficult to arrange exactly forty days into a period which begins and ends on a Sunday. "The Forty Days" was therefore only an approximate description of the number of fasting days in the period, or, for that matter, of the days given to catechetical instruction before Lent.[3]

No doubt the forty days were associated with the temptation of Christ, or with the period spent by Moses on Sinai, or Elijah travelling to Horeb. But it is noticeable that none of these events provide the subjects for the Lenten passages appointed in the Armenian Lectionary, Nos. 18–32.

A fragment of "Eusebius", which may belong to the fourth-century Bishop of Caesarea,[4] says that the forty-day exercise was undertaken for six weeks, and Athanasius mentions the same period in his festal letters. However they calculated their days of

---

[1] Cf. 46.1.

[2] Even fifty years after Egeria's time Rome kept only a three-week Lent according to Socrates, *Eccl. Hist.* 5.22, PG 67.634.

[3] Cyril of Jerusalem speaks of "a penitence of forty days" (*Procat.* 4, PG 33. 341). No satisfactory explanation has yet been given of the scheme according to which his eighteen (or perhaps nineteen) lectures were distributed through the period, but there has been much discussion of the question; see W. Telfer, *Cyril of Jerusalem and Nemesius of Emesa* (London 1955), pp. 34–8; V. Peri, "La Durata e la Struttura della Quaresima nell'antico uso Gerosolimitano", in *Aevum* 37 (1963), p. 40; the important discussions by A. Touttée reproduced in PG 33.155ff, and 447–50, n. 1; and A. A. Stephenson "The Lenten Catechetical Syllabus", in *Theological Studies* 15 (1954), pp. 103–16.

[4] Preserved in *Catenae in Luc.* 22.7.

fasting they reflect a state of affairs which had not yet been complicated by the addition of the "Great Week". To judge from the fact that there was no catechesis in that week according to Egeria,[1] and that according to Epiphanius the full fasting rule was lightened,[2] it seems that the Great Week was regarded as an insertion between the end of the Forty Days and Easter itself. The Forty Days may thus have been regarded as a ready-organized time of fasting and instruction which was not to be disturbed internally, even though it might be moved back as a whole.

The distinction which it is thus possible to draw between the traditional Forty Days and the Great Week, of more recent origin, is blurred by Egeria's explanation of the number of fasting days,[3] an explanation which would have been impossible before the introduction of the Great Week. Lent, as she reckoned it, contained forty-one fasting days, since she excluded all Sundays and Saturdays[4] (except Easter Even), and thus counted eight weeks containing five fasting days and the Saturday of the Paschal vigils, the only fasting Saturday in the year.

Egeria's is in fact the only fourth-century description of Lent in Jerusalem which combines a title in terms of "forty days" with a period described in weeks and a rationale of the actual number of fasting days. She stands unsupported[5] and unchallenged[6] by her contemporaries. We know that she was in Jerusalem not many years after its greatest liturgical upheaval, and it would not be surprising to find that the arrangements for annual feasts had not

[1] See 46.4.

[2] Epiphanius, *Adv. Haer.* 3.2.23 and 75.7, *PG* 42.828 and 511.

[3] See 27.1.

[4] This seems to have been a habit general in Syria; cf. *Canons of Laodicea* 49.

[5] J. Deconinck in his classic review of K. Meister's edition of Egeria (in *R.B.* 7 (1910), pp. 432–45) held that Epiphanius could be interpreted as implying a Lent of eight weeks "if he is consistent with his principles" and compares John Chrysostom, *Hom 18 ad pop. Ant.* 1 and 4, *PG* 49.179 and 187; but this need mean no more than that it was possible to speak of half the Forty Days as "twenty days". A Baumstark defended Egeria's statement on the same ambiguous evidence; see *CL*, p. 195, notes 1–4.

[6] V. Peri's argument that Egeria made a mistake rests principally on his own conjecture about the way in which Cyril's lectures fitted into the Forty Days —which seems inconsistent with the need to place lectures 7-8-9 (like 10-11-12) on successive days—and an inconclusive interpretation of the meaning of the "forty days of instruction" implied by John of Jerusalem, according to Jerome (see *PL* 23.380).

yet settled down into a stable form. We also know from the historians of half a century later that local variations in the observance of Lent were still considerable; thus Socrates wrote:

Those at Rome fast three successive weeks before Easter, except on Saturdays and Sundays. Those in Illyrica and all over Greece and Alexandria observe a fast of six weeks, which they term "The Forty Days' fast" ... It is indeed surprising to me that, differing as they do in the number of days, they should give it one common name. But some assign one reason for it, some another, according to their individual choice.[1]

Sozomen, writing at about the same time, records further variants, but assigns to Palestine a Forty Days of six weeks' duration.[2]

In face of this variety, and since Egeria is our only witness for any details about the late fourth-century observance of Lent in Jerusalem, we are obliged to rely on her. Indeed there is no reason to suppose that she was mistaken, even though the Jerusalem Lent may have lasted only six weeks half a century before and after her time.

[1] Socrates, *HE* 5.22, *PG* 67.634.
[2] Sozomen, *HE* 7.19, *PG* 67.1177.

G The Finding of Job

Miraculous discoveries of saints' bodies began to happen with
some frequency in the late fourth and early fifth centuries. The *
first to be described in any detail is the finding of the sarcophagus
of Job, of which the greater part is preserved in Egeria 16.5.

The discoveries which are recorded took place in Italy, Gaul,
and Africa, as well as in the Holy Land, though the evidence from
Africa is in the form of a vote of censure from a local council.
They occur in the following chronological order

before 384	"many saints' bodies"	in Rome	by Pope Damasus[1]
before 383	Job	Carneas	by a monk of the Ḥaurān[2]
between 379 & 395	Habakkuk and Micah	Ceila and Morasthi	by Bishop Zebennus of Eleutheropolis[3]
386	the Martyrs Gervasius and Protasius	Milan	by Bishop Ambrose of Milan[4]
393	the Martyrs Vitalis and Agricola	Bologna	by Bishop Ambrose of Milan[5]
397	The Third Council of Carthage deplores "the altars which are being set up through the dreams and empty so-called revelations of various men".[6]		
410	Saturninus	Toulouse	by Bishop Exuperius of Toulouse[7]
415	Zechariah	near Eleutheropolis	by Calemerus, a peasant.[8]
415	Stephen[9]	Cafar-gamala	

[1] *Liber Pontificalis* 1.212 (Duchesne) notes this in Damasus' Life.
[2] Egeria 16.5.   [3] Sozomen, *HE* 7.29, *PG* 67.1505.
[4] Ambrose, *Ep.* 22, *PL* 16.1019ff; cf. Augustine, *Conf.* 9.7 (16), *PL* 32.770.
[5] Paulinus' *Life* of Ambrose, *PL* 14.37.
[6] See H. Delehaye, *Sanctus* (Brussels 1927), p. 126.
[7] See H. Delehaye, *Les Origines du Culte des Martyrs* (Brussels 1912), p. 91.
[8] Sozomen, *HE* 9.16, *PG* 67.1628.   [9] Sozomen, *HE* 9.16.

Where these discoveries are fully recounted, they follow what
* appears almost to be a formal pattern. They open with an account
of the favourable circumstances of the time, the good ruler on
the throne or godly bishops over the church. Saint Ambrose discovered Gervasius and Protasius when he was about to dedicate
the Ambrosian basilica in Milan.

There follows an account of the supernatural revelation by
which it was known where to search for the bodies. Sometimes
the place is revealed in a dream, and in Ambrose' case it was by
his own experience of a "prophetic ardour".[1]

Egeria's account begins with the next element in the narratives,
the actual discovery, and this too normally contains a miraculous
element: the bodies may be of remarkable size, or have remained
incorrupt. Here it may be noted that the bodies of Gervasius and
Protasius, like that of Job, seem to have been in named sarcophagi,
unless their names were revealed in Ambrose's prophetic vision.

In some accounts concerning saints of the Old Testament the
bodies are left in position,[2] but the bodies of St Stephen and the
martyrs are removed to a more worthy resting-place, and there is
an account of their reburial or "deposition", which at Milan was
accompanied by the healing of a blind man.

The discoveries or inventions were valued as evidence of God's
grace to the Church as a whole. Sozomen makes it clear that the
peasant Calemerus was no better than his neighbours, but in
recording the finding of Habakkuk and Micah he adds that it
"sufficed for the good repute of the Christian religion". Thus the
discoveries were seen as evidence of the divine favour to the
community.

It is extremely instructive to compare the accounts of these
Christian miracles with Plutarch's narrative of the discovery of
Theseus' body on Skyros.[3] It follows very much the same pattern
as the Christian accounts, containing a supernatural demand that
the body be found, and a sign of its position. Cimon, after finding
the body, brings it to a more worthy resting-place in Athens, and

---

[1] *Ep.* 22.11, *PL* 16.1022-3.
[2] Egeria emphasizes this (16.6).
[3] *Lives, Theseus* 36.1-4, *Cimon* 8.3-6.

at the deposition the Athenians keep festival, and thereafter pray to Theseus as guardian of the poor.

The strength of this comparison probably lies not so much in the realm of literature, for there is no likelihood that there is any conscious borrowing from Plutarch in the Christian accounts. There is rather a psychological acceptance of the discovery of a saint's body as a means of God's revelation, and an expectation that he will choose this series of events as a regular type of miracle. The African Council's vote of censure shows that some of these miracles were spurious, but it does not rule out the possibility that some "inventions" were the products of genuine religious expectation, as can be most clearly seen in the records left by Saint Ambrose and Saint Augustine.[1]

---

[1] See further H. Delehaye, *Les Origines*, pp. 82–108, and H. Leclercq, "Reliques et Reliquaires" in *DACL*, vol. 14, esp. col. 2303.

H *Edessa's Water Supply*

The Bishop of Edessa begins the tour of his city by showing Egeria the palace of King Abgar, which surrounded two pools full of fish (19.7). From these pools the city received its water by means of a "great river of silver" running inside the city, and the Bishop proceeds to tell Egeria a story which explains this unusual water-supply (19.9–15).

This story seems to be an aetiological myth. Thus it is likely to be reliable in its description of the existing system, even if all the rest of the narrative is invention. As he speaks of the water-supply the Bishop reveals:

(*a*) that the water had once come from a hill visible from the pools (19.11);

(*b*) that the Persians diverted the water away from the city "to the side where they had their camp" by digging a channel (19.11);

(*c*) that it was when the channel was finished that the pools appeared (19.12);

(*d*) and that no water ever ran in the channel (19.12).

These points can only be related to the map[1] in one way. The hill which was pointed out to Egeria was one of those by the valley of the River Daiṣan (near A), which flowed down the centre of the valley (B–C) to the city wall, and then through the city and out to the east (C–D). The Persians' diversion can only have been in one place, because of the steep hill traversed by the western wall of the city and the second hill to the north of it. They had no choice but to dig their channel from B to C*. But somehow their plan was a failure in practice. Pools appeared in the city at a point just inside the western wall on the original line of the river-bed, and continued to supply the city; and (at least in the fourth century) their diversion-channel never flowed.

[1] The map is based on that of F. C. Burkitt's *Euphemia and the Goth* (London 1913), following p. 44. But his work is misleading when it deals with levels, and his "Ancient course of the Daiṣan" impossible, since it would make the river run over a hill. See J. B. Segal, *Edessa* (Oxford 1970), Plans 1 and 2, which are now by far the best available.

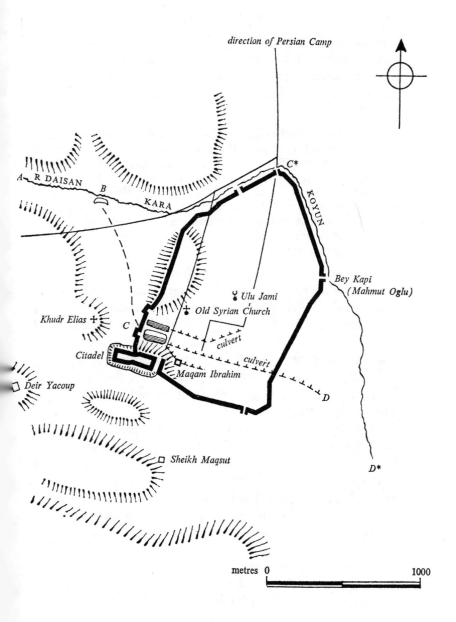

direction of Persian Camp

C*

A — R DAISAN

B

KARA

KOYUN

Bey Kapi
(Mahmut Oglu)

Ulu Jami
Old Syrian Church

Khudr Elias +

C

culvert

Citadel

culvert

D

Maqam Ibrahim

Deir Yacoup

D*

Sheikh Maqsut

metres 0   1000

URFA–EDESSA

In the sixth century Procopius of Caesarea described what
Justinian did for Edessa when it had suffered from a flood.[1] He
seems to ascribe the idea of a diversion-channel to Justinian,
pointing out that without it the river could only run into the city,
and saying,

> [Justinian] constructed a channel which was deeper than the river bed,
> and on the right [i.e. at point B on our map] he erected a huge wall
> of enormous stones. Thus when the river is running with its ordinary
> moderate flow the city still enjoys the advantage of it. But whenever
> the river happens to rise and begins overflowing, there is still a con-
> trolled outflow towards the city along the old channel, but the ad-
> ditional water must flow into Justinian's works . . . Where the river
> comes inside the city he confined it in a straight channel, and built
> up walls on either side in order to prevent it straying from the channel.

The history of the water-supply thus seems to be as follows.
Well before the fourth century the River Daiṣan flowed down its
natural valley and through the city (A–B–C–D). Then a
ditch was dug (B–C★), most probably to avert the danger of
floods. But it was usually dry, and the river-water continued to
follow its old course, though it flowed underground, appearing
in the city as springs[2] in the two pools. When the river was in
flood, it flowed above ground along its old course, causing
considerable damage.

What Justinian did was to increase the effectiveness of the
ditch, now the Kara Koyun (B–C★–D★), and to ensure that all
flood-water was taken down it, at the same time building the dam
at B to prevent any surface waters following the old course of the
river and entering the city at C. The Kara Koyun therefore owes
its present form to Justinian, though what he did was to improve
an existing ditch rather than, as Procopius suggests, to invent
something quite new.

Justinian's "straight channel" inside the city can still be traced
in the culverts which carry the water (and many of the fish) away
from the two pools Birkat Ibrahim and Ain Zilhah.

---

[1] See de Aedificiis Iustiniani 2.7, ed. G. Dindorf, in C.S.H.B. (Bonn 1838),
pp. 228f.

[2] Besides those shown by C. E. Sachau, Reise in Syrien und Mesopotamien
(Leipzig 1883), p. 197, there is an entry for water coming out of the soil at the
west end of the north pool just outside the present wall.

The most recent discussion of the works of Justinian at Edessa is that of J. B. Segal (*Edessa*, pp. 177, 187–90), who accepts Procopius' statement that Justinian was the originator of the dam and "artificial channel". But, apart from the argument outlined above, there are three further factors which make it difficult to * maintain such a position. First, Procopius is likely to ascribe works to Justinian rather than to any one else, and to give the Emperor the credit for them. Secondly, the dam and channel, whatever he may have done to them, proved ineffective, since the disastrous floods continued with the same regularity as before. There had been floods in A.D. 201, 303², 413, and 525. Then the dam was "constructed". But further disastrous floods occurred in 667, 740, and 834–5, which makes it more probable that Justinian adapted the existing system rather than devising something * radically new. Thirdly, there is a late tradition recorded in the *Chronicle to 1234* (see Segal, p. 188) that the Kara Koyun was made by "Seleucus and Nimrod" and the dam by the "Apostle" (Addai). This tradition is obviously not to be taken as literal fact, but it points to a local belief that both channel and dam existed from time immemorial rather than that they owed their origin to Justinian.

I *St Thecla's Martyrium*

Egeria speaks in 23.2 of a holy church at St Thecla's, and in 23.5 tells us of the prayers she says at the martyrium. Beyond saying that the martyrium is very beautiful she gives no further description, and leaves uncertain the spatial connection between the martyrium and the church. The size of the martyrium is insufficient for the large numbers of monks and nuns she saw at the place. But whether the fourth-century church was built over the cave-chapel of St Thecla or near by we cannot tell.

The most detailed plan of the cave-chapel was made by Herzfeld and Guyer in 1912,[1] at a time when it was over half full of debris. But the Turkish authorities have recently removed enough to enable the plan of 1912 to be somewhat revised. In particular the corner of a piece of mosaic has been found (K on the plan) which has been cut by a fifth-century stylobate, and therefore may be assumed to have been the floor in the fourth century. It also establishes the height of the chapel, since the top of the arches are 3.25 metres above the mosaic level.

The cave, believed to be where St Thecla spent the last years of her life, and from which she finally departed alive into the earth,[2] was transformed into a chapel, perhaps early in the fourth century. But, being limestone, it has suffered a good deal since then, particularly when the churches which have been built over it have been in ruins, and water has come in. As a result the limestone walls and ceiling have rotted, and the area of the cave has increased horizontally and upwards, while the limestone has dropped away and formed debris which in the time of Herzfeld and Guyer seems to have reached a height of at least two metres above the mosaic level. In most parts of the chapel the floor is still covered by this debris to a depth of about 75 cm.

The solution to the problem of rotting limestone walls and ceiling was to build retaining walls wherever danger appeared imminent. Not all these walls were observed as such by Herzfeld

---

[1] E. Herzfeld and S. Guyer, *Meriamlik und Korykos* (Publications of the American Society for Archaeological Research in Asia Minor, Monumenta Asiae Minoris Antiqua, vol. 2) (Manchester, England 1930), p. 39.
[2] Basil of Seleucia, *Life of St Thecla*, PG 85.559.

and Guyer, and the dimensions of the earliest building are sometimes greater than those they suggest by the thickness of a retaining wall. Considerable strength had already been added in the
fifth century when Zeno ran a stylobate through the chapel.

The present plans show a tentative conjecture of the state of the
chapel in the fourth century, and Zeno's additions in the fifth.
The apse (A) may in the fourth century have been cut straight
into the limestone,[1] and the same is probably true of chapel B.[2]
More will be said below of chapel C, but it should be borne in
mind that its shape must for the time being remain purely conjectural, since the cave has receded all round it, and the only
opportunity of discovering more about it would be to remove the
limestone debris to its original floor level.

The nave of the chapel (D) has a flat ceiling of rock which is
supported by six columns wedged against it. The columns are
clearly Roman,[3] and were no doubt originally part of some other
building. There is a window (E) at the eastern end of the outer
wall,[4] and though Herzfeld and Guyer show the outside of this
wall on their plan, the inner surface of it can only be conjectural
at present.[5] Steps (G) lead down into a narthex which is joined to
the nave and aisles by two arches,[6] of which only one can still be
seen in its original state. At the northern end of the narthex there
was probably an arched door (J) which led through into a cave
area, and there was possibly a western entry to the cave from the
direction of the relieving arch R.

The corner of mosaic (K) gives the position of the north wall
and north-east corner, but the wall may have been either of rock
or masonry, and it is impossible to relate it to the cave areas near
it, since these have altered considerably.

---

[1] The flint and concrete semi-cylindrical surface which now stretches from
floor to ceiling was probably added at some later stage to take the mosaic
decoration of which pieces still remain attached.

[2] This is at present lined with retaining walls, though HG show the masonry as
rock.

[3] HG only saw the upper part, which looks like Greek Doric, but the lower
part of the columns is now visible, and has fillings between the fluting.

[4] HG had taken it to be a door.

[5] The surface is at present hidden by a wall of masonry, not the rock marked
there by HG.

[6] H was invisible when HG made their plan.

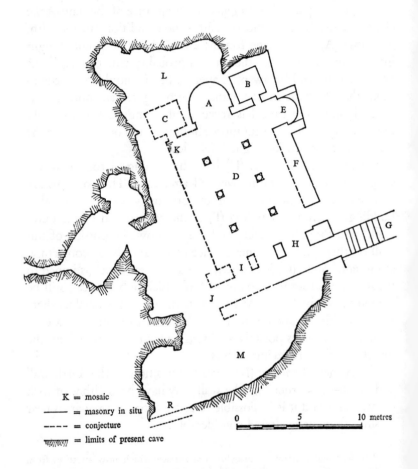

K = mosaic
—— = masonry in situ
---- = conjecture
〰️〰️ = limits of present cave

0   5   10 metres

ST THECLA'S (Fourth-Century State)

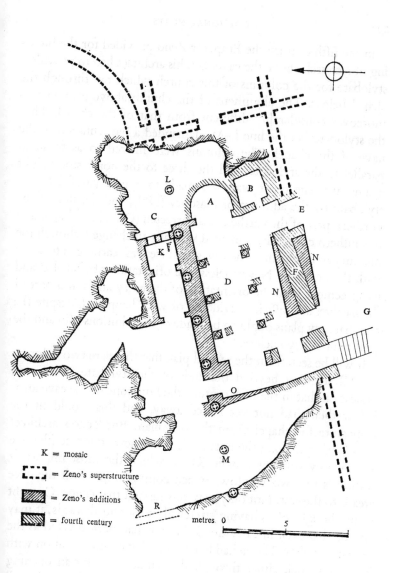

K = mosaic
◼ = Zeno's superstructure
▨ = Zeno's additions
▨ = fourth century

metres 0   5

ST THECLA'S (Fifth-Century State)

In the fifth century the Emperor Zeno provided for the building of a church above the cave. But his architect had to provide a stylobate for the columns of this church which ran through the chapel below. The alignment of the church above ground was moreover considerably different from that of the chapel. Thus the stylobate (on the line L–M) demanded a reorientation of the nave of the chapel. The columns were moved so as to stand parallel to the stylobate, and the three to the north stood right against it.[1] The outer wall was made to appear parallel to the stylobate by the addition of masonry (NN), and the line of the northern part of the narthex was corrected (O). The old apse and its southern chapel (B) remained virtually unchanged, though the masonry which formed their western face was rearranged to agree with the new line. Nevertheless, the orientation of chapel B and its agreement with the orientation of the entry and south part of the narthex are sufficient evidence of what happened, despite the fact that new plans ought to be made of the additions NN and the wall which they enclose.

It will be seen from the second plan that there are two columns (L, M) standing beyond the ends of the stylobate. This is an indication that in the fifth century the limestone of the cave area below them had not yet rotted away, and this would fit the conjecture for chapel C on the first plan. But Zeno's architect made a chapel along the north side of his new stylobate (the one which now contains mosaic K), of which the most important feature is the two windows which communicate with the cave area L to the east. Not only may this suggest that chapel C ought to be thought of as having stretched further northwards; it may also be that even in early times this part had been revered as the cave in which St Thecla had lived,[2] and that communication with it was essential, either through the windows or by an opening which exists today (and may be ancient) through the north wall of the apse.

---

[1] Note that the second plan indicates the fourth as well as the fifth-century positions of the columns.

[2] Not, however, the place where she disappeared alive into the earth, if Basil of Seleucia is to be believed, since he places this miracle "in the very place of ... altar, gleaming with silver and surrounded by columns" (PG 85.559)

J Church Titles

Palestine is one of the countries where the place-names evoke deep associations. Thus a church "on Golgotha" carries with it its own meaning, whether or not it is also called "The Church of the Resurrection". Egeria writes at a time when there was no one standard form of church title, and she refers to church buildings in two main ways. Either she describes the special person or event connected with the building, or else she uses some word or phrase which describes where it is.

Sometimes she describes the person or event in a way which makes it clear she is not exactly reproducing the title in current use. Such is the case when she speaks of the church at Carneas as having been erected "for Job",[1] or when she tells us that the church at Fadana was built "in honour of" the Well of Jacob.[2] But it is only a short step from such explanatory phrases to titles, and it is more likely that titles or, at least, commonly accepted abbreviations of titles are reflected in her phrases about going "to St Thecla"[3] or visiting "the Apostles" in Constantinople.[4]

Egeria explains that the church at Sedima was "where Melchisedech offered pure sacrifices of bread and wine to God". But in the same passage she gives two phrases both of which may have been used as titles: "the church of Holy Melchizedek",[5] and "*Opu Melchisedech*", which is simply the Greek translation of the first two words of her explanation, "Where Melchizedek . . .". Certainly "*Opu Melchisedech*" was a title.[6] Probably "The church of Holy Melchizedek" was one too.

"Where Melchizedek" is a title which says what is commemorated. So are such titles as "Martyrium" or "Lazarium", since both are locative nouns meaning "The place of testimony" or "The place of Lazarus" (indeed they could fairly be rendered "Where testimony" or "Where Lazarus"). But such titles contrast with "Imbomon", which presumably means "On the Hillock", or "On Horeb",[7] since these latter are strictly

---

[1] 16.6. [2] 20.11. [3] 23.2.
[4] 23.9. [5] 15.4. [6] 13.4; 15.4.
[7] 4.1.

speaking phrases which say where the church or chapel has been built. Certainly in the context of a Holy Land these titles carry with them reminders of the person or event commemorated. But the actual form of the title is an indication of place.

Egeria happens to make it clear that "On Horeb" was a title. But there are many such phrases in her book, and it is often hard to be certain whether she is simply saying where something was, or using a title. There is an excellent example of this uncertainty in the case of "the church which is on Eleona, that is, on the Mount of Olives".[1] Does this mean that the church was known by the title "On Eleona"?[2] It may well be so, since in the part of Egeria's text we have, the word "Eleona" is always accompanied by the preposition "On".[3] And if we are right in supposing that "On Eleona" was used as a title, then there is some evidence also for such titles as "On Sion",[4] and "In Bethlehem", even though it must be admitted that the evidence is too scanty to be conclusive.

A characteristic of Egeria's references to churches is that besides giving what may be a title, she does not hesitate to repeat the commemoration at some length.[5] One of the buildings which she tends to introduce in this way is the Martyrium. In this case are we to suppose that the church had one title—Martyrium—and that the rest is explanation? Or were there several titles in common use?

"Martyrium" had certainly been a word connected with this church (or at least with its site) ever since it was built,[6] and was a normal title. To this, at its first mention in connection with the

---

[1] 30.3.

[2] Cf. 33.1; 25.11; 40.1; 43.5.

[3] "On" = in. See Gingras, p. 153, n. 119, and note especially the prepositions in the list given in 39.1: in the Major Church, at the Anastasis, at the Cross, on Eleona, in Bethlehem, and in the Lazarium.

[4] This suggestion is made on the assumption that Egeria uses the preposition in when speaking of the church (e.g. 25.11; 37.1; 39.6) and others, like ad or usque ad, when she is referring to the Mount as a whole (as in 40.2; 43.8; also de in 27.7; 29.1).

[5] 35.2; 39.3.

[6] Eusebius (see p. 165 above) calls the actual Tomb "the Martyrium of the Resurrection". But a document, quoted by Athanasius, but presumably of A.D. 335 (in Apol. adv. Arianos 84) seems to call the church "the Martyrium of the Saviour", and the title Martyrium was certainly in use in 348, when Cyril preached in the church (see, for example, Cat. 14.6).

Jerusalem liturgy,[1] Egeria adds three other phrases, and since she later uses each of them independently, they may all three point to titles.[2] They are: "The Major Church",[3] "Built by Constantine",[4] and "On Golgotha",[5] a phrase to which Egeria sometimes adds the words "Behind the Cross".[6]

Two of these phrases, whether or not they are in fact titles, would support the contention that the Anastasis building over the tomb-cave was a later addition to the Golgotha site as developed by Constantine. Egeria often uses "built by Constantine" to describe the Martyrium, but never applies it to the Anastasis. And while it is true that St Cyril, like Egeria, uses the phrase "On Golgotha" if not as a title, at least as a current phrase attached to the Martyrium,[7] he never adds the phrase "Behind the Cross". It could of course be simply because no cross had been set up in his day.[8] But it is more likely that the phrases "In front of the Cross" and "Behind the Cross" became necessary only when there were two important buildings on the Golgotha site, which needed to be distinguished from each other.

[1] 25.1.

[2] See 30.2; 25.11; 25.8.10.

[3] 25.2, 6, etc. Vermeer, Obs., pp. 103f, suggests that maior has the meaning of "principal": i.e. that it was the church par excellence in the city of Jerusalem. This meaning would also fit the idea that it was a "church with a bishop" (cf. 19.1) and not simply a "church with a priest" (as 3.1).

[4] This may point to a title like "The Church of Constantine". Compare 25.1,6, and the brief expansion in 25.9.

[5] 25.8, 10, 11.   [6] As in 25.1.

[7] See Cat. 1.3; 4.10; 16.4.

[8] See 37.1, where Egeria may well imply that she believed the cross to have been erected recently.

K *Christian—Jewish Relations in the "Travels"*

Jews are mentioned as Jews only once in the texts which can be ascribed to Egeria—in the anti-Jewish story of Christ cursing the synagogue.[1] But the *Travels* provide indirect evidence for relationships which can hardly have been easy. Christians seem to have been encouraged, by the political favour they had enjoyed for the best part of sixty years, to make a take-over bid for everything connected with the Old Testament.

The earliest development of holy places can have offended the Jews only by accident, since there is no evidence that Jews had any special regard for the sites of Golgotha, the Nativity, or the Eleona. Indeed, they may have been as pleased as the Christians when they saw the previous pagan worship suppressed. But the case was otherwise when it came to the use of sites connected with the Old Testament, especially since, in most cases, the Christians relied on late Jewish tradition for the identification of these sites,[2] and were therefore drawn to make use of the same holy places.

The Christians not only acquiesced in the derelict state of the Jewish Temple site. They justified it by reference to Christ's warning that "not one stone should be left upon another", and rejoiced when an earthquake foiled the Emperor Julian's attempt to restore it. Jews must have reacted with horror (or amusement) when Christians displayed the Ring of Solomon and the Horn of Anointing among their relics, or when they began to "discover" the bodies of the Old Testament saints.

However earnestly the Christians may have wished to appropriate the traditions in which they had a part with the Jews, there are signs that they misunderstood the tradition. The Armenian Lectionaries show how less familiar Jewish commemorations give place to those which would be more familiar to the Christ-

---

[1] See PD, V4.

[2] The exceptions are the Tomb of Moses on Mount Nebo (for which there is no known Jewish parallel) and the Tomb of Job at Carneas (which seems to have been an exclusively Christian site).

ians. Thus Jacob the Patriarch is transformed into James, first bishop of Jerusalem,[1] and Zachariah the son of Barachiah becomes Zachariah the father of John Baptist.[2]

Egeria's evidence is specially valuable, since she shows a little of what was going on at the popular level. The most striking illustration of this level of thought is to be seen in the ruins of Capernaum, where in the fifth century a new and beautiful synagogue was built only fifty yards from the site of a new and beautiful church. It is therefore encouraging to remember that ten years after Egeria's visit St Jerome found Jewish collaborators in his biblical studies. At least the lamentable state of affairs reflected in the *Travels* was not the invariable rule.

[1] See note on *AL* 71 (p. 275 above).
[2] See note on PD, E (p. 183, n. 9 above).

L   Jewish Influences on the Jerusalem Liturgy

In describing the liturgy of the Jerusalem Church, Egeria particularly admired the way in which services were arranged to be held at the very time and in the very place which they commemorated.[1] But from her description we can identify two other influences which affected the rite she describes, that of synagogue worship, and that of the rites of the Jewish Temple.

Precisely because Christians owed so much to Judaism, they regarded the many parallels between the two religions with caution. Any undue emphasis on the similarities threatened to blur the distinctions, and for this reason the main body of catholic Christianity ostracised those Christian groups like the Ebionites or the Nazarenes which felt obliged literally to observe the Jewish Law. Where the catholics themselves were concious that they were following Jewish practice, they usually took pains to modify or reform it: thus although they followed the Jews in keeping one day a week for rejoicing and two for fasting they deliberately altered the days, substituting Sunday for the Sabbath and Wednesday and Friday for the Jewish station days, which were Monday and Thursday.

In Jerusalem during Egeria's time the Church may also have been influenced by the way in which the Jews kept the year, for, like the Jews they held three principal feasts which lasted for eight days. For Easter the parallel with Passover had been a permanent and universal feature of the Christian year, though its date had been disputed, and in Jerusalem the parallel was made still closer by the extension of the Easter period to end with Pentecost, as in the Jewish calendar. The other two eight-day feasts observed by the Church in Jerusalem were Dedication and Epiphany.[2] Could these have been arranged to correspond with the Jewish feasts of Dedication and Tabernacles?

Apart from the fact thay they share the same name, the Christian and Jewish feasts of the Dedication have little in common. The Jewish feast (called Hanukkah in Hebrew) takes place in winter, at the end of November or in December, whilst the Christian Dedication was in September. At their feast the Jews commemorated the re-dedication of the Altar on Mount Moriah, whereas the Christian feast came to be known as "The Dedication of the Holy Places at Jerusalem",[3] and celebrated the comple-

1.   For examples of such services see Egeria. 29.5, 31.3, 33.2, 36.2,3, 38.2, 39.4-5, 40.2, 43.2-3.
2.   See Egeria. 25.11, 49.1.
3.   The name given in the Armenian Lectionary of Jerusalem in its early fifth century version: see above, p.274, No.67.

tion of Constantine's Churches. But Egeria tells us that the Christian
feast was held on "the dedication day when Holy Solomon, having completed the House of God which he built, stood before the Altar of God and
prayed, as it is written in the books of the Chronicles".[4]   Now in II Chronicles 7.10, the passage to which she refers, we find that Solomon's dedication coincided with an eight-day feast in the seventh month, which can
hardly have been other than the feast of Tabernacles.[5]   The dedication
of Constantine's buildings on Golgotha may therefore have been arranged
in September to fall roughly at the same time.

There remain two feasts which seem to have only superficial resemblances, Epiphany and Hanukkah. Both were indeed eight-day feasts
which fell at mid-winter, and both involved the lighting of an unusual
number of lamps.[6]   But the date of Epiphany, January 6th, did not exactly correspond with that of Hanukkah, and was derived from Christian practice in Egypt and other parts of the East. Moreover, by about the middle
of the fifth century the Jerusalem calendar included a feast which was
evidently designed to correspond with Hanukkah, "The Dedication of All
the Altars which have been erected"[7]. Its date is not specified in the calendar by a particular day of the month, but since it fell between November
30th and December 25th it was probably designed to coincide with the
date of Hanukkah, which fell between these dates according to the Jewish
lunar calendar.

Since there was no such feast in the Jerusalem calendar of the early
fifth century, it was probably introduced by Bishop Juvenal (bishop from
428 to 458 A.D.) whose episcopate spanned most of the period between
the two calendars. But since Juvenal also suppressed the celebration of
Christ s Nativity on 6th January, and transferred it to 25th December, he
may well have decided to institute the new feast of the "Dedication of All
the Altars" in order to provide the parallel with Hanukkah which had formerly been supplied by Epiphany.

Though the evidence at our disposal is small, it inclines towards the
probability that the Jerusalem Church arranged its liturgical calendar to
match that of the Jews. But if so, the arrangement produced an analo-

4.   Egeria. 48.2.
5.   Lev. 23.23: see Josephus, *Ant.* 8.100, 123, and J. Gray, *I-II Kings,* London 1964
      pp.192, 194.
6.   Egeria. 25.7.
7.   The feast is first mentioned in the late fifth century, as witnessed by manuscript
      P44 of the Armenian Lectionary: se F.C. Conybeare, *Rituale Armenorum,*
      Oxford, 1905, p.526, and A. Renoux, *PO* 35, pp. 196-7. The readings for the
      day, Heb. 13. 10-16 and Matt. 23.12-22, appear to have been chosen with an
      anti-Jewish basis.

gical system of some complexity. Thus at Easter Christians were encouraged to consider the Resurrection in parallel with the original Passover in Egypt, and in the light of the passages in the New Testament which interpret that Passover in relation to Christ. And at the Dedication, Egeria herself reports that the day was chosen not only because of the dedication of the church buildings on Golgotha and the Discovery of the Cross, but also because it was the day of Solomon's dedication of the Temple [8] and thus, if our suggestion is correct, the Feast of Tabernacles. The capacity to draw analogies of this sort at many levels was by no means rare among the scholars who interpreted the Bible in the third and fourth centuries, but it was hardly the province of laymen, and we need not be surprised if Egeria fails to mention all the parallels which were intended by those who had arranged the liturgy.

All over the Christian world the services contained many elements which had been derived from those of the synagogues. But in Jerusalem Egeria reported the existence of a service held on Wednesdays and Fridays in Lent which seems to have been unusually close to that of a synagogue. It was held, so she tells us, "so that the people should continually be learning the Law"[9] and comprised readings which the early fifth-century lectionary shows to have been taken from the Law and the Prophets. We shall notice several further parallels with the ritual of the synagogue, but in examining these parallels we must take account of the fact that the practice of the synagogue was itself designed to correspond with that of the Jewish Temple.

The Temple was, for the Jews, the place where God had "caused his name to dwell", [10] and for this reason they linked their prayers with those of the Temple by turning towards it when they prayed. [11] But in the synagogues there were many other links with the Temple and its service. Thus for instance when priest of a particular course [12] went up to perform their duties in the Temple, the members of that course who did not go to Jerusalem were expected to assemble for prayers and special readings which took place at the same hours as the Temple sacrifices. [13] This practice, together with the fact that the synagogue services were known by the same names as the simultaneous sacrifices in the Temple, symbolised the involvement of every Israelite in the worship which was being offered in Jerusalem. [14]

  8. Egeria. 48.1-2.
  9. Egeria. 27.6: see also above, pp. 264-5, Nos. 19-32.
 10. Deut. 12.11.
 11. See Dan. 6.10 and *b. Ber.* 30a.
 12. See I Chron. 23.1-26.26.
 13. Mishnah, *Taanith* 4.12 (tr. Danby, p.199).
 14. See Danby, *op.cit*, p.199, n.5.

When, in 70 A.D., the Temple was destroyed, and the sacrifices ceased, the synagogue services took on a new importance, becoming the main vehicle of Israelite worship. Indeed one third-century Rabbi believed that the prayers in these services had been instituted to replace the Temple sacrifices.[15] And until the Temple could be rebuilt the synagogue stood as its substitute and, provisionally at least, its *de facto* successor. Many elements in this Jewish understanding of synagogue worship could easily be borrowed by Christians as guides to interpreting the worship of the Church. From the outset Christians had believed themselves as a community to constitute a new Temple "built without hands",[16] with the corollary that Christian worship formed the legitimate successor to the worship of the Jews. This belief held novel attractions for Christians when they came to build their new churches after Constantine's accession, and in about 316 A.D. it received classic expression in a sermon which Eusebius of Caesarea preached at the dedication of the new church at Tyre. It is based on an analogy operating at three levels, for he refers to the building of the Tabernacle and Temple of the Old Testament, to the new church at Tyre, and at the same time to the still greater spiritual Temple in Christian souls. In the building of this new "Temple" at Tyre, Eusebius believed that he saw God's prophecies being fulfilled, and in particular the prophecy (to which he refers three times in the sermon) "The latter glory of this House shall be greater than the former".[18]

Eusebius' evident enthusiasm for his theme is of considerable importance in the history of the Jerusalem liturgy, since he undoubtedly influenced the Emperor Constantine in his plans to beautify the Holy Places and adapt them for liturgy and pilgrimage. Thus ten years after the dedication at Tyre the work began at Jerusalem on the reclamation of the site of the rock-tomb or "Cave" from which the local Christians believed Christ had risen from the dead. Hadrian, two centuries before, had built a Roman temple over the site, and none of those involved in Constantine's works had ever seen the Tomb which they believed to be hidden beneath it. And when Eusebius describes the moment when it was discovered he introduces language properly belonging to the Jewish Temple: Hadrian's temple was removed, and then "as layer after layer of the subsoil came

15. R. Joshua ben Levi, cited in *b.Ber.* 26b.
16. See Mark 14.58: a comparable belief had been held by the sectarian Jewish community at Qumran, see 1QS 8.5-6.
17. See Eusebius, *H.E.* 10.4, especially sections 25-6 and 69 (ed. Schwartz, pp.870, 882).
18. Haggai 2.9, cited by Eusebius, *H.E.* 10.4.3, 36, 46 (ed. Schwartz, pp. 864, 874, 882).

into view, the venerable and most holy '*martyrium* of the Saviour's Resurrection' [19] [i.e. the rock-tomb] became visible: the Holy of Holies, the Cave, was like our Saviour restored to life". [20]   He goes on to speak of the buildings which were erected, and then says, "Thus on the very '*martyrium* of the Saviour' the Emperor constructed the New Jerusalem, facing the one which was famous in former times . . . Opposite to this he built a second and new Jerusalem, heralded by prophetic oracles." [21]

In September 335 A.D., when the new buildings were dedicated, the Cave had been isolated from the rock which had surrounded it, and transformed into a small free-standing building.   At its west end the rock-tomb remained with its chamber preserved in its original state, but on the east a porch had been added, surrounded by a chancel and approached by steps. [22]   The Cave stood at the west of a court with an outcrop of rock protruding into its south-eastern corner, and this rock was identified (though Eusebius strangely fails to mention the fact) with Golgotha, and adorned with a cross.   The eastern limit of the court was formed by the west end of the large basilica called "The Martyrium".   These are the arrangements known to us from the *Life of Constantine*, which Eusebius wrote in 337 A.D., and confirmed by the archaeological discoveries of the last twenty years. [23]   But it appears that the buildings planned were not by then completed, since at some time before 348 A.D. Cyril of Jerusalem implies the existence of an additional building which had been erected to contain the Cave.   This was evidently the large rotunda which Egeria names as the Anastasis or "Resurrection".

In the sermon which he preached at the dedication of the Jerusalem buildings Eusebius "endeavoured to gather from the prophetic visions apt illustrations of the symbols it displayed". [25]   But the sermon has not survived, and we can only guess at what he may have said from the passages we have already quoted.   From these it seems highly probable that he interpreted the '*martyrium* of the Saviour' as the new Temple of Christian

19. See p.165, n.3.
20. Eusebius, *V.Const.* 3.28, above, p.165.
21. Eusebius, *V.Const.* 3.33, above, p.167: the prophecies doubtless included such passages as Isa. 44.28, 52.1f, 9, 54.11f, and Ezek. 40.1-44.7, as well as Hag.2.9.
22. On the form of the Cave and its decoration see Note D, pp.242-52 above.
23. For these discoveries see Ch. Coüasnon, *The Church of the Holy Sepulchre in Jerusalem,* London 1974.
24. Its existence is first implied by Cyril of Jerusalem, *Cat.* 18.33, *PG* 33.1056. In the *Procat.* (Cat.19) 11, *PG* 33.1076, he echoes Eusebius' phrase "Holy of Holies" applied to the Cave, or possibly the Anastasis, and in *Cat.*13.27, *PG* 33. 806 speaks of Golgotha as the centre of the earth, thus recalling the Jewish belief that the Temple was the central point: see Philo, *Leg. ad Gaium* 294 (ed. Cohn-Reiter, p.209) and *Tariĥ. b. Lev.* 78.
25. See *V.Const.* 4.45 (ed. Heikel, p.136).

Jerusalem. At any rate, the idea that the site was the Temple was believed with the crudest literalism by some of the pilgrims of the early sixth century. Thus they were told that the court between the Cave and the Martyrium was the very Temple court "where Jesus found them that bought and sold the doves and cast them out",[26] and that the Golgotha rock was the altar where Abraham had offered Isaac in sacrifice, [27] or in other words the Altar of the Temple on Mount Moriah. Are we to treat these associations between the Golgotha buildings and the Temple as coincidences, or were they part of a broad scheme of comparison which remained in existence from the time of Eusebius onwards?

Egeria, who visited Jerusalem about fifty years after Eusebius' death, shows little awareness that the buildings were to be understood as the Temple. Though, for example, she tells us that they were dedicated on the same day that Solomon had dedicated the Temple,[28] she lays no particular emphasis on this information, and does not enlarge on it. But she gives a number of indications which suggest that the buildings were being used in a way which was designed to correspond with the ritual of the Jewish Temple. The extent of the correspondence can be judged by comparing some of the services which Egeria describes with the Jewish daily morning whole-offering, for which the Mishnah treatise *Tamid* provides detailed instructions. Figure 1 may help the reader in locating the movements described. We begin by comparing the Morning Whole Offering with the Morning Hymns which began each weekday in the buildings on Golgotha.

Tamid	**Egeria**
Daily Morning Whole-Offering	*Weekday Morning Hymns*
1. At about cockcrow (1.2) the officer unlocks the wicket gate of the Temple court: he leads the priests in (1.3) to prepare for the service (1.4).	At cockcrow on a weekday (24.8) the doors of the Anastasis are opened (24.1). (A monastic service is held in the Anastasis, 24.1).

26. Egeria. 43.3, In *Breviarius (a)*, 3, C.C.S.L. 175, p.111, (compare *J.P.B.C.* p.60a lines 82-5), the word *basilica* denotes the Temple court, as in Vulg. 11 Chron. 6.15.

27. *Breviarius (a)*, 2, *J.P.B.C.* p.60a: also Theodosius, *de Situ*, 7, Anon. Plac, *Itin*, 19, and Adamnan, *Loc. Sanct.*1.6.2. (*J.P.B.C.* pp.65, 83 and 97).

28. Egeria. 48.1-2.

2. At daylight (3.2)   When daylight begins (24.2).
    the sacrificial lamb is
    slaughtered (3.5),
    and the great gate of the
    Temple is opened (3.7).

3. The priests and levites recite   they begin the Morning
    prayers in the Chamber of   Hymns (24.2).
    Hewn Stone (5.1).

4. The duty priests and levites
    enter the Temple to finish their
    preparations. Levites take
    their place to sing (5.6).

5. The incense is offered (6.3).

6. The High Priest, followed by   The Bishop and clergy arrive
    the other priests,   and the Bishop at once
    enters the Temple.   goes into the Cave to say
    They prostrate themselves (7.1).   prayers and two blessings (24.2).

7. They come out to stand on   The Bishop comes to stand outside
    the temple steps (7.1).   the chancel rails (24.2).

8. The High priest and the other   The Bishop blesses the people
    priests bless the people (7.2).   one by one (24.2).

                                          It is now daylight, and the
                                          [weekday] service is over (24.2).

9. The High Priest and the other
    priests move from the Temple to
    the Altar, where they offer the
    sacrificial lamb. The levites
    begin their hymns (7.3).

There are evident similarities between these two rites. The timing is marked in the same way, and in each case the main activity begins at daylight (sections 1 and 2). In both cases the chief minister makes his entry after prayers have begun (section 6), and his entry into the sanctuary is a principal feature of the service (section 6). When he emerges from the sanctuary he blesses the people (section 8). But we cannot be certain that any of these parallels were only with the Temple and not also with the synagogue. We know, for instance, that synagogue services followed the same timing as those of the Temple, and that from early times priests had pronounced their priestly blessing in synagogues,[30] as well as in the Temple. We also know that in synagogues certain prayers were said "before the Ark".[31] This "holy Ark",[32] the cupboard containing the scrolls of the Law, was so called in memory of the Ark which had stood in the Holy of Holies of the Temple.[33] The Bishop's prayers and blessings in the Cave (which Eusebius had compared to the Holy of Holies) may therefore derive from the Temple rite only through the rite of the synagogue. Indeed there is one small detail which may incline the evidence in favour of direct dependence on the synagogue: Egeria tells us that the bishop blessed first the catechumens and then the faithful (the first two blessings in section 6) and then blessed the faithful one by one (section 8). If this were seen as three blessings then, by Jewish standards, it would be appropriate to synagogues but not to the Temple.[34]

Egeria describes two other services which are essentially similar to weekday Morning Hymns, though they are held at different times. The first is the version of Morning Hymns used on Sundays which had to be held slightly earlier, so that the resurrection gospel which it contains[35] could be read at the very time, as well as the very place, it describes, namely "early on the Sunday morning while it was still dark" (John 20.1), when Mary Magdalene met the risen Lord. This rearrangement involved the displacement of the monastic service (section 1 above) to an earlier time. The second service described by Egeria and summarised below is *lucernare*, which began at the tenth hour and ended at dusk.

29. Egeria. 26 and Luke 2.2ff: also perhaps Judas' interview with the priests, Egeria. 34 and Matt. 26.14-16.
30. See for instance Mishnah, *Meg.* 4.3,5 (tr. Danby, p.206).
31. *Ber.* 5.4, *R.Sh.* 4.7 (tr. Danby, pp.6, 193).
32. A name deriving from II Chron. 35.3.
33. See for instance Exod. 40.21 and I Kings 8.6.
34. *Sotah* 7.6 (= *Tamid* 7.2), (tr. Danby, pp.301, 588).
35. John 19.38-20.18: see A. Renoux, *PO* 35, pp.158-9, and above, p.270, No.44.

Egeria *Sunday Morning Hymns*	**Egeria** *Lucernare*
(Before cockcrow a monastic service is held in the court outside the Anastasis, (24.8).	At the tenth hour (24.4).
1. At cockcrow the doors of the Anastasis are opened (24.8).	
3. The Bishop enters the Anastasis and goes into the Cave (24.9).	
The congregation enters the Anastasis (24.9).	The congregation assembles in the Anastasis (24.4).
	The church lamps are lit from the ever-burning lamp in the Cave (24.4). [36]
The Morning Hymns are sung (24.9).	The lucernare hymns are sung (24.4).
5. Censers are carried into the Cave (24.10).	
6.	The Bishop and clergy arrive and take their seats "up above" (24.4).
	Hymns and psalms are sung (24.4).
7. At the gates of the sanctuary.	The Bishop comes and stands outside the sanctuary (24.5).
	After a litany the Bishop says a prayer (24.5-6).
8. the Bishop reads the resurrection Gospel (24.10).	The Bishop blesses first the catechumens, then the faithful, and then individuals one by one (24.6).

9. The Bishop and the people move with singing from the Anastasis to the Cross (24.11).

The Bishop and the people move with singing from the Anastasis to the Cross (24.7).

A psalm and a prayer are said (24.11).

The Bishop prays,

The Bishop blesses the faithful and then individuals one by one (24.11).

and blesses first the catechumens, then the faithful, then individuals one by one (24.7).

All go Behind the Cross, where again the Bishop prays, and blesses first the catechumens, then the faithful, and then individuals one by one (24.7).

(It is not yet daylight: see 24.12).

The rite ends at dusk (24.7).

Since the Sunday Morning Hymns are almost a re-enacting of the Resurrection, with the Bishop emerging from the Tomb, we may suppose that in this context the primary reference of the bringing of censers into the Cave (section 5) was to the Holy Women, who brought spices to the tomb and carried them in.[36]   But, as we have already remarked, liturgical analogies might work at several levels at once, and this ceremony recalls also in a striking manner the offering of the incense in the Temple.   But it may also be derived directly from the synagogue, since many synagogue mosaics in Palestine show incense burners[37] which, like most of the other objects shown, seem to have been part of the liturgical equipment of synagogues. Thus it is probable that, despite the silence of the Mishnah on any incense rite other than that of the Temple, incense was used in some Palestinian synagogues.   Again there is a parallel between the ever-burning lamp in the Golgotha Cave and the candlestick or *menorah* which stood in the Temple[38]

36. Mark 16.1, Luke 24.1f. On the pilgrim flasks from Jerusalem now at Monza and Bobbio the women at the Tomb are shown carrying censers: see A. Grabar, *Ampoules de Terre Sainte*, Paris 1958, plates IX, XI, XVIII and XXXV.

37. These shovel like objects are commonly shown in Jewish art of the Byzantine period: see for example the *Bulletin* of the Louis M. Rabinowitz Fund, Jerusalem, I, (1949) Plate XIII and III (1960), Plate XII (3).

38. Egeria. 24.4. Like the *menorah* it was made of bronze: see Anon. Plac, *Itin.*18, *J.P.B.C. p.83.*

but it is not unlikely that synagogues sometimes contained ever-burning lamps, and the possibility therefore exists that in this case also Christians derived their Temple-parallel from a practice of the synagogue.

The two services nevertheless contain one common feature which can hardly be derived through the synagogue. In both services, the Bishop, after he has emerged from the Cave, leads the way over to the Cross or in other words to the Golgotha rock surmounted by its cross. In the light of the idea that the Cave represented the Holy of Holies and the Golgotha rock the altar on Mount Moriah, this procession seems to have been designed to correspond with the movement of the High Priest and his attendants from the Temple steps to the altar of sacrifice. No such procession is recorded in connection with synagogue worship, nor is there any archaeological evidence which would suggest that synagogue buildings would provide for such a possibility.

We may therefore conclude that most, if not all, the correspondences we have noticed between the Christian rites and those of the Temple were intended as direct, even though some of them may have been imitated from practices known to exist in synagogues. And this conclusion receives some support from an accessory of the Cave which was first mentioned by Cyril of Jerusalem before 348 A.D. This was the so-called "Stone of the Angel" [39] which represented the stone which had been rolled across the mouth of the rock-tomb when Christ was buried. If, as the Gospel tells us, [40] the stone had to be rolled it is most natural to think of it as having been like the other rolling stones which have been found at the doors of ancient rock-tombs in Palestine, that is, shaped like a millstone. But in fact the earliest word suggesting its shape describes it as a "cube",[41] or, in other words, very much the shape of the Altar of Incense in the Temple.[42] Here again, if our interpretation is correct, is a feature common to the Golgotha buildings and the Temple which has no known parallel in ancient synagogues.

We have noticed three influences which contributed to the formation of the Christian liturgy in Jerusalem. The first was to make use of the Holy Places at the appropriate times, and this was of necessity a unique

39. Cyril Jer, *Cat.* 14.22, *PG* 33.853.
40. See Matt. 27.60, 28.2, Mark 14.52, Luke 24.2, *Evang. sec. Petrum* 37.
41. Theodosius, *de Situ* 28 and Sophronius, *Anacr.* 20.12 (ed. Gigante, p.123): see also Iacinthus, *Itin*.9, (*J.P.B.C.*pp.70, 91, 123). For stories told to explain the unexpected shape see Theodosius, *loc.cit.* and Adomnan, *Loc. Sanct.* I.3.1. *J.P.B.C.* pp.70, 96.
42. See Exod.30.2.

concern of the Jerusalem Church. The second was the general influence of the synagogue, which affected in some measure all Christian Churches in the world. But the third, though some of its effects may have been suggested by synagogue practice, was evidently a deliberate attempt to shape the Christian liturgy at Golgotha in such a way that it would correspond with the rites of the Jewish Temple. At what date should we suppose that this third influence began to affect the services of Jerusalem?

The evidence of Egeria suggests that the Cave, rather than the Anastasis, represented the Temple proper, and we may therefore seek the origin of the liturgy she describes in the period before the Anastasis had been built. Thus it is probable that the associations between the Golgotha buildings and the Temple were first given liturgical expression under the guidance of Eusebius himself, whose writings give ample evidence that he found such associations attractive. Yet if he had used them to shape the liturgy we need to explain why Egeria, to judge from what survives of her *Travels*, made no direct use of them for, as we have seen, her evidence is almost all in the form of *obiter dicta.*

In fact there is no reason to suppose that, simply because Eusebius had propounded an idea, Egeria must have known it. Indeed Eusebius is the first writer to have applied the term "Martyrium" to the Golgotha site, but its significance is not understood by Egeria, and probably not by many of her contemporaries, because soon after her time it fell into general disuse. [43]   Indeed there may be two reasons why Eusebius' scheme of comparison went out of fashion. The first is the length of Cyril's episcopate, which lasted from 349 to 387 A.D., thus spanning almost the whole period between Eusebius' death and Egeria's stay in Jerusalem. Cyril, to judge from his *Catechetical Lectures*, laid little emphasis on parallels between the Golgotha site and the Temple, at least in his popular teaching, and his lack of enthusiasm may well have affected those who explained the Holy Places and their liturgy to Egeria. Another reason is connected with the offer by the Emperor Julian in 362 A.D. to support the Jews in rebuilding their own Temple. Even though their attempt failed, it exacerbated the already poor relations between Christians and Jews in Jerusalem, and under such circumstances it is hardly surprising that parallels between the two faiths aroused little enthusiasm.

We therefore conclude that Eusebius worked out, on the basis of earlier Christian and Jewish writings, a theological analogy between the Jewish Temple and the new Christian Churches which were being erected in his time. We believe that he applied this analogy in the advice he gave

43: See Egeria. 30.1 and *J.P.B.C.* pp.174b-175a.

Constantine over the buildings at Golgotha, and in the formation of a new liturgical programme for Jerusalem. And the evidence that we have examined suggests that his ideas survived as one of the main influences on that liturgy, even though in time they became less well understood, and eventually degraded into the stock-in-trade of pilgrim guides and their clients.

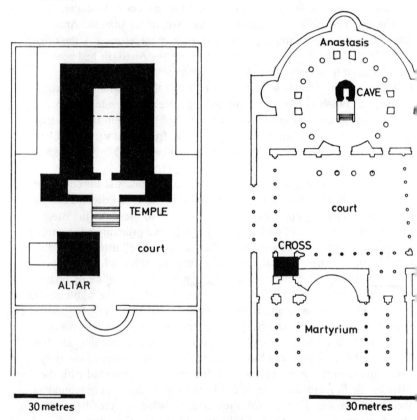

30 metres   30 metres

THE SECOND TEMPLE AND THE BUILDINGS ON GOLGOTHA

The reconstruction of the Temple is based on the description by Josephus, supplemented from Mishnah, *Middoth*. The plan of the buildings on Golgotha in the time of Egeria is based on Ch. Coüasnon, *The Church of the Holy Sepulchre in Jerusalem*, London 1974. Both complexes were laid out from east to west, with west at the top of the Figure.

ADDENDA AND CORRIGENDA

xii. (After J.E.H. add) *JPBC*, John Wilkinson, *Jerusalem Pilgrims Before the Crusades*, Warminster, 1978.

p.9. (Correct the date 351 to 349, and the date 386 (Death of Cyril) to 387).

10-12. (Delete the last sentence at the foot of page 10 and the rest of the paragraph at the beginning of page 12, with the first four lines of the next paragraph. Substitute:)

. . . . We also hear that in about 230 A.D. Origen escaped from Alexandria to Palestine "ostensibly to see the Holy Places",[2] and in his own writings he mentions Bethlehem, the Pool of Bethesda, and the holy wells near Ascalon.[3] But despite these reports it is possible that pilgrimage in the proper sense of the word was a fourth-century development. Later writers may have read back their own motives into these early visits, as have so many who speak of the pilgrimage of Melito of Sardis. Melito certainly visited the Holy Land not long before 190 A.D., but in his letter which is recorded for us by Eusebius he says that he made the journey to verify the names of the books which were included in the Old Testament, and "came to the place where these things [i.e. the events recorded in the O.T.] were proclaimed and done".[1] But he says nothing about any devotional purpose.

Constantine certainly did not invent pilgrimage. Egeria mentions several tombs of Old Testament prophets[a] which seem to have been traditional Jewish holy places revered by Christians. Indeed all three of the "holy caves"[b] over which Constantine erected his churches in the Holy Land had been known and (presumably) revered before his reign.[c] At the least there seems to have been a local cult attached to these places, and if so there is no reason to doubt that foreigners like Alexander and Origen who came to the Holy Land often wished to visit the places and pray there or, in other words, to make pilgrimage to them. But if Constantine was not the creator of pilgrimage he came to see it as a means of encouraging Christianity. By the splendid buildings he erected he helped to transform what may have been an unusual and occasional Christian devotion into a custom welcomed and taken for granted by Christians from every part of the Empire.

In implementing this policy the Emperor received the help of Eusebius, the church historian who, as Bishop of Caesarea, was the metropolitan bishop of Palestine. He first came in contact with the Emperor at the . . .

Notes. a. See for instance above, pp. 186 and 202f.
 b. See above, p. 46 and Eusebius, *VC* 3.43 (Heikel, p. 95)
 c. Bethlehem with its cave is mentioned in the second century (see above, p. 46) and Eusebius implies that Christ's Tomb was known before the time of Hadrian (above, p. 164). The cave on the Mount of Olives is probably the one forming the setting for the event recorded in the *Acts of John* 97 (Hennecke II, p.232), a work probably of the third century, since it is mentioned by Eusebius: see *HE* 3.25.6 (Schwartz I, p.252).

12. Add to note 3. *Comm. John* 5.2 (fragm.6.1, ed. Preuschen, p.532).

13. (Line 6 to begin) Helena. Her visit to found the buildings . . .

13. Note 2 (delete "Note D", substitute) above, pp. 166f.

14. (Line 4, delete "In the year when" and substitute) soon after.

18. (last line but one, delete the last four words, "pool of Siloam, the".)

19. (Delete last two lines of paragraph 4 and substitute) found there a traditional topography whose emphasis had considerably changed.

20. (Lines 3 and 4 of paragraph 2 should be deleted. Substitute) monument is wonderful, but rather because it witnesses to the faith than beca it stimulates devotion. He and Cyril,[3] we may suppose, both contribu to developing this belief . . . .

31. (Delete second half of fourth line of paragraph 3. Substitute) one b one to receive an individual blessing.[3] His . . .

31. (Delete line 8 of paragraph 3, and substitute) as the High priest had led the Jewish priests into the Holy Place of the Temple, so he goes with the clergy into the holy caves, while the congrega- . . . .

31. (Add to Note 6) See also Note L, above, pp. 298 – 310.

39. (In line 2 of Note 3 read "eighth", not "seventh" century.).

40. (Delete last six lines of second paragraph, and substitute) Martyrium[6]. Egeria certainly speaks of a second church building called the Anastasis, which surrounded and enclosed the holy cave. Since the existence of this building was apparently unknown to the Bordeaux pilgrim and Eusebius, but is implied by Cyril of Jerusalem,[a] we may assume that it was built between 337 and 348 A.D.

Note a. In *Cat*.18.33, *P.G.*33. 1056.

40. (Add to Note 1) The fullest available account of the buildings is still the late Father Ch. Coüasnon's *The Church of the Holy Sepulchre in Jerusalem,* London 1974. A new comprehensive work by by Father V. Corbo is in the press.

42. (Delete lines 7 and 8 and substitute) but its exterior was carved into a polygonal block, which was supplied with columns, a porch, and a roof.[2] This in itself . . . .

43. (Delete the sentence beginning "At one stage" in line 5 and the rest of the paragraph. Substitute) This was a natural enough name for it, since there was a cross set up on the rock.[1] Since this rock is mentioned by both the Bordeaux pilgrim (593, see above, p. 158) and by Cyril of Jerusalem (who tells us that it was "rent"[2]) it is hard to understand why Eusebius made no mention of it.

43. (Delete last word of paragraph 4, "market" and substitute) street.

43. (Delete Note 1 and substitute) Egeria in 37.1 calls it the cross "which stands now", probably to distinguish it from the Holy Wood of the Cross, which was a small relic preserved in the chapel nearby. See also *JPBC*, p.177a.

48. (Delete second and third paragraphs and substitute)
The Emperor Justinian (527-65 A.D.) is said by a later writer to have enlarged the church. If he did he must have taken this action in the last years of his reign, since his contemporary, Procopius of Caesarea, mentioned no work at this church in *The Buildings of Justinian,* which he wrote before 558 A.D. In any case the enlargement involved the destruc-

tion of all but the foundations of Constantine's church, and a radical alter-
ation of the part near the holy cave. Only in 1934 were archaeologists
able to identify what was left of the earlier church and reconstruct its general plan.[2] At the time of the discovery it was assumed that the sanctuary was in the form of an octagon attached by an arch to the square
nave. But although the mosaic floor above the cave has an octagonal design, the foundations discovered between the supposed octagon and nave
were narrower than those of the outer walls, and may have supported
nothing more substantial than a chancel rail. It thus seems wiser to picture the sanctuary as an angular projecting apse with an octagonal altar at
its centre.[4]

The excavators found no solid indications of the way in which clergy
and pilgrims gained access to the cave in the earlier church.[3] Though
stairs were discovered at the east end of the nave they have not been precisely . . . . (continue at top of page 49).

Note 4. See B. Bagatti, *Gli antichi Edifici di Betlemme,* Jerusalem 1952, pp.33-41.

49. (Delete line 3. Substitute) Constantine's Church on the Mount of
Olives, or Eleona, is

49. (First line of paragraph 3 to read) The cave was, as the White Fathers
and Father Hugues Vincent discovered in their campaign . . .

49. (Paragraph 4 should begin) The building on the near-by Hillock (or . .

53. (Add to end of first paragraph) The date of the building may affect
our judgement on the date of Egeria's visit (see above, p. 239).

53. (Second paragraph. Delete lines 6 to the end, and substitute) places
were a stone's throw apart from each other, and though Egeria (36.2) tell
us that the people were so tired that they went slowly from one to the
other, she does not imply that they were far apart.[4] We may therefore
assume that Egeria understood the prayer to have taken place at the site
of the present Church of All Nations, and the arrest at the Gethsemane
Cave. Thus the foundations discovered when the Church of All Nations
was being built are probably those of Egeria's "graceful church".

53. (Note 4, line 2, to begin) the prayer was further up the Mount of
Olives at the site now called . . . .

53. (Delete present Note 5, and substitute) Egeria's evidence thus seems to agree with Jerome's statement that there was a Gethsemane church "at the foot of the Mount of Olives". See his elaboration of *On. Gethsemane.*

54. (Line 13 to begin) containing a wealth of details, which . . .

55. (Note 1. Delete first sentence and substitute) Cyril was bishop from c.349 to 387.

60. (Note 2 to end) and contrast Egeria 35.2.

61. (Note 1 to end) See also above, p. 72.

62. (Note 3: read) *competentes.*

63. (Paragraph 3, line 1. Delete "Throughout" and substitute) During

63. (Paragraph 3, lines 5-7: delete and substitute) received. Egeria's account connects this teaching with Anastasis, which suggests that in her time it could not have been given on the Wednesday and Friday of Easter week, since on those two days that Thanksgiving, if there was one, was not in the Anastasis. Probably she was writing at a stage when the number of mystagogical lectures had already been reduced to five.[6]

63. (Note 1: before the word *Myst.* insert "Ps-Cyril").

64. (In paragraph 2, line 3, delete the word "privately").

65. (THE FIRST SERVICE ON SUNDAYS: this paragraph as here revised should follow the end of the section THE OFFICES, which begins at the foot of the page. Delete Notes 1-5 at the foot of the page.).

Despite its elaborations the first service of Sunday morning appears to be essentially a version of the Morning Hymns which took place on weekdays. It had to be held slightly earlier in order that the timing of the Resurrection Gospel at the Anastasis would be correct, since that had to take place "early on the Sunday morning, while it was still dark" if it was to agree with St. John 20.1,[2] and thus to be at the very place and time when Mary Magdalene came to the tomb. The parallels between this Sunday service and that held on a weekday are as follows: both take place in the Anastasis.

WEEKDAY (24.2) at dawn	SUNDAY (24.8-11) at cock-crow
	The Bishop enters the Cave.
"Morning Hymns" (probably psalms like those of Sunday). The Bishop arrives and enters the Cave to say the Prayer for All.	Three psalms with their prayers.
	The prayer for All.
	Censers are taken into the Cave.
	Bishop reads Resurrection Gospel from door of Cave.
	All go to the Cross for a Psalm with its prayer.
The Bishop blesses the catechumens. There is a prayer. He blesses the faithful.	The Bishop blesses the people.
The people come to his hand.	The people come to his hand.

Although Egeria's wording in 44.2-3 is somewhat confusing, she seems to treat the weekday and Sunday services as closely related.[a]

Note a.   Some of the special features of the Sunday Service are discussed in Note L above, pp. 298 – 310.

67. (Delete last four lines of text, and first four on page 68.   Substitute) began at its usual time in the Anastasis.   Egeria's text as we have it does not tell us clearly . . . .

67. (Add to Note 2).   The eleventh or twelfth century *Typicon* which describes the services then held at the Anastasis shows that "spice-bearing women" or *myrophoroi* continued to play a part by carrying incense to the tomb in the liturgy of Easter morning: see A. Papadopoulos-Kerameus (ed.), *Analecta Hierosolymitikes Stachyologias*, vol. 2, St. Petersburg 1894, pp.191, 199 (where there are also deacons who carry incense), and J. Mateos, "La Vigile cathédrale chez Egérie" in *Orientalia Christiana Periodica* 27 (1961) pp.291f.

68. (Delete the table of services, and substitute)

TIME	WEEKDAY	SUNDAY
Cock-crow		First Service (i.e. Solemn Morning Hymns
First Light	Morning Hymns (ferial)	
Full Daylight		Eucharist
9 a.m.	Minor Office (only in Lent)	
11 a.m.		Thanksgiving
Noon	Minor Office	
3 p.m.	Minor Office	(Minor Office?)
4 p.m.	Lucernare	Lucernare.

72. (Note 6, line 1. Delete the parenthesis after the word "singular".).

75. (Paragraph 3, line 3, delete "the mountain".).

76. (Last line of text, delete "in Sion". Substitute) on Sion.

76. (Note 2: delete and substitute) 36.6-7; see *AL* No.43 and note L above, pp. 298 – 310.

76. (Note 3: delete and substitute) 37.8; see *AL* No.43.

77. (Delete last two lines of text and first line of p.78. Substitute) it seems likely that the main eucharistic celebration must in Egeria's time have been elsewhere, since it does not seem that Poemenia had by then built her church at the Imbomon, we still have to explain Egeria's . . .

81. (Paragraph 3, line 10, delete "takes place". Substitute) is held.

83. (Delete the last two lines of paragraph 3, and substitute) to his hand" individually, which probably means that he laid his hand on each one in blessing.[9]

83. (Delete Note 9. Substitute) 24.2, 24.6, etc. The Greek version of Canon 19 of Laodicea uses the phrase "coming under the hand" of the bishop in describing the blessing of catechumens and penitents, and the same basic notion of blessing probably underlies the imposition of hands on individual penitents which is mentioned by Optatus, *Schism. Don.* 1.19 2.20 (*CSEL* 26.21, 56) and by Sozomen, *HE* 7.16 (*GCS* 50.323).

84. (SUBSEQUENT MODIFICATIONS: delete first paragraph and substitute)

During the fourth century the expansion and development of the Jerusalem liturgy probably kept pace with the building of new churches. At any rate Egeria, who is our first detailed witness, links most of the liturgical activity to buildings. Hence we may picture a pattern, perhaps originally formulated under the guidance of Eusebius, being constantly elaborated by the Bishops of Jerusalem, and especially by Cyril. In consequence the Jerusalem ritual of Egeria's time was so burdened with activity that, as she herself hints from time to time, it was beginning to make unreasonable demands on the energies of those who took a full part in it. On Pentecost, for example, the people were expected to attend services almost continuously from dawn until midnight.

85. (Add to Note 5) and above, p. 254.

87. (Delete first line of Note 9, and substitute) The veneration of relic of the Cross continued in East and West. But the veneration on Good Friday itself was dropped from the Eastern rites ....

91. (Paragraph 2.1, line 4 should read) wide,[n] and we had to pass throu this valley before we reached the ...

95. (Paragraph 2 (4.3), last line should begin) we arrived anywhere, I al ways ...

102. (Paragraph 2 (8.5), last line but two should end) ... children of Israel had escaped ....

105. (Paragraph 2 (10.3), delete "Jericho stretch" in line 6, and substitute) Jericho side ...

108. (Delete line 6, and substitute) Also from this spot they pointed over to Peor,[3n] once a city of ...

108. (Paragraph 2, line 7, first word to read) Jerusalem .. . .

111. (Headline: delete SALEM, substitute) SALIM.

111. (First paragraph (15.3) line 12, delete "St. John's Garden" and substitute) 'Holy John's Garden',

123. (Third paragraph (24.2, line 6) should end) comes up to have his hand laid on them. He . . . .

123. (Fourth paragraph, (24.3) should end) they come to have his hand laid on them.

124. (End of first paragraph (24.7 should end) one by one to have the bishop's hand laid on them.

124. (The reference number 7 in the margin should be placed opposite the beginning of the second paragraph, beginning "Then, singing ...").

124. (Second paragraph (24.7), delete fifth line from bottom and substitute) places they come to have the bishop's hand laid on them, as they did in the ...

125. (Last line of first paragraph (and 24.11) should end) everyone comes to have his hand laid on them.

125. (Second paragraph, end of line 3, delete [n].)

140. (Delete last word of line 6. Substitute) on . . . .

142. (Delete line 9 of third paragraph, and substitute) great doors which face the market street are opened, and the bishop and . . . .

143. End of line 3 and beginning of line 4: delete and substitute) everyone goes to have the bishop's hand laid on them, and at about ...

146. (48.2: add to last line but one the word "holy" to read) holy Solomon.

151. (Delete last sentence of paragraph 3, and substitute) Probably this promise had never been included in the Greek versions of the letter. Like several other passages it is not included in the version preserved by Eusebius[3].

153. (Below marginal reference 585.7, against the line beginning "who gave much" insert marginal reference 586.).

153. (Note 6: after the word "Bath", insert) or baptistery, ...

154. (Line 6, beginning "Aser". Delete marginal reference 586 and substitute) 587.

154. (Line 8 beginning "according": delete marginal reference 587.).

154. (Delete present Note 4, and substitute) The pilgrim makes no mention of the tomb of the martyr Basil, which was in Scythopolis. The present name of the place is Beth She'an or Beisan.

154. (Delete last sentence, beginning in Note 7, line 7, and substitute) But Jerome, who had at first accepted the view of Eusebius (see *Lib.loc.* 69.19-21) later came to place them near Neapolis (see *Ep.* 108.13). The two traditions evidently continued, as evidenced by the Madaba Map, made in about 600 A.D., which names the mountains in both localities.

154. (Note 8, line 2: after the word "Jerusalem" insert) See 2 Chr.3.1.

155. (Second paragraph: first word of last line should be not "bath" but) baptistery . . .

155. (In the continuation of Note 11 from p.154, in lines 3-4 and 6 delete "Antoninus" and substitute) the Piacenza pilgrim.

155. (Add to end of Note 2) Like the roughly contemporary shrine of St Babylas near Antioch, this church had a cruciform plan, though we first learn the fact only in the seventh century: see Adamnan, *Loc.sanct.* II.21. 2, and his plan, *JPBC* pp.108 and 193, Plate 1.

155. (Delete present Note 6, and substitute) The pilgrim thus believed that the events of Peniel (Gen.32.30) took place at Bethel, a mistake not made elsewhere in the literature of the period. This error is like his belief (586 above) that David killed Goliath in the plain of Jezreel.

156. (Line 1 should begin) left, built by Solomon, [1] and further inside the city ..

156. (Note 2, end of line 1 and beginning of line 2 should read) by aqueduct from Birket el Miya'a at the head of the Kidron valley. Eusebius ...

156. (Add to end of Note 2) See also *JPBC*, p.170.

156. (Note 5: delete the first name "Mark". Substitute) Matt.

156. (Add to end of Note 6) See his article in *Jerusalem Revealed* Jerusalem 1975. pp.26f. and 35.

156. (Note 7, middle of first line should read) single stone may be the one which later ...

157. (Add to end of Note 4) One of Antoninus' names was Hadrianus, and an inscribed stone giving both names has been re-used in the perimeter wall of the Haram esh Sharif. If, as is likely, this stone was part of the plinth of one of the two statues, we can understand how the Bordeaux pilgrim came to think that there were two statues of Hadrian.

157. (Delete Note 6, and substitute) The most likely candidate for the pilgrim's "House of Hezekiah" is the rock plinth supporting the ruins, such as they were, of the Antonia fortress at the north-west corner of the Temple enclosure.

157. (Delete Notes 7 and 8, and substitute) The pilgrim appears to be saying that of the two pools he describes the one called Siloam was inside the wall and the other (Birket el Hamra) outside. The arrangement suggested in the map on p.37 above perhaps has something to commend it: see the arguments in *Levant* 10 (1978), pp.116-25.

157. (Note 9, line 4, for "pilgrim" read) writer.

157. (Add to end of Note 10) But in 333 A.D. it was still at the site of Caiaphas' House. It may have been moved into the Church on Sion as soon as it came to be rebuilt. The name "Sion" can apply to the whole ridge running along the western wall of the city up to the citadel (see the map on p.37 above), and we are thus left without any sure knowledge of the line of the "wall of Sion". Perhaps it enclosed a rectangle with the citadel at its north-west corner, but leaving the site of the House of Caiaphas outside it to the south: this had at least been the area which in 70 A.D. Titus had assigned to the garrison, the Tenth Legion which remained to guard the city: see Josephus, *War* 7.1-5.

158. (In the last line of the translation delete "bath" and substitute) baptistery.

158. (Add at the beginning of Note 1) The buildings taken to be David palace were no doubt those on the site now occupied by the Citadel, sinc one of them, a tower built by Herod the Great which still survives, has been known since the sixth century as the "Tower of David": see Piacen Pilgrim, *Itin*.21, *C.C.S.L.* 175, p.140.

158. (Delete beginning of first line of Note 2 and substitute) See Isa.1. The Church on Sion, which was outside the "wall of Sion" is not mentio and had not by the time of the Pilgrim's visit been rebuilt. Is it perhaps to be identified with the one remaining "synagogue" mentioned above? In any case the site was the Christians' traditional . . .

158. (Delete Note 3, and substitute) The pilgrim speaks as if he was leaving the rectangle of the walled area of Sion by some exit near the no east corner. See further *Revue Biblique* 1969, pp.266-8.

158. (Delete first sentence of Note 5, and substitute) The Piacenza pilgrim (23, *C.C.S.L.* 175, p.141) shows that the church later built at the House of Pilate was to the east of Valley Street, perhaps somewhere in t housing block between the present Gate of the Chain and Gate of the Cotton merchants.

158. (Delete present note 6, and substitute) The name Golgotha is her used to refer to the rock outcrop rather than to the whole site: see p.42 above.

158. (In last line of Note 8 delete "Cf." and substitute) Contrast the meaning of the word as Egeria uses it in 24.8.

158. (Add to end of Note 10) See also C. Tinelli, *L.A.* 1973, pp.95-104.

159. (Delete Note 1 from line 2 to the end, and substitute) present name "St. Stephen's Gate" is probably connected with the Church of St. Stephen in the Kidron Valley, which is not mentioned until the twelfth century A.D., and comes to be regarded as important in the two centuries following.

159. (In Note 2, line 1, instead of "Yahwe" read) Yahweh.

159. (Delete the first paragraph of Note 3, and substitute) The evidence discussed above, p.53, seems to favour the site of the present Church of All Nations for the Agony, and the Gethsemane Cave for the arrest of Jesus in the topography of Egeria's time. At the time of the pilgrim of Bordeaux the arrest, if it is indeed commemorated at the rock now in the Church of All Nations, was not yet kept as a separate commemoration, but both were in one place, possibly the spot identified as "Gethsemane". See also p.184 and note 3 below.

160. (Note 6 continued from previous page, first paragraph, line 2 should be deleted. Substitute) Jeremias, *Hg*, pp.61-6) and since only two tombs are mentioned it seems reasonably certain that they are the two still visible. Some of the other tombs which had been in the area had long been lost, owing to a

160. (Note 6 from previous page, delete last paragraph and substitute) The present "Tomb of Zechariah", like the neighbouring tomb of the Benei Hezir (or "Tomb of James the Less") was probably made in the middle of the second century B.C.

160. (Note 1 to begin with the words) The Church on the Eleona was . . .

160. (Note 6. The second sentence on the subject of Justinian should be deleted).

162. (Note 2 should begin) Like the Church on the Eleona.

162. (Note 3, line 6: delete third word "Antoninus" and correct as in p. 155, Note 11).

162. (Note 5, line 2 should end) rebuilt in or before.

165. (Note 1, line 6: the reference should be) *Ep*.58.3, *PL* 22.531, ...

165. (Note 1: delete from line 9 to end of the note, and substitute) we are told by Eusebius. Thus Jerome believed that the site of the Resurrection contained the city's Capitoline Temple, which is also represented on one of Hadrian's local coins: the temple shown contains the figures of Jupiter, Juno and Minerva, but not of Venus.

165. (Add to the end of Note 3) Both words appear in the Greek version of Zephaniah 3.8, which Cyril of Jerusalem quoted in reference to the Golgotha site before 348 A.D. (*Cat*.14.6, *P.G.* 33.832), and it is likely that this text is here in Eusebius' mind. This unexpected application of the text probably provides the origin of the name "Martyrium" for this site, but it was too obscure for most people, and Egeria gave a different and simpler explanation (30.1, p.132 above). The Golgotha site is not described in any literature later than the fourth century by the name "Martyrium" except in passages which appear to be quoted from fourth-century sources: see *JPBC*, pp.174-5.

165. (Note 4, line 2 to begin) which Bord. 593-4 calls "Golgotha". . . . .

165. (Note 4, line 3 to end) and became a commonplace

165. (Note 4: add to end of line 4) See Note L above, pp. 298 – 310.

166. (Note 3: delete line 1 and substitute) The word *basilica* evidently means "church" in this letter. But it was not yet universally used in this .

167. (Line 3 of Note 1 to begin) when she came and founded the church

167. (Line 3 of Note 3 to end) but here the exterior of . . . .

168. (Delete Note 1, line 8, and the rest of the first paragraph. Substitute) added the Anastasis. Probably it had been part of the original complex planned by Constantine's architects, but for some reason it was not finished by the time the complex was dedicated in 335 A.D. Comparable delays attended the buildings of Constantine at Trier.

168. (Delete Note 2, and substitute) Excavations have so far revealed little in the area of this church, but its inscribed apse has been found at the western end, as in Constantine's churches at Trier and at St. Peter's and St. John Lateran in Rome. All the Emperor's other churches in the Holy Land had their apsidal sanctuaries in the eastern end.

169. (Note 1: delete last line of note and substitute) assembled with stones brought from the ruins of the outer wall of the Temple precinct.

169. (Delete the first sentence of Note 3, and substitute) The Church on Golgotha thus had five aisles, like the Church at Bethlehem.

170-1. (Delete the first sentence of Note 6).

172. (In line 1: delete the date "c.350" and substitute) before 348.

181. (Add to the end of Note 1) On the use of the word "temple" see Note L, above, pp.298-310.

181. (Note 2, For "Adamnan" read) Adomnan.

181. (Delete Note 4 from line 2 to the end. Substitute) earth, also quoting Ps. 74.12. In the seventh century Adomnan speaks of a column in another part of Jerusalem which casts no shadow at midsummer, thus proving that Jerusalem was at the centre of the earth (*Loc.sanct.* 1.11, *C.C.S.L.* 175, p.195), and in the ninth century the centre-point was marked in the court of the buildings on Golgotha (Bernard the Monk, *Travels* II, ed. Tobler-Molinier, p.315). These ideas are an adaptation to Golgotha of the Jewish belief that the Jerusalem Temple was the centre-point of the earth (*Tanh. B. Lev. 78* and *b.Sanh.* 37a). In this passage the ancient ideas seem to be expressed in a twelfth-century form: compare Daniel 10, *IRO* p.14.

181. (Add to end of Note 10) except the Piacenza pilgrim, *Itin.*19, *C.C.S.L.* 175, p.139. See also the end of section C3 below.

182. (Note 1 to begin) Compare the equally inaccurate mention . . . .

182. (Add to end of Note 1) Peter the Deacon makes no attempt to harmonise the correct identification of the site of the Jewish Temple with

the treatment of Golgotha as the Christian Temple which seems to under-
lie the language of section C1 above.

182. (Add to the end of Note 2) See the end of section E below, and
contrast the same commemoration made in Anastasis, according to the
Breviarius 3(a), *C.C.S.L.* 175, p.110, which was written in about 500 A.D.

183. (Add to the end of Note 6) These "pinnacles" were the corners of
the wall of the temple precinct rather than of the Temple itself. Their
massive stones had proved too heavy to be removed by the efforts of Titus'
army in A.D. 70, and one of them still stands almost to its full height.

184. (The first sentence of section I may well be derived from Egeria, and
should not be printed in italic).

184. (Delete the last two lines of Note 9, continued from the previous page
and substitute) opinion, and *Protev. James* 23.1-3, Hennecke I, p.457 of
about 150 A.D., which is at least fifty years earlier than Origen.

184. (Delete Note 3, and substitute) The expression is not clear, but it
is possible that Peter is adapting a passage from Egeria. Although there is
no archaeological evidence of any church built above the Gethsemane
cave, the cave itself was in Christian use from time at least as early as the
fifth century. See V. Corbo in *La Terra Santa* 33 (1957), pp.167-71, and
Ricerche Archeologici al Monte degli Ulivi (*Pubblicazioni dello Studium
Biblicum Franciscanum* 16) Jerusalem 1965, pp.1-57.

184. (Note 6 to begin) All that was left of the Church on the Eleona
after . . . .

184. (Note 6 last line on the page to begin) of the cave on the Eleona . . .

185. (Delete last word of line 4 of Note 1 and first word of line 2.
Substitute) seems in consequence to have been treated as

185. (Note 2: delete first line and substitute) Luke 22.44. The "place"
was the rock in the present Church of All Nations at the foot of the

185. (Note 5: delete line 2 and substitute) upper pool" (cf. also Isa. 7.3),
at some point on the watercourse now known as the Low-level Aqueduct
which comes in from Bethlehem round Mount Sion and into the Temple
precinct. The

188. (Continuation of Note 8 from previous page: delete lines 8-10 and substitute) Bayāzīd el Bastānī, and at Kh. Siya, the small hill to the east, are the remains of a church: see R. de Vaux in *R.B.* 1946, pp.267-9.

190. (The first sentence of section P1 is probably of twelfth-century origin, and should be set in italic type).

190. (Note 1, line 3, for "Adamnan" read) Adomnan.

190. (Note 2: line 1 to end) a roof" must surely be the Ḥaram.

190. (Note 4, line 6, correct as on p. 155, Note 11).

191. (Note 2: delete lines 2-5, and substitute) Mount Sion till the late fifth century (the probable date of Hippolytus of Thebes' composition of *Texts* 1.4, ed. Diekamp, p.5) and the Last Supper not till the early fifth century (if we are correct in thinking that Hesychius of Jerusalem wrote *In Ps.* 49.23, ed. Faulhaber, p. 1197). Neither commemoration was mentioned by Jerome when in 404 A.D. he described Paula's visit to Sion. (*Ep.*108.9).

192. (Delete present note 3, and substitute) 2 Kings 4.8-10. *On, Sonam* suggests that Eusebius did not know the location of the village.

192. (Delete Note 5, and substitute) This may well refer to a resurrection appearance, such as the one described in St. Mark 16.14 ff, or the expanded version preserved in the *Gospel of Nicodemus* 14 (Hennecke I, p.462).

193. (Note 3: delete line 2, and substitute) Annunciation. B. Bagatti judged that there had been a cult of the Blessed Virgin Mary at this site from the third century, and that the first church there was built not later than the fifth. See his summary of the argument in his *Excavations at Nazareth,* Vol. 1, Jerusalem 1969 (*Pubblicazioni dello Studium Biblicum Franciscanum* 17) pp.172f.

193. (Note 5, line 1: delete name "Antoninus" and substitute) 5 *C.C.S.L.* pp. 130-131, *JPBC*, p.79.

196. (Note 3: delete line 1 and substitute) Now the writer, presumably Egeria, begins to describe et Tabgha, which the archaeological evidence

suggests was a monastic site. Here, as at Mount Sinai, a number of biblical commemorations are clustered together in one small area, probably
as a result of the monks' own interpretation of the place where they lived.
The four steps still exist beside a . . . .

196. (Note 4, line 1, to end) (p.195) adapted from . . .

196. (Note 4, line 5, to end) the Arabic name et Tabgha.

196. (Note 5, line 4, to begin) that, though the origins of this and . . . .

202. (line 8, for Socoh read) Sochoth.

202. (Add to end of Note 8) See *JPBC* 165a (Morasthi) and pp.20, 25
and Map 4.

205. (Note 7, correct as on p. 155, Note 11).

208. (Note 3: delete from the last word of line 1 to the end of the note.).

208. (Note 1, line 1, correct as on p. 155, Note 11).

213. (On 1.1, *The Graves of Craving*: add to end of note) and O. Bar-
Yosef and others in *I.E.J.* 27 (1977), especially pp.65-70. In this context
the word *nawamis* is the plural of a word deriving from the Greek *naos* and
meaning "tomb" rather than of the similar word meaning "mosquito".

215. (On 3.8, *Egypt and Palestine*: Note to begin) In Egeria's time the
area of Mount Sinai formed part of Palaestina III. Both the Red Sea . . . .
(In the last line of the same note delete the words "and Palestine".).

215. (On 3.8, *Saracens*: line 1 and beginning of line 2, to read) This
word derives from the same Semitic root as the Arabic . . .

215. On 4.1, *the church called "On Horeb"*, line 1: delete the name
"Antoninus" and substitute) the pilgrim.

216. (On 7.1, *The Land of Goshen*: delete last line and substitute) (i.e.
near Gezirat el Khadra and Tell el Kebir); see 7.9.

217. (On 7.8, *sixteen miles*: delete line 1 and substitute) Heroöpolis is just over sixteen miles east of Tell el Kebir, which was near the . . .

220. (In lines 1 and 2 at top delete the name "Antoninus" and substitute) the Piacenza Pilgrim.

220. (On 12.10, *The Viewpoint*: line 5 to begin) plateau below Nebo , ...

221. (On 13.2, *Carneas*: last line but two to read) to note the emphasis with which Jerome rejects its authenticity (*On, Dannaba, . . .*

221. (On 13.3, *Sedima*: add to end of first line) Indeed Jerome, *Ep.*73, *P.L.* 22.680, said that at that time (398 A.D.) it was still called Salem.

221. (Same note, line 11 to begin) Vol. 3, (London 1867), p.315 and agrees . . .

224. (On 19.1, *Batanis*, line 3: for "thought" read) supposed

225. (On 19.5, *the holy bishop*, line 2: dates to read) 379-87.

229. (On 23.1, *Pompeiopolis*, line 3: delete word "pillars" and substitute) columns

230. (On 25.3, *the tomb, the cave itself*: delete rest of line 1, and substitute) Latin, *martyrii speluncae,* "of the martyrium, the cave". Here Egeria seems to be speaking of the edicule as a martyrium, but . . . . .

231. (On 37.1, *the column*: line 1 to begin) Bord. may have seen the column in Caiaphas' House on Sion (see 592, p.157 above), but Egeria does not say where on Sion it was in her day.

237. (After the word "provides" in line 7 add) Thus B. Bagatti has shown that Egeria must have visited Livias before 431 A.D. [a]

237. (Place additional note (a) between notes 1 and 2, to read) B. Bagatti "Ancora sulla data di Eteria", *Bibbia e Oriente* 10 (1968), p.75, points out that in 10.8 Egeria speaks of a presbyter of Livias, whereas by 431 A.D. the city had a bishop, who attended the Council of Ephesus.

239. (After the last paragraph add)

To this dating, however, three objections have been made which particularly demand comment. B. Bagatti[1] has pointed out that Egeria mentions a church on Sion, and argues that her visit must therefore have been made some time after 387 A.D., when John II became bishop. Bagatti cites a passage in the eighth-century *Kanonarion* of Jerusalem[2] which states that "Archbishop John of Jerusalem" (whom Bagatti takes to be John II) "first founded" the church on Sion. But already before 348 A.D. St. Cyril was speaking of a church on Sion,[3] so its existence tells us nothing new about the date of her visit. Indeed it is possible that the *Kanonarion* was referring to John I in the passage quoted, who was the seventh in the short Jewish succession of bishops of Jerusalem from the time before the Emperor Hadrian. The suggestion that the earlier John founded the church would accord well with the tradition of its great antiquity.

Another argument is held to show that Egeria must have visited Edessa after August 394 A.D.,[4] because at that time his body was brought from the martyrium outside the city, and placed "at the beginning of the north portico" of a church inside the city walls.[5] This argument depends on the assumption that when Egeria wrote "*perreximus ad ecclesiam et ad martyrium sancti Thomae*",[6] she meant "we hastened to St. Thomas' Church and martyrium", that is, to a single site containing both. But this assumption is not made necessary by her language, which equally well mean "we hastened to the church, and to St. Thomas' martyrium. The second interpretation would be consistent with a visit to two separate sites. Unfortunately for our present purpose Egeria never repeats "ad ... et ad" in the rest of her text as we have it, and we are thus deprived of comparisons. Thus we may only conclude that her language is here so ambiguous that it can give no certain indication of the date of her visit.

Thirdly it has been suggested that the developments near the martyrium of St. Thecla[7] are so elaborate at the time of Egeria's visit that they are likely to be late rather than early, especially as the other churches in the area of the martyrium belong, at the earliest to the middle years of the fifth century. But against the lateness of the major building campaign at the site we should set the antiquity of the cult of St. Thecla, which was first attested in about 200 A.D.[8] The martyrium of this renowned saint is likely to have an early origin, and its alignment beneath the fifth-century church[9] shows that it belongs to some earlier period, though the date has not yet been determined archaeologically.

A fourth argument, this one in favour of the date we have adopted, also merits attention. It has been noticed that Egeria speaks of a "place" but nowhere of a "church" at the Imbomon,[10] and this has been taken to imply that she was residing in Jerusalem at a time before Poemenia had built her circular portico at the site of the Ascension. Since Jerome mentions the cross (which surmounted the portico) in a work composed at some point in the years from 389 to 392 A.D.[11] we would thus receive support for the earlier dating of Egeria's visit.

The Imbomon,[12] or "place from which the Lord ascended into the heavens",[13] was evidently supplied with an altar before the time between 417 and 438-9 A.D., since in the Armenian Lectionary[14] it is mentioned as the setting of a eucharistic celebration. But other services had already been held there in Egeria's time, and in all probability she is speaking of a building at the site, since she tells us that every one sat down.[15] Given the possibility that in Egeria's time the Imbomon had not yet been supplied with an altar, and that for this reason it seemed appropriate to avoid calling it a church, and given the further possibility that Poemenia may have built the building at any time between 379 and 392,[16] it is hard to deduce from Egeria any clear evidence connected with the Imbomon which might have a bearing on the date of her visit. Certainly the evidence, if any, does not reduce the probability that she was in the Holy City between 381 and 384 A.D.

Notes.
1. *Bibbia e Oriente* 10 (1968), p.73.
2. M. Tarschnichvili, *Le Grand Lectionnaire de l'Eglise de Jérusalem, C.S.C.O.* 189 (*Scr. Iber.* 10), Louvain 1959, p.80, No.565.
3. In *Cat.*16.4, *P.G.* 33.924 Cyril calls it "the Upper Church of the Apostles".
4. See G. Morin, *Rev. Bénédictine* 1913, p.179.
5. See J.B. Segal, *Edessa, the Blessed City*, Oxford 1970, p.175, citing the usually reliable *Chronicle of Edessa.*
6. See 19.2 above.
7. See 23.2, 4 above.
8. See Tertullian, *de Baptismo* 17, CSEL 20, p.215.
9. See Note I, pp.288-92 below.
10. See P. Devos, "La Servante de Dieu, Poemenia", *A.B.* 87 (1969), p.200.
11. Jerome, *Comm. Zephaniah,* 1.15f, *C.C.S.L.* 76, p.678.
12. Meaning "On the Hillock" (as confirmed by Cyril of Scythopolis, *Life of Sabas* 56.9: see also A.J. Festugière, *Les Moines de l'Orient,* III.2 1962, p.62, n.65). This form of title is comparable with those of several other churches described by Egeria: see Note J, pp. 293-5 above.
13. See 31.1 above, repeated exactly at 39.3, and with minor variants at 35.4 and 43.5.
14. See *A.L.* No.57, p. 273 above, and for the position of the altar, Adamnan, *Loc Sanct.* 1.23.2, *C.C.S.L.* 175, p.199.
15. 31.1 above.
16. See Devos, *op.cit.* p.206.

240. (Paragraph 3, line 1: delete "In 347, however, twelve", and substitute) Twelve

240. (Add to end of Note 4) The *Letter to Constantius*, which may not be Cyril's, contains the statement (in section 3) that the Cross was discovered under "your father Constantine", see *P.G.*33.1168.

241. (Delete line 10, and substitute) by the title, Rufinus states that the title was found by itself, and Christ's

242. (Line 14 to begin) (*Cat.*2.14).

244. (Add to Note 6) See also J. Wilkinson "The Tomb of Christ: an outline of its structural History," *Levant* 4 (1972) pp.83-97.

248. (Note 1, correct as on p. 155, Note 11).

255. (In second paragraph, line 10, for "Council" read) Canons

255. (Note 6, delete "Council of Nicaea".).

258. (First paragraph, last line but three to end) was in the Church on th

258. (Second paragraph, line 3: delete date "386" and substitute) 387

263. (Delete Note 15^c and substitute) 15 ^{c} Cyril, d.387.

270. (No. 45 to read) Mark 15.42 - 16.8.

275. (Note 71b, line 3, correct as on p. 155, Note 11).

277. (Delete Note (a), and substitute) Though Egeria (47.1, 2) speaks mystagogical instruction after the dismissal in the Anastasis on every day of Easter Week, she also shows that it was unlikely on the Wednesday an Friday, because she tells us that on those days the eucharist took place o the Eleona and Sion respectively. She therefore seems to witness to the use of the five mystagogical lectures we now have, though Cyril himself (*Cat.* 18.33, *P.G.*33. 1056) had originally promised one for each day of week. The number had evidently been reduced, and the fact that there had originally been more than five is confirmed by the survival of a sixt reading, for which see A. Renoux, "Le Codex Erevan 985", in *Armenia* Venice 1969, No. LII ter, pp.190ff.

281. (Line 2, second sentence to begin) One of the ...

287. (Line 5, for "three" read) two

287. (Line 14: delete to end of paragraph, and substitute) adapted the existing system rather than that he devised something radically new.

288. (Lines 5-7: delete the sentence beginning "The size of the martyrium ...".

341. (Entry "Antoninus" should begin Piacenza, pilgrim of, and be transferred to p.344)

345. (After "Aijalon" delete "16" and read) 17

346. (After "Cross" read) 20, 43, 137, 168; apparition ....

348. (At bottom of first column read) Mary's spring 193-4.

349. (For Socoh read) Sochoth.

SELECT BIBLIOGRAPHY

EDITIONS

J. F. Gamurrini, *S. Hilarii tractatus de Mysteriis et hymni et S. Silviae Aquitanae peregrinatio ad loca sancta, quae inedita ex codice deprompsit J. F. G.* (including Peter the Deacon "On the Holy Places"). Biblioteca della Accademia storico-giuridica, vol. IV. Rome 1887.

J. F. Gamurrini, *S. Siluiae peregrinatio ad loca sancta*, in *Studi e documenti di storie e diritto*, IX (1888), pp. 97–174.

J. Pomialowsky, *Peregrinatio ad loca sancta saeculi IV exeuntis edita, rossice uersa, notis illustrata* (Scripta Societatis Rossicae Palaestinensis). St Petersburg 1889. Pp. 257ff, the emendations suggested by M. Cholodniak.

L. Duchesne, *Origines du culte chrétien*, Appendice 5e (*Itin.* capp. XXIV–XLIX). Paris 1889. Ed. Va (Paris 1925), pp. 510–42.

J. H. Bernard, *The Pilgrimage of S. Silvia of Aquitania to the Holy Places circa 385 A.D.* translated with introduction and notes. Palestine Pilgrim's Text Society. London 1891. Latin text, pp. 79–136.

P. Geyer, *S. Siluiae, quae fertur, Peregrinatio ad loca sancta.* Corpus scriptorum ecclesiasticorum latinorum, vol. XXXVIII, Itinera Hierosolymitana saeculi IIII–VIII, pp. 35–101. Vienna 1898.

W. Heraeus, *Siluiae uel potius Aetheriae Peregrinatio ad loca sancta.* Sammlung vulgärlateinischer Texte, herausg. von W. Heraeus und H. Morf, Heft 1. Heidelberg, ed. IIIa, 1929; IVa, 1939.

E. Franceschini, *Aetheriae Peregrinatio ad loca sancta.* Testi e documenti di storia e di letteratura latina medioevale, fasc. II. Padua 1940.

H. Pétré, *Ethérie. Journal de voyage. Texte latin, introduction et traduction.* Sources chrétiennes, vol. 21. Paris 1948.

O. Prinz, *Itinerarium Egeriae.* Sammlung vulgärlateinischer Texte. Heidelberg 1960 (ed. 1–4 by W. Heraeus).

E. Francheschini and R. Weber, *Itinerarium Egeriae.* Corpus Christianorum, Series Latina, vol. 175 (Turnhout 1965), pp. 27–90; vol. 176, Indexes.

ENGLISH TRANSLATIONS

J. H. Bernard (see above).

M. L. McClure and C. L. Feltoe, *The Pilgrimage of Etheria.* Translations of Christian Literature, 3rd ser., Liturgical Texts. London 1919.

G. E. Gingras, *Egeria, Diary of a Pilgrimage* (*Ancient Christian Writers*, ed. J. Quasten, W. J. Burghardt, and T. C. Lawler, No. 38). Westminster, Md. 1970.

THE TEXT AND LATINITY

E. Löfstedt, *Philologischer Kommentar zur Peregrinatio Aetheriae. Untersuchungen zur Geschichte der lateinischen Sprache*. Uppsala 1911 (ed. IIa, ibid., 1936).

W. van Oorde, *Lexicon Aetherianum*. Amsterdam 1930.

A. Ernout, "Les mots grecs dans la *Peregrinatio Etheriae*", in *Emerita* XX (1952), pp. 289–307.

R. Weber, "Note sur le texte de la *Peregrinatio Aetheriae*", in *Vigiliae Christianae* VI (1952), pp. 178–182; "Note sur *Itinerarium Egeriae*", XXVIII, 4, ibid. XII (1958), pp. 93–7.

E. Wistrand, "Textkritisches zur *Peregrinatio Aetheriae*", in *Göteborgs Kungl. Vetenskaps = och Vitterhets = Samhälles Handlingar*, F. 6, Ser. A, Bd. 6, no. 1 (Göteborg 1955), pp. 3–25.

J. G. Préaux, "Panis qui delibari non potest", in *Vigiliae Christianae* XV (1961), pp. 105–15.

O. Prinz, *Bemerkungen zu einer Neuausgabe des Itinerarium Egeriae*, in *Archiuum Latinitatis Medii Aeui* XXX (1960), pp. 143–53.

G. F. M. Vermeer, *Observations sur le vocabulaire du Pélerinage chez Égérie et chez Antonin de Plaisance* (Latinitas Christianorum Primaeva 19). Nijmegen 1965.

THE DATE AND AUTHORSHIP

M. Férotin, "Le véritable auteur de la Peregrinatio Siluiae, la vierge espagnole Etheria", in *Revue des Questions historiques* LXXIV (1903), pp. 367–97.

K. Meister, "De Itinerario Aetheriae abbatissae perperam nomini S. Siluiae addicto" in *Rheinisches Museum für Philologie* LXIV (1909), pp. 337–92.

J. Deconinck, in *Revue Biblique* XIX (1910), pp. 432–55, reviewing Meister's theory.

A. Baumstark, "Das Alter der Peregrinatio Aetheriae", in *Oriens Christianus*, N.S. I (1911), pp. 32–76.

A. Bludau, *Die Pilgerreise der Aetheria*. Studien zur Geschichte und Kultur des Altertums, herausg. von. E. Drerup, Band XV, Heft 1–2. Paderborn 1927.

C. Jarecki, "Siluaniae Itinerarium appelé Peregrinatio ad loca sancta", in *Eos. Commentarii Societatis philol. Polonorum* XXXI (1928), pp. 453–73; XXXII (1929), pp. 43–70; XXXIII (1930), pp. 241–88.

A. Lambert, "Egeria. Notes critiques sur la tradition de son nom et celle de l'Itinerarium" in *Revue Mabillon* XXVI (1936), pp. 71–94; "Egeria, soeur de Galla", ibid. XXVII (1937), pp. 1–24; "L'Itinerarium Egeriae vers 414–416", ibid. XXVIII (1938), pp. 49–69.

A. Vaccari. "Itinerarium Egeriae", in *Biblica* XXIV (1943), pp. 388–97.

P. Devos, "La Date du Voyage d'Egérie", in *Analecta Bollandiana* 85 (1967).

B. Bagatti, "Ancora sulla data di Eteria" in *Bibbia e Oriente* 10 (1968), pp. 73–5.

THE JERUSALEM LITURGY

F. Cabrol, *Étude sur la Peregrinatio Siluiae. Les églises de Jérusalem, la discipline et la liturgie au IVe siècle.* Paris 1895.

E. Dekkers, "De datum der *Peregrinatio Egeriae* en het feest van Ons Heer Hemelvaart", in *Sacris Erudiri* I (1948), pp. 181–205.

J. G. Davies, "The *Peregrinatio Egeriae* and the Ascension" in *Vigiliae Christianae* VIII (1954), pp. 93–100.

Chr. Mohrmann, "Missa", in *Vigiliae Christianae* III (1958), pp. 67–92.

G. Garitte, *Le Calendrier palestino-géorgien du Sinaïticus 34* (xe siècle). Subsidia Hagiographica, 30. Brussels 1958.

A. Renoux, "Un manuscrit du Lectionnaire arménien de Jérusalem (cod. Jérus. arm. 121)", in *Le Muséon* LXXIV (1961), pp. 361–85; LXXV (1962), pp. 385–98.

J. Mateos, "La vigile cathédrale chez Egérie", in *Orientalia Christiana Periodica* XXVII (1961), pp. 281–312.

A. A. R. Bastiaensen, *Observations sur le vocabulaire liturgique dans l'Itinéraire d'Egérie.* Latinitas Christianorum Primaeua, 17. Nijmegen 1962 (cfr. V. Peri, in *Aeuum* XXXVII (1963), pp. 188–93).

V. Peri, "La durata e la struttura della Quaresima nell'antico uso ecclesiastico Gerosolimitano", in *Aeuum* XXXVII (1963), pp. 31–62.

A. Renoux, "Liturgie de Jérusalem et lectionnaires arméniens: Vigiles et année liturgique", in Mgr Cassien et B. Botte, *La Prière des Heures* (Lex Orandi 35) (Paris 1963), pp. 167–99.

R. Cabié, *La Pentecôte: L'évolution de la cinquantaine pascale au cours des cinq premiers siècles* (Tournai 1965), esp. pp. 163–78.

R. Zerfass, *Die Schriftlesung im Kathedraloffizium Jerusalems* (Liturgie-wissenschaftliche Quellen und Forschungen 48). Münster-Westfalen 1969.

A. Renoux, *Le Codex Arménien Jérusalem 121* (= F. Graffin *Patrologia Orientalis* 35.1, No 163). Turnhout 1970.

SCRIPTURAL INDEX

Note: This index does not include passages in the Old Armenian Lectionary

PERSONAL NAMES

Aaron: 95, 97; statue 102; throne 204, 209

Abel, F. M. 221

Abgar: 113, 115–17, 151–2, 225; palace 115, 117; statue 115; tomb 117

Abisalom see Peter Abshelama

Abishag 192

Abner, tomb 190

Abraham: 110, 117–19, 154; house 118, 163; cave 188; tomb 163, 188

Absalom, tomb 159, 243

Adamnan, abbot 162, 181, 194

Addai 151

Adonis see Thammuz

Ahab, king 95, 112, 154

Albright, W. F. 221

Alexander, bp of Jer. 10

Amalek 209

Ambrose, saint 241, 281–3

Amico, B. 244, 251

Amos, prophet, tomb 186

Ananias, courier 113, 116–17, 151–2

Andrew, ap., 275

Anna, prophetess 128

Anonymous: *Abgar, Letter of* 117, 226; *Addai, Doctrine of* 151, 225; *Armenian Lectionary* 253–77; *Liber Glossarum* 8, 235; *Liber Pontificalis* 184; *Pèlerinages, Les* 181; *Philocalian Calendar* 71; *Typicon* 181

Antoninus of Piacenza 155, 162, 190, 193, 205, 208, 215, 220

Antony, hermit 14, 22, 24–5, 263

Aphrodite, temple (Jerusalem) 164

Araunah 154, 183

Arculf, bishop see Adamnan

Asaph, tomb 162

Asenath, house 204

Augustine, saint 283

Avi-Yonah, M. 153, 157

Bagatti, B. 39, 185, 200

Balaam 108

Balak 108

Banna'a, rabbi 190

Bar Cochba 36

Basil of Caesarea, saint 9, 14, 23, 26, 237

Basil of Seleucia, bishop, 288, 292

Baumstark, A. 80, 88, 237, 264

Bede, Venerable 27, 179–80, 194

Beni Ḥezir, tomb 160

Bernard, J. H. 5, 7

Bethuel, tomb 119, 227

Black, M. 80

Burchard, pilgrim 193

Caleb, tomb 190

Calemerus, peasant 281

Cassian see John Cassian

Chaldeans 120

Chedorlaomer 110

Chitty, D. 26

Chrysostom see John Chrysostom

Cimon 283

Constantine, emperor 9–10, 12–13, 38–9, 46, 48, 79, 82, 125–7, 158, 160, 163–71, 193, 272

Conybeare, F. C. 78, 253, 255

Corbo, V. 184, 194, 218

Cornelius, house and bath 153

Crassus, Lucius 227

Cross, F. L. 258

Cuntz, O. 153

Cyril, bp of Jer. 9, 14, 20, 36, 39, 55, 59, 61, 83–4, 86–7, 172–3, 240, 257–8, 263

Daniel, higoumen 181, 194

David: 275; and Goliath 154, 202; house 190; palace 157; tomb 162

Davies, J. G. 78

Deborah 154

Deconinck, J. 279

Dekkers, E. 78

Devos, P. 53, 78, 238, 272

Dinah 155

Dracilianus, prefect 166

Duchesne, L. 68, 129

Dugmore, C. W. 69

341

PLACES AND MONUMENTS

GENERAL INDEX

Councils: Carthage III 281; Constantinople I 9, 237; Nicaea 9–10, 255
creed 144–5
crusaders 19, 39
curtains 82, 127

day, the liturgical 66–9, 123–6
deacons 32–3, 56–7, 83, 123–5, 137
deaconesses 33, 121, 229
December 25th 71, 87, 254, 275
decoration 79, 82, 127, 139, 168
Dedication (Encaenia): 71, 79, 146, 275; Jerusalem Temple 79, 146; Temple of Jupiter Capitolinus 80
destruction of pagan shrines 12
diocese 31
dismissal 57–8, 74, 83, 123

Easter: Day 27, 29, 61, 71, 73, 76, 79 81, 111, 118, 128, 139, 147, 270; Tide 71, 77–8, 128; vigil 63, 76, 138; Week (before) 132; (following) 63, 77, 139, 145; see also Fortieth Day
Egeria: character 3–5; date 9, 237–9; home land 3, 115, 174; journey 9, 27–8; name 174, 178, 235–6; sources 5–6; style 5
electi see Baptism
Encaenia see Dedication
Epiphany 70, 80–1, 87, 102, 126–8, 139, 147, 262, 276
Eucharist (the Offering): 31–2, 34, 58–9, 63, 71, 74, 76–7, 81, 95–6, 129–31, 135, 137, 141, 172, 214, 223; time of celebration 60–1, 67, 70, 72, 77, 80, 85, 96; twice in one day 60, 74, see 76, 79, 87, 94, 134, 141, 215
eulogiae see "Blessings"
exorcism 33, 62, 144

"faithful" 33–4, 57, 123, 144
fasting 34, 69–73, 77, 79, 128, 130, 135, 140–1, 143
fathers see Baptism (godparents)
"Feast" see Lent
festal additions 64, 133, 140, 142
Fiftieth Day see Pentecost
finding: Cross 79, 146, 231, 240; Job 112, 281–3

first service: weekday 54; Sunday 65, 67, 78, 124, 141
fish 116, 207
Flagellation see Sion (scourging)
flasks see ampullae
font 63, 139
Fortieth Day: from Easter (Ascension) 71, 77–8, 141; from Epiphany (Presentation) 38, 71, 80, 128, 263
Franks 39
Friday: 67, 69–73, 79, 141, 143; in Easter Week 77; in Great Week 66, 76, 85, 136–8, 269

gobala 255, 267–8
Gospel: 58, 60, 64, 66, 74–6, 80–1, 131–6, 138, 140, 142, 256; of resurrection 58, 65, 76, 86, 125, 128, 139–41, 143; "of Thomas" 225
Great Church see Martyrium
Great Week 71–4, 81, 87, 132–9, 145, 266–70
Greek see languages
groans see applause

"hallowing" 84
hand, "coming to" 83
Hanukkah 80
heathen 119
hebdomadarii 73, 130
"hemisphere" 170
Heortai (Feast) see Lent
hermits 23–4
history, sacred 81
Holy: of Holies 31, 38, 165; Fire 83, see 123; Land 10–13; men 213 (see also saints)
Holy Places : clearing 13, 165; concealment 165; Jewish 19, 154, 157, 159, 162, 186, 190, 201, 218, 296; Muslim 19, 155–6, 182, 190, 227; Pagan 119, 162; Samaritan 18, 154–5, 186
Horn of Anointing 137, 181, 231
hospitality 24, 93, 102, 106, 214
hour services: 67–8, 72, 143; 9 a.m. (Third) 72, 77, 129, 133–4, 138; noon (Sixth) 123, 129, 133–4, 138; 3 p.m. (Ninth) 68, 72, 123, 129, 133, 138